More praise for RANGERS AT WAR

"Excellent . . . Fascinating . . . The author covers an important part of the war ignored by many."
Richmond Times-Dispatch

"A significant contribution to the operational history of the Vietnam War . . . Not every fire fight was a victory, not every Ranger a hero, but in Stanton the men in black berets have a worthy chronicler."
Publishers Weekly

Also by Shelby L. Stanton:

VIETNAM ORDER OF BATTLE
ORDER OF BATTLE: U.S. Army, World War II
THE RISE AND FALL OF AN AMERICAN ARMY
GREEN BERETS AT WAR
ANATOMY OF A DIVISION
AMERICA'S TENTH LEGION
SPECIAL FORCES AT WAR
U.S. ARMY UNIFORMS OF THE VIETNAM WAR
U.S. ARMY UNIFORMS OF WORLD WAR II
SOLDIERS: A Portrait of the United States Army

RANGERS AT WAR
Combat Recon in Vietnam

Shelby L. Stanton

IVY BOOKS • NEW YORK

To those soldiers assigned or attached to U.S. Army reconnaissance and ranger units who sacrificed their lives in Southeast Asia

Ivy Books
Published by Ballantine Books
Copyright © 1992 by Shelby L. Stanton

Library of Congress Catalog Card Number: 91-35114

ISBN 978-0-345-48493-2

This edition published by arrangement with Orion Books, a division of Crown Publishers, Inc.

Manufactured in the United States of America

144912319

CONTENTS

ACKNOWLEDGMENTS

The author expresses his sincere appreciation for the expert assistance provided by innumerable individuals and government agencies contacted during the research for this book. In addition to the many ranger veterans themselves, the author wishes to extend special thanks to Richard Boylan at the Suitland Reference Branch of the National Archives for his cooperation in accessioning important patrol documents; Brig. Gen. Harold W. Nelson, Dr. David W. Hogan, Romana Danysh, and other members of the U.S. Army Center of Military History for material concerning ranger operations and lineage; ranger regiment commander Col. David L. Grange and his 75th Infantry staff at Fort Benning for detailed information on ranger activities; Lt. Col. Robert H. Huckabee of the Army Special Operations Branch for general support; fellow members of the 75th Ranger Regiment Association and the Ranger Regiment Association for insights and contacts; Assistant Secretary for Veterans Liaison Allen B. Clark Jr. and John P. Lawton at the Department of Veterans Affairs for helpful insight; and the Director of Freedom of Information and Security Review at the Department of Defense for expeditious review.

The author also wishes to express his appreciation to all at Orion Books who helped get this story between covers, including (but not limited to) James O'Shea Wade, Stephen Topping, Candace Hodges, Pamela Stinson, Ted Johnson, Leonard Henderson, and John Sharp.

INTRODUCTION

The U.S. Army combat reconnaissance and ranger campaign of the Vietnam war represented an important military adjunct to regular operations throughout the prolonged conflict. Patrol units were formed as field expedient organizations out of battlefield necessity, and their employment varied according to higher command objectives and terrain dictates. This book examines the actual methodology and contrasting experiences of Army long-range patrol elements by describing recon and ranger operations on a unit-by-unit basis. In this manner, the author has endeavored to provide an accurate and useful account of ranger utilization and lessons learned during the Vietnam era.

This volume describes Army combat reconnaissance by focusing on Army long-range patrol units as they originated and were incorporated into ranger components. An overview of ranger advisory and training efforts is also presented. To ease the process of historical review within the context of the larger Vietnam conflict, the reconnaissance record of each command is addressed separately. An overall chronological sequence would have clouded important wartime considerations that determined separate ranger development in different geographical regions. Likewise, strict adherence to the final lettered series (A–P) of the 75th Infantry ranger companies would have infringed unfairly on earlier patrolling organizations with other regimental sequences.

The original variant spelling of "Lerp" instead of "Lurp" is preferred within this text. Some recon veterans might be troubled by this relatively minor aspect of terminology, but both alternatives stem from vowel-inserted pronunciations of the official Army abbreviations LRP and LRRP for Long-Range Patrol and Long-Range Reconnaissance Patrol, respectively. In the early 1960s the first

European-based LRRP detachment members used Lerp as an extraction of long range reconnaissance patrol, a spelling also influenced by the prevalence of "e" as in Germany or Europe. The earlier version is used in this book out of respect for historical seniority, although Lurp later gained more acceptance in Vietnam and among many postwar publications.

Ranger elitism is a popular concept, but military history cannot become anchored on fabled exaggeration. Modern ranger concepts must be grounded on a solid foundation of historical objectivity, where a true understanding of ranger strengths and weaknesses might still contribute significantly to today's national defense. The Army's combat reconnaissance and ranger record of the Second Indochina War was highlighted by individual valor accented by dedicated professionalism, but it was also marred by occasional tragic misapplication, inadequate training, and general inexperience inherent within the one-year combat tour rotation policy. The narrative thus encompasses ranger successes as well as failures in Vietnam, but latter examples were selected solely to illustrate doctrinal lessons and not intended to disparage unit or individual integrity.

During the compilation of this book the author was ably assisted by many ranger and recon veterans, and well served by the military historical records that preserved many facets of the true ranger story in Vietnam. The author is indebted foremost to his excellent ranger instructors while becoming qualified as a Ranger School graduate and to his ranger comrades and superiors while serving as a wartime ranger detachment officer. This primary experience was coupled with the later acquisition of a legal education that facilitated a thorough review of many primary taped combat interviews, court-martial records, official reports of inquiry, and unit after-action reports. These primary sources were either surveyed during the war or researched in government and military archival collections, and they are specified in the endnotes.

MAP A. REFERENCE MAP OF SOUTH VIETNAM

Scale 1:1,250,000

Corps Tactical Zones renamed as Military Regions in July 1970

Map by Shelby Stanton

1

RANGER DEVELOPMENT

RANGER BACKGROUND

The United States Army ranger traditions were forged in the European struggle for the North American continent that predated the birth of the nation. During the Imperial Wars from 1689 to 1762, the British raised contingents known as American Provincials for specific campaigning operations against Spanish and French forces. These units were formed outside the standard colonial militia system. Officers of the Provincials were selected on the basis of their fighting experience and individual reputations for bravery. The troops were recruited from hardy woodsmen and other rugged volunteers who responded willingly to the prospects of wilderness adventure and inducements of hearty bonuses.

Perhaps the most celebrated service rendered by these American Provincials was that of a band of northern colonial rangers led by New Hampshire Major Robert Rogers. His separate Provincial companies, known collectively as "Rogers' Rangers," were raised during the French and Indian War. These early rangers accomplished several important tasks, and the passage of centuries has elevated their deeds to near-legendary status. The companies provided valuable reconnoitering services for the regular forces invading Canada, and they performed several long-range raids against both the French and their Indian allies. The term "ranger" became a matter of upcountry or frontier preference, and this title was bestowed on several mounted outfits during the American Revolutionary War.[1]

The ranger companies of the Vietnam conflict reflected a very close operational link to Rogers' Rangers. Both backwoodsmen

Provincials and Vietnam-era ranger personnel gained recognition as capable but fiercely independent warriors. The leaders of ranger companies represented carefully selected and seasoned professionals. Troops possessing desired soldiering attributes were offered promotions, extra payment, extended leave, and other incentives to join the ranger ranks. Perhaps even more telling, both types of ranger companies existed as separate ad hoc entities raised beyond the established military structure to undertake special tasks. Like Rogers' Rangers, the ranger companies in Vietnam were first formed as expedient patrol units to conduct long-range reconnaissance and raids across an extended battleground.

During World War II the Army rangers earned considerable combat acclaim. Six ranger infantry battalions and one provisional ranger battalion achieved notable successes while spearheading Allied amphibious assaults and performing special raids in both Europe and the Pacific. These elements shaped a vital part of modern Army ranger legacy. During the Vietnam conflict, however, regular ranger and patrol units were denied any official connection to that ranger service. Instead, the rangers of the Vietnam era traced their lineage to another expedient long-range penetration force: the 5307th Composite Unit (Provisional), popularly known as "Merrill's Marauders."[2]

Merrill's Marauders were a select group of soldiers led by Brig. Gen. Frank D. Merrill during 1944. General Merrill's force was given the hazardous assignment of penetrating deep behind Japanese lines and executing a crucial military drive across the mountain jungles and malarial valleys of northern Burma. This task was part of a coordinated push by Chinese Army forces that cleared the way for building the Ledo Road and reconnecting China with Allied logistical bases in India.

The extended march of the marauders, cut off from overland supply sources and supplied by radio-directed parachute drops, was designed to disrupt enemy communication lines and reach distant Allied objectives. In true ranger fashion, the foot soldiers had to rely on deception, raiding prowess, and skirmishing mobility to stifle or confuse organized Japanese resistance. The final target was the key airfield at Myitkyina on the Irrawaddy River. The capture of this airfield—the only all-weather airstrip within the remote mountain fastness of upper Burma—would enable consolidation of Allied control over the region.

The possibility of maneuvering troops deep in enemy territory had already been verified by British Brigadier Orde C. Wingate's raiding expedition of February–June 1943. The composite British,

Indian, Burmese, and Gurkha columns sliced through north Burmese territory, cutting railways and creating widespread havoc, and then dispersed into smaller groups that successfully evaded pursuit battalions and returned to Allied lines before the monsoon rains. This daring exploit captured Merrill's imagination, and he set about to raise a much larger force that would seize the offensive and clear the pathway for the Ledo Road.

In September 1943 the Army began organizing three special battalions known as the Galahad Force. Gen. George C. Marshall, chief of staff of the United States Army, ensured that these battalions were composed of physically hardened volunteers who were acclimatized to the tropics. The troops were derived primarily from veterans of the Solomon-New Guinea campaigns, defenders of Trinidad and Puerto Rico, and well-qualified stateside infantrymen. By the end of October all three battalions arrived in India, where they trained intensively under Brigadier Wingate's overall supervision through January 1944.

On 1 January 1944 the Galahad Force was officially designated as the 5307th Composite Unit (Provisional) at its training site of Camp Deogarh, India. Acting on Brigadier Wingate's advice, the Americans split each battalion into two jungle columns with proportionate supporting forces. The resulting self-contained 475-man units were color-coded as the Red, White, Blue, Green, Orange, and Khaki Combat Teams. The soldiers received intense training in scouting, marksmanship, jungle movement, and platoon tactics.[3]

On 9 February 1944, Merrill's Marauders went into combat. Toward the end of the month, led by scouting platoons, the raiders infiltrated along a maze of forested trails and set up positions behind Japanese defensive lines on the southern rim of the Hukawng Valley. The American blocking positions were concentrated in the vicinity of Walawbum, a grassy clearing in the midst of river-laced jungle. The Japanese tried to dislodge the raiders with a series of furious attacks through the fog-shrouded underbrush and stream ravines, but broke off the engagement on 6 March and withdrew from the valley.

The long-range unit continued its relentless pursuit of the retreating Japanese 18th Division by marching south toward the narrow Mogaung Valley. Part of the American force sidestepped the main valley road by going on a left-flank hike through the rough hill country. Their forward movement was snared by heavy foliage and occasional Japanese delaying actions, but the marauders chopped pathways through the bamboo thickets and traversed leech-infested streams. The exhausting trek forced the soldiers deeper into heavy jungle, and they slipped past the main Japanese forces. On 28 March the 1st Battalion reached the Japanese-held rear junction of Sha-duzup in the upper Mogaung Valley and made a surprise night attack. After over-running the Japanese camp with a classic bayonet charge, the marauders set up a crucial roadblock and held it against repeated counterattacks.

In the meantime, the 2d and 3d Battalion columns used native footbridges to cross the Tanai River, while horses and pack mules forded the four-foot-deep water, and established another unex-pected block against the Japanese at Inkangahtawng. The raider lines were anchored in heavy jungle patches among grassy lowland clearings, and numerous Japanese counterattacks were defeated in the open elephant grass. On 25 March, both battalions withdrew westward and clashed with a Japanese flanking move on Shaduzup. Sharp fighting escalated with alarming frequency along wooded trails, often ankle-deep in mud, and General Merrill ordered the 2d Battalion to hold the high ground at Nhpum Ga village. The 3d Battalion was charged with maintaining backup positions at the Hsamshingyang airstrip and keeping a trail segment open to Nhpum Ga.

By 31 March 1944, several determined Japanese onslaughts com-pletely surrounded and isolated the Nhpum Ga perimeter, and even captured the crucial water hole that supplied the American defend-ers. This loss forced the raiders to drink swamp water from stagnant pools in a draw littered with mule carcasses. The battle for Nhpum Ga lasted ten days and consisted of enemy artillery barrages and relentless infantry assaults against the beleaguered village position. The 3d Battalion desperately counterattacked to reach its battered comrades at Nhpum Ga, but was thrown back several times. The heavy combat included persistent attacks up sheer slopes domi-nated by Japanese machine gunners and grenadiers. Finally, on 9 April, relief forces broke through to Nhpum Ga and the Japanese withdrew.

By this stage of the Burmese campaign the original ranks of Merrill's Marauders were so seriously eroded that complete reor-ganization was mandated. Cumulative battle losses, malaria and dysentery, and accidental injuries sustained during 500 miles of prolonged jungle maneuvering had already caused the loss of 700 soldiers. Following the battle of Nhpum Ga the depleted 2d Bat-talion, which suffered nearly 50 percent causalities, was bolstered with 300 Kachin tribal irregulars and reorganized as M Force. The 1st and 2d Battalions retained their dual combat team organization, but were reinforced with a Chinese infantry regiment each and labeled as H and K Force, respectively.

On 27 April 1944, General Merrill ordered his command to continue toward the Myitkyina airfield. This last drive consisted of a punishing march over the jagged spine of the Kumon Range in seasonal rains and oppressive tropical humidity. The marauders trudged up highland ridges dominated by dense, gloomy rain forests. The large trees towered over the winding pathways and their leafy canopies virtually blocked all sunlight. The dank jungle floor was layered by thick decaying vegetation that wrenched ankles and made footing treacherous. Clearings on the eastern slopes of the ridges were covered by razor-sharp elephant grass and vine-tangled undergrowth. The K Force was delayed by two village battles, but H Force managed to close against Myitkyina by the middle of May.

The advance of Col. Charles N. Hunter's H Force was temporarily stalled when its Kachin guide, Nauiyang Nau, was bitten and lamed by a poisonous snake while wading rice paddies in the overcast darkness of 15 May. Captain Laffin and Lieutenant Dunlap took turns sucking poison from the guide's swollen foot for over two hours, and then mounted him on Colonel Hunter's horse. On 17 May the colonel led a midmorning attack on Myitkyina. The Chinese regulars stormed the airfield as the Red and White Combat Teams seized both ferry sites to block Japanese reinforcements from crossing the Irrawaddy River. The marauders were so exhausted, however, that even the arrival of K Force could not force the Japanese from Myitkyina itself, and the battle for that location was not finished until 3 August.

The struggle for Myitkyina represented the final victory of the decimated 5307th Composite Unit, and it was dissolved as a field unit. On 10 August 1944 the army consolidated it with the 475th Infantry Regiment at Ledo, India. Among its many singular honors, the 5307th was credited as being the first United States ground combat force to meet the enemy on the continent of Asia during World War II. The marauders paid a heavy price for this privilege. From February to June 1944 the recorded losses among Merrill's Marauders totaled 424 battle casualties and 1,970 cases of amebic dysentery, typhus fever, malaria, tropical fevers, and psychoneurosis. Actual casualties were much higher. The number of wounded at Nhpum Ga alone exceeded the official total for the entire campaign, and nearly every member of the command suffered some degree of malaria.[4]

The successor command to Merrill's Marauders, the 475th Infantry Regiment, became part of the 5332d Brigade (Provisional)

"Mars Task Force." The regiment and its Mars Task Force command were also special long-range penetration forces fashioned for Burmese operations. On 15 October the refurbished regiment moved south along the Ledo Road and continued the offensive to open a supply route to China. In mid-November the 475th Infantry marched into battle to assist the Chinese 22d Division near Si-u and attacked during early December to restore positions near Mo-hlaing. The regiment held the Mo-hlaing and Tonkwa sector, repelled strong Japanese counterattacks, and succeeded in establishing contact with the British 36th Division on 15 December.

During January 1945 the Mars Task Force turned eastward. The 475th Infantry struck once more into enemy territory by marching toward Mong Wi. The regiment fought its last battle at Loi-kang Ridge during 3–4 February. The Japanese severed contact by retreating their last elements southward, and the regiment was relocated to garrison the Lashio area in March. On the following month the 475th Infantry was airlifted by transport planes into China, where it became responsible for training and supervising the equipping of several Chinese divisions. The regiment remained on this assignment until inactivated on 1 July 1945.[5]

Nine years later, on 21 June 1954, the Army redesignated the inactive 475th by shortening its numerical identity to the 75th Infantry. On 20 November the regiment was activated on Okinawa by Col. John D. Lawton, in order to replace the 29th Infantry. The latter regiment transferred its personnel and equipment to the 75th Infantry and then departed Okinawa for its traditional home post of Fort Benning. The 29th Infantry's homeward journey only consisted of a fifteen-man escort group that returned the colors. The 75th Infantry remained on Okinawa and was inactivated there on 21 March 1956.[6]

The legacy of Merrill's Marauders—which the Army ascribed first to the 475th Infantry and then to the 75th Infantry in the immediate post-Korean war period—was destined to become the basic heritage of all Army ranger companies raised in Vietnam. This connection is entirely appropriate, because many of its singular characteristics befitted both ranger organizations.

Merrill's Marauders, like the American Provincials and later Vietnam campaign patrollers, was created as a field-expedient contingent of volunteers designed for a specific campaign. The unit was the first U.S. ground combat force to reach mainland Asia during World War II and fought in Southeast Asia, where the Vietnam-based rangers also served. Finally, Merrill's Marauders were pioneers in long-range penetration tactics through tropical terrain, fighting on foot while largely reliant on aircraft-delivered sustenance. This experience provided the foundation for the jungle warfare style of ranger raiding and reconnaissance exhibited in Vietnam.

KOREAN WAR RANGER EXPERIENCE

Merrill's Marauders provided the underpinning of the ranger heritage in Vietnam, but the Army rangers of the Korean war established much of the practical foundation. The Army ranger battalions of the Second World War were multicompany organizations that assaulted strategic objectives in support of high-level commands. The rangers of the Korean war were companies with tactical scouting and small raid assignments that paralleled ranger attributes on the Vietnam battlefield.

The Army rangers of both the Korea and Vietnam conflicts were organized into companies that operated in a limited war environment, where infiltration of enemy-held territory was a premium requisite. Both types of rangers were designed to provide direct reconnoitering and raiding support to the field army or field forces, divisions, and brigades or regimental combat teams. The only striking difference was that the Army decided against further ranger employment when the Korean battlefield became mired in static warfare, whereas the fluid regional warfare of Vietnam kept the rangers occupied there for the duration of Unites States military participation.

Ranger service in the Korean emergency, as in Vietnam, commenced with several field-expedient organizations. The first ranger company was the 8213th Army Unit (Eighth Army Ranger Company), which was activated in Japan on 25 August 1950. In October the rangers entered Korea and underwent five weeks of special training near Pusan prior to being committed to action. Until late November, the rangers engaged in anti-guerrilla fighting behind the main front.[7]

The Eighth Army Ranger Company then joined Task Force Dolvin in a thrust aimed at the Yalu River, but became embroiled in the massive Chinese counteroffensive. At Ipsak the rangers held a critical hill against overwhelming odds and were nearly annihilated. The ranger commander, 1st Lt. Ralph Puckett, was critically wounded by mortar blasts and enemy rifle fire while directing the action from a forward position, but Pfc. Billy G. Walls succeeded in carrying him to safety through a hail of enemy bullets. The fierce fighting practically destroyed the company.

In December 1950 the battered ranger company was withdrawn from Hwang-ju in northern Korea and reorganized in southern Korea at Kaesong. Ranger commander Capt. John P. Vann relocated the refurbished company on the 200-square-mile island of Kangwha-do off the western Korea coast. The rangers patrolled the island, established observation posts, and watched for enemy landings. The company mission was to warn the Turkish Brigade of any attempted enemy amphibious move behind the Eighth Army's main battle lines. Averaging only 68 personnel, the ranger company was discontinued in March 1951.[8]

A provisional raider company of American and Korean commandos, later designated as the 8245th Army Unit, was raised by X Corps commander Maj. Gen. Edward M. Almond. The raiders specialized in executing surprise night amphibious raids along the western Korean coast. On 12 September 1950 the unit conducted a deception raid against Kunsan port to confuse enemy forces about intended corps amphibious targets. Four days later, as part of the main corps landings at Inchon, the company attempted a seaborne assault to seize Kimpo airfield. Unfortunately, the mission had to be canceled at the last minute because the element of surprise was lost.

The provisional raider company continued to support X Corps, but its mission switched by November from waterborne to screening operations in northeast Korea. The raiders patrolled the passes of the Taebaek Range and the frozen valleys north of Hamhung to detect Chinese infiltration groups, while the corps maneuvered to evacuate the region. In December the raiders were expanded into a special attack battalion of two companies and shifted to southern Korea, where they prepared to assault Sinbul-san Mountain on the main Eighth Army front.

On 22 December 1950 the two raider companies of the special attack battalion climbed and crawled up a narrow goat trail to reach the top of the snowy mountain pass leading to Sinbul-san Mountain. The Korean and American commandos traversed the rocky, iced-over mountainside in blizzard conditions that threatened to hurl the troops over the sharp ridges. The raiders succeeded in securing three of the knolls, but their charges against the summit were defeated by North Korean machine-gun, sniper, and mortar fire. The worsening weather, survivor exhaustion, and plunging night temperatures forced the raiders to withdraw. The 8227th Army Unit (Special Activities Group) reorganized the raider companies and shifted them to an anti-guerrilla role.[9]

Commencing in October 1950, regular airborne ranger infantry companies were activated and trained by the Ranger Training Command at Fort Benning, Georgia, and then attached to combat divisions and selected field commands. The ranger companies, "organized and equipped for rapid movement and brief and decisive engagements, for aggressive action, day or night, were not intended to be employed in sustained combat. Their attacks were to be made by employing surprise, stealth, heavy automatic fire, rapid movement, and short, hard action at the objective." The unit personnel were volunteers selected on the basis of their patrolling leadership qualities, mental alertness, and physical stamina. The first three ranger infantry companies (1st, 2d, 4th) reached Korea in December 1950, followed by three more ranger infantry companies (3d, 5th, 8th) during March 1951. The last two ranger infantry companies scheduled for Korean duty (10th, 11th) were inactivated in Japan before reaching the combat theater.[10]

During the Korean conflict, the ranger companies averaged 125 soldiers and were designed with the specific mission of infiltrating through enemy lines and attacking command posts, artillery positions, tank parks, and key communications centers or other facilities. The rangers were also expected to conduct reconnaissance and intelligence-gathering operations by penetrating the hostile combat zone. To achieve these results, the rangers had to be able to infiltrate through enemy lines; to cross all kinds of terrain, regardless of weather or night conditions; to seize and hold key areas when so directed; and to execute parachute, glider, or even amphibious insertions.[11]

The Korean combat record of the ranger companies was worthy. The commander of the 2d Infantry Division praised his rangers as "outstanding without exception" and noted their adeptness at night operations. On one occasion the division's attached 1st Ranger Infantry Company (Airborne) was credited with infiltrating eight miles into enemy territory and severely damaging an enemy command post. In other actions the company captured prisoners and created confusion by deep forays into enemy territory. During one early 1951 incident the rangers infiltrated behind Chinese positions and placed antipersonnel mines across enemy escape routes.[12]

The 3d Infantry Division used its attached 3d Ranger Infantry Company (Airborne) for specific missions before, during, and after attacks. In the former case, patrol teams conducted raids across the Imjin River to determine how many of the innumerable trench works were actually occupied by enemy troops, and sometimes made more distant patrols into Chinese rear areas to establish ambushes and observation posts. During the divisional attacks the rangers per-

formed chores such as accompanying armor and setting up blocking positions; taking selected mountain peaks to prevent enemy
utilization; and patrolling the flanks in rugged terrain. After an
offensive the rangers searched out bypassed Chinese or Korean military forces and sometimes pushed forward to harass withdrawing
enemy columns.[13]

The 2d Ranger Infantry Company (Airborne), composed of black
enlisted personnel, earned high praise from both the 7th Infantry
Division and the 187th Airborne Regimental Combat Team. The
former command found the rangers "valuable because of their capabilities in mountainous terrain on independent long-range penetration missions." The latter command noted that it employed both
the 2d and the 4th Ranger Infantry Company (Airborne) on a variety of assignments, including the notable parachute assault at
Munsan-ni on 23 March 1951. The 2d was used to provide infantry
support for tanks and the 4th was attached to a parachute battalion, where it contained strong enemy forces on the unit's open flank.
Regimental combat team commander Brig. Gen. Frank Bowen Jr.
noted that the rangers were employed in a predominantly infantry
role and that "all missions assigned were accomplished in a superior manner."[14]

The significant problem of the Korean War ranger experience
was the attachment of 105-to 107-man companies to infantry divisions engaged in battle. The division commanders and staffs were
not trained in the employment of rangers and too preoccupied to
learn.

The 24th Infantry Division commander stated on 12 April 1951
(only twelve days after their arrival) that the diminutive size of the
8th Ranger Infantry Company (Airborne) made it unable to undertake desired night deep-penetration missions. The rangers felt that
ranger/commando history showed that success in such operations
depends not on numbers, but on stealth, surprise, and a timely
withdrawal.

On 15 April 1951, the thirty-three Rangers of the 3d Platoon 8th
Airborne Ranger Company ambushed a large Chinese force behind
enemy lines. They killed an estimated seventy Chinese, with fifty
actually counted dead.

In the Chinese fifth-phase offensive of late April 1951, the 6th
Republic of Korea Division retreated 21 miles leaving the right
flank of the US 24th Infantry Division open to envelopment. Ninety
men of the 8th Airborne Rangers made a long night-climb that
revealed that the division flank was exposed. Ordered to return, the
rangers opened a battle by striking the rear of a Chinese force

assembling to attack the flank of the 24th Division. Though some eight miles into enemy territory, the rangers—assisted by air and artillery—disrupted the Chinese preparations and fought through to a meeting with the men of the 3rd Platoon, Company C, of the 6th Medium Tank Battalion, who voluntarily came forward to link up.

The specialized infiltration advantages of the rangers were not utilized in Korea to the extent anticipated by the Army. The airborne capability of the ranger companies was used only once, during the Munsan-ni parachute assault. On another occasion, "one ranger company was alerted for a drop intended to cut off the escape routes of high-ranking enemy personnel, but this operation was cancelled." Ranger amphibious capability was employed only once, on 11 April 1951, when the 4th Ranger Infantry Company crossed the Hwachon Dam reservoir in assault boats to make an enveloping move as part of a 7th Cavalry regimental attack. Ranger adeptness at night infiltration was seldom used because higher commanders were reluctant to commit rangers on nocturnal missions. They believed that the enemy tendency to "maneuver during darkness would probably force the rangers to deviate from preplanned routes and thus disarrange planned artillery fires."[17]

Lt. Gen. Matthew B. Ridgway, who commanded the Eighth Army from late December 1950 until April 1951, reached the conclusion that expectations for ranger companies were highly unrealistic. He believed that ranger employment on extended missions, to destroy hostile installations, was beyond their actual capability and invited destruction. Gen. James A. Van Fleet assumed command of Eighth Army on 14 April 1951 and promptly ordered an internal review on the status and possible future employment of the rangers. His army operations officer, Brig. Gen. Gilman C. Mudgett, also new to the job (since 21 March), carefully surveyed the senior officers for their views on the subject. Within a month, on 14 May, General Mudgett reported the "conclusion that a ranger battalion at Army level would meet with general approval."

General Mudgett's report summarized how the six ranger companies could be consolidated into a battalion organization large enough and flexible enough to overcome objections against the companies. He also noted the crux of the whole ranger problem by commenting, "From a broad viewpoint, the underlying objection to any special units lies in the evil of 'creaming' the Army for volunteers who might be more useful as leaders in line organizations, and the belief that any line infantry organization should, and could with special training, perform the special missions equally well."[18]

On 17 May, General Van Fleet sent details of the proposed ranger battalion to General Ridgway, who was now commander in chief of Far East Command. Van Fleet related that the envisioned Eighth Army ranger battalion would be attached to the 8086th Army Unit (Miscellaneous Group), with the mission of penetrating the enemy rear for harassment, gathering intelligence, and destruction behind the lines, as well as supporting overt partisan activities. The ranger battalion would be capable of either strategic (deep) penetration missions directed by the 8086th Army Unit, or a range of tactical (shallow) missions. The latter assignments encompassed activities such as raids in corps or division sectors, airborne envelopments with the 187th Airborne Regimental Combat Team, and acting as an army reserve to eliminate enemy infiltration elements. Depending on mission dictates, any part or all of the ranger battalion could be used.[19]

General Ridgway was not swayed by the battalion concept and recommended instead "that all ranger companies in the Far East Command be inactivated." Ridgway considered the rangers especially limited by Korean combat conditions and wasteful of highly trained manpower. The rangers, in his opinion, were too small for deep penetration, could not overcome "language and racial recognition barriers," and risked personnel to increased chances of capture—a particularly disturbing prospect because of the "failure of the communists to adhere to legal and humane treatment of prisoners of war." General Ridgway secured Van Fleet's agreement that "ranger units, even of battalion size, could not exploit their full capabilities under existing conditions" in an Asian combat zone.[20]

Army chief of staff Lt. Gen. J. Lawton Collins consented to a mass disbandment of ranger units in Korea that August. General Collins had been pleased with the significant and favorable public response to ranger activations and divisional attachments, but he also was concerned about the alleged mission difficulties caused by their small size, language unfamiliarity, and nonindigenous ethnic background. He sent a message to subordinate commands that carefully explained the official army version of the circumstances necessitating combat ranger inactivations:

> One of the compelling reasons for the decision to inactivate these companies was the fact that deep patrol missions by small units for which the rangers are intended, are made most difficult in the Far East command by reason of the racial differences between the oriental and the Caucasian.[21]

The wartime ranger companies of the Korean conflict served as an important prelude to the continuing development of small patrol and ranger units—despite the temporary severance of ranger organizations—and this chain of service was eventually relinked by the Army. In the meantime, Korean combat experience demonstrated that rangers were extremely valuable for performing close-in patrols and raids to gain intelligence and secure prisoners; setting up ambushes; establishing observation and listening posts; accompanying and protecting mechanized patrols; seizing and occupying prominent terrain features to deny enemy use; sending out flank patrols to maintain contact with nearby friendly elements; and combating guerrilla activities in rear areas. These were essentially the same ranger tasks assigned in Vietnam.[22]

RECONNAISSANCE ON THE EVE OF THE VIETNAM CONFLICT

Ranger infantry companies were discontinued during the stalemated confrontation between linear-placed armies in the midst of the Korean war. Many senior officers believed that ranger-style reconnaissance was important as an additional infantry tactic, but that specific ranger units were unsuccessful in Korea and therefore not needed in peacetime. Maintaining ranger companies as part of the postwar ground force structure was dismissed, and in 1960 the Army lineage branch transferred all ranger heritage to the newly created Army Special Forces.

During the years between the Korean and Vietnam conflicts, the most dangerous arena of confrontation between opposing land armies was the "Iron Curtain" border separating western Germany from communist-controlled eastern Germany and Czechoslovakia. The Seventh Army, a bulwark of American military commitments to the North Atlantic Treaty Organization (NATO), was responsible for a 300-mile length of the German border in Hesse and Bavaria. Powerful enemy forces arrayed against this region were expected to advance swiftly through six major corridors into the American zone, requiring the Seventh Army to stretch all available resources. These circumstances revitalized the merits of long-range infantry reconnaissance units.[23]

In 1958 the Seventh Army reacted to several war-threatening crises. These included renewed Soviet pressure against the access zones leading to West Berlin and the emergency dispatch of military forces to Lebanon. Both situations prompted immediate Seventh Army efforts to upgrade its response posture, with emphasis on combat surveillance and target acquisition abilities.

On 1 July 1958 the Seventh Army established the U.S. Army Surveillance Unit, Europe. The unit was equipped with observation aircraft, fire-control radar, counter-mortar and ground-surveillance radar, and mobile photographic instruments. Several interim forty-four-man surveillance platoons were organized in infantry and armored division reconnaissance squadrons. By September 1959 new intelligence-gathering devices, such as the AN/TPS-25 long-range ground-surveillance radars, reached several divisions in Seventh Army.

The Seventh Army also sharpened its focus on longer-range surveillance and countermeasures in case of general nuclear war. Special nuclear weapons and Atomic Demolition Munitions added new dimensions for infiltration patrols, but they required airborne-qualified soldiers who could parachute into objective areas, scout forward to targets, and fight as infantry in defensive situations. During early 1960 the Seventh Army investigated the feasibility of each subordinate corps forming a patrol company.

The V Corps, located across the Hessian and Bavarian front north of the Main River, faced four of the six most likely Soviet penetration corridors into the German heartland. The corps commander expressed reservations about forming a patrol company that took personnel from other corps units, and preferred to test the patrols in field exercises before making a definite decision. The VII Corps commander, charged with guarding Bavaria against a Soviet thrust out of Saxony and Czechoslovakia, requested permission to form such a patrol unit immediately, because of wartime employment opportunities in the forested Fichtel Mountains and Bohemian mountain passes.

In the late summer of 1960 the Seventh Army planners decided that the personnel slots for two 160-member airborne patrol companies could be gained by reorganizing the 8th Infantry Division. In September the Seventh Army directed V and VII Corps to organize two experimental eighty-member scouting companies. The half-strength units participated in Exercise WINTER SHIELD II and confirmed the effectiveness of long-range reconnaissance patrols in a special target acquisition role. In March 1961, U.S. Army Europe approved the formation of two corps-level patrol companies, composed of 166 paratroopers each, for the purpose of infiltration on special tasks that included team placement of T-4 Atomic Demolition Munitions and locating enemy battlefield targets for Army tactical nuclear delivery systems.[24]

On 15 July 1961 the Seventh Army activated the U.S. Army Long Range Reconnaissance Patrol Company (Airborne), Wildflecken, for V Corps. The provisional company, organized under Table of

Distribution (TD) 3779, had no numerical designation but was known as the "Victory Lerps." The Victory stemmed from V for V Corps, and Lerp was a contraction of long-range reconnaissance patrol or LRRP (later Lerp became indifferently spelled as Lurp, by approximating its pronunciation). The company mission encompassed extensive patrolling missions in the Bad Hersfeld, Fulda, Bad Kissingen, and Coburg corridors.[25]

On 15 July 1961 the Seventh Army also activated the U.S. Army Long Range Reconnaissance Patrol Company (Airborne), Nellingen, for VII Corps. The provisional company, organized under Table of Distribution (TD) 3780, had no numerical designation but was known as the "Jayhawk Lerps." The Jayhawk was derived from the corps' fighting Jayhawk symbol, a bird sporting an overseas cap and baring sharp teeth. The company was entrusted with patrolling missions in the Hof and Fürth corridors, leading toward Nuremberg and Munich respectively.

Both companies were assigned extremely dangerous missions and required selected paratroopers who could perform special skills, such as demolitions and long-distance communications, and complete demanding winter warfare and mountain courses. The companies filled slowly at first, but the Berlin crisis in the early fall of 1961 increased command pressure for both units to reach full operational readiness. By the end of the year the V Corps' Wildflecken LRRP company contained 128 troops, and the VII Corps' Nellingen LRRP Company mustered 144 personnel.[26]

In January 1962 the Department of the Army responded to the growing need to update ranger tactics by publishing a new field manual on ranger training and operations. Ranger operations were defined as overt operations by highly trained infantry units, to any depth into enemy-held areas, for the purpose of reconnaissance, raids, and general disruption of enemy operations. The manual set forth programs of realistic and tough ranger training that covered airmobile operations, establishing ambush and roadblock positions, cliff assaults, extended operations, small-unit waterborne employment, and anti-guerrilla techniques. Ranger methods governed the commitment of infantry long-range patrol units, but the two companies stationed in Europe remained their only practitioners.

The ranger task in Europe was given new impetus as the Army began upgrading its tactical nuclear warfare capability. The "Honest John," a free rocket employed at division and corps level, was joined by the smaller "Little John" version adopted for airmobile operations. The "Sergeant" and "Pershing" guided missiles provided supplementary nuclear weapons, with greater range, for both the corps and the field army. During wartime the rangers would support these systems by finding targets and making assessments of their low-yield nuclear strikes.

The solid-fuel, medium-range Sergeant missile could deliver nuclear, chemical, or biological fires at ranges from 46 to 140 miles. In September 1964, the last of five Sergeant-equipped missile battalions deployed to Europe, where they replaced the less accurate liquid-fuel "Corporal" missiles. That same year the Army began deploying long-range Pershing nuclear ballistic missiles into Germany, where they assumed the quick reaction alert role for Seventh Army nuclear fire programs during 1965. Additionally, the Army's 8-inch howitzer nuclear capability was bolstered by newly developed warheads for 155mm howitzer tubes.

As a result, during the spring of 1965, the European-based provisional corps-level long-range reconnaissance patrol units were transformed from their original Table of Distribution status to regular components of established infantry regiments. On 15 May 1965, Company D (Airborne Long Range Patrol), 17th Infantry, was activated using the assets of the discontinued Wildflecken LRRP Company. On the same day, Company C (Airborne Long Range Patrol), 58th Infantry, was activated using the personnel and equipment of the old Nellingen LRRP Company.[27]

The Company D "Victory Lerps," under V Corps, practiced combat reconnaissance for operations in the Frankenwald and Thuringian mountains, and across the river-segmented highlands of the Bad Hersfeld–Giessen, Fulda–Hanau, Bad Kissingen–Würzburg, and Coburg–Bamberg corridors. The recon paratroopers also rehearsed deep penetration missions scheduled against likely Thuringian targets that were typified by the Soviet Weimar-Nohra air installation and army facilities around Ohrdruf and Jena.

The company C "Jayhawk Lerps," under VII Corps, routinely parachuted into the south German hills to conduct patrolling through the Fürth–Munich and Hof–Nuremberg corridors. The recon teams also prepared for deep-penetration missions against enemy communication lines in western Czechoslovakia, as well as crucial Saxon targets like the Soviet air base at Altenburg. The company boasted annual first places in the European-hosted international four-day marching tournaments. Patrol team preparation for this strenuous event consisted of hiking twenty-five miles daily, with fully loaded gear and weapons that totaled eighty to ninety pounds per soldier, through the hilly pathways of rural Bavaria.

During typical training missions, the company reached its target areas by parachuting sixty-five-member contingents from flights of three C-130 aircraft. The paratroopers were organized into teams of ten each, called "sticks," and each stick contained a leader responsible for making sure his troops were equipped correctly and briefed on jump tactics and weather conditions before the airborne infiltration exercises. The troops carried heavy loads of gear and weapons in H-harnesses, kit bags, and personnel equipment containers.

A typical training exercise was reflected by the July 1965 jump over Leonberg, Germany. As the transport carriers approached the upcoming drop zone at an altitude of 1,200 feet, Safety NCO Staff Sgt. David D. Glenn grabbed an interior railing of the lurching aircraft and leaned out of the open door. He peered into the gale-force winds to watch for "drop" or "no-drop" smoke signals from the ground. Spotting the signal to proceed, Sergeant Glenn turned back inside and signaled for the first man to jump out. The lead troop was Sp4 Frederick Kennedy, the "wind dummy," who parachuted first to allow the aircraft navigator to observe his parachute drift and make last-minute course corrections.

Stick leaders Sgt. James R. Jackson and Staff Sergeant Dudley readied their sticks by moving into final positions at the side aircraft doors, where they awaited the order to jump. Their T-10 nylon parachutes were static-line-operated, and Safety NCO Staff Sgt. James P. Hart had already checked all parachute static lines to ensure they were hooked up securely to the overhead anchor-line cable. Upon receiving the command "Go!" the stick sergeants led their paratroopers out the door.

The teams exited the aircraft and descended under blossoming white T-10 parachutes. The paratroopers were equipped with reserve parachutes in case of dreaded main parachute malfunctions, most of which were "Mae West" semi-inversions (occurring when a portion of the skirt was blown through adjacent or opposite gores). The Jayhawk Lerps landed routinely, however, without suffering any mishaps, and proceeded smoothly into the ground portion of their training mission.

These parachute-capable infantry patrol units fulfilled a command necessity for ranger-style raiding and military intelligence operations that did not ordinarily exist in peacetime. No similar units were organized elsewhere. The Army at large remained oblivious to the urgent requirements for conventional ranger-style tactical reconnaissance units until regular military forces entered Vietnam. The Army continued to insist on airborne-qualified personnel wherever possible, but the abundance and rugged dependability of new-model helicopters rendered parachute insertions superfluous to patrol operations.

In those last golden days of the prewar drafted army, the airborne long-range patrol companies were composed entirely of highly trained infantry volunteers. During the constant field exercises in cold German morning mists, lines of recon troops moved in orderly procession to board bright metallic C-130 Hercules aircraft that were parked neatly on concrete ramps. The paratroopers wore tightly strapped main-and-reserve parachute harnesses and chin-strapped helmets that gave them unmistakable combat appearance, but their jump boots gleamed with polish and their field-jacketed uniforms were adorned with full-color emblems. They exuded the pride and confidence of professional warriors.

Within a year many of the same troops would be patrolling through the rain forests and trackless marshes of Vietnam. There the soldiers were attired in rip-stop tropical combat fatigues, burdened by ammunition-crammed rucksacks instead of parachutes, substituted jungle flop hats for helmets, and wore jungle boots plated with steel soles to deflect punji stakes. The patrol leader sergeants and their patrollers became seasoned combat veterans. The combat reconnaissance teams—apart from other army units in Vietnam—displayed the proud cohesive esteem bonded by the ranger legacy.

2

AMERICAL INFANTRY DIVISION

AMERICAL RANGERS

COMBAT RECONNAISSANCE IN VIETNAM

United States Army long-range patrol and ranger units in Vietnam were raised as field-expedient elements to perform extended scout and raiding coverage for larger formations employed in a territorial security role. The impact of limited warfare in Southeast Asia, combined with the lack of a well-defined front, mandated greater reliance on ground combat reconnaissance.

Small patrol teams were fielded to discern the fragmented battlefield and detect enemy activity in difficult tropical terrain. These patrollers, later designated as rangers, were tasked to operate in the remote countryside and gather intelligence, perform terrain analysis, monitor key areas, acquire targets, and conduct small precision strikes.

This heightened combat reconnaissance endeavor was also influenced by the irregular nature of the battlefield. The Army adopted an essentially reactive posture to militarily safeguarding its areas of responsibility in South Vietnam, and the frequency and intensity of army operations were conformed to the reported strength and movement of opposing forces. For this reason, Army reconnaissance tactics were inseparably linked to the nature of its adversaries: the Vietnamese National Liberation Front, known to the Americans as the Viet Cong (VC); and the People's Army of Vietnam, labeled commonly by Americans as the North Vietnamese Army (NVA).

The Viet Cong armed insurgency movement was composed of both armed "local force" partisans and "main force" combat units.

The shadowy and fluid local Viet Cong bedeviled many patrols. North Vietnamese Army and main force Viet Cong units were organized in regular units, but soldiers sometimes intermixed with guerrilla outfits, and some NVA components merged with elements of their southern compatriots. The North Vietnamese Army and Viet Cong regular forces fought conventionally, if possible, only under favorable circumstances and resorted to ambush and elusive tactics if challenged by larger forces or superior firepower.

Extended ground combat recon operations were the domain of Long Range Reconnaissance Patrol (LRRP) units, later redesignated as ranger companies. These were organized into platoons and infantry companies that consisted of a small command and control headquarters, a sparse support element, and a number of recon teams. The number of authorized teams varied according to the Army hierarchy: twenty-eight teams for each field force, sixteen teams for every division, and eight teams for a separate brigade. Ordinarily, the operating efficiency of the patrol or ranger unit was divided by thirds, a third of the teams being active in the field while remaining teams were cycled through rest and preparation stages.

Long-range patrol and ranger companies in Vietnam were combat recon units. In other words, they were capable of performing both reconnaissance and combat missions—either separately or in combination. Reconnaissance patrols were surveillance expeditions that garnered information by observing the enemy surreptitiously. Contact with the enemy was avoided, and if the enemy became aware of the presence of the patrol, it was considered "compromised" and evacuated as quickly as possible. Combat patrols raided enemy forces by performing ambushes, capturing prisoners, or directing artillery shelling and air strikes. Teams that combined reconnaissance and combat usually watched the enemy and struck opportune targets.

Combat recon team size varied with mission requirements and personnel availability, although four patrollers was the minimum considered prudent for actual deployment. Some teams were reinforced with an indigenous guide, a turncoat Kit Carson scout, or a sniper. Teams could also be supplemented by specialists, such as pathfinders or engineers, on missions requiring additional expertise. Two teams operating inside a highly dangerous area were often combined into "heavy teams" for firepower advantages, but they were noisier and prone to create more visible signs of trail-breaking and foliage disruption.

The long-range patrol, recon team, or ranger team was a team in its truest sense. The members developed confidence in their own abilities and relied on those of their comrades, and this mutual trust counted for everything. The team leader was a combat-experienced veteran, usually a sergeant or specialist promotable to sergeant, who demonstrated leadership traits, mastery of reconnoitering skills, a knack for maintaining surprise against the enemy during patrol infiltration and movement, and a measure of either real or ascribed luck in keeping fellow team members alive. Rank was a secondary consideration in determining team positions.

The assistant team leader was usually the next-most-accomplished senior scout. The remainder of the team consisted typically of two or three scouts and a radiotelephone operator. The radioman usually doubled as a forward observer who could adjust artillery and aerial fire support. Other team members doubled as medical specialists and marksmen. All team members were handpicked volunteers carefully selected for scouting qualities, hard soldiering ability, and mature judgment. Team members received constant training in scouting and extended patrolling, either in the field or through individual schooling—such as that offered by the MACV Recondo School or division and brigade courses.

Team objectives were often far inside tropical rain forest, jungle-clad razorback ridges, or trackless swamps. The teams were air-landed by helicopter, lowered by rope, or delivered by small boat or armored personnel carriers, or simply walked into its area. A recon team normally received its mission a day or two in advance. This time enabled the platoon leader and team leader to accomplish the necessary planning, coordination, and preparation for the mission.

Ideally, the aerial reconnaissance took place twenty-four hours before the planned insertion and was accomplished by a one-time overflight of the objective. The helicopter was preferably piloted by the same aviator who would conduct the actual insertion, and he flew the leaders over the mission area to select landing zones and see the layout of the countryside. Mission details were finalized after the aerial recon flight. Unfortunately, many Vietnam patrols were scrambled into action under much briefer and even crash circumstances, where morning overflights (if available) were followed by afternoon insertions.

Long-range patrols in Vietnam were routinely scheduled for five days. The time period was chosen to give adequate surveillance opportunities for distant patrols working inside unknown territory. However, the same period also gave short-duration patrols (assigned a point target or other quick assignment) time allowances for adverse weather or enemy-reaction contingencies. The long assignments mandated portage of enough equipment, rations, water, supplies, weaponry, and munitions to sustain the patrol for several successive days. The team members carried all the equipment and supplies for which a need could be anticipated and stamina allowed. Individual patrolling loads varied from sixty to seventy pounds per man, and only rarely under fifty. Once in the field, resupply from outside sources was avoided to prevent jeopardizing the mission and endangering the team.

Team armament varied according to the type and expected duration of the assigned mission. Reconnaissance patrols were armed primarily with M16 rifles or CAR-15 submachine guns, the latter being favored but not readily available until 1968. The M16 and its modified CAR-15 version were highly effective at jungle-fighting ranges, where their lethality caused fatal heartbeat reversal even on shoulder hits. Each team usually carried an M79 grenade launcher, a compact and dependable weapon that extended the range of hand-thrown grenades. Other patrol weapons included occasional shotguns, sniper rifles, and a variety of fragmentation, white phosphorus, and CS-gas grenades and mini-grenades. M18 claymore mines, designed to stop close assaults by spewing out 700 steel balls in a 60-degree arc of destruction, were the principal ambush instruments used by Army patrols in Vietnam.

Combat patrols demanded heavier firepower than reconnaissance patrols. The addition of an M60 machine gun offered superior firepower advantages that offset its relatively heavy twenty-three-pound weight and sometimes troublesome auto-gas operation. M72 Light Antitank Weapons (LAWs) were hand-held, single-shot rocket launchers periodically used against bunkers. Some teams were also equipped with enemy weapons, such as captured AK47 assault rifles and RPG-2 or RPG-7 rocket-propelled grenades. Foreign weapons were used primarily either to create deceptive fire or to confuse enemy spotters who glimpsed a lead patroller (point man) with enemy equipment. The patrollers carried a variety of weapons and a lot of ammunition, but they knew this mattered little if they were opposed by a determined and numerically superior enemy force.

Team observation items included AN/PVS-2 starlight devices for night visual enhancement as well as binoculars and a 35mm camera. The team hauled backpack and emergency radios, extra batteries, strobe lights, pen flares, flashlights, aircraft signal panels, signal mirrors, and flare pistols for communications and signaling purposes. Each patroller also carried a knife, compass, map, three to five canteens of water, combat rations, poncho, extra socks, carabiner with a climbing rope, weapons-cleaning items, and a medical kit with one or two blood-expander units. A lightweight protective mask was brought along in case gas was used to facilitate patrol escape and evasion.

Patrollers were not only burdened with their own military apparel and gear but became loaded with the team equipment and ammunition distributed among them. One mid-1969 ranger team recorded the following material carried on missions:

> 2 PRC-25 radios with long antennae and 3 handsets (1 extra), spare radio batteries, 1 Starlight scope, 4 strobe lights, 6 trip flares, 4 star clusters, 4 parachute flares, 4 VS-17 panel markers, 4 WP grenades, 4 CS grenades, 4 LAWs, 1 M60 machinegun, 1 M79 grenade launcher, 1 XM21 rifle with sniper scope, 2 White Phosphorus rifle grenades with crimped cartridges for M16 use, 1 pair 6×30 binoculars, 900 rounds of M16 ammunition, 1500 rounds of M60 ammunition, 300 M14 rounds, M79 ammunition to include 120 HE rounds, 10 canister rounds, and 6 parachute flare rounds. Each man also carried an M16 (except for the sniper, grenadier, and machine gunner), 8 quarts of water, 2 smoke grenades, 2 compasses, a protective mask, 2 signal mirrors, 2 battle dressings, 6 M26 or M33 grenades, 2 claymore mines, a knife, weapons cleaning equipment, wrist watch, poncho, 50 salt tablets, insect repellent, and a length of parachute suspension line.

The great cumulative weight of all this gear was truly staggering, and severely hindered the mobility of even the hardiest soldiers. A great deal of ranger knowledge was not required to understand that Army patrols in Vietnam broke the cardinal scouting rule of traveling "light and fast." The patrol team was inspected just prior to insertion to ensure that all prescribed equipment was carried. Later in the war, standards slipped and patrols became less disciplined. The final prefield inspections included checks for prohibited cigarettes, reading matter, commercial radios, and other material that might have compromised the team's position or contributed to inattentiveness.

Patrol insertions were supervised by the field platoon leader or sergeant, who flew in a command and control aircraft circling the area at a high altitude. The aerial platform enabled the platoon leader to radio patrol directions or coordinate required assistance. The command helicopter was the guide aircraft for the flight, and was followed by the utility helicopter carrying the team. The utility helicopter flew at much lower altitude or even at treetop level. The third "chase" helicopter in flight was a recovery aircraft that could lift out the team and aircrew if the utility helicopter was downed in a landing zone mishap. The reserve helicopter was automatically put on flights because emergency situations left no time to call a replacement helicopter from base. A pair of armed helicopter "gunships" escorted the formation and provided aerial firepower.

Helicopter delivery was deliberately varied to avoid predictable schedules, but twilight landings were preferred. The timing allowed enough daylight for the aviators and permitted the team to move some distance away from the landing zone before nightfall. Helicopters landed in different spots with closed doors and conducted numerous "false insertions" as a deception technique to disguise the team's exact drop-off point. North Vietnamese or Viet Cong leaders, however, posted trail-watchers near likely clearings or sent scouts to investigate probable locations. For this reason, the first two hours after insertion constituted the team's most dangerous interval and mentally strenuous period.

Once a team was on the ground, it moved to the nearest cover, such as the row of trees ("tree line") at the end of the landing field. As soon as the team reached jungle overgrowth the members formed a small defensive circle and reverted to a quiet listening mode. Further patrol activity did not occur until the team leader was satisfied that the location was secure. He established communications with the overhead command helicopter as well as the base tactical operations center. When the patrol moved again, it moved rapidly but cautiously in a direction away from the landing zone.

Night movement across treacherous tropical jungle was often considered hazardous, and primitive light enhancement ("night vision") devices were in their infancy. Patrols had trouble navigating, and their noises were more likely to be heard. Therefore, teams seldom moved at night except for short distances. During the evening the team chose a tentative overnight position, usually nestled in a dense jungle thicket, but did not move in immediately. Instead, the team observed the chosen location from a safe distance and watched for any danger signs until dusk. Hand signals substituted for words, and talking consisted of hushed whispers or crisp reports using faint sounds over radio handsets.

Teams tried to select overnight, ambush, or surveillance positions that would help a small patrol hide from the enemy, see all approaches, maintain good radio contact, and escape quickly if detected. Sometimes these characteristics were mutually exclusive. For example, thick underbrush gave concealment but hampered observation of the surrounding area. Where tropical foliage was thickest and the best concealment existed, along a streambed or jungle hollow, radio receptivity was marginal because higher ground interfered with transmission signals.

At nightfall the team occupied a small circular laager position and the patrol members formed a tight perimeter by huddling close together so that everyone was within easy touch contact. The radio was centrally located to facilitate passing the handset. Sometimes the team leader was in the center of the circle. Throughout the night, the patrollers posted guard on a rotating basis. The patrol moved at first light and left no evidence of their presence in the area.

Later in the morning the members found another vegetated spot and consumed a quick meal. The patrollers carried a minimum amount of food and water, and their lightweight, 1,000-calorie long-range patrol food packets were the first freeze-dried combat rations in the military. The substance was a precooked, freeze-dried meal (typically beef hash, pork, or chicken stew) that could be eaten dry or rehydrated using cold water—both techniques avoiding telltale fires. Good patrollers were careful to leave no trace of their presence in the area and carried all trash with them.

Patrols moved slowly in file. The formation made less noise, was easier to control, and left fewer broken branches and other signs of human movement in its wake. The file could be compact, with patrollers within arm's reach and never more than six feet apart, or extended with team members just keeping visual range. The team file moved long distances in a tropical hinterland that included vine-choked dense jungle, jagged forested mountains, ankle-wrenching rice fields, and brackish swamps. "Heavy teams" or teams with more than six personnel caused more broken branches, overturned rocks, and other trail clues that inevitably attracted enemy attention.

The Viet Cong and North Vietnamese Army troops were prone to take a midday two-hour siesta or "pock time," usually from about 11:30 or 12:00 to about 1:30 or 2:00 P.M. During the lull, the enemy set up defensive perimeters and guarded them with trail-watchers and outposts. Long-range patrols moving at this time incurred a greater risk of being detected, especially if they moved inadvertently into an enemy area. For these reasons, American patrols also remained stationary during the same two-hour period. The soldiers rested under the blistering tropical sun or dank jungle canopy and often made a quick radio check.

Radio communication was essential to every patrol. Radios were used by patrols to transmit the current situation, inform headquarters about the enemy, and coordinate supporting firepower or arrange evacuation. Patrols tried to give situation reports at least two or three times a day. The succinct patrol summaries gave the team location, direction of movement, and condition of the terrain and trails. Any information about observed enemy activity was transmitted immediately, on a priority basis, as circumstances allowed.

The radios of the Vietnam era were inadequate to patrolling demands. The better radios of the long-range AM variety were of little use because they required apparatus that was difficult to erect in emergencies. Some radios, like the PRC-64 high-frequency set, performed well in the continuous-wave mode but the voice mode was unreliable—and the lack of trained key operators prevented their employment. The sturdy Special Forces GRC-109, a continuous-wave radio that worked well despite Vietnam's tropical terrain and atmospheric conditions, was shunned because patrollers disliked the hand-cranked generator and were usually unable to transmit in Morse code.

Patrols resorted primarily to carrying PRC-25 short-range FM radios. These were modular and transistorized except for a power amplifier tube. The twenty-pound radio sets were heavy to backpack, especially when the weight of necessary auxiliary components and spare batteries was added. In addition, the radios had certain parts that tended to malfunction or break. Many teams lugged along an additional PRC-25 in case the primary radio became inoperable. The extra equipment added more weight, but the backup was highly desirable. The completely solid-state design of the PRC-77 radio classified it as an improved version of the PRC-25, but it was only slightly more reliable than the older model and actually possessed less power. The PRC-77 radios came into common infantry use after 1968, but many recon teams stayed with the PRC-25 radios.

Vietnam's rugged geography, dense tropical foliage, and adverse weather sliced into the PRC-25 radios' advertised five-mile radio ranges. Mountains and ridges blocked transmissions and hindered signal receptivity. Severe electrical storm disturbances, which were common enough in any season, endangered any radio work. Wet weather caused radio handsets to fail almost automatically. To provide moisture-resistant barriers, teams sealed batteries in plastic bags and taped plastic around handsets, but these remedies were only partially successful.

Dense jungle made the normally reliable RC-292 ground antenna impractical, unless it could be hoisted into upper forest canopies. To increase signal range, teams were often forced into noisy and time-consuming constructions of field-expedient signal contraptions, including the building of wave and vertical half-rhombic antennae. Such makeshift apparatus often included trees or bamboo poles for support, and claymore wire or WD-1 wire strung up as vertical and ground-plane elements. Lines were passed through branches, regular antennae were elevated into trees, and antenna lead-ins were connected. A team exhibiting enough patience, ingenuity, machete power, tree-climbing expertise, and hard work might be able to establish radio contact.

On more distant patrols, direct communication was outside the realm of possibility. Teams on these missions had to depend on passing their signals through aerial or ground radio relay stations. Such patrols were at the mercy of rotating aircraft shifts and the operating safety of other radio bases. Emergency radios like the URC-10 were useful only in situations where distress signals could be directed at aircraft directly overhead.

Equipment problems were secondary to the ordinary hardships that patrollers endured in the tropical environment. The Vietnamese climate was hotter and more humid than any tropical region of the United States. During the dry season temperatures soared well over 100 degrees, with humidity frequently exceeding 90 percent, and body strength was rapidly sapped. During the wet season, torrential monsoon rains caused severe physical discomfort and increased the chances of personal injury by turning streams into raging cascades and inundating lowlands.

Diseases and fevers of unknown origin were endemic in tropical regions and often sliced through the patrolling ranks. For example, the trombiculid mite proliferated in the high grass of mountainous Vietnam and accounted for the high patrolling incidence of scrub typhus. Gastrointestinal diseases were especially acute and debilitating. Team ranks were thinned more often by parasitic diseases such as hepatitis and other diarrheal ailments than by combat. In the Americal Division sector, patrols operating in the disease-ridden Antenna Valley were subjected to very high malaria rates as well as amebic dysentery and other illnesses. Persistent moisture in Vietnam encouraged fungus infections and rotted boot leather.

Streams and waterways in Vietnam were infested with leeches, and infestation of the nasal leech produced nosebleeds and hemoptysis. Neurotoxic snakes, including Asian cobras and the banded krait, thrived in significant numbers. The bamboo viper of the rain forest was dreaded by all soldiers, including those from rattlesnake-infested areas in the United States who normally displayed little fear of reptiles. The bamboo viper was often referred to respectfully as "Mr. Two Step" or the "cigarette snake," because, once bitten, a person supposedly lived for two steps, or alternatively for enough time to smoke a cigarette.

One Americal Division ranger was bitten in the arm by a snake while preparing to leave a night ambush area. Another medic-qualified ranger applied a tourniquet to his arm while the patrol leader killed the snake with a machete. The patrol carried the reptile back, just in case an antivenin was needed, and placed it in the custody of the "rather hesitant door gunner" on their extraction helicopter. In reality, most snakebites were made by nonvenomous snakes, and venomous bites from even the arboreal green bamboo viper rarely proved lethal to American soldiers.

Teams terminating their patrols moved into positions about 300 yards from the extraction zone. They spent the night there, moved to the pickup point early in the morning, and checked the area for any signs of human activity. The teams formed a final defensive perimeter and waited for the arrival of the helicopters. The patrollers often used a mirror to signal the helicopter and confirmed the reflection by displaying a ground panel. Smoke or flares were used only as a last resort. The team leader also radioed the pilot information about the best direction of approach, the winds, and any obstacles.

Patrols were normally extracted when the teams boarded helicopters. Enemy action or heavy forestation sometimes barred the helicopters from landing. In these invariably adverse cases, the lift-out helicopter hovered above the team and descended as low as possible over the jungle. Three rope assemblies—the "McGuire rigs" developed by Special Forces and named in honor of Project Delta Sgt. Maj. Charles T. McGuire—were dropped to the ground, weighted by sandbags. The team members below the helicopter hooked into the ropes by releasing the sandbags, shaking out all the loops, and stepping into the lower part of the harness while fastening their carabiners to the D-rings farther up the rigs. Once the patrollers were securely fastened into the McGuire rigs, the pilot lifted them out.

McGuire rig extraction, however, remained the absolutely last alternative available to patrols and was employed only when a team was in trouble and could not reach the normal pickup zone. In such cases, the surrounding jungle could be thick and double- or triple-canopied, and the team was probably being pursued closely by NVA/VC forces. The extraction helicopter had to hover low over the site and drop lines. If the patrollers were fortunate enough to have gunships in support, the dense jungle often forced them to rely on sound to make firing-pass adjustments. The aerial support had to be directed around both the patrol pickup point and the extraction helicopter. Once the helicopter crew initiated the McGuire extractions, it was a very slow process for the aircraft to pull the patrollers up before it could begin flying forward. Both aircrew and patrollers knew significant enemy fire might cause serious hits against the aircraft and, if necessary, the ropes would have to be chopped.

On extremely dark nights, during emergency situations, pilots used homing devices on their helicopters in an attempt to locate recon teams. The team depressed its radio handset and broke squelch at ten-second intervals while the control helicopter homed in on the signals. Command helicopters using this method were able to determine when they were over a patrol's position. When the helicopter was directly overhead, the patrol employed a strobe light to signal it for final extraction.

Whether the team boarded its helicopters normally or was lifted out in exigency, it was transported back to the base camp or mission support site and debriefed. The team members then entered "standdown" for three or four days. The time between missions was spent resting, rehearsing patrol techniques, perfecting teamwork, honing individual scouting skills, and finally preparing for another patrol mission.

Break-contact drills were rehearsed constantly during standdown, and teams practiced this vital patrol survival facet daily. The drill was finalized by a live-fire exercise where the point man fired up the front, the patroller behind him first threw a grenade and took up the fire as the point man "broke contact," and the sequence was repeated at dizzy speed until every team member was through the rehearsal. The exercises invariably wounded people, and higher commanders chafed at the lack of safety, but ranger leaders steadfastly refused command pressure to "institute safer measures"— because no substitute existed for the precise lifesaving reaction required in an emergency.

The individual patroller depended foremost on stealth and vigilance to complete his mission and return to fight another day. He lived by a motto only slightly modified from the instructions of Rogers' Rangers of the French and Indian War period: *Keep alert, report what you see, remember what you hear, and think before you act.*

BURNING ROPE PATROLLERS

During early 1966, Gen. William C. Westmoreland, commander of U.S. Military Assistance Command Vietnam (MACV), ordered all Army divisions and separate brigades in Vietnam to form long-range patrol detachments and increase their reconnaissance capability. General Westmoreland wanted the units created on a priority basis, even while final Army Department approval was still pending. Shortage of properly trained soldiers and pressing operational requirements, however, prevented this measure from being carried out immediately in many units.

The separate 196th Infantry Brigade arrived in Vietnam during August 1966, well after General Westmoreland's directive, but was unable to form the directed long-range patrol detachment until January 1967. The brigade was first dispatched to Tay Ninh Province and then brought into action to fight Operation ATTLEBORO—where lack of proper ground reconnaissance almost led to disaster. During the first few months of combat, the inadequacy of the original brigade reconnaissance assets became manifest. The brigade's conventional recon component, Troop F of the 17th Cavalry, was neither organized nor equipped for extended foot patrolling operations.

On 2 January 1967 the commander of the 196th Infantry Brigade, Brig. Gen. Richard T. Knowles, organized a Long Range Reconnaissance Detachment (LRPD) because "to increase the brigade's intelligence collection capability, organic [intrinsic] highly trained reconnaissance teams were needed." Prospective personnel were interviewed throughout the brigade, but the process was hampered by four months of Vietnam service. Brigade troops were battle-experienced enough to know the hazards of such duty, and unit commanders were reluctant to release good soldiers. By the end of the month, only thirty soldiers were assembled out of sixty-seven authorized.[1]

The 196th Infantry Brigade Long Range Patrol Detachment was assigned to the brigade intelligence section but administratively controlled by Troop F, 17th Cavalry. The recon troops were known as the "Burning Rope Patrollers"—a term reflecting the common soldiering interpretation of the 196th Infantry Brigade's shoulder insignia. The blue shield patch was embroidered with a yellow looped, double-headed match (from the days of the matchlock musket) lighted at both ends to ensure readiness. Most brigade soldiers saw the insignia as depicting a burning rope. The long-range patrol detachment adopted the phrase as its nickname.

Burning Rope teams were organized and began training in patrol techniques, helicopter employment, land navigation, radio handling, rappelling, intelligence reporting, and adjustment procedures for artillery fire or air strikes. The training period was compressed into several weeks and the teams were declared ready. Brigade patrols generally sought information about enemy dispositions, intentions, and movements for brigade analysis, but some patrols were also assigned bomb damage, ambush, and artillery assessment missions.

One of the first missions involved a night ambush patrol led by Sgt. Anthony Mazzuchhi. The six patrollers were crossing a clearing in the jungle when they heard noises behind them. Sergeant Mazzuchhi ordered the team to return into the woods and establish a hasty ambush to discourage pursuit. The recon members crouched in the dense foliage, their weapons at the ready, while assistant patrol leader Pfc. Caro Velleri and the rear security man watched the open field.

A few minutes later, three Viet Cong soldiers appeared along the forest trail. Sergeant Mazzuchhi's troops opened fire, and the unfortunate trio were eliminated quickly by rifle fire and grenades. Mazzuchhi realized these Viet Cong might be a point element for a larger column, and he hand-signaled his men to withdraw to Private Velleri's position immediately. The team formed a small circle and radioed for artillery fire against the suspected VC force deeper in the forest. The patrol was extracted, and allied units later found evidence that the team-directed shelling had destroyed a platoon of the 271st VC Regiment.[2]

During early February the 196th Infantry Brigade LRPD conducted a scouting patrol along the fog-shrouded, steep granite face of Nui Ba Den. This mountain peak jutted high from the otherwise flat Tay Ninh provincial countryside and contained an American signal relay post on the summit. The mountain's maze of natural caverns, deep-seated caves, and underground tunnels still served as a transient Viet Cong base area.

The Burning Rope Patrollers created several cave-exploring "tunnel rat" teams, each composed of two recon members and two indigenous scouts from Special Forces. One team entered a small opening under a huge boulder and found an inner passage leading to more subterranean chambers. The walls had painted directional arrows. They followed one narrow tunnel twisting 300 yards through the rock until it ended abruptly only ten yards above the original entrance. Another team searched a tunnel higher on the rocky hillside and found discarded cooking utensils and small parcels of rice. The detachment charted some of the tunnels and recorded information about possible occupancy.[3]

At the end of February 1967 the 196th Infantry Brigade commenced Operation JUNCTION CITY in concert with several other allied formations pushing into War Zone C. During March, recon team leader Sp4 Robert Webber led a recon patrol that established a night observation post only five yards from a suspected Viet Cong infiltration lane. Specialist Webber reported that "a ten-man Viet Cong patrol came upon our rear. We all froze and almost stopped breathing, and the VC went on by us." The six team members remained stationary for "what seemed hours" and quietly watched as other Viet Cong elements passed on the trail.

Later in the night the patrollers heard rustling in the nearby bushes and watched thirty-five Viet Cong soldiers cooking and talking right behind them. Pfc. William Connor heard noises to the left of his flank position and saw three Viet Cong walking straight at him. Connor waited anxiously to see if the enemy would turn away, but they did not. He opened fire on full automatic and killed the first enemy soldier in the file. Pfc. Mark Brennan also fired into the same group and killed the other two. The recon troops retreated from their hiding places as Pfc. Vick D. Valleriano and Paul Rosselli threw grenades to cover the patrol's withdrawal. The stunned Viet Cong did not pursue, and the patrollers reached the landing zone safely for emergency extraction. Private Connor described the mission as a deliberate ploy: "We pulled the same tactics Charlie [the VC] uses: we hit and ran. After all, there were all those VC still behind us."[4]

During April 1967 the 196th Infantry Brigade was relocated from Tay Ninh Province, in the lower portion of South Vietnam, to Chu Lai, thirty miles from Da Nang along the northern coast. The brigade was merged into a provisional division-sized organization called Task Force Oregon. The brigade would remain in this new territory for the rest of its Vietnam service, first under Task Force Oregon and then under the Americal Division. The landscape consisted of well-cultivated rice lowlands and rugged interior mountains, and represented a completely different patrolling environment from the previous brigade region.

The 196th Infantry Brigade LRPD fielded nearly fifty patrols in this new operational area during the remaining six months of its existence, from May through October. The pace of eight patrols per month imposed a serious drain on the small detachment and threatened team integrity. During the summer a combination of factors—lack of replacements, personnel hospitalized by disease or injuries, scheduled mid-tour R&R (rest and recreation) departures, and special and emergency leave cases—disrupted teams severely.

Patrols started going into the field with four soldiers instead of six. Detachment commander Lt. Frank Pratt changed team composition to seven men, so R&R and leaves could still be programmed and teams would not be trimmed below viable size. The change gave each team an adequate "personnel pool" of well-acquainted members who could function easily together in the field, but the measure further reduced the total number of available recon teams.[5]

The Burning Rope Patrollers maintained mountain outpost sites on Hills 213 and 707 northwest of Chu Lai. During June 1967 a patrol led by Sgt. Michael W. Daniels was helicoptered onto a small hill at twilight to function as a three-day observation post. The team members heard rifle shots coming from the other knoll on the long forested ridge. The troops believed that Corp. William Davis's team was signaling them from the other hilltop, and fired some rounds in the air to acknowledge the signal. Shortly afterward, they listened as the sounds of firing increased and realized that Davis's team was actually under attack. A helicopter soon extracted the other patrol in the gathering darkness.

Nightfall descended, and Daniels's isolated patrollers feared that their hasty firing could have alerted the Viet Cong. Within minutes, scattered rifle fire began striking the team positions and verified their belief. Sergeant Daniels knew that helicopter extraction was unlikely before dawn, and directed the placement of trip flares around the small perimeter. He also radioed for artillery salvos against the surrounding jungle. At 9:15 P.M., two flashlight beams were spotted and Pfc. Mark Brennan set off a hand illumination flare. The sudden light exposed several enemy soldiers in the draw, but they were too close to call for protective artillery barrages.

A brisk firefight erupted, and the patrol might have been overrun immediately except for the sharp night vision of Pfc. William Connor. He detected an enemy squad maneuvering up a side ravine, grabbed his M60 machine gun, and ran through sporadic gunfire to deliver point-blank automatic fire into the enemy flankers. The concentrated machine gun fire forced the Viet Cong squad to retreat into the valley. The patrollers also stopped another enemy assault force approaching the summit along the other side of the hill.

Two helicopter gunships from the 161st Aviation Company arrived overhead and began rocketing and strafing the flare-lit hillside continuously. The enemy returned fire and hit a helicopter door gunner, who fell back into the aircraft as his machine gun spun out of control and sprayed the patrol-defended hilltop. Fortunately, the errant burst of fire caused no casualties. Sergeant Daniels radioed for more artillery and stopped another Viet Cong charge, but he knew that their situation was now hopeless. The patrollers abandoned the fire-swept peak and slid down the jagged rocks of the slope. They heard Viet Cong moving around and searching the original perimeter, but the enemy soldiers never ventured down the darkened boulder-strewn hillside. The patrollers waited until dawn, when they were rescued by helicopter.[6]

On 14 July 1967 a typical Burning Rope patrol led by Sp4 Cecil A. Crosby was inserted to investigate enemy sightings southwest of Thanh My Trung. The team was scratch-built for the assignment, and the members worked together as a unit for the first time during the mission. Specialist Crosby's team was helicoptered onto the crest of a wooded hill and infiltrated through the waist-high grass into an adjacent patch of forest. As soon as Crosby made radio contact, he was asked to observe an air strike in the valley. The team pushed through the dense jungle but could not locate a suitable observation point.

The team called for overhead aircraft to guide them toward another clearing before nightfall. The recon team established its "harbor" or night rest area in the thickest possible foliage. Every hour the radio relay station on Hill 707 contacted the patrol with the code word "Novel." When the team member on guard heard the code word, he keyed the handset twice without speaking, a signal that "broke squelch twice" and signified a "no change" situation report. At dawn, Specialist Crosby, scout Sp4 Gary Beecher, and point man Pfc. James R. Davison moved thirty yards down the hill while the other three men stayed at the original overnight position.

Specialist Crosby climbed thirty feet up a tree to gain a better vantage point to observe artillery fire and radioed for marking rounds. Then he climbed down and Davison took over the treetop post. Suddenly assistant team leader Pfc. David J. Ohm, at the original position, saw a khaki-uniformed Viet Cong soldier walking along the hillside near the tree. The VC soldier did not notice anyone. When Crosby was informed of the sighting, he decided to keep moving rather than occupy a static observation post around enemy troops.

About an hour before midnight on the second night, Private Davison was on radio watch when he saw three faint yellowish lights, like flashlights with weak batteries. He woke up Crosby, but the lights went out and nothing further was seen. Just before 5:00 A.M., Davison performed guard duty again. This time he saw pinpoints of light in the distance and smelled marijuana odor. The Viet Cong frequently used marijuana in the area, and he radioed for a white phosphorus burst over the cigarettes. Davison reported, "As soon as [the burst] went off I saw three figures jump up and take off towards the rice paddies." The team was extracted later that morning and headquarters credited them with three dead VC, although Crosby later stated sarcastically, "I don't have any idea how any died since all three jumped up when the WP [white phosphorus] went off. They must have died from heart attack."[7]

At the end of September, Brig. Gen. Frank H. Linnell's 196th Infantry Brigade began preparing for absorption into the American Division, raised to replace Task Force Oregon. Brigadier General Linnell attempted to retain his reconnaissance unit by submitting a proposal to incorporate the patrol detachment permanently into Troop F, 17th Cavalry. General Westmoreland disapproved the recommendation in October, and all Burning Rope Patrollers were transferred out to a newly formed division patrol detachment by November.[8]

AMERICAL DIVISION PATROLLERS AND RANGERS

On 25 September 1967, General Westmoreland ordered the transformation of Task Force Oregon into the American Division (later designated 23d Infantry Division). The new division was headquartered at Chu Lai and assigned one of the largest Vietnam operational areas, a huge swath of territory encompassing all of Quang Ngai and Quang Tin provinces and part of Quang Nam Province. The division operated against the 2d NVA Division and Viet Cong guerrilla forces of communist Military Region 5, a military and political command that controlled much of the Vietnamese population between Da Nang and Cam Ranh Bay. The territory was characterized by multicanopied mountain jungle in the west, rugged hills overgrown with tropical forests and brushwood in the middle, and rice-cultivated lowland along the eastern coast.

The American Division assumed a flexible offensive posture to counter persistent enemy threats. The large area and limited division forces necessitated the frequent shifting of battalions in response to NVA or VC maneuvering. The division held the coast with preemptive operations and concentrated on neutralizing previously immune enemy units and base areas in the mountainous regions. The NVA/VC maintained combat viability by avoiding major confrontations with the American Division and breaking down into small groups to avoid entrapment. The American Division increased the tempo of its own small-unit operations by fragmenting larger units into squad- and platoon-sized patrols. Long-range reconnaissance was ideally suited to render assistance to division screening, surveillance, and raiding tasks.

On 22 November 1967, division commander Maj. Gen. Samuel W. Koster formed the American Long Range Patrol Detachment (Provisional). The 196th and 198th Infantry Brigades were tasked to provide personnel for this new unit, but the majority of combat-experienced personnel within both brigades were completing their required one-year Vietnam tour of duty and going home. Additionally, the 198th Infantry Brigade contained no intrinsic patrolling element. As a result, a small nucleus from the 196th Infantry Brigade Long Range Patrol Detachment formed the basis of the new divisional patrol detachment. The American Long Range Patrol Detachment's mission was to provide the newly consolidated division with a long-range reconnaissance surveillance and target acquisition capability.[9]

The 11th Infantry Brigade arrived from Hawaii in late December, but its own reconnaissance element no longer existed. The brigade's former 70th Infantry Detachment (Long Range Patrol) had been authorized only while the brigade was a separate response force for U.S. Army Pacific. The detachment, formed under Capt. Ralph Clark on 15 August 1967, had never reached operational status and was quickly broken up at Schofield Barracks once the brigade was alerted for overseas assignment along with a revocation of its separate status. Thus, the embryo unit patrollers were parceled directly into the brigade line battalions and the 70th was deactivated in Hawaii on 19 December 1967—without ever reaching Vietnam.[10]

In the meantime, the provisional Americal Long Range Patrol Detachment at Chu Lai in Vietnam existed less than a month before being formalized on 20 December 1967 as Company E (Long Range Patrol), 51st Infantry. Maj. Gen. Charles M. Gettys, who took command of the division during April 1968, described the patrol company's mission rather poetically: "to tear away the cloak of darkness that the enemy has enjoyed." The patrollers referred to themselves as the Americal Patrollers, after the division title. The company recon teams were named after states, cigarette brands, and so on.[11]

Company E conformed to the standard organization prescribed for 118-member division-level long-range patrol companies (see Appendix C) in Vietnam. Company commander Capt. Gary F. Bjork pushed his men through a rigorous ten-day physical hardening and preparatory course prior to a three-week "finishing school" taught by crack Special Forces instructors at the MACV Recondo School in Nha Trang. Staff Sgt. Earl L. Toomey recalled Bjork's conditioning:

> The first few days are composed of a strenuous physical training period, forced marches with thirty-pound rucksacks in the morning and a five to seven mile run in the afternoon. Special attention is given in the classroom to map reading and radio communications. This is probably the toughest part of the course. We cover in ten days what the men will receive in more detail at the recondo school. The highlight of the course is rappelling, or insertion into difficult places by means of rope and snap links [carabiners]. We rappel from fifty-foot cliffs first, then from a fifty-foot water tower, and finally a hundred feet from a helicopter. It takes determination and will. It is by no means an easy course. [12]

On 29 April 1968, Bjork's prep school was standardized into the Division Recondo Course, with the mission of giving scheduled fundamental and refresher patrol instruction to Company E members. The course typified the division-level reconnaissance schools throughout Vietnam that implemented patrolling basics taught by the Army Ranger School and MACV Recondo School.

Americal recon company patrols were sent routinely into widely scattered regions of Quang Tin, Quang Nam, and Quang Ngai provinces. Patrol action was generally light, but teams were confounded by mines and booby traps saturating many of their areas. Teams deployed into the Que Son Valley and Antenna Valley regions, inside the eastern sector of the WHEELER-WALLOWA operational area, encountered much higher combat levels. For example, several teams were used to disrupt VC secret base area 116. On 3 July 1968, team Old Gold uncovered a major North Vietnamese secret base area in the Song Re Valley while supporting 11th Infantry Brigade operations. Thirteen days later, a helicopter carrying team Camel was driven from its intended landing zone by heavy fire but succeeded in reaching base with no casualties to the team.

On 1 January 1969 the Department of the Army reorganized the 75th Infantry in the combat arms regimental system for the purpose of linking the various long-range patrol regiments—then serving field forces, divisions, and brigades as components of different infantry regiments—and transforming them into commonly designated ranger companies. During the Vietnam era the 75th Infantry perpetuated the heritage of "Merrill's Marauders," but it was denied any official ranger lineages already bestowed on Army Special Forces.

On 1 February 1969, in accordance with Army directive, 23d Infantry Division (Americal) commander Major General Gettys activated Company G (Ranger), 75th Infantry. Personnel and equipment for the rangers were obtained by simultaneously deactivating Company E, 51st Infantry. The mission of the ranger company was to provide intelligence collection, long-range surveillance, and target acquisition to the Americal Division. The rangers referred to themselves as either "Golf Rangers" (G in conformity with ICAO phonetic alphabet adopted by the U.S. military in 1956) or the "Americal Rangers" after the formation's title.

Company G was organized initially as a binary ranger company and authorized 118 soldiers. The company was organized into a company headquarters of eighteen personnel and two fifty-man field platoons, each organized with eight six-man patrols and a two-man headquarters. Personnel shortages later curtailed the total number of patrols from sixteen to twelve, and internal arrangements were altered to three platoons with four teams each. Ranger teams within the company were named after states.

The division employed the rangers on combat recon assignments that were based on the recommendations of either headquarters intelligence or operations section. The ranger company was satellited with the 16th Aviation Group for administration, helicopter transport, and aerial or ground assistance. The company commander supervised the patrol teams through intermediate platoon headquarters, and the platoons were collocated with the tactical operations center of the brigade being supported. Missions were assigned by the division or brigade, but the ranger company commander and his platoon leaders were responsible for planning the assigned missions, for ensuring proper patrol preparation, and for debriefing the teams after patrol completion.[13]

The 23d Infantry Division (Americal) insisted on high standards for its rangers, including successful completion of the Americal Recondo Course. The division sought qualified individuals for the ranger company on a voluntary basis by offering certain emoluments. Rangers were given priority consideration for accelerated promotion, as well as special attention for awards and decorations. An additional R&R (rest and recreation) at a selected resort outside Vietnam was also authorized as a reward for voluntary service on hazardous operations.

On 18 March 1969 the 23d Infantry Division and the 2d Army of the Republic of Vietnam (ARVN) Division merged their formerly unilateral operating zones. Units of both countries were realigned to make the Americal zone a joint American-Vietnamese responsibility. Ranger Company G was directed to share in the partnership by creating experimental combined teams. Two "showcase" teams were built to demonstrate mutual patrolling confidence, but each contained only two ARVN rangers. They were assigned as front and rear scouts—the most dangerous duty, because either file end was likely to be hit first during an action.

Lt. Jack Harrison reported, "The ARVN rangers have provided a sharpness to our patrols in the field that they didn't have before. They usually walk point and provide rear security on our missions because they have real knack for spotting enemy activity or movement. Most of them can tell you the difference between an enemy soldier and a local civilian just by listening to them walking through the jungle." Whatever combined patrol benefits were claimed, the serious language barrier and other problems confined most of their field utility to securing helicopter landing zones—a routine pathfinder task and not a regular ranger job.[14]

The Americal Division Reconnaissance Zone extended from the interior mountains to the Laotian border and was often known as the "Suicide Zone." The remote border region was so dangerous that the Army Special Forces had already abandoned the area after two garrisons, Ngok Tavak and Kham Duc, were smashed by 2d NVA Division regimental assaults. The Americal Rangers engaged primarily in reconnoitering activity and strived for twenty-four-hour completion on missions inside the Reconnaissance Zone. The ranger staff reasoned that most teams could verify enemy presence or lack of presence in one-day sorties. Longer missions would only expose the teams to undue risk of annihilation.[15]

Capt. Anthony Avgoulis's ranger Company G conducted crucial divisional combat reconnaissance and intelligence-gathering patrols. The patrols were led by team leaders who were the key to mission success and the driving force behind actual patrolling proficiency. The ranger team leaders owed primary allegiance to accomplishing the mission and safeguarding the lives of their men. One outstanding Americal Ranger team leader was Staff Sgt. Robert J. Pruden of ranger team Oregon.

On 14 November 1969, Staff Sergeant Pruden led ranger team Oregon on a road surveillance mission west of Duc Pho. The rangers ambushed ten Viet Cong dressed in black peasant clothing mixed with military attire. Several enemy soldiers in the column were killed at close range with tunnel weapons, powerful .44-caliber modified magnum revolvers with special ammunition. The rounds were of trapped piston design, each containing fifteen shot pellets, and gave the rangers a low-noise, multiprojectile weapon.[16]

Four days after being extracted from the area, Staff Sergeant Pruden's team Oregon volunteered to return to the same valley road and capture a prisoner. The rangers landed on a hill, moved into the rice fields, and established two three-man positions alongside the road under team leader Pruden and assistant team leader Sgt. Danny L. Jacks. One element intended to conduct the prisoner snatch while the other provided security, depending on the direction of enemy travel.

During the preparation of the ambush site, twelve Viet Cong approached the ranger area. The team ceased all movement, let the enemy pass by, and then continued setting up claymore mines and preparing the ambush zone. One team member crawled forward, positioned his claymore mine, and had begun moving back when he was suddenly spotted. Six Viet Cong soldiers pinned him down with rifle fire. Another enemy force began firing on the rangers from the opposite direction near the road bend.

Staff Sergeant Pruden realized that his team was in grave danger, and one of his rangers was exposed directly to enemy marksmen. Pruden leaped onto the trail from his jungle hideout and charged directly toward the road bend while firing his CAR-15. The enemy soldiers were startled by this unexpected assault and shifted their fire toward the charging ranger while the other soldier crawled out of the road.

Pruden was hit and knocked to the ground but regained his footing and continued forward until hit a second time. He fell to the edge of the trail, reloaded his submachine gun magazine, and staggered to his feet. By this time he had killed four enemy soldiers and wounded several others. The unnerved VC fled the area as they fired final shots in his direction, and the solitary ranger was hit a third time. He collapsed only fifteen yards from the enemy-held berm with five bullet wounds in the chest and abdomen. In the meantime, the team defeated the other enemy soldiers.

Rangers Sergeant Jacks, Sp5 John E. Schultz, Sp4 John S. Gaffney, Sp4 James R. Gromacki, and Sp4 Robert B. Kalway ran to Pruden's aid and established a hasty perimeter around him. The fallen team leader was still conscious and realized that his team, low on ammunition, could be overrun if the enemy decided to return. Pruden forced himself to remain conscious despite great pain, and attempted to speak on the radio to obtain armed helicopter support and immediate extraction for his team.

Pruden, however, was no longer able to speak above a whisper. As his breathing became difficult, Pruden was given mouth-to-mouth resuscitation, and he temporarily regained his breath. Staff Sergeant Pruden asked quietly for the status of his team members, reiterated the order to get his team extracted, and then lost consciousness and died. A few minutes later the extraction helicopters arrived and withdrew team Oregon from the skirmish site. The gallantry of the ranger team leader was alone responsible for the defeat of two flanking enemy squads and the safe return of his patrol.[17]

On 17 November a heavy team, composed of Staff Sgt. Lonnie D. Miller's ranger team Ohio and Staff Sgt. George I. Beach's ranger team Texas, found a well-used trail fifty yards from a landing zone. The heavy team moved south along the trail and uncovered a small, hastily abandoned enemy encampment with two twenty-foot-long huts built over underground bunkers. The rangers found corn still cooking and numerous green North Vietnamese Army uniforms hanging on branches. The rangers set fire to the huts and left the area as exploding ammunition ripped through the burning structures. Team Texas scored an important prisoner snatch shortly afterward, while moving down the mountain. The rangers saw a North Vietnamese soldier through the window of another hut farther downslope. Staff Sergeant Beach leaped through the grass roof and grabbed the startled NVA officer while the other rangers killed the sentry. The team was evacuated without further incident.[18]

On 30 December 1969, Staff Sgt. Ralph B. Dunham's ranger team Alabama performed a surveillance mission and logged the following report: "At this location the reconnaissance element observed six enemy without packs or weapons. One caucasian was observed with the group. He had blond hair, was approximately six feet two inches in height, and carried an unidentified weapon and small pack. The enemy moved back into the jungle and could no longer be observed." The probability of the "caucasian" being a foreign journalist, renegade American, or Soviet adviser was listed in that order.[19]

On 20 April 1970, ranger team Hawaii, led by Staff Sgt. Robert W. Hammond, had a harrowing experience. The team was spotted by NVA soldiers outside a bunker complex and fled the area, occupying a new evening vantage position near a large boulder. The team leader climbed atop the rock and saw a North Vietnamese squad holding flashlights and approaching fifty yards away. The rangers evaded along a stream to a pickup point in the triple-canopy rain forest, fought off enemy soldiers, and attempted an emergency helicopter extraction by McGuire rig.

The helicopter gained an altitude of 250 feet above the dense vegetation before suddenly dropping because of power loss. Three rangers riding the McGuire rig were slammed into the tropical hardwoods and became entangled in the trees. The mission commander cut the ropes to free the helicopter and the injured rangers managed to climb down to the jungle floor. The team reached another overgrown clearing, blew up obstructing trees with claymore mines and explosives, and were finally rescued.[20]

Company G averaged sixty patrols per month during 1970, although monsoons and adverse weather—such as October tropical storms Kate and Joan—periodically curtailed patrols. Additionally, during the fall, most patrols were assigned to shield the national election campaign in the coastal region against possible NVA/VC encroachment from the western mountains. The mission was typical of the political considerations influencing tactical responsibilities. On 18 August 1970, for example, ranger team Tennessee suffered three wounded in a duel with a North Vietnamese rocket squad trying to get closer to Quang Ngai city and disrupt the 30 August South Vietnamese senate elections.[21]

During 1971, the 23d Infantry Division Americal Rangers became increasingly involved in responding to data gathered by electronic sensor devices. Ground radar and line sensor strings began to dominate ranger employment, as teams reacted to data collected from remote data readouts. In the fall the rangers were notified of pending disbandment as part of the Army's Keystone Oriole-Charlie redeployment from Vietnam. The ranger company ceased combat activity, commenced stand-down procedures on 14 September, and was reduced to zero strength ten days later. On 1 October 1971, Company G (Ranger), 75th Infantry, was officially inactivated.

The 196th Infantry Brigade, the first of three separate brigades eventually fused together into the Americal Division, had arrived in Southeast Asia woefully unprepared for either Vietnam-style area warfare or its combat reconnaissance demands. The brigade organized its Burning Rope Patrollers to help reconnoiter War Zone C, a long-standing Viet Cong wilderness stronghold that defied allied suppression throughout the conflict. This unit later formed the basis of the Americal Patrollers in a different region of the country.

The Burning Rope Patrollers, Americal Patrollers, and Americal Rangers performed commendably despite shortages of personnel and very tough operating sectors in Vietnam. The most salient historical feature of their service was their incredibly disorganized evolutionary development. In this instance, the series of ad hoc components marked a rather confused but ultimately successful Army attempt to patch together adequate combat reconnaissance capability.

3

1ST CAVALRY DIVISION

CAVALRY RANGERS

THE PERSHING LERPS

The 1st Cavalry Division deployed to Vietnam in September 1965 as the Army's first airmobile division. It arrived lavishly equipped with helicopters and well organized for flexible area warfare. Division combat reconnaissance was initially furnished by the aerial 1st Squadron of the 9th Cavalry. The squadron's scout helicopters and aero-rifle platoons provided the division with tactical intelligence about terrain characteristics and North Vietnamese or Viet Cong activities. The aerial cavalry squadron sought out and located the enemy so effectively that no initial requirement existed for other patrol units.[1]

The Cavalry Rangers—Company H of the 75th Infantry—were finally raised to provide specialized patrol reconnaissance. The rangers supplemented the 9th Cavalry's 1st Squadron, but did not evolve from squadron components. The antecedent of the Cavalry Rangers was the small long-range reconnaissance patrols formed nearly eighteen months after the 1st Cavalry Division arrived in Vietnam.

Division commander Maj. Gen. John Norton required sustained ground patrolling support for Operation PERSHING, an extended search and destroy campaign covering most of eastern Binh Dinh Province. The vast 1,032-square-mile operational area covered northern Binh Dinh and southern Quang Ngai provinces. The terrain varied from coastal plains to narrow jungle valleys and rugged mountains. Higher elevations were composed of steep-sided ridges covered by dense jungle or tall elephant grass. Many hillside caves

43

and trails were hidden by thickly forested slopes and granite boulders that made observation difficult from the air. Additionally, heavy fighting in the campaign's opening stages exhausted the 9th Cavalry's ability to meet all but the most urgent requirements.

On 2 February 1967 the division Long Range Reconnaissance Patrol (LRRP) component was raised by Capt. James D. James and First Sergeant Frederick J. Kelly for sustained jungle penetration. Provisional teams were formed by using arriving replacement sergeants with recon experience, pathfinders, and headquarters volunteers. The patrollers were nicknamed "Pershing Lerps" after their assigned mission, Operation PERSHING, and Lerp. The first team was attached to the 1st Brigade in the An Lao Valley, and the second team joined the 2d Brigade in the Kim Son Valley.

During April 1967, Maj. Gen. John J. Tolson III assumed command of the 1st Cavalry Division. He attached the LRRP component to the division intelligence section and used the teams to collect information about terrain conditions and enemy movement for processing by the 191st Military Intelligence Detachment. He also expanded the trial LRRP element into the provisional 1st Cavalry Division Long Range Patrol Detachment (LRPD), with a strength of 118 U.S. Army soldiers, eighteen Montagnard tribal warriors, and eighteen South Vietnamese scouts.[2]

The initially high combat level of Operation PERSHING tapered off at the end of May. North Vietnamese and Viet Cong forces avoided open battle, reverted to guerrilla warfare, and evaded division forces whenever possible. The Pershing Lerps rendered valuable advance reconnaissance for the brigades. From three to nine teams served interchangeably, depending upon requirements, within each brigade sector. During the summer, three new teams were deployed to support an independent task force of the 2d Battalion, 7th Cavalry, operating farther south along the Vietnamese coast.

By August 1967 the Pershing Lerps were an important adjunct to division reconnaissance. The teams achieved numerous sightings and initiated several contacts with small North Vietnamese and Viet Cong elements. From August through October over twenty detachment troops learned combat recon techniques at the Special Forces-run MACV Recondo School in Nha Trang. Starting in November, all recondo school quotas for the divisions were reserved solely for LRPD volunteers.

On 24 September 1967, Capt. Warren Gooding assumed command of the Pershing Lerps from Captain Tucker. At this time Captain Gooding's detachment reached a strength of ninety-seven

Americans and twenty Vietnamese and Montagnard native scouts. Ground recon patrolling proceeded briskly during the last months of Operation PERSHING. The cavalrymen sighted or engaged scattered groups and solitary Viet Cong almost daily, but could not find any major enemy troop concentrations.

The most important patrol intelligence windfall of Operation PERSHING occurred late on the afternoon of 5 December. A team inserted the previous day to search the jagged mountains of the lower Suoi Ca Valley spotted and ambushed three Viet Cong wearing green uniforms, killing one and capturing the others. The prisoners were flown to the division interrogation center, where it was discovered that the patrol had intercepted a high-ranking VC delegation from the communist Binh Dinh provincial headquarters. The dead Viet Cong was identified as a battalion executive officer. Among the pair of captives was a senior Viet Cong intelligence captain fresh from a two-year course of study in the Soviet Union. The division obtained extremely useful information of enemy organization, intentions, and operating techniques from this individual.[3]

December fighting escalated into some of the largest battles of Operation PERSHING. The effectiveness of the division's patrol concept was beyond dispute. The Army Department granted approval for the division to officially activate a long-range patrol company. During the last two months of the year the Pershing Lerps unit conducted a total of 105 patrols from its bases at Phan Thiet, Landing Zone English, and Landing Zone Uplift. These missions accomplished over 350 sightings of enemy personnel and gained formal recognition of an airmobile division requirement for ranger-style reconnaissance.[4]

FIRST TEAM PATROLLERS

On 20 December 1967 the 1st Cavalry Division activated Company E (Long Range Patrol), 52d Infantry, at Camp Radcliff outside An Khe. The new company absorbed the 1st Cavalry Division Long Range Patrol Detachment and gave the division patrolling unit a distinct numerical entity and regimental association. The unit was commonly known as the "First Team Patrollers" because the 1st Cavalry Division was known as the "First Team" in Vietnam.

In January 1968 the First Team Patrollers were parceled out according to brigade needs on widely separated fronts. Just prior to the Tet-68 holiday period, the 1st Cavalry Division relocated the bulk of its maneuver units to reinforce I Corps Tactical Zone. Company E dispatched seven reconnaissance teams northward to help secure division bases at Gia Le and Camp Evans outside Hue. Time was required to brief and familiarize recon teams with the new territory. Only one patrol was launched on a long-range mission in 1 CTZ before the enemy Tet-68 offensive. The rest of Company E remained at Camp Radcliff with patrols divided between the interior An Khe and coastal Bong Son sectors.

The First Team Patrollers were thus scattered over wide areas when the surprise Viet Cong Tet-68 offensive struck the country-side. Only a few patrols could be spared to hinder North Vietnamese supply lines leading into the Hue and Quang Tri battlefields. Up to nine recon teams were retained to shield Binh Dinh Province and assisted 2d Brigade efforts to monitor VC activity in the Crescent, Nui Mieu, and Cay Giep mountains. Several teams were kept on guard duty just outside the main perimeter of Camp Radcliff.

During March the division assembled Company E at Camp Evans as part of its stepped-up counteroffensive in the wake of the Tet-68 onslaught. This marked the first time that all patrol teams were joined together in one location. The company was assigned the mission of reconnoitering suspected enemy mountain strongholds in eastern and central Quang Tri Province. Reconnaissance emphasis was placed on the enemy jungle havens of secret base areas 101 and 114. The North Vietnamese and Viet Cong forces attempted to regroup and replenish supplies and tried to evade allied detection efforts.

From May through July 1968 the First Team Patrollers fielded sixty-one patrols and observed the enemy on ninety-eight separate occasions. The rangers killed twenty-eight North Vietnamese regulars by direct fire, and suffered five patrollers killed and four wounded in exchange. The company performed an average of twenty patrols per month, and scheduled most of them for ninety-six hours. However, emergency extractions were required on twenty-three missions. These and other circumstances forced early termination of roughly a third of all patrol assignments.[5]

During July, Maj. Gen. George I. Forsythe took command of the 1st Cavalry Division and maintained Company E's steady pace of mountain patrolling. The company deployed sixty-six patrols from August through the end of September, but the North Vietnamese and Viet Cong continued to hide and avoided significant unit movement. As a result, patrol sightings dropped drastically. Company E patrollers made a total of fifty-two observations and killed twenty-two enemy soldiers by direct fire.

Team mission duration was ideally set at four or five days but averaged just over three days, or approximately eighty-two hours. These were still very long patrols in hostile domain, especially while probing dangerous mountain regions. Most mission shortening was caused by either mission changes or team emergencies. During the fall trimester, seven teams were detected by numerically superior enemy forces and extracted under adverse circumstances.[6]

Company E operations were more seriously impeded by command and control problems than by enemy action. The situation reflected unsatisfactory arrangements that never changed from the original Pershing Lerp period. For instance, the long-range patrol company commander could only exercise marginal supervision because teams were still parceled out and stationed at the various brigade command posts, where they were held under tight brigade control.

Furthermore, patrols were unevenly employed by the brigade commanders, who used them in different ways. Some patrols were used as close-in scouts for maneuvering infantry. Other patrols performed listening post and sentinel duties around forward locations, especially fire support bases. Improper utilization canceled the intelligence-gathering benefits of highly trained long-range patrol personnel, endangered teams, and stifled patrol tactics. Patrols used in a "short-range" environment experienced greater difficulty with extra-alert enemy troops, as well as problems securing artillery or aerial support while operating in proximity to other friendly forces.

The dispersion of company assets also caused administrative difficulties. There were problems reallocating personnel among the teams to make up losses resulting from injuries, illness, or individual combat-tour rotation. Any real degree of unit training was virtually impossible while company assets remained unconsolidated. The shortage of veteran recon troops and recondo-qualified personnel was worsened by brigade insensitivity to instructional needs. Ongoing mission requirements prevented soldiers from attending either formal recondo training or informal company refresher courses. Throughout the year, Company E managed to receive only eight graduates from the MACV Recondo School every three months.[7]

On 18 October 1968, General Forsythe resolved the division reconnaissance situation by consolidating Company E under the operational control of the 1st Squadron, 9th Cavalry. Company commander Capt. George A. Paccerelli recalled that the change was both welcome and troublesome: "This transition from direct G-2 [division intelligence] control to the Squadron was not, in its initial stages, a smooth operation. Due to an apparent inability [on the part of squadron leaders] to comprehend our [long-range patrol] mission and mode of operation—and a direct attempt to smother the company's identification and restrict its employment—the relationship was often strained between the two general support reconnaissance elements of the division.''[8]

The greater efficiency and advantages of grouping all formation reconnaissance elements soon became so apparent that both organizations expressed mutual satisfaction. Company E centralization reduced previous requirements for extra support personnel and increased the number of active teams. Patrols were employed consistently, and long-range missions were based on timely information secured by helicopter scouts. Patrol sightings were acted upon more expeditiously, and aero rifle platoons were available to reinforce promising situations. The best consequence for Company E was the ready availability of squadron helicopter support.

During the fall the 1st Cavalry Division was relocated south from the northern I Corps Tactical Zone to the III Corps Tactical Zone, in order to help screen the approaches to Saigon. Company E utilized naval transport, and became the only Army recon unit to execute a sea transfer between combat zones in the Vietnam conflict. At the beginning of November the company moved to Tan My, the embarkation port, and boarded the Military Sea Transportation Service tank-landing ship LST-532 Chase County. The ship was an ex-Navy vessel manned by contracted South Korean crewmen. The voyage through the South China Sea and into Saigon took a full week. The company completed unloading at the Newport docks on 5 November.[9]

Ground reconnaissance operations in the III Corps Tactical Zone commenced soon after Company E reached its new headquarters at Phuoc Vinh. The 1st Cavalry Division established a picket line of fire support bases in Tay Ninh, Binh Long, and Phuoc Long provinces. The airmobile cavalry division was tasked to provide surveillance and armed reconnaissance astride the principal NVA/VC infiltration routes leading from Cambodia toward the capital, Saigon.

The First Team Patrollers sent teams against identified North Vietnamese resupply lanes that were coded by allied intelligence offices. The routes included the Jolley Trail along the boundary between II and III Corps Tactical Zones; Adams Road in the western portion of War Zone D around Bu Dop; Serges Jungle Highway from the Fishhook region of Cambodia; the Western Corridor or X-Cache Route running through War Zone C; and the historical pirate avenues from the Cambodian Angel's Wing and Parrot's Beak areas into Saigon.

Company E experienced problems adjusting to the new operational area. Instead of mountains and coastal valleys, the terrain consisted of inland rice fields, jungle plains, and marshy swampland. The North Vietnamese Army and Viet Cong style of warfare in the south differed substantially from the style in the northern provinces. About the only thing that remained the same was the enemy preference for nighttime movement, daylight use of camouflage capes or nets with fresh foliage, and confinement to trails having good overhead concealment.

Teams encountered many unexpected enemy tactical variations. Patrollers hearing shots to either side of their position learned that these were often enemy signals to keep ranks abreast during area sweeps. The spacing between shots became shorter as enemy units closed the gap. Patrols seldom fired captured AK47 rifles to confuse the enemy, because such a mistake spelled annihilation if their own position was given away. Instead, patrols tried to disrupt the pattern by calling for artillery fire. The shelling kept enemy maneuvering units off balance and muffled rifle noise.

On 17 November 1968, recon team 36 discovered another enemy technique while operating northeast of Special Forces camp Minh Thanh. The patrol members realized that they were being followed by a few enemy soldiers, circled back, and killed three Viet Cong. However, when the team members continued their movement they heard barking from enemy tracker dogs behind them. The patrol managed a close escape, and after this incident all Company E teams began carrying black pepper. The rear scout spread it periodically behind the patrol to nullify dog pursuit.

Another unpleasant surprise for patrollers, accustomed to sparsely populated upland wilderness, was finding domestic animals, such as chickens and pigs, and plenty of people in the war zone. The people were never young men (of military age) but always old men, women, and children in groups of five or seven who watched the patrols closely. After darkness, the recon troops sometimes heard people nearby throwing rocks or twigs as a locating gimmick. Team members learned to disregard the nuisance and avoid compromising their overnight positions. Teams withheld fire unless fired at, or someone refused to surrender in the ambush zones. Artillery fire was used to discourage the searchers.

The war zones contained many large, well-camouflaged bunker complexes. Many patrollers were unnerved when they found themselves unexpectedly surrounded by fortifications. They learned,

however, that an alert enemy would never let them get that close.
If the patrol saw the bunkers first, this indicated that the North
Vietnamese were either not present or lax in their security. In either
case, the patrol would experience little trouble passing through. If
the patrollers were spotted inside an occupied encampment, the
enemy clacked bamboo pieces together as an alarm, but the sound
also gave teams time to react.

In the latter part of December there was a sharp increase in patrol
clashes, especially when patrols were checking small bunker complexes. The enemy disengaged, however, as rapidly as possible and
evaded the teams rather than offer resistance. Most patrols found
and observed mobile North Vietnamese soldiers during hours of
darkness. Several clashes occurred between the patrols and the enemy units moving south. The patrols inflicted heavy casualties on
some of these groups by judiciously using field artillery, aerial
rocket artillery, and tactical airpower and refraining from direct
engagements.

Prisoners were considered one of the most treasured prizes by a
patrol sent to gather intelligence information. On 13 December
1968, Staff St. Ronald J. Bitticks led recon team 39 on a mission
to locate enemy forces reported four miles northwest of Phuoc Vinh.
Team 39 moved through thick bamboo until it reached a well-used
trail. While Staff Sergeant Bitticks was examining the pathway,
front scout Sgt. Edward Malone spotted a pair of North Vietnamese
soldiers moving toward the patrol. Staff Sergeant Bitticks decided to obtain a prisoner and jumped onto the trail in front of the
two startled soldiers. He yelled for them to surrender by shouting, "*Chieu Hoi!*," which is Vietnamese for "Open Arms," an
anti-guerrilla program giving enemy soldiers the chance to switch
sides and rally to the established government (Republic of Vietnam). A *Hoi Chanh* was a former enemy soldier who had rallied
to the South Vietnamese side under the *Chieu Hoi* program. Bitticks
recalled, "It was evident by the surprised expression upon their
faces that they didn't believe what they saw. For a few seconds they
just stared; then they went for their weapons. I opened up with my
M16, killing one while the other managed to escape into the bamboo thicket."

The botched prisoner snatch started an unfortunate chain of
events. Team 39 hastened back into the jungle and advanced slowly
to avoid rustling the underbrush with loud noises. The patrollers
pushed through the dense foliage only to come across the same trail
after it made a sharp L-turn, nearly 300 yards farther along. The
bamboo was so thick that the patrol members could barely see the

pathway. They saw several large groups of enemy soldiers, and Bitticks radioed for air support. Within ten minutes the Cobra gunships arrived overhead. In the meantime, an enemy search party stumbled across the team position. The patrollers opened fire, killing the trio, and received a heavy volume of return fire from all directions.

The team 39 personnel, outnumbered and surrounded, set off smoke grenades to mark their position as the first gunship "rolled in hot." Two Cobras strafed the enemy ranks repeatedly. As each aircraft made its run, the brunt of heavy enemy automatic weapons fire was shifted against the overhead threat and away from the team. Staff Sergeant Bitticks stated, "This went on for over two hours. If it hadn't been for the gunships we never would have got out alive. At one point a machine gun opened up on us from only twenty-five feet away. It cut a path between us, raking our position first horizontally and then vertically, slitting the bamboo all around us."

The patrollers broke out of their entrapment by coordinating their movement through radio contact with the aviators, and advanced closely behind three gunship runs to a small pickup zone in the jungle. Covered by circling gunships, Sergeant Bitticks and Sgt. Howard Fatzinger III frantically hacked down trees to make the clearing large enough for extraction. The heroism of team members and supporting aircrews discouraged the superior enemy force from attempting an overrun attack, and team 39 was lifted out that evening.[10]

The Company E members often suffered exhausting and harrowing experiences in the field, but could always look forward to returning to base camp and a well-deserved rest period. Their reception by the other cavalrymen was usually in the spirit of warmhearted gratitude and admiration. In the late-war period, however, there were a few isolated cases of troop discontent against "gung-ho" troops. Reconnaissance officers and sergeants were singled out for increasing violence from rear-echelon malcontents. Just after midnight on 1 January 1969, company commander Captain Paccerelli met with Sergeant-Major Denison, the field lieutenants, and six sergeants near the company orderly room. Without warning, a fragmentation grenade exploded nearby and injured two team leaders. At first everyone in the group thought it was a mortar shell, but Captain Paccerelli remembered an earlier smoke grenade being thrown into the company area "as a warning." Staff Sergeants Barnes and Torres investigated and confirmed that the grenade attack was a fragging attempt by rebellious members of another company.[11]

THE CAVALRY RANGER SCREEN

On 1 January 1969 the Department of the Army gave its long range patrol companies a common numerical designator with range heritage and reorganized the 75th Infantry as the parent regiment Effective 1 February 1969 the division activated Company H (Air mobile Ranger), 75th Infantry, using the First Team Patrollers a; its basis and deactivating Company E of the 52d Infantry. The rangers were known as either "Hotel Rangers" (H in conformity with ICAO phonetic alphabet adopted by the U.S. military in 1956 or as "Cavalry Rangers" because of their 1st Cavalry Division assignment.

Company H remained headquartered at Phuoc Vinh under the operational control of the 1st Squadron, 9th Cavalry. The Cavalry Rangers kept three ranger liaison personnel and two ground radic relay sections located at the brigade tactical operations centers. Actual ranger teams were sent in response to brigade requests for sector reconnaissance coverage. The division intelligence section maintained final authority to approve or disapprove the requests for ranger assistance.

Prior to the Tet-69 period, the Cavalry Rangers heightened patrol activity in response to reports of fresh 5th NVA Division activity and stockage of logistical depots. The rangers found several hidden camps. The teams also located enemy units moving through the jungles, along roads, and on canals and other waterways. There was an increased enemy willingness "to stand and fight," and the rangers countered with team-directed air strikes and artillery bombardment. Reaction forces were inserted on several occasions to react to patrol observations. Inevitably, some patrols became embroiled in disadvantageous contacts and required emergency extraction. More helicopters on routine lift-out missions sustained damage from unexpected hostile fire. Company H directed unengaged patrols to monitor pickup zones for eight hours prior to helicopter arrival. If enemy presence was detected the patrols tried to find alternate fields.

The dangers of the intensified ranger reconnaissance campaign were demonstrated by ranger team 41, led by Sgt. Tony Griffith. On 4 February the patrol was infiltrated along Serges Jungle Highway north of An Loc. The rangers saw no enemy troops but heard them hunting and cutting wood. The team radioed for artillery fire on the estimated enemy locations and established an overnight position. Two hours after midnight the team members heard noises on a nearby trail, followed by the sounds of truck engines. Sergeant

Griffith sent two scouts to investigate the situation at daybreak, while he remained at the observation point with another pair of patrollers. The scouts returned to find North Vietnamese infantrymen in combat against the patrol location. The NVA troops, fearing the appearance of American reinforcements, fled the area after the returning scouts opened fire. The rangers found that Sergeant Griffith had been killed and the other two rangers seriously wounded.

The North Vietnamese also introduced new weapons in an attempt to inhibit ranger patrols. On the afternoon of 24 February, on the third day of its mission, ranger team 34 killed a North Vietnamese soldier while investigating an enemy motorbike unit in Tay Ninh Province. Almost immediately the team received concentrated enemy fire. As the rangers fought back, they were engaged at close range with B-40 rocket fire. The rockets severely wounded four rangers and produced considerable psychological shock. An extraction helicopter braved a gauntlet of direct enemy fire to reach the stranded team, although it was severely damaged during the emergency extraction. Warrant Officer Parker, however, managed to nurse his crippled helicopter back to a friendly airfield.[12]

The ranger company took steps to counteract the B-40 rocket threat by equipping each ranger patrol with one or more M72 LAWs (Light Antitank Weapon). The LAW was normally used in Vietnam for bunker busting. The rangers discovered that the M72 LAWs delivered an effective "counterpunch" to B-40 rocket employment. The use of the LAW also demoralized the North Vietnamese troops. After some firefights the rangers discovered that enemy troops abandoned dead comrades and valuable equipment to get away from LAW rocket blasts.

Throughout March the rangers intensified efforts to gather more intelligence data by capturing documents and prisoners. Many valuable papers were sewn or hidden in material not found in hasty searches, and rangers began stripping enemy dead completely to bring all clothing to military intelligence analysts. Company bulletin 9-69 stated:

> Patrol Leaders are reminded to pick up wooden nickels prior to departing on patrol. When stripping the enemy dead, a wooden nickel will be placed on the body. Remember your company's motto "Qui me Tangent Paenetabit" [sic] (Who Touches Me Will Regret It). In our ever increasing campaign to gain hard intelligence concerning the enemy and to win his hearts and minds, we hope that his fear of our elements will cause him to move in larger groups, resulting in more lucrative targets for the Artillery and Air.[13]

Former ranger commander Captain Paccerelli recalled, "The wooden nickels had started when we were still Company E (Long Range Patrol) 52d Infantry. I had ordered a thousand of them printed with the Indianhead on one side and the company's identification on the other. They would be used for many purposes such as calling cards, thank-you tokens for the helicopter crews who put us in and took us out, and most importantly, for the reason stated in the bulletin, to spread fear in the minds of the enemy. They must have been effective, our patrols ran into too many enemy recon elements who were looking for someone."[14]

Company H was also directed to seize more prisoners. The Cavalry were trained to use nightsticks and quietly suppress captives with minimum harm. One example of a successful prisoner snatch mission occurred when ranger team 32 was inserted to check possible Viet Cong movement through a "No-Fire area" set aside for Vietnamese woodcutters. The rangers established their positions on both sides of a road. Within fifteen minutes a Viet Cong suspect was spotted on the road by the flank scout, who snapped his finger twice and alerted the other rangers. The first four rangers let the man pass until he was next to the patrol leader, who served as the team "snatch man." The patrol leader leaped in front of the individual and demanded immediate surrender. The enemy soldier reached for his pistol but was overpowered by the patrol leader. The captive was bound and gagged, led to a pickup zone, and extracted to an interrogation center. He turned out to be a knowledgeable lieutenant of the Viet Cong 301st Local Force Company.

Toward the end of March 1969, the rangers began encountering renewed enemy activity. Ranger field platoon leaders and platoon sergeants were also in the thick of combat. They accompanied patrol leaders on helicopter sorties to select landing and pickup zones and escorted the insertion and extraction flights. On 27 March, ranger Lt. William B. Bell's helicopter was returning from a patrol insertion northeast of Dau Tieng. The helicopter was struck by a fusillade of accurate antiaircraft fire and crashed, killing all on board. Ranger duty was one of the few Army occupations in which all unit members routinely faced the same level of danger, regardless of rank or position.

Ranger patrols observed many enemy bicycle-mounted units along the X-Cache Route in northern Tay Ninh Province. The majority of these cyclists lacked accompanying security units and fell prey to ranger ambush and sniping. The patrols also reported truck traffic on several routes leading south from Cambodia. The rangers attempted to block vehicular travel with antitank mines. Mine-planting patrols received thorough training in the employment of mines and carefully planned minefield locations. An engineer sergeant was usually attached to the patrol and recorded mined areas. The seven-man patrols used charges consisting of four M7A2 antitank mines placed over a slab of C4 explosive. The mines destroyed two Soviet-style trucks and stopped further enemy motorized traffic in War Zone C.

Throughout April, ranger patrols participated in the Operation MONTANA SCOUT/MONTANA RAIDER series by searching for North Vietnamese regroupment areas. Continuous surveillance was posted along southward infiltration routes, but sightings dwindled as the month progressed. Patrols were still able to conduct ambushes with regularity against small groups of four to seven individuals and obtained documents and equipment. Most enemy troops operating in War Zone C were identified as belonging to either the 1st NVA or 9th VC Division. The rangers upgraded ambush potential by arranging multiple sets of clustered claymore mines connected together by demolition cord and blasting caps. The command-detonated mine clusters were very effective in covering their intended kill zones.

In May 1969, Maj. Gen. Elvy B. Roberts assumed command of the 1st Cavalry Division. During the same month, ranger patrols uncovered more bunker complexes as part of Operations MONTANA SCOUT and MONTANA RAIDER. The rangers usually found food and gear in the fortifications, a certain indication of recent use. Daytime ambush teams near bunker locations reported a buildup in enemy traffic. North Vietnamese movement in daylight hours was unusual, and indicated that reinforcements were being hurried into the battles around division fire support bases Grant, Jamie, and Phyllis. Nocturnal ranger missions observed long columns of bicycles and oxcarts transporting heavier loads. The rangers used artillery fire, often preplanned by patrol leaders during insertion area overflights. The large enemy movements tapered off as the month closed.

Ranger ambushes began using more M14 antipersonnel mines. The rangers favored using the mines as warning devices, because the enemy often mistook them for artillery bursts instead of patrol-placed weapons. The mines were extremely effective when connected by detonating cords to claymores that covered multiple approaches. The patrol could either wait for the enemy to step on the M14 mines or detonate the connected mines with electrical blasting caps. The latter method was sometimes used to destroy the mines in place before the patrol departed the area. This precaution prevented accidental harm to friendly troops or future patrols, but noiseless collection of the devices was preferred.

During June 1969, ranger night ambushes were reemphasized as daytime enemy movement waned. For instance, on 26 June, ranger team 41 established an overnight ambush near Song Be, at a trail intersection near a recently used bunker complex on the Adams Road infiltration route. Patrol leader Staff Sgt. Guy R. McConnell observed three flashlights and the silhouettes of twelve enemy soldiers. The rangers selectively opened fire on the column from both ends and succeeded in forcing the survivors to run into a second kill zone lined with six claymore and M14 antipersonnel mines.

More North Vietnamese troops gathered in the area and tried to overwhelm the five-man team in a violent confrontation that lasted until dawn. The rangers repulsed several enemy charges with the assistance of aerial rocket artillery and illumination rounds. The patrol was saved by the collective valor instilled by the wartime bonding of its individual members.

Sp4 Kenneth E. Burch held a strobe light aloft to mark the team position for overhead aircraft, and was wounded in the arm. Staff Sergeant McConnell scooped up an enemy grenade and was wounded trying to toss it away from his comrades. When communications were severed because of poor transmission, radioman Specialist Germany stood up and shielded the radio with his body. The extra height succeeded in restoring radio contact, and Germany maintained his post although wounded severely in the side. When Private Taijeron's rifle jammed during a duel with enemy infiltrators, Specialist Leerburg knocked him to safety and accepted the brunt of enemy return fire, being wounded seriously. The gallant rangers exhibited the highest sense of teamwork and fought until daybreak, when cavalry reinforcements arrived.

From March through July 1969 the 1st Cavalry Division interdicted a major North Vietnamese offensive against Saigon. During this campaign, the Cavalry Rangers deployed 328 patrols and made 143 enemy sightings—118 resulting in team actions. Armed helicopters from the 1st Squadron of the 9th Cavalry reacted to 80 percent of these sightings, and combined ranger-aerial fire killed 128 NVA soldiers. Larger ground reaction units responded to half of all ranger contacts. The rangers suffered six dead and forty-two wounded during the trimester.

The type of person who volunteered for division ranger duty was often atypical of the general soldier populace, as shown by the following letter received by Company H headquarters:

My name is Sergeant Paul J. Salminen. I'm presently serving with Headquarters Battery, 2nd Bn, 20th Artillery. Briefly, Sir, I am trying to become a ranger and need your help. I submitted a DF [Disposition Form] for transfer to H Company (Ranger) 75th Infantry, which was approved by my battery and battalion. At division level it was disapproved—a new regulation states that ranger volunteers must be airborne qualified: I am not. The ranger company First Sergeant had taken the DF to the Division Adjutant for a ruling. I was informed today that it will again be disapproved. Sir, I want to be a ranger very badly. If an exception could be made for me I would be very much in your debt.

Below is a brief background and what I believe are my qualifications for the job. I write you, Sir, because I feel I have no one else to turn to. I did not utilize the I.G. [Inspector General] because I feel this is in no way a complaint; I'm not trying to get out of anything. I requested transfer to the 1st Cavalry [Division] the day I arrived at my first duty station in Dong Ha. I requested transfer to the Rangers the day I arrived at the 20th Artillery. . . . I served on active duty from November 1962 to November 1965. . . . I came back on active duty in November of 1968 under a fifteen-month reserve enlistment specifically to complete a one year tour of Vietnam. . . . When I returned to active duty my military obligation was already fulfilled. I didn't have to come but I wanted to see this war for myself, to form my own opinions. And I wanted to see combat. I never felt that I had done anything my first tour and it seemed strange to have been in an Army for three years and not to have done what soldiers are trained to do.

I won't lie to you, Sir. I don't believe in this war, but I believe in our system and I believe a man should first be willing to accept the responsibility for it. Then if he desires, he can strive for change. When I leave I want to be able to say that I've done the toughest job this war has to offer, done as much as any man. I believe the Rangers represent this. I recognize the need for support personnel, but I'm willing to fight and want the opportunity, and firmly believe that the Army will be getting the maximum milage out of me in this capacity. I am twenty-five, single, have two years of college and an Army GT score of 142. I'm in top physical condition and I run every day. I've had twelve fights in the Michigan Amateur boxing competition. I lost a split-decision to the open light-welterweight champ in the 1968 Golden Gloves. I believe I can be a good combat soldier if I am just given the chance.

Sergeant Paul J. Salminen was accepted for ranger duty and quickly rose to become assistant patrol leader of a premier reconnaissance team. Company H selected the patrol to perform a special ranger demonstration for the commanding general. On 24 July the rangers conducted a final rehearsal in full equipment. They were scheduled to move in single file onto the stage, turn to the right, and place a sign at their feet listing the equipment they were carrying.

Patrol leader Sgt. Stanley J. Lento held a thirty-minute practice session and then told the men to line their equipment up for review by the first sergeant. When Sp4 Archie H. McDaniel Jr. removed his rucksack, one (possibly two) claymore mines inside exploded accidently. The blast killed McDaniel, Lento, and Salminen. Sgt. James W. Kraft and Sp4 Fred R. Doriot were wounded in the head, and Sp4 Charles M. Steele suffered a punctured chest. Only Specialists Michael Bakkie and Henry Morris escaped injury.

The building caught fire and partially burned down. An Explosive Ordnance Disposal (EOD) team under Capt. Chester H. Heidl swept the scene of destruction and investigated. Captain Heidl's men found extra safety precautions had been taken by the deceased rangers. Hand grenades and trip flares attached to their belts and packs were well taped. The EOD team were forced to cut away tape on both sides of all handles to remove them. The grenade pins were thoroughly wrapped in tape to prevent any accident. The chance of foul play was investigated thoroughly by the division Criminal Investigation Detachment and ruled out. The cause of the explosion that wiped out the company H demonstration ranger team was never determined. [15]

Field accidents, especially those involving helicopter crashes over remote territory, also necessitated ranger deployment. The rangers routinely dispatched search teams for downed helicopters. For example, on 14 July 1969 a ranger team was assembled to locate possible survivors after a gunship and observation helicopter crashed near Song Be. The team was led by Captain Paccerelli and contained assistant patrol leader Staff Sgt. David O. Mitchell, radioman Staff Sgt. Stephen C. Virostko, and machine gunner Sp4 Ernest Squire. At 10:30 P.M. the ranger team rappelled into the darkened jungle where several burning fires marked the crash site.

The team searched the scattered wreckage near a large crater created by the detonation of the UH-1B helicopter impacting the ground. The rangers set up defenses and called out, "Hello, is anybody there?" and "If you're hurt and can't make talk, make some noise." There was only silence, however, as Captain Paccerelli walked past scattered fires, twisted debris, and smoldering body parts. He used a red-filtered flashlight to check one body segment, a head and upper chest cavity of a black man. The forward portion of the shattered helicopter was still burning intensely and could not be searched because of unexploded aerial rockets nearby. However, Captain Paccerelli found the severely burned bodies of the pilot and copilot nearby. He also identified enough scattered human remnants to report that the fourth crewman probably died. An hour later the ranger searchers were extracted, using a jungle penetrator.

In the morning the 9th Cavalry aerial scout platoon was inserted to retrieve the bodies found during the night. The platoon recovered the bodies of the pilot and copilot but could not locate any other body parts identified by the rangers. Captain Paccerelli was initially puzzled upon returning to the scene, because the presence of helicopter weapons and ammunition indicated that enemy soldiers had not disturbed the site. The mystery was solved when Paccerelli found flame-resistant DuPont Nomex nylon twill aviator uniform fragments, smaller body pieces, and animal tracks farther off in the woods. He surmised that wild pigs had carried off all human remains east of the crater, but had been discouraged by the large fire from reaching the bodies of the two aviation officers. Based on the ranger report, Staff Sgt. Roy G. Davis and Pfc. Dewey R. Butler were declared dead, although only Maj. Thomas M. Felton and CW2 Earnest D. Burns were positively identified.[16]

The 1st Cavalry Division continued to screen the Vietnamese-Cambodian border region through the rest of the year. Capt. Richard K. Griffiths took over Company H in September 1969. Ranger patrols scouted possible shifts in enemy infiltration networks but found scant signs of enemy movement. A typical ninety-day ranger period covered the months of November 1969 through the end of January 1970. During this time, Company H employed 110 patrols, thirty-nine of which resulted in twenty-seven engagements and thirty-seven North Vietnamese troops killed by direct ranger fire.[17]

Many patrols resulted in brief contacts, and the rangers were capable of placing abundant firepower on favorable targets. On 3 November 1969, ranger effectiveness was demonstrated by team 45, inserted to monitor the Jolley Trail vicinity near the Dak Kat river in Phuoc Long Province. The team carried typical equipment. Team leader Sgt. Milford P. Harvey carried an M16, and assistant team leader Sp4 Larry Robinson carried an M79 grenade launcher and an emergency URC-10 radio. The radioman, Pfc. James F. Rogers, back-packed the main PRC-25 radio and carried an M16 rifle, as did medic Charles F. Coffin. The rear scout, Sp4 David

Torres, carried an M14 rifle with twenty magazines. Rangers liked to employ the M14 because it resembled the sound of an M60 machine gun if fired on full automatic, and the enemy would refuse to engage what they thought was a larger unit. Each member also carried eleven grenades, spare ammunition, two claymore mines, and six flares.

Sergeant Harvey picked out a landing zone in advance of the actual patrol. During the insertion, as the helicopters were making the final approach to the ground, Specialist Robinson saw a hard-packed trail in the woods beneath them and pointed it out to Harvey. The helicopters deposited the rangers in their selected field, and the team conducted a ten-minute wait to ensure radio transmission and to check for possible enemy response. After the halt, the team moved through scattered brush vegetation toward the trail previously seen by Robinson.

Just before nightfall the patrol set up a trail-monitoring position. Within a half hour the rangers observed a rocket-carrying platoon of twenty-four khaki-uniformed soldiers pass their positions through the woods. Private Rogers radioed for armed helicopters, and the gunships fired into the area until dark. The ranger team remained undetected throughout the night, calling in artillery and aviation fire on several other groups. Just before dawn, several North Vietnamese passed the patrol position carrying litters.

At sunrise the size and frequency of the enemy groups became smaller. Sergeant Harvey decided to ambush the next few enemy soldiers who passed through their kill zone and capture a prisoner. Just before 7:00 A.M., two North Vietnamese walked into the ambush zone. Unfortunately, the claymore mines were not "double-primed" and they failed to fire when the detonator was pushed. There was a loud clacking noise and then silence. The rangers froze, hoping the enemy soldiers would think some animal had broken a twig. One North Vietnamese soldier began looking into the brush with his AK47 at the ready. Robinson shouted, "He's seen me!" and Harvey opened up with his M16 rifle at virtually point-blank range. As the rangers began firing, Robinson hooked another detonator into the claymores and successfully fired them.

There was no return fire. One North Vietnamese body lay in the trail, and the other wounded NVA soldier crawled away. Later the rangers linked up with a 9th Cavalry aero rifle platoon dispatched to their location. A large North Vietnamese force engaged the combined American force, wounding Robinson and another cavalryman. The Americans retreated to a clearing under the covering fire of armed helicopters strafing the enemy lines. Ranger team 45 was extracted just before 10:00 A.M. Later infantry sweeps of the vicinity counted forty-three NVA bodies in the area where the rangers called for artillery and air strikes, as well as quantities of abandoned enemy equipment.[18]

Ranger harassment of enemy supply columns was typified by the experience of ranger team 41 on the morning of 17 November 1969, while they were monitoring another branch of the Jolley Trail. During midafternoon the rangers observed a North Vietnamese squad moving past their location and decided to wait for a larger target. Two hours later, forty Vietnamese and one water buffalo moved into the kill zone. Every third native carried a heavy pack, signifying an enemy resupply column. The rangers exploded claymore mines and decimated the lead elements, but came under heavy rifle and B-40 rocket return fire from a flanking direction. Two rangers were killed and another wounded. The patrollers called in gunships that rocketed and strafed the enemy attackers. The aerial firepower enabled the rangers to reach a medical evacuation helicopter with their casualties.

Another typical patrol occurred on 28 January 1970. Ranger team 35 landed by helicopter and patrolled for 350 yards uneventfully until they spotted a North Vietnamese soldier crossing a wide field. The rangers then listened to someone singing in the distance and heard the sounds of bamboo being cut in the opposite direction. The team members halted and set up an overnight ambush. Late in the evening the team killed an enemy soldier and received rifle fire from several directions at long range. Then the firing stopped and the rangers saw a wavering row of flashlights low off the ground as the enemy crawled toward them. The rangers opened fire on full automatic, and the lights were quickly doused. The ranges radioed for gunship suppressive fire and retreated safely to a nearby clearing for a nighttime extraction.

CAVALRY RANGERS FROM CAMBODIA TO CEASE-FIRE

From December 1969 until 22 April 1970, Company H (Airmobile Ranger), 75th Infantry, participated in Operation DONG TIEN. This exercise paired 1st Cavalry Division elements with the South Vietnamese Airborne Division. The Cavalry Rangers worked closely with their South Vietnamese paratrooper counterparts to impart American patrolling methods and communications techniques. The rangers temporarily formed two joint teams of three Americans and three Vietnamese for field operations during this operation.

The rest of the ranger spring 1970 campaign served as a prelude to the impending incursion into Cambodia. Capt. William S. Carrier III replaced Capt. Richard K. Griffiths as Company H commander. The Cavalry Rangers continued to seek out enemy routes of infiltration and from February through April fielded ninety-five patrols. These patrols made forty-seven observations, participated in twenty contact situations, and killed six NVA soldiers by direct fire.[19]

Patrolling during this period was typified by the 7 February encounter of ranger team 43. The patrol established a trail ambush along the Western Corridor. After dark a bicycle-riding North Vietnamese platoon halted right in front of the rangers' carefully hidden claymore mines. The rangers detonated the mines and heaved grenades into the startled cyclists. The North Vietnamese abandoned their bicycles and ran off, leaving five bodies and twelve 220-pound bags of rice among a twisted pile of bent bicycle frames. The rangers were lifted out of the area an hour later.

One ranger team was particularly unfortunate. In the first instance, on 9 March, team 52 was occupying an overnight position in dense jungle when the assistant team leader suddenly went into convulsions. A medical evacuation helicopter was requested. The "dust-off" pilot insisted that the rangers mark their position with smoke, and the sick individual was hoisted out using a jungle penetrator. Unfortunately, the cloud of smoke compromised the ranger location and forced the rest of the team to request night extraction from an emergency pickup point.

The lofty triple-canopy jungle mandated the use of the jungle penetrator for the patrol lift-out. The jungle penetrator, lowered by cable from a helicopter winch, consisted of a three-foot metal projectile that unfolded like an anchor to form seats. Designed for hoisting casualties without gear, the device's safety straps could not be used if full rucksacks were worn. The weight of heavy equipment also tended to pull the men backward off the jungle penetrator seats. As the last two remaining team members were being hoisted to the hovering aircraft, one ranger lost his grip. He fell 125 feet through the darkened triple-canopy jungle to his death.

In May 1970, Maj. Gen. George W. Casey took over the 1st Cavalry Division and commanded the formation during the Cambodian invasion. Ranger Company H, with just over a hundred troops, led the advance of both the 1st Cavalry Division and the South Vietnamese Airborne Division. The rangers performed critical ground reconnaissance for the two divisions despite intense hostile fire, adverse weather conditions, and hazardous landing zones. From 1 May until the end of June the Cavalry Rangers conducted fifty missions into Cambodia ranging from the "Fishhook" border region to Bu Krak.

These patrols resulted in thirty-eight major enemy sightings, fifteen significant contacts, and numerous enemy killed by direct ranger fire or ranger-directed artillery and air strikes.[20]

The scope of ranger activities was best exemplified by the experience of ranger team 51. The patrol was in an overnight position when it observed seventeen individuals moving on an adjacent trail. Sixteen soldiers wore normal enemy gear, but the final person appeared to be a high-ranking official. The rangers then spotted fifty-five additional soldiers. The team leader radioed for aerial and artillery bombardment that devastated a large North Vietnamese troop concentration in the area.

During the Cambodian invasion, ranger team 52 suffered its most catastrophic incident. On 13 June the team received orders to search the area between O'Rang in Cambodia and the Vietnamese border (see Map B). The team was flown into Fire Support Base David, an advanced outpost inside Cambodia, on the following day. Upon arrival the patrol leader went to the base aid station and was medically excused from the patrol because of an infected foot cut. On 15 June, Staff Sgt. Deverton C. Cochrane was sent to team 52 as the replacement patrol leader. On the same day the team's assistant team leader was medically excused from the patrol because of an eye infection. That evening Sp4 Carl J. Laker was designated as the new assistant patrol leader. The other team members were radioman Sergeant Ronald M. Andrus, medic Sp4 Royce D. Clark (another replacement), and rear scout Staff Sgt. Dwight D. Hancock.

Staff Sergeant Cochrane executed an overflight of the Cambodian forest on the afternoon of 16 June and selected the landing zone on high ground, and team 52 was inserted by helicopter at 4:45 P.M. Sergeant Andrus secured radio contact using a long-whip antenna, and Cochrane moved the patrol to overnight positions about 300 yards into the jungle. The team rendered squelch-break negative situation reports over the radio at each hour throughout the night. On the following morning, team 52 discovered an empty North Vietnamese defensive position full of ammunition and flares. The patrol continued to move through the jungle and was soon drenched by a tropical rainstorm.

At 3:35 P.M., in the driving rain, team 52 moved to the top of Hill 717 and found a small bunker complex. Staff Sergeant Cochrane decided not to report this finding until that evening, to lessen the chance of communications interception. The team walked down the other side of the forested hill. At 5:30 P.M., Cochrane approached the edge of the woods, near an open field, and motioned that he heard voices. As he began to hunch down, a burst of automatic weapons fire swept through the trees from a machine gun nest in the woods directly across the field. Cochrane fell, muttering, "Oh God, I'm hit." Enemy automatic rifle fire ripped through the team positions. Sergeant Andrus radioed, "Contact 52! 52 in Contact!" But the signal was never picked up. The team was on low ground with only the short antenna on its PRC-25 radio.

Specialist Clark saw the head of a North Vietnamese soldier protrude from the distant shrubbery and fired three M14 rounds into him. Staff Sergeant Hancock threw grenades at the enemy until the firing stopped. During the temporary lull, Specialist Laker yelled for Andrus to bring him the radio and ordered his men farther back into the woods. Laker tried to reach Cochrane but was shot in the head by a sniper and fell on top of Hancock. Hancock saw that "Laker had a bullet hole above the left eye and the back of his head was blown out." Sergeant Andrus was shot in the chest as he affixed the long antenna. The radio was shattered by several more rounds in quick succession. Specialist Clark was hit in the leg by a sniper bullet that shattered his thigh.

Staff Sergeant Hancock tried frantically to find the team's emergency URC-10 survival radio among the dead and wounded rangers but could not locate it. He picked up Clark and carried him from the fire-swept area as Andrus, although seriously wounded, gave covering fire. The three rangers moved back into the thick undergrowth. Hancock administered emergency first aid and covered Andrus and Clark with vegetation. Hancock then gave his rifle and ammunition to Andrus and told them he was going to get help.

The weaponless ranger sergeant stayed close to the trees and avoided several fields. Fortunately a heavy ground fog rolled across the patches of jungle and mixed with the rain to cover his evasion. Hancock traveled for miles, passed nocturnal North Vietnamese machine gunners covering the highway near O'Rang, and finally reached an American outpost near Fire Support Base David. He ignited a hand flare to light the darkness and stood waving a piece of white parachute cloth while shouting, "Don't shoot! I'm Staff Sergeant Hancock of the rangers!"

At daybreak on 18 June, ranger Captain Carrier and Hancock led a reinforced search team of cavalrymen and rangers back to the skirmish site. Both Andrus and Clark were found. Despite an extensive search of the area, neither Deverton Carpenter Cochrane of Brookline, Massachusetts, nor Carl J. Laker were ever found. Both men were carried as missing in action until an official Army investigative panel declared on 28 June 1970:

The Board [of officers] believes that Sp4 Laker died as a result of wounds received in the action on 17 June 1970. The nature and extent of the wound and the testimony of the witnesses present leave no doubt in the minds of the Board that Laker is in fact dead and should be classified as killed in action. The Board, however, was unable to be as conclusive about Staff Sergeant Cochrane. The seriousness of Cochrane's wounds were not verified, and since the body was not thoroughly checked before the remaining members of the team pulled back, a definite decision as to the status of Staff Sergeant Cochrane cannot be determined. The Board therefore concludes that Staff Sergeant Cochrane should be considered as Missing in Action.[21]

The Cambodian campaign inflicted other casualties also, among them 1st Cavalry Division commander Major General Casey, who was killed in a helicopter crash on 7 June. In July the division departed Cambodia. Maj. Gen. George W. Putnam Jr. assumed division command as the American military withdrawal from Southeast Asia escalated sharply. There was increased political pressure to lower combat activity and reduce Army casualties among units remaining in Vietnam. This concern led to the Cavalry Rangers being ordered to terminate missions immediately upon direct contact with enemy troops. Additionally, ranger patrols were redirected closer to the division's protective web of fire support bases.

In April 1971 the bulk of the 1st Cavalry Division redeployed to the United States. From 27 March to 2 April, ranger Company H was reduced by seventy-three authorized personnel spaces and restructured as part of the separate 3d Brigade. The brigade operational area included all of Long Khanh and Binh Tuy provinces and large swaths of adjacent territory that encompassed 3,000 square miles—the largest area assigned to a U.S. brigade in Vietnam. The ranger teams were based at Bien Hoa and provided surveillance by identifying enemy penetration routes and capturing documents. During the six months from May through October, for example, Company H fielded 110 patrols and made seventy sightings of enemy personnel. These patrols killed ninety-four NVA or VC soldiers (from all causes, including ranger-directed artillery and airstrikes), detained thirteen suspects, and recovered approximately 150 pounds of enemy documents.[22]

From June 1971 until its withdrawal from Vietnam, Company H consisted of ranger teams 71–79. During December the 3d Brigade was reconcentrated to guard the Saigon-Long Binh logistical complex and the scope of ranger operations was further restricted. These installations were surrounded by "rocket belts" from which enemy rockets could be fired. The Cavalry Rangers spent the final months of the war patrolling the rocket belts just outside these final bases. The rangers interdicted many North Vietnamese rocket troops and recoilless rifle gunners venturing near the capital region.

The few line battalions of the separate 3d Brigade represented the only American infantry left in this crucial area of Vietnam. North Vietnamese regiments moved into vacated regions and safely operated much closer to once-secure airfields and supply depots. On 9 June 1972 the Cavalry Rangers suffered their final Vietnam losses when ranger team 76, led by Sgt. Elvis W. Osborne Jr., was inserted on a reconnaissance patrol near Tan Uyen. The team point element walked into a well-concealed enemy bunker complex and spotted several enemy soldiers without being detected. Sergeant Osborne pulled his men back and radioed for gunships to rocket the area. The helicopters expended their ammunition and departed.

The ranger team reentered the smoking base camp to assess damage. The rangers came under fire but maneuvered forward. Suddenly the team was hit by either concentrated enemy rocket fire or a command-detonated bomb rigged as a mechanical ambush device. The resulting explosions killed Sergeant Osborne and radioman Jeffrey A. Maurer, and wounded secondary radioman Sp4 Donald E. Schellinger. He courageously kept fighting despite serious wounds and, along with three other patrol members (Sgt. Robert Roy, Sgt. Thomas Heiney, and Sp4 Michael Pratt) managed to reach and defend the extraction site.[23]

The action represented one of the last significant ranger encounters in Vietnam. On 27 June the Cavalry Rangers were relieved from the separate 3d Brigade of the 1st Cavalry Division and assigned to the ''Garry Owen'' Task force of the 1st Battalion (Airmobile), 7th Cavalry. The company ceased combat operations after mid-July and began final phase-out procedures. On 15 August 1972, Company H (Airmobile Ranger), 75 Infantry, was officially inactivated as the last Army ranger unit in Vietnam.

The Pershing Lerps, First Team Patrollers, and Cavalry Rangers were highly motivated and imbued with the same team spirit that permeated the 1st Cavalry Division during the Second Indochina War. The units demonstrated the validity of ranger reconnaissance and extended patrolling techniques in an airmobile helicopter-oriented division. The integration of ground patrols with a ranger-cognizant division air cavalry squadron offered an excellent combination for long-range operations. The patrol forces operated successfully in three dissimilar corps tactical zones and spearheaded cavalry screening functions. Company H also achieved the longest continuous combat tenure of any ranger outfit in American history.[24]

4

1ST INFANTRY DIVISION

IRON RANGERS

WILDCAT RECONNAISSANCE

The 1st Infantry Division completed its deployment to Vietnam in October 1965. Throughout its service in Vietnam, the division battled Viet Cong and North Vietnamese Army units in their strongholds north and west of Saigon. The division secured Highway 13, which both connected Saigon with Cambodia and formed the general partition between enemy-held War Zones C and D. The division was primarily responsible for the line of communications and surrounding territory. Division reconnaissance was principally mounted from bases at Di An, Phu Loi, Lai Khe, and Phuoc Vinh. Patrols were conducted throughout the predominantly jungle- and marsh-covered regions of War Zones C and D, the Iron Triangle, the Trapezoid, the Michelin Rubber Plantation, the Long Nguyen Secret Zone, the Song Be Corridor, and the Vietnamese frontier with Cambodia. Sometimes division reconnaissance was launched farther afield to cover other operational areas, such as the Rung Sat Special Zone.

Division reconnaissance initially relied on the armored 1st Squadron, 4th Cavalry. The squadron also included an aerial unit, "Dark-horse" Troop D, that contained an aero rifle platoon that had limited patrolling capability. The platoon's mission involved rapid response to scout helicopter sightings and security of downed aircraft, and this task precluded the platoon's employment on longer ground patrols. During April 1966, Maj. Gen. William E. DePuy remedied the situation by forming a provisional division Long Range Reconnaissance Patrol (LRRP) contingent. The

"Lerps" specialized in ground searches that stretched over several days inside hostile territory. The patrol contingent was attached to Troop D for aerial weapons (armed helicopter) and aerial rifle (reaction force) platoon support.

The 1st Infantry Division LRRP contingent received the radio call sign "Wildcats." The patrols were ideally composed of combat-experienced volunteers who displayed a mastery of land navigation, radio communications, and patrolling skills. For instance, LRRP operations sergeant Sfc. Donald Wallace was chosen because of his previous advisory tour with the South Vietnamese Army in 1962. The requirement for battlefield experience and top recon credentials secured many volunteers who extended their Vietnam service by six months to join the unit. Troop D airlift platoon commander Capt. Richard Murphy inserted and extracted many of the patrols. He remembered, "I could tell of many daring insertions and extractions. It takes a great deal of teamwork and that's what we were—a team. Sometimes the chopper hovered over a bomb crater to put the patrol into the jungle and days later it was picked up at the edge of a rice paddy several miles away."[1]

In late April 1966, several Wildcat Lerp teams were utilized in Operation BIRMINGHAM, at that time the deepest conventional allied penetration of War Zone C in northern Tay Ninh Province. The teams rappelled into heavy jungle along the Cambodian border and eastern bank of the Cai Bac River, but were quickly detected by numerically superior Viet Cong forces. All patrols were forced to abort their missions under emergency circumstances. This premature compromise of division assets necessitated reliance on Special Forces Project Delta for the majority of operational reconnaissance during BIRMINGHAM. In June 1966, more Lerp teams returned to the field to scout enemy positions ahead of Operation EL PASO. On 13 June, during a recon expedition near Special Forces Camp Loc Ninh, Sgt. Rudolph Algar Nuñoz became the earliest division LRRP contingent member killed in action.[2]

During wartime operations the 1st Infantry Division still relied heavily on battalion reconnaissance, especially while the LRRP contingent was still forming or in a provisional mode. Sample battalion reconnaissance platoons included the 2d Infantry's 2d Battalion "Double Devil Recon"; the 18th Infantry's 1st Battalion "Recon Swamp Rats"; the 18th Infantry's 2d Battalion "Recon Vanguards"; and the 28th Infantry's two "Black Lion Recon" platoons. Such units provided a ready source of reconnoitering expertise when long-range patrols were eventually formally authorized at division level.

The most notable battalion reconnaissance platoons in the development of division rangers were the original "Recon Rangers" of both 16th Infantry battalions. Their professional excellence was sharpened by 1st Battalion commander Lt. Col. Rufus C. Lazzell and 2d Battalion commander Lt. Col. Joseph Ulatoski, who were both superb ranger leaders. Lazzell was a 1956 graduate of the ranger school and a 1961 company commander of the British Parachute Regiment. Ulatoski was a 1951 ranger school graduate who commanded the 5th Ranger Company and a guerrilla force of the 8240th Army Unit, Combined Command for Reconnaissance Activities, during the Korean conflict. These officers molded the "Recon Ranger" platoons into highly proficient combat recon units capable of operating independently for extended periods in a jungle patrol environment.[3]

The "Recon Spaders" of the 26th Infantry "Blue Spaders" represented two other battalion reconnaissance platoons that contributed significantly to division patrolling techniques. In early 1967, one 1st Battalion reconnaissance venture experienced the swift VC disappearing act that often occurred if the enemy did not desire confrontations. The battalion's four-man ambush teams were situated along a trail network leading to a Viet Cong assembly area in an old pottery factory. Sp4 Albert Weaver Jr. spotted three Viet Cong approaching along the moonlit trail. Pfc. Joseph Fordham recalled, "One of the three Viet Cong tripped our flare and he froze, either from fright or hoping that he might blend in with the brush if he didn't move." The patrollers killed the lead VC soldier, but his two comrades somehow escaped the ensuing rifle fire and grenade explosions. One enemy soldier scrambled into the jungle and the other plunged into a nearby hidden tunnel. Weaver and Fordham tossed a grenade down the entrance, but surmised that the fleeing Viet Cong was already far underground.[4]

The "Leopard" reconnaissance platoon of the 1st Battalion, 2d Infantry, likewise pioneered many division reconnaissance methods—especially against Viet Cong tunnels and bunkers. One typical incident took place during Operation MANHATTAN, an April 1967 attempt to ferret out VC troops of the Binh Duong Province Committee located between the Iron Triangle and the Michelin Plantation. Sgt. Harry W. Warlick was point man on a Leopard recon patrol that discovered several pits with punji stakes pointed exclusively down-trail. Patrol leader Staff Sgt. Louis Santos decided to reverse direction to find the VC base camp. Sergeant Warlick found a discarded cartridge belt farther along the trail, and the team followed the path until it ended in a thick pile of vines and foliage. Underneath the camouflaged mat was a steel door with a view slit.

Staff Sergeant Santos tried unsuccessfully to open the door with a rope. Platoon commander Capt. Gilbert Wichert tried to pry the door open next, but was wounded by a Viet Cong firing through the aperture. Santos then devised a field-expedient ''shaped charge'' by packing high explosives in front of a claymore mine and electrically detonated it against the door. The blast ripped through the door,·and Santos tossed a grenade into the open pit. When the smoke cleared the patrollers heard someone cry ''Save me'' in broken English, followed by a dazed Viet Cong emerging from the tunnel entrance. The prisoner related that four more Viet Cong were in the tunnel, one of them already dead.

Staff Sergeant Santos led part of the team into the narrow tunnel past the body of a dead sentry behind the door. They traveled only ten yards before finding another Viet Cong. The team leader was forced to shoot his way deeper into the labyrinth as the enemy soldier retreated through the curving underground passage. The tunnel-crawling recon patrol was unable to relocate the defender, who probably fled through a hidden escapement. The tunnel crew returned to the surface and evacuated their sole captive.[5]

One of the more memorable division reconnaissance episodes occurred in October 1966. During the Vietnam era, United States homeland defense relied directly on the strategic DEW (Distant Early Warning) Line spanning the area from Alaska to Greenland. One division recon force ''duplicated'' the DEW line on a much smaller scale. A 2d Brigade recon team moved into an ambush site along the Song Saigon, only to find a flock of domestic ducks already occupying the preselected locality. The ambush patrollers decided to use the canal bank anyway, established their positions, and waited quietly until the disturbed ducks settled down. Hours later the men were alerted by quacking ducks and spotted a Viet Cong sampan attempting to slip through the darkened canal. The ''Duck Early Warning'' line gave the patrollers enough time to sink the vessel with concentrated rifle and grenade fire.[6]

On 28 September 1967, division commander Maj. Gen. John H. Hay Jr. secured permission to formalize the Wildcat Lerp unit. General Hay was an experienced mountain battalion commander of World War II, and his decorations included the International Gold Medal for skiing proficiency as well as the Swiss Bergführer (''Mountain Leader'') Badge. He took measures to upgrade ranger-style warfare within the division by expanding the first patrols into a long-range detachment authorized 118 reconnaissance personnel.

Once formed, the provisional 1st Infantry Division Long Range Patrol Detachment (LRPD) at Lai Khe was controlled by the division intelligence section. The patrol detachment was organized with a headquarters, operations section, communications section, and two patrol platoons, each containing eight long-range patrols of six men. The nature of its mission and intrinsic hazards mandated the patrollers' continued status as strict volunteers. Individuals were accepted only after personal interviews determined their actual capabilities and strong desire to be members of the detachment.

The unit building period lasted from September to the end of October. The recon members consisted of the original LRRP cadre and additional troops drawn from the battalion reconnaissance platoons. Special training for long-range missions required each team to undergo a twelve-hour daylight area recon, a twelve-hour night trail monitoring mission, and a twenty-four-hour combined problem under combat field conditions. During October the "training teams" located a new enemy base camp under construction, located an old enemy base camp being repaired, and killed several Viet Cong by direct fire.[7]

Long-range detachment patrols were designed to infiltrate objective areas prior to division operations and obtain information on enemy locations and perform terrain analysis. Lengthy ground searches were required, because many trails and streams were covered by thick jungle canopies and not observable from the air. One patrol found an Olympic-size concrete swimming pool, complete with adjoining dressing rooms, in the midst of tropical forest outside Lai Khe. The structure had been built years before by French plantation owners, and years of green moss, tropical undergrowth, fallen trees, and stagnated water engulfed the huge pool.

During the detachment training phase, the teams rehearsed reconnaissance techniques. Each mission required advance scheduling of artillery, airlift support, and other patrol factors that necessitated several days of advance coordination. This included a helicopter overflight on the day prior to the actual mission, conducted by the recon team leader in conjunction with the LRPD commander or operations officer. They selected checkpoints and possible insertion areas. The pilot of the overflight helicopter usually inserted the patrol. A detailed plan was then drafted and issued as the patrol order.

Airmobile team insertions required command, infiltration, and recovery helicopters, as well as a hunter-killer team of one scout and one armed helicopter. The 1st Infantry Division had access to only limited aviation support, and securing adequate aircraft support was a constant problem. For example, sometimes it was even difficult to obtain helicopters for recon overflight purposes. Several missions were aborted either because of aircraft nonavailability or adverse weather. The division adopted a wide range of infiltration practices that "stretched" aviation resources. "Stay-behind" recon teams entered areas surreptitiously as part of larger infantry forces and stayed behind in ambush positions after the regular unit departed. Unfortunately, this stay-behind method was impractical if the reconnaissance was needed before operations actually started.

Other problems involved communications and personnel qualifications. The detachment was initially authorized only ten PRC-25 radios, not enough for all patrols, and the equipment was incapable of transmitting from many areas without intermediate relays or construction of slant- or tree-rigged directional antenna rigs. The advanced patrol knowledge needed to create such devices was taught by the Special Forces–run MACV Recondo School at Nha Trang. Unfortunately, the division could initially spare only forty-one students for formal training at the school. Division operational demands restricted the flow of other recondo-bound students to a monthly average of ten detachment members.

The detachment was declared fully combat-ready in October 1967. LRPD patrols reconnoitered NVA/VC concentrations around Loc Ninh and Bu Dop, uncovered rocket caches northwest of Phuoc Vinh, and scouted west of Highway 13 and into the Michelin Plantation through the end of the year. The early patrols were typified by the five-man team led by Sgt. Edward Davis. On 24 October the recon team was inserted to check enemy use of an area near War Zone C. The team members established an overnight position, observed Viet Cong soldiers passing their location after midnight, and followed the enemy trail at sunrise.

The patrollers stalked the VC for several miles and then turned toward their scheduled extraction point. They reached the landing site, where they were surprised and subjected to heavy fire from a large Viet Cong contingent. Sergeant Davis's men killed seven enemy soldiers with rifle and grenadier fire before being chased into a rice field. Radioman Pfc. Wilber J. Latin radioed for gunships that kept the pursuing Viet Cong from overrunning the patrollers. A utility helicopter extracted the team from the fire-swept rice paddy, and Sergeant Davis returned with detailed confirmation of enemy strength and activity.[8]

Army patrol success depended foremost on team leaders who

possessed the recon expertise and skill required to complete demanding mission assignments while ensuring the safety of their men. The team leaders were almost always incredibly young and brave. In November 1967, Sgt. Kenneth A. Siegel led a long-range team that was directed to verify a suspected Viet Cong troop concentration within the dense jungle northeast of Lai Khe. Shortly after being inserted, the team spotted a Viet Cong platoon moving along a distant trail. Sergeant Siegel and his point man went forward and saw a Viet Cong outpost near the side of the path, preparing to open fire on the American intruders.

Sergeant Siegel quickly fired his M16 rifle and killed the VC security troops. He then continued to fire several magazines into the Viet Cong platoon hastening up the trail. His firing gave the team radioman enough time to radio for extraction. Siegel signaled the patrollers to get to the designated pickup zone while he delayed the VC pursuit force with a hasty ambush. The team leader remained at the edge of the clearing while his men scrambled on the helicopter and continued firing as the last man aboard, killing one Viet Cong soldier next to the tail rotor. Sergeant Siegel's courageous leadership enabled the patrol to complete its verification assignment and return promptly without incurring casualties.[9]

DANGER FORWARD PATROLLERS

On 20 December 1967, in accordance with Army Department directives, the 1st Infantry Division activated Company F (Long Range Patrol), 52d Infantry. The new company was derived from the 1st Infantry Division Long Range Patrol Detachment and received a new call sign. Company F was designated as "Danger Forward Reconnaissance" after the radio code for the advanced division command post, Danger Forward. Company teams were given a standard prefix code of "Remote Trails," signifying RT or Recon Team, and numbered sequentially, such as Remote Trails 7.

The company's first duty was providing part of the sixty-man honor guard for President Lyndon B. Johnson when he visited Vietnam on 23 December. In January 1968, actual reconnaissance work started in reaction to division intelligence assessments. One report concluded that "a major attack by fire [122 mm rocket and heavy mortars] launched in coordination with a major [VC] ground assault against Phu Loi [base camp] by a regimental or larger force is highly probable." General Hay realized that a successful attack on Phu Loi, where division aviation was chiefly concentrated, would severely restrict his formation's maneuverability. Company F was withdrawn from field patrols and posted to provide heightened security around all major division installations, including Phu Loi.

On 31 January a Company F patrol led by Sgt. Ronny O. Luse manned a forward night observation position outside the Phu Loi base camp. At 10:05 P.M., Sergeant Luse detected about twelve Viet Cong moving toward his position and radioed the sighting. The recon team prepared to routinely ambush the enemy soldiers, but the VC turned and moved into the far woods before reaching ambush range. An hour later, Sergeant Luse watched with incredulity as he saw at least one full battalion of Viet Cong emerge from the darkened trees and begin to cross the rice paddies. He radioed the division tactical operations center, "I see a large number of Viet Cong on line moving towards us—several hundred of them!"[10]

The division recalled the small patrol to the perimeter and relayed the reconnaissance sighting to division artillery. An illumination helicopter equipped with a xenon searchlight was scrambled into the air. As the helicopter prepared to flood the fields with artificial light, a division battery of 105mm howitzers fired volleys of fuze-timed shrapnel directly into the advancing enemy ranks. The Viet Cong scattered into the adjacent village of An My. Unable to advance further, they engaged the perimeter with weapons fire.

The Danger Forward Patrollers had detected and foiled the main Viet Cong Tet-68 offensive against the 1st Infantry Division. The battle for An My and the outskirts of Phu Loi lasted through 3 February. Information gathered from the battlefield revealed that two battalions of the Viet Cong 273d Regiment and a Dong Nai regimental battalion were involved. The powerful Viet Cong forces were prevented from surprising and reaching their objective because one miniscule reconnaissance patrol stood in their way.[11]

Following the Tet offensive the depleted Viet Cong units pulled back to regroup. Patrols noted that all enemy movement was greatly diminished. Observations on VC inactivity were equally important in division determinations of probable enemy action. Late in February, Lt. Paul Mattox led a ten-man heavy patrol on a night ambush mission against a normally well-used Viet Cong supply trail near An Loc. The patrol crossed a chest-deep swampish stream, reached a desired section of the trail, and installed ten claymore mines to cover the kill zone. The patrollers, pestered by swarms of mosquitoes, monitored their mines closely. Staff Sgt. Jack Leisure, the rear security guard, waited patiently and listened for any careless noises from the new volunteers accompanying the mission.

Five minutes past midnight, several members of the ambush

group thought they heard footsteps on the trail, but Lieutenant Mattox detected nothing through his starlight scope. The night passed uneventfully. In the morning the patrol collected the claymores and returned through dense bamboo thickets to recross the river and return to their perimeter. The patrol was logged as a "no sightings, no contact" mission, an important result for intelligence-gathering purposes. The division was informed about the lack of enemy area presence and adjusted its search and destroy plans accordingly.[12]

In March 1968, Maj. Gen. Keith L. Ware assumed division command. Soon afterward, a Company F long-range patrol led by Sgt. Franklin Jones was inserted west of Lai Khe. The recon team members set up positions in the underbrush as several Viet Cong walked past them along a trail. Sergeant Jones radioed for artillery to land in front of the enemy soldiers, hoping they might reverse direction back into his team's kill zone. When the artillery shelling commenced, dozens more Viet Cong began running out of the nearby jungle. Sergeant Jones remarked that his "men were shocked to see so many Viet Cong when they were expecting only a few . . . the enemy must have really been surprised when the artillery rounds began hitting." Fortunately the patrollers had never ambushed the original enemy, who turned out to be flankers attached to a larger Viet Cong force.[13]

During June, one four-man Danger Forward Reconnaissance patrol was evacuated under fire by a Cobra gunship in the enemy-held Catcher's Mitt area. The recon team, led by Sgt. Robert P. Elsner, was just beginning to leave the jungle and cross a rice paddy during the night. Sp4 William P. Cohn Jr. and Gerald W. Paddy thought they saw movement across the field at the other edge of the darkened woods. Sergeant Elsner verified enemy movement through his starlight scope. Assistant patrol leader Sgt. David M. Hill stated, "We all got down on our stomachs to go back into the jungle when the enemy opened up on us." The team was pinned down by concentrated fire while Elsner called for artillery and gunships.

When the helicopters arrived overhead he popped flares at the enemy positions. The North Vietnamese troops aimed automatic weapons at the circling gunships and began massing troops against the stranded team. Elsner radioed they were about to be overrun. Suddenly a sleek AH-1G Cobra gunship swooped into the center of the rice field. The isolated rangers climbed aboard—two on the skids, one on a rocket launcher, and one on the small wing—and the Cobra attack helicopter lifted off. The incident was one of the only "Cobra extractions" of the Vietnam war.[14]

On the afternoon of 13 September 1968, Maj. Gen. Keith L.

Ware helicoptered from Loc Ninh toward Quan Loi and disappeared. Reconnaissance teams were airlifted into an area of thick bamboo and brush after a rising column of distant smoke was reported. The recon members reached the wreck while it was still burning and confirmed seven human corpses and one animal body, later identified as Major General Ware's faithful canine companion King. The aircraft had been struck by heavy machine gun fire that tore off the tail boom and caused it to crash with such force that the transmission was buried three feet in the ground. Only one person, Sp4 Raymond E. Lanter, was never accounted for. He either jumped or fell from the helicopter as it crashed and landed some distance away. Brig. Gen. Orwin C. Talbott, the assistant commander, was placed in charge of the division immediately. Upon learning of his appointment, Talbott stated, "I would have given anything, I say again, anything to have had it been under other circumstances."[15]

Company F continued operations in a variety of battlefield screening and intelligence-gathering assignments. On some occasions the long-range patrols were exposed to extremely dangerous situations. During late November 1968 a reconnaissance disaster caused the loss of team 11. The incident was long remembered with bitter resentment by the patrollers as a supreme example of senseless headquarters "march or die" staff work. At the time, Company F was commanded by Capt. Allen A. Lindman, a very professional officer who cared greatly for his men. Lindman's company was operating under the control of the 1st Brigade, 1st Infantry Division, in one of the most dangerous areas of South Vietnam.

The brigade was operating west of the Rach Thi Thinh on a sweep through a Viet Cong–occupied slice of territory known as the Trapezoid. The Danger Forward Reconnaissance company was assigned to watch for enemy movement east of the Thi Thinh river, between the Trapezoid and the Long Nguyen Secret Zone, in conjunction with the brigade sweep. Captain Lindman was directed to send his teams to reconnoiter either possible Viet Cong movement away from the brigade and across the Rach Thi Thinh, or potential North Vietnamese Army reinforcements arriving from the Long Nguyen Secret Zone and marching to cross the Rach Thi Thinh and hit the brigade flanks.

On 20 November 1968, Captain Lindman inserted four teams of six men each to look for enemy activity in the assigned reconnaissance sector (see Map F). All four teams were helicoptered to their areas between 3:00 and 3:30 in the afternoon, and they reported enemy activity within an hour after landing. Recon team 3 was airlanded in the sector's northernmost portion, near the stream junction of the Rach Thi Thinh and Suoi Ho Da. An hour later the patrol skirmished against fifteen Viet Cong, killing one, and was extracted. The other patrols also experienced close encounters.

Recon team 5 was helicoptered into the reconnaissance sector's midsection, close to the Rach Thi Thanh and south of Ap Bo Cang village. The team sighted three water buffalo, moved southward, and heard a Vietnamese female yelling, dogs barking, and some chickens cackling. Farther along, the recon troops observed a company of seventy-five Viet Cong wearing black shirts and shorts and a mixture of steel helmets and flop hats, and carrying AK47 automatic rifles, carbines, and light machine guns. The patrollers noticed that one man in the center of the column carried no weapon but was wearing a white shirt and a Panama straw hat. The formation included female nurses and wounded soldiers walking on crutches. As the column passed east of the patrol, another line of seventy-five enemy soldiers went by in the distance on the other side of the team's position. The team waited quietly until well after dark and was extracted.

Recon team 10 was inserted directly along the Rach Thi Thanh. The patrol engaged in a desultory firefight against four Viet Cong and killed one of them. The patrol leader also waited until evening before being extracted. Recon team 9 scouted the sector's lower corner, close to the river, and clashed with fifteen Viet Cong. The team claimed one enemy soldier killed in the firefight, requested twilight extraction, and was lifted out in the evening.

That night Captain Lindman recommended against employing new teams on the following day, because the area was apparently saturated with enemy troops, as confirmed by all four patrols. The 1st Brigade executive officer in charge of operations, Lt. Col. Dudley T. Bunn, seconded Captain Lindman's opinion. Based on the patrol observations, 1st Brigade commander Col. Earl W. Fletcher also recommended that no further teams be sent into the reconnaissance zone. Captain Lindman later explained his reasoning to a formal investigative board:

LTC Cassels [Investigating Officer]: "Captain Lindman, do you feel there are any lessons to be learned in the employment of LRRP teams that you would care to discuss based on the operation of team 11?"

A [Answer]: "Yes Sir. The lesson I feel that should be learned concerns the basis on which a LRRP team should be inserted. The basis for inserting team 11 was to confirm the report made by team 5 the previous day. Team 5 reported seeing one hundred and twenty black-pajamaed personnel in that area, carrying AK's [assault rifles], carbines, and what appeared to be belt-fed machine guns. These personnel were observed moving in a trail formation. Team 5 also reported water buffalo, chickens, dogs, and women's voices. The decision to put LRRP team 11 in the same area the next day may have been a misuse of a reconnaissance element, since it had already been determined that the area had been occupied by a large number of enemy troops. A better method of using reconnaissance might have been an aerial reconnaissance of the area utilizing electronic sensor devices. A reconnaissance-in-force might also have been effective, as a larger force could have fixed the enemy in position until air support or additional troops arrived.''[16]

The division operations section insisted, however, that at least two fresh teams were required in the same reconnaissance zone on the following day, 21 November. One high-ranking witness later explained that the division operations section reached the conclusion because it expressed a general disbelief about the original recon reports:

Four LRRP insertions were made in the LRRP area of operations to screen the east flank of the two battalions operating in AO [Area of Operations] Devil. Within approximately two to three hours after these four teams were inserted, three of them were pulled out based on requests of the LRRP detachment commander and information from the teams that they had been in contact with VC forces on the ground. One team, after reporting it was surrounded, then broke contact and made their way back to the original LZ [landing zone]. The fourth team which was located in the vicinity of where LRRP team 11 was inserted on the 21st, was extracted at approximately 2230 hours on the 20th after reporting enemy sightings, but having no physical contact with enemy forces. Reports from the three teams extracted initially made the credibility of the information that they gave questionable. Based on the reports of fire, contact, and being surrounded, but actually having no injuries or no indications of fire fights when debriefed by the S-2 [intelligence section].[17]

The division operations colonel devised a plan to put new recon teams on the ground to reconfirm enemy presence. If combat resulted, he wanted to ''build up'' the fighting by airlanding the Troop D aero rifle platoon next. If the battle escalated and demanded more reinforcements, a company of the 28th Infantry would be standing by to assist. Later termed a ''calculated risk'' by an official investigating board, the division operations section was prepared to go to battalion and brigade pile-on effect. This plan was clearly very dangerous for the initial six-man team that would be put into the mousetrap. Additionally, for the scheme to work, both recon teams needed to be positioned in a manner advantageous to brigade maneuvering west of the river. This rationale meant ordering at least one recon team back into the western midsection of the reconnaissance zone, near the exact vicinity of the earlier team 5 observation.

Despite his misgivings, Captain Lindman was ordered to send two teams into the area. He decided to use recon team 11, because it was on standby for the teams sent previously. At daybreak on 21 November, Captain Lindman told the patrol leaders to prepare their teams for insertion and handed out specific map locations for the desired insertion point. At 8:30 A.M., Captain Lindman accompanied the patrol leaders on an overflight of the area. Their helicopter was flown by CW2 David R. O'Dell, the same pilot who would make the insertion. Following the morning recon flight, the men returned to Lai Khe base camp, where teams 4 and 11 put on their equipment, drew ammunition, were briefed, and passed their final inspection.

At 11:43 A.M., Warrant Officer O'Dell airlanded recon team 4 in the wooded marshlands of the reconnaissance zone. The helicopter returned to Lai Khe, picked up recon team 11, and flew back to the reconnaissance zone. At five minutes past noon, Warrant Officer O'Dell guided his helicopter toward the preselected field. He lowered the helicopter over some small trees and descended into a rice paddy. Heavy jungle dominated both sides of the clearing. Recon team 11 clambered out and O'Dell prepared to lift off.

Enemy gunfire abruptly smashed into the aircraft. One round tore through the chin bubble, knocked out the Plexiglas, and hit O'Dell in the leg. The right door gunner was under the impression that the recon members never realized enemy bullets were striking the helicopter. The last patroller to exit the helicopter, however, stopped and looked back at the gunner with a puzzled expression. The door gunner motioned with his hand to get down and the rear scout squatted for a minute in the rice field and then kept moving away.

The helicopter lifted off as O'Dell executed a left turnout while both door gunners fired into the nearby trees. The helicopter was riddled with bullets as the wounded pilot completed his left-pedal turn and flew off. He managed to transmit that he was receiving fire before communications were severed and fuel began gushing through the air. Warrant Officer O'Dell, although wounded, skillfully piloted the crippled aircraft into Lai Khe.

Another helicopter high above the same field carried Troop D commander Maj. Robert H. Haley, Captain Lindman, and Lieutenant Colonel Bunn, who were monitoring the insertion. The officers heard O'Dell report that the "LZ was hot and I'm coming out!" Further efforts to reach either O'Dell or the team by radio were unsuccessful. Major Haley circled the helicopter closer to the ground and abruptly heard a brief radio transmission: "We're in contact! Get us out of here! Get us out of here!"

Major Haley did not request immediate gunship support because he was unable to ascertain the team's location. Frantic attempts to get a situation report from team 11 failed until a very muffled radio transmission was received: "This is Eleven [pause]. . . . They're all dead [pause]. . . . They're all dead [pause]. . . . I'm dying." Captain Lindman requested that the aero rifle platoon be landed at once. In the meantime the officers kept circling over the field trying to regain visual or radio contact with the team. Then they picked up a radio signal in English with a Vietnamese accent (possibly an enemy terminal or even the seized team radio): "Their last transmission was: All are dead, all are dead, and I'm dying."

The team's fate was resolved when the sole survivor, severely wounded Private First Class Comyers, was rescued 500 yards from the original insertion point. He related that the team departed the aircraft and moved into the nearest tree line. As soon as they reached cover, the team leader opened his map and tried to orient it with his compass. Suddenly several rocket-propelled grenades exploded among them. The six recon members fell dead or wounded as a platoon of Viet Cong, wearing black uniforms and firing AK47s on full automatic, emerged from the underbrush and stormed through the position. Private Comyers was hit once in the chest and spun to the ground. He was then "finished off" by Viet Cong soldiers who shot him in the back. Comyers later managed to crawl painfully to the edge of a rice paddy and waved a hand mirror to signal a rescue helicopter.

An official inquiry was convened by the division shortly after the incident. During the course of questioning witnesses to the event, patrol proficiency was called into question:

LTC Cassels [investigating officer]: "Major Haley, do you have any recommendations to make pertaining to lessons learned from experience gained on 21 November in the insertion of LRRP team 11 that you would recommend at this time?"

A [Answer]: "Yes Sir. The first transmission I heard from the LRRP team on the ground was 'We're in contact! Get us out of here! Get us out of here!' I feel these words were wasted. If they had said, 'We're in contact, direction of fire is in a certain heading, we are popping smoke to identify our position location,' I could have immediately started gunship runs in the area, laying down suppressive fire, and could have started my backup slick [helicopter] into the area to extract these men. But without gunship runs and suppressive fire, I felt that it would have been too dangerous to try to attempt an extraction at that time."[18]

The official inquiry concluded that recon team 11 was destroyed because of its own negligence, and that the division operations section was not to be faulted for taking a "calculated wartime risk":

The death of five team members subsequent to insertion was attributed to the hazards of war and not to any one individual. . . . Indications are that the team was completely surprised and that little or no security was posed while the leader was using the map to get oriented. . . . Move as far from the LZ on an initial predetermined azimuth as necessary to find an area with concealment and cover if possible before taking time to get oriented on the map. . . . Smoke was not used to mark friendly troop location nor was the direction of the enemy attack identified. This was probably due to the violence of the enemy attack. A situation report and location by the team on the move away from the LZ would have enhanced the possibility of assistance from the gunships overhead. . . . LRRP teams should be composed of our very best combat soldiers who have been seasoned in battle. LRRPs [sic] must make every effort to avoid contact with the enemy.[19]

The team 11 catastrophe was one of the last missions of Company F, 52d Infantry "Danger Forward Reconnaissance." Some members suggested that an entirely new slogan might be appropriate. Following the destruction of recon team 11, the old nickname was considered an unlucky portent of potential eventualities. Within weeks following the tragedy, company operations sergeant Sfc. Warren D. Massey was notified by the 1st Infantry Division staff that a new ranger company would be raised.

IRON RANGERS

On 1 January 1969 the Department of the Army reorganized the 75th Infantry as a parent regiment under the combat arms regimental system to give long-range patrol companies a common heritage. On 1 February 1969, Major General Talbott activated Company I (Ranger), 75th Infantry, by using the personnel and equipment from Company F, 52d Infantry, which was inactivated.

The rangers referred to themselves as either "India Rangers" (I in conformity with ICAO phonetic alphabet adopted by the U.S. military in 1956) or as the "Iron Rangers" because Company I harmonized with the "Iron Brigade," the nickname of the 3d Brigade that the company predominantly served. An alternative nickname introduced by minority members was the "Bro Rangers"—BRO being the division's Vietnam-era abbreviation for "Big Red One" and coinciding with black slang "bro" for "brother," meaning comrade.

Company I numbered its patrols sequentially by field platoon. The first platoon teams were numbered 1 through 8. Second platoon teams were assigned three-digit codes, 909–916. Company I ranger teams having double-digit sequences were heavy patrols representing mission-specific combinations of two other teams. For example, ranger team 91 was composed of teams 915 and 916 during one particular assignment in June 1969.

The 1st Infantry Division began Operation TOAN THANG ("Complete Victory") with the objective of clearing and pacifying Binh Duong Province. As part of this effort, reconnaissance patrols were sent into such enemy base areas as the Iron Triangle, the Trapezoid, the Long Nguyen Secret Zone, the Mushroom, the Easter Egg, and the Heart-Shaped Woods. Throughout the remainder of division service in Vietnam, the Iron Rangers monitored menacing NVA/VC formations in these hazardous locations. The ranger teams stressed area reconnaissance and night ambush tactics to identify and interdict enemy concentrations, and worked extensively with the 3d "Iron Brigade."

Another routine but deceptively precarious ranger task involved furnishing advance picket duty around forward fire support bases and outlying allied logistical avenues. The short-range missions deprived the rangers of long-range reconnaissance flexibility and tied them to static night ambush positions or close-in patrol sweeps. Teams were jeopardized because the enemy was wary of American forces in these areas and very alert to any type of patrol activity.

The dangers of ranger security duty were demonstrated by two late-February patrol experiences in support of 3d Brigade.

On 20 February 1969, ranger Company I commander Lt. Jerry M. Davis inserted eight teams along the Song Be river-infiltration corridor and in the Long Nguyen Secret Zone to monitor enemy reinforcement and supply lanes. As part of this assignment, ranger team 3 was positioned outside Fire Support Base Thunder II, an advanced division outpost near Highway 13 in the vicinity of Ap Bau Bang near the boundary of Binh Duong and Binh Long provinces.

The ranger team was led by Sp4 Raymond Cervantes Jr. and threaded its way through thick jungle to reach the Song Be. Almost an hour after being inserted, point man Sp4 Michael P. Cannon heard some faint coughing and movement near the patrol. At the same time, assistant team leader Sp4 Daniel R. Wiggins heard movement behind them and spotted an enemy soldier. Specialist Cervantes hand-signaled his team to move quickly to their preselected pickup zone, a marshy clearing in the Suoi Ong Bang tributary of the Song Be. The rangers planted claymore mines around their positions at the extraction site as pace man Sp4 Robert D. Law covered the patrol rear.

The Viet Cong interception unit followed the withdrawing ranger team, and a brief firefight erupted at the edge of the field. The rangers fought a delaying action until gunships arrived overhead. The arriving helicopters strafed and rocketed the enemy ranks, giving the rangers a temporary lull. The team took advantage of the aerial support to detonate most of its claymore mines and run into the jungle stream. Radioman Pfc. Bill G. Powell called for immediate extraction. Higher headquarters denied this request because it was almost dark, the team was no longer under fire, and no one was hurt.

Later that night, Specialist Cervantes led the team farther down the tropical stream as it flowed through the dense forest. They reached a spot where the stream emerged from the jungle and crossed another open tract of swampland. A small footbridge over the Suoi Ong Bang was situated halfway across the clearing. When the rangers reported the structure they were instructed to perform surveillance at that location. The six rangers established defensive positions at the bridge and watched the stream-crossing point throughout the following day and night.

Shortly after 8:00 A.M. on 22 February the rangers spotted three Viet Cong soldiers moving toward the footbridge. Two were armed with AK47 assault rifles, and the third carried a light machine gun.

The enemy soldiers suddenly saw the patrol position and opened fire. The rangers returned fire with their rifles on full automatic, detonated three claymore mines covering their front, and then switched to semi-automatic fire to conserve ammunition. The Viet Cong trio were wounded but began throwing fragmentation and gas grenades at the team position. Anticipating the arrival of enemy reinforcements, Specialist Cervantes radioed for artillery and gunship support.

During the initial exchange of fire, Specialist Law moved to the right edge of the team's location so he could aim accurately at the prone enemy troops. Suddenly a grenade landed near Private Powell and grenadier Sp4 Robert A. Rossien. Specialist Law immediately fell on the grenade and absorbed the blast, shielding the other team members at the sacrifice of his own life. The ranger team killed all three opponents, searched the bodies and recovered some documents, and were extracted by helicopter back to Fire Support Base Thunder II.

The patrol could be summarized as a case study of the problems inherent in ranger employment near American bases. Cervantes's team encountered a Viet Cong interception force almost immediately after insertion. The resulting firefight compromised the mission and endangered the continuing safety of the patrol. Much later, three Viet Cong scouts approached the bridge cautiously, probably aware that the rangers might still be in the area. Their heightened vigilance enabled them to discern the ranger position and fire first. The close fighting also allowed the enemy to reach grenade range and kill one of the defenders. More ranger casualties would have resulted if Specialist Law had not covered the grenade explosion.

On 23 February 1969 the North Vietnamese Army commenced its Tet-69 offensive by attacking division base installations. The rangers remained situated around selected 3d Brigade fire support bases in a short-patrol screening mode. On the evening of 27 February, seven-man ranger team 8 was mauled by a strong Viet Cong force while guarding the brigade sector. Three rangers were killed, three were wounded, and both PRC-25 radios were rendered inoperable by battle damage. The surviving rangers—without radio communications and unable to secure assistance—experienced a harrowing night under fire. Aircraft attempted to locate the shattered team throughout the night. Finally, at 8:00 A.M. on the following morning, a helicopter skimming the jungle at treetop level spotted signal mirrors and smoke. A new radio was dropped to the team, enabling emergency extraction to be coordinated. Still under fire, the remaining patrol members were lifted out later that morning.[20]

Ranger Company I suffered high cumulative losses resulting from death or injury on close-in patrolling assignments. Comparisons between division ranger methodology showed that patrols operating at greater distances (i.e., on long-range missions) were ultimately safer because the enemy was not expecting them. Ranger teams employed on extended missions were able to gain better surprise opportunities, inflict heavier casualties, and sustain fewer losses—even though they were infiltrated in the midst of larger enemy units or traditionally contested areas. Later in the year the division began installing more ground radar around base perimeters, a development that eventually relieved most ranger teams from picket duty.

During March 1969 the Iron Rangers shifted emphasis to longer-range patrols in the Michelin Plantation and Trapezoid vicinity. On 1 April, ranger Company I was officially attached to the 3d Brigade and remained in that status for the duration of the war. Throughout May and June, the rangers conducted numerous bomb damage assessments in the Trapezoid and provided critical information about the effects of B-52 strategic bombing sorties used in an operational role. During these expeditions, the rangers patrolled the demolished jungle and found hundreds of destroyed bunkers, significant quantities of food and documents, and the remnants of a large munitions factory. The rangers found various molds and several tool-and-die kits within the destroyed factory complex and confirmed its previous use as a production center for antitank mines and bangalore torpedo casings.[21]

In August 1969, Maj. Gen. Albert E. Milloy assumed command of the 1st Infantry Division. The Iron Rangers continued to participate in Operation TOAN THANG as a vital component of the formation's "protective umbrella" across the northern and eastern fringes of Binh Duong Province and War Zone D. For example, on 13 October, ranger team 1 reported enemy troop movement in the upper portion of the Michelin Plantation region. The ranger team sighting enabled the division to react immediately with Time-on-Target salvos from three artillery batteries, followed by five Air Force tactical air strikes. A subsequent search of the battlefield showed that the ranger-initiated bombardment completely disrupted a column of the 101st NVA Regiment.[22]

The ranger excursions were increasingly supplemented by and contingent on sensor fields. The Iron Rangers were heavily involved with planting, upgrading, and replacing these devices. For instance, the rangers helped to place electronic screens along the periphery of the rugged Razorback and the banks of the upper Saigon River. Division intelligence officers began using ranger patrols to verify patterns of NVA/VC movement based on the changing intensity of sensor readings. The division also used Nighthawk aircraft, Navy river patrol boats, and infantry companies to respond to readouts from the ranger-placed sensor fields.

From late October until mid-December 1969 the Iron Rangers provided reconnaissance expeditions north of Lai Khe and monitored the Long Nguyen Secret Zone and the Song Be Corridor along Highway 13. These NVA–controlled staging areas continued to bedevil the division's security efforts until the very end of its Vietnam service. On 15 December the 1st Infantry Division was alerted to begin redeployment to the United States as part of Operation KEYSTONE BLUEJAY. Planning commenced immediately, and ranger operations were scaled down accordingly.[23]

In March 1970, Brig. Gen. John Q. Herrion assumed command of the division and ordered the Iron Rangers to cease combat operations and stand down effective 7 March. Within three days the company released its personnel and equipment and was reduced to zero strength. Company I (Ranger), 75th Infantry, was officially inactivated on 7 April 1970.

The Iron Rangers suffered a very high casualty rate during the Vietnam conflict, uncannily similar to that of the "Iron Brigade of the West" in the American Civil War. In proportion to its numbers, the Iron Brigade of a hundred years earlier sustained the heaviest loss of any Union brigade in that war. Likewise, the relative aggregate of Iron Ranger casualties was not exceeded by any other ranger company (Company L's 60 percent casualty rate was larger, but the company served much longer). The only debate is whether this figure was attributable to "being in the thick of fighting" or being under an overzealous and aggressive division operations section. Whatever the reason, the Iron Rangers performed with valiant determination in reconnoitering some of the most persistently dangerous enemy strongholds in South Vietnam.[24]

5

4TH INFANTRY DIVISION

HIGHLAND RANGERS

RECONDO-HAWKEYES

During September 1966 the 4th Infantry Division completed its deployment to Vietnam as part of the main United States military buildup. Allied units were already guarding Vietnam's coastal cities and rice lands. Reinforcements were needed farther inland, and the newly arriving division was sent into the country's central interior. The formation was assembled in the western Central Highlands, near Pleiku, to safeguard Vietnam's tri-border region with lower Laos and upper Cambodia.

The 4th Infantry Division's combat arena was far larger and more remote than other divisional battle zones in Vietnam. The hinterland territory consisted of a Connecticut-sized area of operations blanketed by wild grasslands, scrub forests, and jungle-covered mountains. The tropical forests, rolling wooded plains, and red-clay plateaus were bisected by seasonal streams and countless logging and hunting trails used by the North Vietnamese as infiltration corridors.

The 4th Infantry Division was organized conventionally for linear battlefront warfare and not for area security operations. Division commander Maj. Gen. Arthur S. Collins Jr. realized that the division's frontier screening assignment demanded far more reconnaissance capacity. He incorporated the area Special Forces surveillance camps into his reconnaissance network and used their Montagnard tribal companies for flanking and scouting assignments. The division coordinated intelligence activities with the

South Vietnamese 24th Special Tactical Zone in the Kontum-Pleiku sector.

Major General Collins still lacked enough intrinsic division reconnaissance. On 1 November 1966 he established the 4th Infantry Division recondo program at brigade and battalion level. The recondo teams were designed for combat reconnaissance in the high-mountain tropics, but the embryonic program was initially a very austere trial concept. Collins was unsure whether it was feasible to use American reconnaissance-commando teams in the extremely rugged and dangerous Central Highlands environment. The first recondo patrols were used to seek landing zones or provide warning of ambush positions ahead of advancing regular units.

In January 1967, Maj. Gen. William R. Peers assumed command of the 4th Infantry Division. He decided to secure the division's 8,000-square-mile block of territory by launching brigade-sized punitive expeditions throughout the tri-border front. Remote brigade operations were field-tested in Operation SAM HOUSTON, following the deployment of Special Forces and a few division recondo teams across the Nam Sathay river.[1]

The division recondo patrols learned many valuable lessons while scouting the tropical mountain wilderness. All teams contended with rainy weather, low cloud ceilings, and dense fogs in the higher elevations. Retrieving patrols by helicopter presented serious problems. Colored smoke from grenades and flares dissipated in the soupy haze of rain and mist or failed to penetrate the towering forest canopies. Recondo teams adopted the Special Forces technique of "breaking squelch" by keying their radio handsets in fifteen-second spurts. The brief transmissions enabled aviators to follow the signals through their helicopter homing devices and locate patrol positions within a few hundred yards. The helicopter crew then narrowed its search and normally spotted signal panels, mirrors, beacons, or smoke smudges of the ground patrollers.

The recondos discovered that North Vietnamese soldiers moved into areas after patrols passed by, and sometimes even followed the teams at a distance. The recondos modified their patrolling techniques and began weaving back and forth in zigzag or cloverleaf patterns that covered specific areas and then circled back. The variable-pattern patrols passed twice or more over any locality and often ensnared trailing parties or other enemy units infiltrating into territory behind them.[2]

The patrollers found enemy activity prevalent within the tri-border region. One 2d Brigade recondo patrol rappelled through the dense forest north of Fire Support Base Oasis between Pleiku and the Cambodian border. The patrol moved through the dense undergrowth by following a creek for several days. Just after refilling canteens, the team members approached a bend in the stream. Point man Sp4 Joseph L. Seals heard a "flopping" noise in the water and thought the sound might be a waterfowl. Specialist Seals rounded the bend and saw an NVA patrol. Both sides opened fire as Specialist Seals emptied his rifle into an NVA soldier wearing a flop hat and blue shorts. Seals withdrew under the covering fire of Sgt. Cornelius Strotters. Sgt. Steve Steffens led the team to safety by climbing 500 yards up a steep jungle incline. Radioman Sp4 David Cabeceiras called for artillery, and the patrol was successfully extracted from the hillside by helicopter.[3]

During Operation SAM HOUSTON the division reconnaissance program was strengthened. A division sniper course was instituted, and some expert sharpshooters were assigned to recondo patrols. Three specialized recondo countermeasures patrols were formed, one per brigade, to eliminate enemy couriers, officers, or sentries in surveillance areas. "Hawkeye" teams were raised by Major General Peers after he witnessed the success of Special Forces–led native troops. The hawkeye team paired two division recondo members with two Rhade tribesmen who exhibited hunting and terrain prowess. Each hawkeye team completed a ten-day course to learn mutual signaling and survival skills.[4]

There was an initial doctrinal separation in recondo and hawkeye employment. The recondo teams were trained for three main jobs: (1) Trail Watching: observing and reporting enemy movement along infiltration and resupply routes; (2) Terrain Analysis: checking jungle density and mountain or valley characteristics, and finding suitable helicopter landing zones; and (3) Screening: active patrolling to guard the front or flanks of regular infantry formations. On the other hand, hawkeye teams were intended to supplement recondo missions by executing assignments requiring native skill. For example, hawkeye teams were used as stay-behind forces to watch vacated base sites, radio for artillery on NVA/VC scavengers, and then evade pursuit forces despite swamp thickets or other obstacles and exfiltrate back to friendly lines.

The doctrinal difference between recondo and hawkeye patrols became blurred in actuality. Contrary to initial expectations, there was a great degree of interchange between their capabilities. Both types of teams became skilled at hit-and-run ambushes and gathering battlefield intelligence. In some instances, the recondo and hawkeye teams were combined to lure enemy troops into revealing their positions. The most dangerous tactic was entrapping enemy troops with artillery or other patrol ambuscades. A decoy hawkeye team feigning patrol trouble was used to entice enemy pursuit troops into a certain area and, if successful, would escape intact while a recondo team or sudden artillery bombardment destroyed their pursuers.

The actual size of patrols varied, although organizationally recondo teams were authorized five soldiers and each hawkeye team contained two soldiers and two irregular warriors. However, teams fielded three to eight men depending on patrol assignments. Lengthy patrols usually included an extra soldier trained in emergency medical procedures. Patrols operating near native habitations commonly included an area tribesman or Special Forces specialist. Teams engaged in terrain analysis were accompanied either by pathfinders or combat engineers when searching for and preparing landing zones.

Each maneuver brigade was authorized a sixty-two-member reconnaissance platoon. The platoon was organized into a headquarters section (commander, executive officer, operations sergeant, and six radiomen), eight recondo teams, and three hawkeye teams. By the first week of April the brigade reconnaissance platoons were fully operational and participated throughout the division's major western campaign of Operation FRANCIS MARION. Reconnaissance teams fielded during the operation "had the broad mission of infiltrating into enemy controlled areas to observe [enemy activities] and/or conduct harassing activities."[5]

On 19 May 1967, one typical four-man patrol from the 2d Brigade reconnaissance platoon was inserted to reconnoiter the Chu Goll-Chu Pa mountain region. The team patrolled a valley during the first day but only found footprints around a small water hole. On the following afternoon the patrol spotted North Vietnamese soldiers and radioed for air strikes. Patrol leader Lawrence R. Willey reported, "Two of the secondary explosions were enough to yank trees out of the ground." The patrol members were establishing overnight positions when they heard noises nearby. Willey commented, "They were definitely looking for us." The patrol created a hasty ambush along the abutment just off the hilltop. Soon a North Vietnamese platoon marching toward the nearby summit passed into the team's kill zone.

The patrollers opened fire, killing five NVA soldiers, but the resulting firefight wounded Sp4 Charles Ditterman, Sp4 Russell Oliver, and Staff Sgt. Lloyd W. Lee. Sergeant Willey directed the wounded men to try to reach an emergency pickup point while he remained temporarily behind. Willey stated, "Two more NVA came

over the hill and I cut them down. Then I followed the others.''
The thick jungle at the evacuation site was broken slightly by a
small hole in the canopy, mandating extraction by rope. Armed
gunships strafed the surrounding forest as the team members were
hoisted individually into a hovering helicopter.[6]

During June, Major General Peers formalized the provisional 4th
Infantry Division Recondo Detachment to supplement the brigade
reconnaissance platoons. The division-level detachment contained
eight recondo and three hawkeye teams but no command section.
The division-level recondo detachment was commanded and staffed
as part of the intelligence section and administratively assigned to
the 1st Squadron, 10th Cavalry. The arrangement gave the 4th Infantry Division Recondo Detachment helicopter support and backup
from the 10th Cavalry's Troop D aero rifle platoon.

The 4th Infantry Division recondo-hawkeye surveillance screen
was still stretched thin by its mandated coverage of Pleiku Province
as well as large swaths of Kontum and Darlac provinces on either
side. Teams operated close to main enemy supply lines and staging
areas, and the strain of these long-range remote-area missions was
high. The effect of these factors on overall division reconnaissance
capacity was noted in a U.S. Army Vietnam (USARV) report:

> From experience, it was found that the average number of teams
> operational in the [4th] division AO [area of operations] is about
> twelve or thirteen or about 35–40 percent of the total [note: the
> percentage was actually closer to 32 percent because forty-four teams
> were involved]. The fatigue and tension resulting from these opera-
> tions is considerable. Therefore, whenever possible, they are given
> at least one day off to rest and recuperate for every day they are in
> operation. This, combined with personnel on R&R [authorized
> leave], hospitalized and the like, reduces the division capability to
> about twelve or thirteen teams.[7]

During 8–12 June 1967 an example of the dangers attending
tri-border reconnaissance was experienced by a 2d Brigade reconnaissance patrol. The five-man team occupied a mountaintop overlooking the Ia Ayun and transmitted highly valuable reports about
NVA troop traffic in the river valley beneath them. The North Vietnamese finally detected the observation point and silently climbed
the steep mountainside until they were within grenade range of the
Americans.

The enemy attacked suddenly at 8:00 P.M. on 12 June. Sp4 Russell Oliver, now a patrol leader, radioed for extraction. The head-

quarters replied to "hold on" because it was estimated "the recon [team] could hold off a company trying to storm their position." Specialist Oliver retorted, "If you wait until morning to get us out of here, there won't be anyone here." When radioman Sp4 Joseph F. Camper's situation report was interrupted by the third NVA assault, he kept the radio keyed to the sound of gunfire and bursting grenades to emphasize their worsening predicament.

Air Force C-47 aircraft lit the night sky over the mountain with flares, and A-1E Skyraiders finally arrived overhead during the fourth NVA attack. When the forward air controller asked where the patrollers desired the air strike, Specialist Camper stated, "Feel free to do anything!" The propeller-driven Skyraiders skimmed the mountain sides unleashing bombs and rockets. The North Vietnamese charge faltered on the rim of the summit. When asked for results, Camper replied, "Where's the ship to get us out of here?" One hour before midnight the isolated team was finally extracted. As the helicopter departed, Specialist Camper directed a concentrated barrage of heavy 175mm shells against North Vietnamese infantrymen swarming over the mountain.[8]

The extended nature of the 4th Infantry Division operations caused its patrols to operate routinely at far greater distances than other divisional long-range reconnaissance units in Vietnam. Furthermore, the division engaged in operations located far from established base camps having adequate communications facilities. The 4th Infantry Division Recondo Detachment teams were often sent to check future operational areas well beyond normal radio range and used overhead relay aircraft. The brigade reconnaissance patrols operated independently at extended ranges, especially when the line battalions were scattered, but encountered more trouble securing radio relay aircraft services.

During October, 4th Infantry Division Recondo Detachment Sgt. Jean-Guy Sejourne led a three-man patrol that experienced radio trouble on the first day of their mission. The radio could not transmit voice messages, but Sergeant Sejourne managed to communicate with another patrol, led by Sgt. Denis H. Robinette a mile away, by breaking radio squelch in coded patterns. Sejourne decided to continue the mission and established a trail-ambush position on the second day. A large North Vietnamese column passed in the morning. No further enemy movement occurred until late afternoon, when two men came into view, dressed in tiger-striped camouflage and bush hats that matched the recondo uniforms. Both sides saw each other but the patrollers withheld their fire, initially uncertain whether the men were indigenous Special Forces troops. Both NVA scouts dodged into the jungle.

At 6:03 P.M., fifteen North Vietnamese troops moved cautiously down the trail and spotted the patrol's claymore mine. One soldier started following the wire to the patrol position while five stood behind him. Sejourne reported, "I remember thinking, six guys standing around a claymore. That is too much." The sergeant detonated the mine, killing all six, as Sp4 Troy O. Ashenfelter and Pfc. Steve J. Reed opened fire with CAR-15 submachine guns. Sejourne broke squelch four times in quick succession, the agreed signal to Robinette's recondo team that they were in combat. Sergeant Robinette radioed the aero rifle platoon and Sejourne's patrol was extracted. Major General Peers decorated the trio in a division formation, announcing that "they insisted on remaining in a position along a jungle trail despite failing radio communication with their unit. I want to tell all of you what a great job this team did."[9]

One of the most unusual FRANCIS MARION encounters was recorded by Staff Sgt. Charles L. McKee's patrol. The patrol completed their mission and waited for helicopters at the designated landing zone. A seventeen-foot python and its serpentine family slithered past the motionless Americans and toward an NVA platoon that suddenly ran in front of the team, disturbing the snakes. The helicopters landed and Staff Sergeant McKee's men clambered aboard. There was no sound from the enemy until a burst of fire peppered the helicopters lifting off. McKee credited the long interval to North Vietnamese trouble with snakes: "I think that python was on our side. He may have gotten a couple of enemy soldiers before the gunships came in."[10]

During Operation FRANCIS MARION, from 6 April to 11 October 1967, the 4th Infantry Division recondo-hawkeye forces achieved remarkable surveillance results that pinpointed the changing locations of both the 1st and 10th NVA Divisions. The patrols completed 555 missions that produced 366 sightings of enemy personnel. During the eighty-two patrol clashes, ninety NVA/VC soldiers were killed by direct patrol fire. There were fourteen emergency patrol extractions under fire, but only one American was killed. Division reconnaissance provided further assistance during Operation MACARTHUR around Dak To, and by the end of the year accomplished 698 missions, made 411 observations of enemy units, and earned a reputation as one of the finest recon units in Vietnam.[11]

ECHO FIFTY-EIGHTH PATROLLERS

One of Major General Peer's last acts before departing the division was elevating his provisional recondo-hawkeye forces to the status of an official long-range patrol company. On 20 December 1967 the division activated Company E of the 58th Infantry (Long Range Patrol) using the 4th Infantry Division Recondo Detachment. The company was known as "Echo Fifty-eighth" in conformity with the ICAO phonetic alphabet adopted by the U.S. military in 1956. Operational readiness of the new recon company, however, was postponed by the Viet Cong Tet-68 offensive against Kontum, Pleiku, and Ban Me Thuot.[12]

In January 1968 the new division commander, Maj. Gen. Charles P. Stone, initiated a program to teach patrol tactics to the Vietnamese 23d Division strike company. From 23 April to 21 June 1968, thirty South Vietnamese personnel were trained and integrated into Company E. There was a noticeable lack of interest by the South Vietnamese Army. The second class contained only Regional Force conscripts. Following strenuous division protests, the South Vietnamese sent forty ranger recruits to the third training cycle on 14 October. Unfortunately, twenty-two were unfit for physical or disciplinary reasons. In the meantime, conflicts with other graduates threatened the safety and efficiency of the original jointly manned reconnaissance teams. The experiment was finally ceased that November.[13]

From 24 May until 21 June 1968, several Company E teams were sent into the rugged western mountains of Kontum Province as part of 1st Brigade Task Force Mathews. The patrols worked closely with Special Forces Project Omega to thwart the 325C NVA Division moving toward special Forces Camp Ben Het. The patrollers traversed jagged ridges despite torrential rains and directed strategic bombing runs that blunted the enemy advance. The reconnaissance reports were instrumental in directing thirty-nine arclight bombing sorties by B-52 bombers in front of Camp Dak To and Camp Ben Het, and another eleven arclight bombings near Dak Pek. Throughout the campaign, the Echo Fifty-eighth patrollers performed important surveillance and bomb damage assessment, although only six North Vietnamese soldiers were killed by direct team fire.[14]

During September a three-man Echo Fifty-eighth patrol led by Sp4 Emory Spraggins was dropped off by helicopter in a bomb crater outside the besieged Special Forces outpost of Dak Seang, close to the Laotian border. Specialist Spraggins stated, "It was supposed to be a forty-eight-hour mission at the most. Just to clear a landing zone and blow a tree that was standing in the way." The patrollers moved through thick jungle obscured by fog and rain, located the field, and packed the roots of two trees with high explosives. Knowing that NVA forces were in the area, Spraggins decided not to create an explosion until an extraction helicopter was on station. Heavy rains prevented helicopter flight, so the patrol stayed mired in their bleak surroundings for four days. Out of food and subsisting on rainwater, the patrol members were about to risk destroying the trees on the sixth day when they received radio instructions to clear out immediately.

The team pushed through dense sloping jungle that veteran assistant patrol leader Sp4 Harold Thompson called "the worst terrain I've ever been in." A poisonous viper dropped behind Pfc. Mike Overturf as they crossed a swift jungle stream. The weary team members were ordered to keep moving through the night and told that a B-52 bomb strike was targeted for their area. Specialist Thompson said, "I was too tired to care, but they kept screaming over the radio to keep going." The team members tied ropes to each other as they fought through the darkened tangle of vines and lush foliage. The thick brambles tore their camouflaged uniforms to shreds. The patrollers finally collapsed on a steep hillside the next day and radioed they could go no farther.

Headquarters replied to take cover, and the men hid between the roots of a six-foot-thick hardwood tree while pulling ponchos over their exposed skin. The ground rumbled and heaved as the bombs landed in the distance. Private Overturf remembered, "The whole sky turned red. We could hear things flying over our heads." On the eighth day the patrollers weakly continued their trek and climbed another mountain only to find a North Vietnamese bunker complex. They smelled rice and knew the enemy was not far away. Fortunately, the men found enemy tools and helmets and put on as much enemy gear as they could locate before hurrying back into the jungle.

The men were now almost delirious with hunger and fatigue. Private Overturf remembered, "For some reason I looked up and saw a head." They were facing an American patrol that aimed its rifles right at the three men. Overturf tore off his North Vietnamese pith helmet and yelled, "Don't shoot! I'm a Lerp! I'm a Lerp!" They reached the lines of a forward infantry company located on a rain-drenched summit. The unit was also unable to secure supplies. With all helicopters grounded, headquarters ordered the infantry company to march out. The recon patrollers spent another two days struggling through more jungle. Infantrymen began to pass out around them from lack of sleep and heavy equipment loads. The storm finally subsided after a full week, and Specialist Spraggins's patrol was airlifted to Dak To. The Echo Fifty-eighth staff congratulated the trio for accomplishing the longest recorded division mission. Spraggins recalled, "Somehow, it didn't seem to matter."[15]

The division's wide sector, difficult landscape, and dreadful weather caused acute problems in maintaining sufficient reconnaissance coverage. A short-range patrol (SRP) program was devised to bolster the long-range patrols. The SRP concept was an expedient measure that tasked each rifle company to furnish five four-man teams for advance picket duty of forty-eight hours' duration. This gave each line battalion a theoretical reconnaissance screen of up to twenty teams.

Unfortunately, ordinary riflemen were generally too inexperienced in reconnaissance work to function as independent patrollers. One battalion commander (2d of the 35th Infantry) got his SRP teams into position outside Ban Me Thuot by having them follow artillery "marking rounds" to reach their destination. Some patrols were so inexperienced that they disregarded strict division orders not to initiate ambushes. In September, for instance, an SRP team ambushed an NVA squad and then left its positions to count the enemy dead. Some wounded North Vietnamese pulled back into a ravine and machine-gunned the Americans, killing all four. Two other SRP teams were attacked near Kontum after hostile Montagnards followed their daylight trek into outpost positions. On a lighter note, one SRP led by Sp4 Toil Smith checked fire after they discovered their target was a long-armed orangutan jumping from tree to tree.[16]

The use of short-range patrols underscored the importance of having properly trained and experienced reconnaissance personnel perform actual combat recon duties. Reconnaissance patrolling and ranger-style tactics represented a learned military science. The disadvantages of the 4th Infantry Division short-range patrols were echoed by division chief of staff Col. Warren D. Hodges:

> One of the most significant problem areas SRP members have reported is psychological strain and the fatigue which this strain produces. The fact that the teams are relatively isolated and have difficulty obtaining sleep affects morale and effectiveness. Most patrol members interviewed felt that the anxiety created while in position could be reduced significantly through additional training in

the basic fundamentals of recon patrolling. Refresher training in these fundamentals at brigade or battalion level can instill confidence in the individuals who make up the SRP teams. All units singled out this problem and are attempting to remedy this through additional training and by keeping the time the teams are in position to an operational minimum.[17]

The short-range patrol concept allowed 4th Infantry Division staffers to claim fielding nearly 200 patrols per month, instead of the average twenty teams inserted by Company E. In actuality the short-range patrols were not ranger activities but merely battalion sentinel posts. The Echo Fifty-eighth reconnaissance task was not greatly assisted by the SRP endeavor.

By October 1968, Company E was also experiencing alarming deficiencies in some operations. The problems were created by the loss of experienced veterans to the one-year combat rotation policy, the shortage of MACV Recondo School graduates, and lack of qualified rangers. For instance, on 20 October, recon team 28 was inserted near Ban Me Thuot to conduct a three-day surveillance mission. The team leader was a private first class with only regular infantry training and less than a year in the Army. Pfc. Dickie W. Finley led the patrol through the upland plateau forest and selected an overnight position. The first night passed without incident, and the team monitored an adjacent trail uneventfully throughout the following day.

The Echo Fifty-eighth patrol reoccupied its previous overnight position. At 7:00 P.M., Private First Class Finley radioed reports of enemy movement to platoon leader Capt. Donald E. Conneville, who ordered the patrol to relocate. Private Finley, however, decided to take a group vote about leaving their current location. The other four team members decided against repositioning, and the team stayed where it was. After waiting thirty minutes, Finley ordered radioman Pfc. Robert E. Hamby to relay a false report that they had completed the ordered move.

For the next hour the team radioed a stream of frantic messages reporting enemy trails were "all over the team's AO [area of operations]," that "there were noises all around them," and a "flashlight was seen." At 8:30 P.M., Private Finley called for artillery fire, and within half an hour signaled "Contact" while requesting emergency night extraction. Less than ten minutes later Finley radioed that the team was low on ammunition and, just after 9:00 P.M., reported that all ammunition was expended.

The helicopter arrived and hovered over a pond on the flare-lit landing zone. The aircraft commander was unaware that the puddle was shallow and wanted to avoid landing in deep water. The five patrollers bunched up along the aircraft starboard side. Boarding attempts were complicated by the unsteady rocking of the helicopter off the ground. Radioman Hamby was finally shoved on from behind, Pfc. Bernard C. Pisarcik managed to hoist himself onto the cabin floor, and Sp4 Gerald O. Hancock was halfway aboard. The helicopter hovered about three minutes before the pilot asked, "Are we up?" The door gunner claimed that one of the recon members told the pilot to take off. The pilot asked again, "Is everyone on?" and the door gunner replied, "I think so." The helicopter took off as Hancock pulled himself inside.

As the helicopter gained altitude, Private Pisarcik yelled to Hamby, "Where's the other two guys?" Private Hamby looked over the helicopter side, saw someone hanging from the skid, and shouted back, "Finley's on the skid!" Pisarcik peered next over the edge but saw nothing but trees. He screamed at the pilot, "You've left two people back there!" as the door gunner reported that a man had fallen off. The helicopter pilot circled back but landed at another location. The patrollers exited, saw the clearing was covered by vines and tall grass, and reboarded the helicopter saying, "This is the wrong field." The helicopter pilot circled the woods and returned to Ban Me Thuot.

An extensive ground search began at daybreak. The body of assistant team leader Sp4 Luther A. Ghahate was found along the helicopter flight path where he had fallen from a great height. Later that afternoon, Captain Conneville uncovered the team's night location and found evidence that the team had never moved as ordered. He also found claymore mines, ration wrappers, cigarette butts, and empty cigarette cartons strewn carelessly over the ground. The 4th Infantry Division convened an official inquiry into the incident. Private First Class Hamby testified:

Capt. Melton [investigating officer]: "Did you see anybody at all that night?"

A [Answer]: "I kept hearing more things in front of me. Finley and Pisarcik thought they saw a gook. Everybody was frightened. I heard something or someone, I thought near my claymore. I thought someone was walking out there. It was silent for a while, then I saw a flashlight to my front about thirty meters away. The others heard noises. I thought I heard somebody dragging along the ground, like somebody crawling. Finley started calling artillery. The first two rounds were close. I heard shrapnel flying over us. I thought I heard movement. Finley requested extraction and gunships after the artillery was fired. He was asked to make a fake extraction. Finley said 'No, we're getting on that bird!' Finley said 'Blow the claymore.' I blew mine. Finley blew his. We sprayed the area on the way to the LZ [landing zone]. I shot up two magazines. I had the radio in my [back]pack. Finley was behind me with the handset in one hand and a strobe light in the other. We set up around Finley at the LZ. We would fire and pause. Finley said 'Keep firing' several times. I fired forty magazines, mine and Finley's, and then threw two grenades. I didn't see anybody firing at us."[18]

Private Pisarcik testified:

Capt. Melton [investigating officer]: "Did you see anybody out there that night?"
A [Answer]: "Finley and Hamby thought they heard something. I thought I saw a dink or a shadow. I was arranging my pack when the claymore went off. Finley said to move to the LZ. I sprayed the area to my front and heard firing [from other team members] behind me. I fired five magazines from the NL [Night Location] to the LZ. My weapon jammed at the LZ. Then I used my M79 [grenade launcher] firing in a circle around the team. I fired fourteen rounds I had, fired six Finley had, then six of Ghahate's. Hamby threw two grenades, I threw one. I didn't see any gun flashes and couldn't say if we were being fired upon."[19]

Specialist Hancock, who possessed more service time than the other patrol members, testified:

Capt. Melton [investigating officer]: "Did you see anything out there that night?"
A [Answer]: "I fixed up my poncho to go to sleep. Pisarcik and Finley thought they heard movement. It was getting dark. I went to sleep. Five or ten minutes later Ghahate woke me and told me to pack up, that they were sure they had seen a light and heard movement. Finley was on the radio and calling in artillery. Artillery started coming in. The first two rounds came in close. I told Ghahate that Finley was adjusting wrong. I told him how Finley should do it. Ghahate talked to Finley about this and gave him a compass. Finley said he had orders to fake an extraction by running to the other side of the LZ. I think he had ships in the air by then. He said, 'When that bird comes, we'll get on it.' Finley told us to blow our claymores. I blew mine. Ghahate and I talked and didn't think there

were any gooks out there. I fired my CAR-15 on the way to the LZ, two magazines on automatic. I was covering the rear. At the LZ I was last in line, covering the west. The others were firing east and south. I fired eight magazines on automatic. There was no incoming fire. I did not hear any movements.''[20]

The division board of inquiry concluded that the patrol panicked on 22 October, failed to conserve ammunition, and probably encountered no opposition. The board ruled that the helicopter crew lifted off improperly before everyone was aboard. The investigative panel presumed that Private First Class Finley fell from the skids. Dickie Waine Finley of Sweet Springs, Missouri, remains missing in action.[21]

On 30 November 1968, Maj. Gen. Donn R. Pepke assumed command of the 4th Infantry Division. Renewed emphasis was placed on Echo Fifty-eighth patrols with seasoned noncommissioned officers and Montagnard scouts. The value of loyal native expertise was displayed during a trail-monitoring patrol led by Sgt. George Douglas east of Dak To. The four-man patrol contained no first-termers, the other members being Sgt. Emory Spraggins, Corp. Don Hartman, and Montagnard scout Y-Truck.

Sergeant Douglas was about to fire on a lone North Vietnamese soldier walking on the trail when Y-Truck motioned him to desist. Douglas was puzzled but eased his finger off the trigger. Twenty more North Vietnamese soldiers soon appeared around the jungle bend, spaced at twenty-foot intervals. After completing its road surveillance, the Echo Fifty-eighth patrol was intercepted moving to the pickup point. Sergeant Douglas's rifle was blown out of his hands by a sudden burst of enemy fire, and he was again saved by Y-Truck. The Montagnard killed an NVA soldier about to shoot the weaponless team leader. Douglas then grabbed the fallen opponent's AK47 and rejoined the fighting. The team eliminated the opposing squad, set off smoke grenades, and was picked up by helicopter without further incident.[22]

HIGHLAND RANGERS

The Department of the Army reorganized the 75th Infantry to give each long-range patrol unit a common tradition under the combat arms regimental system. On 1 February 1969, Company K (Ranger), 75th Infantry, was activated under the command of Capt. Reuben H. Silverling by converting the ''Echo Fifty-eighth.'' The war in the Vietnamese western Central Highlands demanded continuing recondo proficiency in mastering basic mountaineering and swift-stream-crossing procedures. The division's ranger specialty of traversing mountain jungle became the hallmark of Company K, known foremost as the "Highland Rangers." The unit was known alternatively as the "Killer Rangers," a modification of K for "Kilo" in the ICAO phonetic alphabet adopted by the U.S. military in 1956.

The ranger company mission was to "provide long range reconnaissance, surveillance, harassment, and target acquisition patrol capability at division level." The 4th Infantry Division continued to hold a 200-mile front extending the length of Vietnam's central border—from the northern An Lao Valley of Kontum Province, across Pleiku and Darlac provinces, to Bu Krak in western Quang Duc Province. The Highland Rangers were entrusted with reconnaissance coverage corresponding to this large territorial frontage. Major General Pepke placed premium reliance on his rangers, as he related:

A maximum number of long-range [ranger] patrols were operational at all times. Long-range patrols were normally inserted into a landing zone some distance away from their assigned areas of operation; they then moved to the assigned area of operation. Long-range patrols were not extracted routinely when a contact developed or when they detected enemy in the vicinity of their location. Long-range patrol sightings and contacts normally were exploited by the [cavalry] aero rifle platoon followed by elements of an airmobile battalion.[23]

This ideal support was not always possible or readily forthcoming. Four days after the rangers were activated, on 5 February 1969, Company K team 3-C was inserted to monitor a jungle river valley in Pleiku Province. Patrol leader Sgt. Kenneth Hess radioed on the second day that he was feeling ill but declined extraction. On the morning of 8 February the four-man patrol reported that everything was normal and they were waiting at the pickup zone. No further contact was ever made, and aircraft searches failed to locate the team.

On 10 February two companies of the 1st Battalion, 35th Infantry, were landed in the area. On the following morning the advancing infantrymen mistook Ju Hmok—the missing patrol's Montagnard scout—for a "wounded but armed NVA soldier" and killed him at a distance. That same day the aero rifle platoon found the remains of Pfc. Nathaniel Irving and a grave containing the body of Sergeant Hess. Eight days later the 35th Infantry captured NVA Sgt. Do Van Luong of the 95B NVA Infantry Regiment. The captive stated that a wounded American wearing tiger-striped camouflage, with reddish-brown hair and a mustache, was being carried on a stretcher to the North Vietnamese B-3 Front headquarters. The description of the prisoner matched Pfc. Don A. MacPhail, who was returned after the 1973 cease-fire agreement.[24]

Company K did not operate at full efficiency until the brigade reconnaissance platoons were integrated with the ranger company. The final absorption of brigade reconnaissance resources ended disparate reconnaissance arrangements and the field duplication of ground surveillance efforts. The three added platoons gave the rangers extra manpower and allowed the company to reach its authorized 220-member strength level.

On 6 October 1969 the ranger company completed this consolidation under the command of Capt. Kim H. Olmstead, and was placed under operational control of the division operations section while assignment to the 1st Squadron, 10th Cavalry, was retained. Company K was authorized a fifty-three-man company headquarters and three field platoons, each containing a headquarters section, five five-man ranger patrols, and five six-man hawkeye ranger patrols (the sixth person being a native scout). Ranger teams were given an alphabet-numerical combination standardized as R-1 through R-27.

The opportunity to demonstrate improved ranger capability developed shortly after Company K reorganization. The 4th Infantry Division became involved in a major battle for An Lao Valley and was forced to reinforce the engagement by withdrawing the 2d Brigade from its "swing position" north of Pleiku. The brigade displacement uncovered a crucial stretch of western Highway 19A. Major General Pepke anticipated that the North Vietnamese might sever the road, but was uncertain of their strength and timing. He ordered the Highland Rangers to screen the unguarded sector.[25]

Company K sent a full field platoon with a control headquarters and twelve ranger teams to Special Forces Camp Plei Mrong, located near Highway 19A. The ranger platoon used the Special Forces compound as a staging and communications relay point. The dozen rangers teams were rotated regularly so that eight teams were always patrolling the NVA approaches west of the highway. While eight patrols were in the field, the other four teams were debriefed, rested, and prepared for further missions.

On 12 October 1969 the 24th NVA Regiment began moving east from the Chu Goll-Chu Pa mountain region toward Highway 19A.

The enemy maneuver was calculated to take advantage of adverse weather conditions. Aerial observation of movement underneath the clouded valleys and fog-shrouded ridges was impossible. The ranger teams, however, detected the regiment as it crossed over the jungle-cloaked ridges and neared the highway. The Highland Rangers tracked and harassed the enemy columns with four days of radio-directed artillery shellfire and air strikes. Portage parties were ambushed and stragglers killed.

The ranger teams endured casualties from return fire, injuries in the vine-snarled tropical foliage, and near-drownings in hillside rapids—but they provided the essential warning needed for division reaction. Major General Pepke sent the mechanized 2d Battalion, 8th Infantry, to Plei Mrong, and armored blocking forces were arrayed against the 24th NVA Regiment as it emerged from the mountains. The North Vietnamese troops were defeated and withdrew toward Cambodia. The Highland Rangers were credited with preempting an enemy regimental offensive by careful surveillance and persistent tactics.[26]

The ranger reconnaissance barriers were found inadequate a month later, when Viet Cong sappers assaulted the division's Camp Radcliff installation at An Khe. The rangers could not spare teams to cover more than the Alpha sector of the base perimeter. On 15 November 1969 the enemy infiltrators achieved complete surprise and stormed the camp using B-40 rockets, assault rifles, and satchel charges. The enemy demolition parties knocked out guard towers, dynamited hospital wards, and destroyed nineteen helicopters before escaping.[27]

The successful sapper raid against Camp Radcliff in the "division backyard" was partially explained by the adverse personnel turbulence in the ranger company ranks. During the same period, October 1969 through January 1970, Company K absorbed 108 new replacements—a turnover equal to over half the company's total strength. In addition, from 12 November to 24 December the rangers were under the 7th Squadron of the 17th Cavalry and not technically under direct division control.[28]

Maj. Gen. Glenn D. Walker took over the 4th Infantry Division in November 1969 and directed a series of ranger retaliatory missions. On 24 November a ranger patrol led by Sgt. Bill Ten Kate entered the An Lao Valley to interdict elements of the 18th NVA Regiment. Sp4 David Flannery reported, "We had been in the field only a few hours and found an enemy platoon-sized base camp, two cave complexes, three high-speed trails, and a small food and water supply point." Sergeant Kate established a hilltop observation post and spotted a North Vietnamese squad crossing the rice paddies beneath them. He pre-targeted artillery on the nearest cover, a grove of trees, and then radioed for artillery on top of the rice field. The enemy soldiers ran as predicted for the group of trees, where more artillery annihilated the entire squad.

On the following day another NVA squad carrying AK47 rifles and rucksacks traveled across the same rice field. Sergeant Kate repeated the same tactics and the enemy squad dashed into the same trees, only to be eliminated by the second artillery salvo. Two days later a larger force of thirty-five North Vietnamese soldiers was sighted wading along the edge of a stream and heading directly toward the patrol's hill. The patrol leader stated, "They stopped at the foot of the hill and pointed up to our positions. Then they broke into two groups and headed up the hill. One group took the ravine to our right and the other came right for us." The rangers radioed for standby gunships, routed the advancing platoon, and were extracted.[29]

During mid-February 1970 the Highland Rangers participated in a prison rescue mission known as Operation WAYNE STAB II. Captain Olmstead concentrated the entire ranger company together for the raid on the reported jungle compound. On 16 February the 1st Infantry Brigade ringed the suspected area with three sudden battalion airmobile assaults while the ranger company was air-assaulted into the "doughnut hole."

The rangers reached the compound before noon, clashed with the enemy, and liberated one captive, who stated the others had just been moved. There were indications that South Vietnamese 22d Division staff members tipped off the VC at the last minute. The enemy broke into small groups and laid a web of skillfully disguised mechanical ambushes and punji-stake pits that delayed the ranger pursuit. By nightfall on the first day, eleven helicopter sorties were needed to evacuate wounded rangers from the multitude of traps.

The rangers widened the band of patrols to reconnoiter their circle of exploration as rapidly as possible. Small teams rappelled through aircraft-blasted drop zones in the triple-canopy jungle, while gunships and scout helicopters of the 7th Squadron, 17th Cavalry, surveyed the rugged area overhead. On 19 February, the 2d Battalion of the 35th Infantry occupying ambush positions killed ten enemy soldiers and captured a female nurse. Heavy blood trails marked the enemy escape route, and the rangers were redeployed vainly in pursuit. The guards slipped through the allied net with their prisoners.[30]

The rangers participated next in division Operation EICHEL-BERGER BLACK, the invasion of enemy base area 226 in central Binh Dinh Province. Unfortunately, rainy weather delayed the division jump-off until 19 March, and the enemy began withdrawing from the targeted area. The division trimmed its attack forces to one brigade, and Company K participation was trimmed to a single platoon. As a result, the Highland Rangers could not maintain an effective screen on both the flanks and in front of the advancing brigade.

The dense jungle and steep ridges of base area 226, however, added another ranger tactic to the Vietnam experience. The Company K rangers teamed up with combat engineers from the 4th Engineer Battalion and produced three unique ranger-engineer rappelling teams. These highly proficient teams were employed throughout the operation to establish small landing zones and destroy caves. The ranger-engineers rappelled into preselected locations every afternoon, cut landing zones and cleared out cavern-tunnel complexes, and were extracted on the following morning. The technique proved extremely beneficial and was continued until the operation's conclusion on 24 April.[31]

During the spring of 1970, Highland Ranger responsibilities were shifted eastward as the 4th Infantry Division moved into coastal Binh Dinh Province. Border security was turned over to the South Vietnamese, and the 3d Brigade was inactivated on 10 April. With the exception of the Cambodian offensive in the following month, the division was relieved of its previously formidable task safeguarding the western border.

Surprisingly, ranger Company K did not participate in the 4th Infantry Division's cross-border invasion of Cambodia on 5 May. Major General Walker decided not to use the ranger company, despite obvious reconnaissance requirements occasioned by the division's intrusion into completely unknown territory. He dispersed Company K throughout Binh Dinh Province as an "economy of force" measure while the division invaded Cambodia. The division report for Operation BINH TAY (Cambodian activity) explained, "While the bulk of the division was deployed into Cambodia, the 3-12 Inf and K/75 Rangers continued operating in the division permanent [Vietnam] area of responsibility. K/75 Rangers continued to deploy teams generally north and northwest of Camp Radcliff to gather information and intelligence on enemy locations and dispositions."[32]

The lack of division ranger support was keenly felt during the Cambodian invasion, and the substitution of a field force ranger company—Company C, 75th Infantry—generally proved unsatisfactory (see chapter 9). In the meantime, the Highland Rangers penetrated the communist Gia Lia secret base area during May and June. The rangers also operated against enemy infiltration routes along the Suoi Kon and Song Ba rivers. These economy-of-force activities were important, but ranger Company K might have been more gainfully employed in a traditional reconnaissance function: providing advance patrol support for the Cambodian incursion.

The Highland Ranger personnel situation remained critical. From November 1969 through July 1970, Company K casualties were ten killed and forty-seven wounded rangers. The rangers received 291 new replacements but lost more through normal attrition caused by rotation, transfers, and emergency leaves. The continuing shortage of qualified soldiers hampered replacement selection. During the same period the company received only thirty MACV Recondo School graduates. Fortunately, the general division withdrawal from border security duties and the dismantling of 3d Brigade greatly diminished ranger support requirements.[33]

In July 1970, Maj. Gen. William A. Burke took over the 4th Infantry Division. The following month he sent Capt. Larry E. Penley's Company K in the Nui Mieu mountains to support joint operations with the 1st Brigade. Other South Korean and South Vietnamese units in the same area forced the rangers to use multifarious coordination channels. Teams spent an inordinate amount of time trying to secure permission for artillery and air strikes while lucrative targets slipped away. The patrols were reduced to near-ineffectiveness by the procedural restraints, and Captain Penley reported the episode as an unproductive ranger assignment.

The rangers were summoned back to Camp Radcliff, now the division main base. Many line battalions were preparing for redeployment to the United States, and the Highland Rangers were used primarily as a stopgap infantry force. For example, from 26 September until 10 October, Company K operated as part of the 2d Brigade and searched the Tiger mountains with an attached artillery battery. The rangers saturated the area in sweep patrols, much like a regular infantry battalion, and artillery was employed conventionally in direct support. The rangers were used again as ''fire brigade'' infantry during Operation WAYNE SABER, conducted southwest of Camp Radcliff.[34]

The 4th Infantry Division rangers were notified of pending disbandment as part of Increment V (Keystone Robin-Bravo) of the U.S. Army redeployment from Vietnam. On 12 October 1970 the Highland Rangers commenced stand-down procedures, but continued limited field operations until 22 November. On the morning of 26 November, Major General Burke mustered the rangers for a final review and decorations ceremony. The unit was then reduced to zero strength. Company K (Ranger), 75th Infantry, was officially inactivated on 10 December 1970.[35]

The 4th Infantry Division combat reconnaissance units performed herculean service in monitoring Vietnam's tri-border region during a large part of the Second Indochina War. The recon effort was especially perilous because it covered a wider area and often lacked the same amount of artillery, aerial, and communications support available to other long-range patrols. The Highland Rangers combated an influx of well-trained and confident North Vietnamese regiments. Despite these dangers, Company K and its predecessor recon organizations rendered significant military service by detecting considerable enemy infiltration across the western II Corps Tactical Zone border.

The recondo-hawkeyes, Echo Fifty-eighth patrollers, and Highland Rangers played a vital role in locating and identifying key enemy elements; interdicted many North Vietnamese supply networks, base areas, way stations, and storage points; and actively screened and guarded regular formation flanking maneuvers. Its large area of operations caused Company K to consistently cover more territory and shoulder greater reconnaissance responsibilities, over a wider area, than most other division ranger companies in Vietnam.

6

9TH INFANTRY DIVISION

RIVERINE RANGERS

WAR EAGLE RECONNAISSANCE

During the fall of 1966 the 9th Infantry Division was at Fort Riley, Kansas, completing preparations for its scheduled December movement to Vietnam. The subordinate units were concluding their training programs, and soldiers were on their final leaves before overseas deployment. At this time, division commander Maj. Gen. George S. Eckhardt flew to Vietnam on an orientation tour of the combat theater and noted how each division contained a long-range patrol unit. Major General Eckhardt arrived back at Fort Riley and ordered the immediate organization of a reconnaissance platoon for his own division.

Capt. James Tedrick, Lt. Winslow Stetson, and Lt. Edwin Garrison were chosen as the officers for the division Long Range Reconnaissance Patrol (LRRP) Platoon. The provisional unit was known as the "War Eagle Platoon." The three officers interviewed and screened the records of 130 soldiers who volunteered to join the new unit. Forty of the best troops were selected. In November 1966 the division LRRP Platoon went to Panama and completed the Jungle Warfare School. Following the regular two-week course, Captain Tedrick conducted an extra week of tropical training. The platoon members returned to Fort Riley, took leaves, and were shipped to Vietnam in January 1967.

Upon arrival in Vietnam, Lieutenant Garrison flew to the Special Forces MACV Recondo School at Nha Trang with ten soldiers and completed the three-week course. Other groups attended the school until the entire 9th Infantry Division LRRP Platoon was recondo-qualified. The original policy required troop attendance at the MACV Recondo School for "basic recon training," followed by advanced team training within the platoon.

In the meantime, the 9th Infantry Division was adjusting to its combat operating area. Throughout the war the division operated primarily in the lowlands south of Saigon, the Rung Sat Special Zone, and the Mekong Delta. The entire region was extremely flat and covered by rivers, numerous tributaries, and canals. Most of the land consisted of soft soil or silt that became inundated during the rainy season, from May through October. Heavy rains caused regular flooding and left only a few areas dry, such as stream banks or rice paddy dikes.

From a military reconnaissance standpoint, the division's zone presented unique complications. Many sectors contained vast swamp forests and trackless marshes. The rest of the region was an extremely fertile and densely populated alluvial plain known as the "rice bowl of Asia." The predominant form of vegetation was wet rice sown in July, transplanted in September, and harvested in January or February. The well-cultivated ricelands were filled with people, which rendered undetected patrol activity almost impossible. The channelization of the waterways created thick underbrush and rows of nipa palms and other trees, giving the enemy excellent concealment and ambush opportunities. The Viet Cong constituted a popular resistance movement, and the guerrillas could easily hide their weapons and disappear among the general population.

The uniform flatness and wetness of the Mekong Delta terrain was especially troubling. Patrols were often compromised while trying to cross wide, open fields. Near villages or towns, large numbers of people often observed patrol activity. These conditions necessitated reliance on night movement and travel through narrow, vegetated lanes where booby traps and mechanical ambush devices proliferated. Helicopter insertion was generally unsuccessful, because all aircraft landings, even those involving false insertions and other tricks, were always watched closely by the inhabitants. Helicopters remained essential, however, for quick extraction and reinforcement purposes.

Torrential rains in the monsoon season and year-round water exposed patrollers to high rates of disabling skin disease. Reconnaissance troops were often unable to get completely dry for days at a time and suffered extensive inflammatory lesions and rampant skin infections. Neither treatment nor preventive measures were particularly satisfactory, although the prevalence and severity of the infections were directly related to the amount of exposure to the water and wet clothing. Nearly three-fourths of all 9th Infantry Division infantrymen, including patrollers, had clinically recognizable infections by the fourth month of tropical service.[1]

Immersion injuries of the feet and jungle rot were very common and greatly hindered patrolling operations. The pain and swelling were often so severe that recon personnel took off their boots and socks, only to discover they could not replace their footwear. Troops suffering from prolonged tropical immersion foot were evacuated to rear hospitals and not returned to the field. Wet sock abrasions caused lesions and such discomfort that sufferers could no longer walk. Patrollers in the 9th Infantry Division used standard canvas-and-leather jungle boots and cotton-nylon socks throughout the conflict. Lightweight shoes were developed for Mekong conditions later in the war, but recon units could not use them because the extremely thin soles offered no protection against stones and hard ground objects.[2]

Serious bacterial infections, typified by skin ulcers and multiple boils, also disrupted individual combat availability. Treatment for these cases varied widely, and affected men were often simply placed on weeks of light duty (non-patrolling) status until their lesions healed sufficiently. Fungal infections, typified by ringworm, also plagued recon troops. The infections were commonly acute and covered large areas of the body. Additionally, noninfectious diseases such as heat rash, ruptured blisters, and leech infestation caused severe problems in waterlogged areas.

Reconnaissance elements were not authorized replacements while soldiers, no matter how disabled, were still carried on unit rolls. The high incidence of terrain-associated medical and related problems presented great difficulties in sustaining the 9th Infantry Division reconnaissance effort. The combination of medically incapacitating diseases and enemy observation limited 9th Infantry Division patrols in the Mekong Delta to a maximum length of twenty-four to forty-eight hours. The dangers of keeping patrols operating beyond that time span were too great. Even short-duration patrols were prone to lose effectiveness quickly.[3]

The division was concentrated initially in the Bear Cat-Long Thanh area east of Saigon while a permanent base camp was constructed by dredging the My Tho river to produce enough fill to build a major installation in the Mekong Delta. The new base, named Dong Tam, was located five miles west of My Tho in Dinh Tuong Province. Action on both fronts, around Bear Cat and in the Mekong Delta, was relatively light until March 1967.

Some of the first 9th Infantry Division LRRP Platoon combat operations were conducted with the jungle-experienced 1st Australian Task Force. On 9 April 1967, as part of 1st Brigade Operation PORT-SEA, a four-man long-range patrol led by Sp4 Raymond A. Hulin was inserted into the southeastern portion of Phuoc Tuy Province. The team reached its surveillance position and spotted a column of the 5th Viet Cong Division. After waiting ten minutes, point man Sp4 James L. Elder stepped out onto the trail to see if it was clear. He suddenly saw more enemy soldiers and hand-signaled to Specialist Hulin that there was no time to fade back into the jungle.

The men froze in position, and the first enemy soldier passed by without seeing the Americans. He was shouldering his rifle and looking solely at the ground. The second VC soldier stopped right in front of Hulin, who recalled that "it shocked him, like he didn't know what to do." Specialist Hulin responded by firing a full M16 magazine into the man. The other patrol members, Sp4 Freddie D. Jenkins and Pfc. Danny C. Phillips, opened fire, and the team withdrew back into the jungle, where they set up a small defensive perimeter. Helicopters extracted the team under fire while gunships raked the enemy ranks.[4]

In June 1967, Maj. Gen. George C. O'Connor assumed command of the 9th Infantry Division. The Mobile Riverine Force began sustained operations in the Mekong Delta. The combined naval-infantry force combined the 2d Brigade with Navy River Assault Flotilla One and contained over a hundred Navy vessels, ranging from barrack ships to armored troop carriers and monitor gunboats. The strike force even contained floating Army artillery barges. The Mobile Riverine Force ferried Army and Vietnamese Marine units into action throughout the meandering waterways of the Mekong Delta and Rung Sat Special Zone.[5]

During the same month the division LRRP Platoon at Bear Cat was alerted that it would be expanded to a full company-sized unit with 119 men. The MACV Recondo School notified Captain Tedrick that its academy was not equipped to handle such a large influx of personnel. Tedrick established his own intensive two-week training program, based on the doctrine of the MACV Recondo School. The course prepared new members in specialized reconnaissance skills. Military emphasis was placed on map reading, navigation, military intelligence, communications, supporting fires, and patrolling fundamentals.

On 8 July 1967 the 9th Long Range Patrol Detachment (LRPD) was formalized, but the division staff carefully regulated the initial tempo of reconnaissance activity in accordance with medical dictates and terrain operating conditions. Requirements were kept at controlled levels that did not overtax recon capability. Other divisions engaged in area warfare and territorial security could not afford the same degree of controlled reconnaissance flexibility.

The 9th Infantry Division Long Range Patrol Detachment was "well brought up," borrowing General Marshall's World War II phrase referring to the carefully trained units of that conflict. The pre-Vietnam preparation, the large percentage of cadre graduates from the Panama Jungle Warfare School and the MACV Recondo School, and the relatively slow pace of initial recon operations enabled the detachment to develop in an orderly fashion. Additionally, many patrollers received special instruction from Australian cadre experts in jungle warfare. Marine Lt. Col. James S. G. Turner, who was placed on duty with the division headquarters by the Commandant of the Marine Corps as riverine operations observer and liaison officer, ensured that some teams received advanced training in boat and shore tactics from Marine instructors.

During July, the still-forming division LRPD sent some recon patrols into Phuoc Tuy and Long Khanh provinces alongside the 1st Australian Task Force and two battalions of U.S. Marine-advised Vietnamese Marines. Staff Sgt. Richard T. Cottrell led a typical LRPD patrol through the jungle surrounding Long Thanh. He was a graduate of the MACV Recondo School and a previous commander on twelve successful recon platoon combat missions. His assistant patrol leader was Sp4 Dennis L. Marble, an honor graduate of the MACV Recondo School and a veteran patroller. On the third day of their mission the team members reached an old pathway cut by allied tank tracks. They were surprised to discover a multitude of recent, well-used foot trails in the immediate vicinity. The team moved farther along the maze of hard-packed footpaths until the men spotted a shelter fabricated of ponchos draped as a roof over upright poles and camouflaged from aerial view by fresh-cut banana leaves. Metallic ammunition boxes and fifty-five-gallon barrels gleamed in the sun under the poncho.

Staff Sergeant Cottrell decided to sweep the patrol wide around the suspicious shelter and approach it from the other side. The point man volunteered to make the necessary diversion for this maneuver. As expected, the Viet Cong defenders were waiting for the patrol to hit them from the front and listened to noises made by the decoy point man. When the enemy thought the patrol was within range they tossed a grenade. The resulting blast sent the point man crumpling to his knees, but fortunately the enemy was using poor-quality Chicom grenades and he was only stunned.

At that instant, Staff Sergeant Cottrell and the others stormed the Viet Cong perimeter from the other direction. The enemy desperately tried to correct their mistake and shift firing, but they were too late. The patrollers overran the VC squad position and triggered an ambush on the first relief force. Faced with more arriving VC troops, Cottrell directed his men into a predetermined fire and escape plan. The patrollers emerged from the incident unscathed and returned to Bear Cat with valuable information locating the 4th Viet Cong Main Force Battalion of Thu Duc district.[6]

During June and July the 9th Infantry Division LRPD completed forty-three patrols and clashed eighteen times with enemy forces. The detachment remained engaged in surveillance of southern III Corps Tactical Zone, where teams reconnoitered the Viet Cong stronghold of base area 302, east of Highway 2 in lower Long Khanh Province, and base area 303, also known as the Hat Dich Secret Zone. The patrols successfully provided the division with a general overview of expected resistance in areas they were assigned to reconnoiter.[7]

Throughout August and September the division intelligence section continued to fill the LRPD. By October the detachment reached full authorized strength of 119 personnel and was rated as fully operational. The detachment headquarters controlled patrol operations, communications and supply functions, and the two patrol platoons. Each platoon contained a command section and eight six-man teams.[8]

The 9th Infantry Division LRPD patrols were actively engaged in extensive operations. Some teams rendered reconnaissance for 2d Brigade during Operation CORONADO and entered the Viet Cong Cam Son secret base area. Other teams supported 1st Brigade during Operation AKRON and swept the jungles east of Bear Cat, uncovering a massive underground system of enemy tunnels and bunkers. The enemy complex was so large that patrollers and brigade soldiers spent two weeks recovering huge quantities of weapons, crates of clothing supplies, and boxes of ammunition.

During Operation RILEY, Staff Sgt. Arlyn P. Wieland led a LRPD patrol into the canal-laced loop of the Song Nha Be near Nhon Trach. The recon team selected a surveillance post in a marsh thicket and watched Viet Cong troops unloading boxes of mortar projectiles from sampans beached on the shore. The patrollers were too close to radio for gunships and were forced to wait motionless until dark before trying to exit the area. At nightfall the team moved slowly away from the enemy shoreline through the swamp grass. When the pointman spotted dozens of khaki-clad Viet Cong, he signaled the team to get down. The patrollers crawled through the grassy quagmire and past the enemy lines without being detected.

Staff Sergeant Wieland radioed for armed helicopters as soon as his patrol was a safe distance away. Gunships from Troop D, 3d Squadron of the 5th Cavalry, strafed and rocketed the enemy encampment for fifteen minutes. Wieland later reported, "We could hear the VC screaming, trying to get away." The team radioed for artillery bombardment and extraction. The patrollers boarded the helicopters as the artillery shelling stopped, and Air Force F-101 Super Sabre fighter-bombers hit the target next. The patrol was credited with destroying a munitions depot of the Viet Cong 84th Rear Services Group.[9]

During another night encounter, an LRPD patrol led by Sgt. Hilan Jones had neared its extraction field outside Long Thanh when the team point man noticed movement around a lighted house window. The team crouched in the thick brush and watched the house as three people carrying weapons went inside. Sergeant Jones radioed for permission to investigate the house and relocated his patrol within yards of the door. Jones related, "I called for them to come out and when they heard me, I saw them run for their weapons. So I threw a grenade in and we opened fire." The patrol killed six VC, captured four pounds of intelligence documents from the dwelling, and detained one suspect. When the report was radioed to headquarters, the patrol was told to stay there and await the 5th Cavalry aero rifle platoon exploitation force.

Less than an hour later, helicopters of the 5th Cavalry's 3d Squadron appeared overhead with the aero rifle platoon. As the helicopters descended, an enemy machine gun crew located in a neighboring house opened fire. Sergeant Jones's team close-assaulted the machine gun nest as it was firing at the aircraft and killed one of the Viet Cong gunners. The aero rifle platoon landed and swept the area. Two additional bodies were found, along with fifty pounds of military gear and 500 pounds of rice. Sergeant Jones's patrol was credited with knocking out a Viet Cong company assembly point of the C240 Local Force Battalion and preventing damage to the airmobile insertion.[10]

The LRPD conducted important military intelligence tasks for the Mobile Riverine Force within the Mekong Delta. Attached patrol teams were used to obtain specific information about regional waterways. Working closely with riverine survey teams, the patrollers gathered vital data on area rivers, streams, and canals. The LRPD teams measured waterway depths and bank conditions, gauged clearances underneath bridges, and reported natural and artificial obstacles. The assessments precluded combat except on an incidental basis. For instance, teams clashed periodically with the enemy while providing security for underwater demolition teams and explosive ordnance detachments removing enemy channel obstructions.

Mekong Delta operations demanded a new set of reconnaissance techniques. Patrols engaged in point reconnaissance missions looked for particular targets in short time intervals, as opposed to longer area reconnaissance missions of a general "search and contact" nature. For example, helicopters operating near Dong Tam reported receiving automatic weapons fire from hostile sampans. In August, assistant division intelligence Capt. William F. Balfanz dispatched several recon patrols to search specifically for the enemy gunboats, with each patrol covering a certain waterway for only a few hours.

Staff Sgt. Elbert Mullen's patrol spotted a well-camouflaged flotilla of Viet Cong gunboats on a tributary of the My Tho river, three and a half miles southwest of Dong Tam. He reported, "From our position about thirty meters away, we could see that the boats were piled high on each end with coconuts and in the middle of each we could see the thirties [.30-caliber machine guns]. The light machine guns were mounted on tripods lashed to platforms about a foot and a half above the deck." The recon sighting provided the first ground verification that the enemy was arming its wooden sampans in the division's eastern region of the Mekong Delta.[11]

On 1 November 1967 the 3d Brigade coordinated with Vietnamese officials in Long An Province and organized a highly effective Combined Reconnaissance and Intelligence Platoon (CRIP). The platoon was composed of twenty-five American and twenty-four South Vietnamese soldiers. The platoon's mission was to verify and respond militarily to intelligence reports. The CRIP received advanced training in reaction and ambush patrols and became a valuable division asset. The unit was not part of the LRPD but often operated in close support.[12]

The division intelligence section acknowledged that assigned Vietnamese personnel would greatly improve the LRPD reconnaissance capability. Teams accompanied by natives fluent in the language could gain valuable and timely intelligence from on-the-spot interrogation of local farmers or suspects. During November, teams trying to duplicate the CRIP success used regular South Vietnamese Army scouts for linguistic support. Unfortunately, some ARVN soldiers were unwilling to go on extended patrols if danger or hard work was involved.

Later that month the LRPD operations sergeant went to the Bien Hoa "Chieu Hoi" center, cash in hand, and hired three Hoi Chanhs. The Hoi Chanhs were former North Vietnamese and Viet Cong prisoners who had agreed to work for the Americans. The monetary arrangement proved to be an excellent solution and gave recon teams a source of dedicated and uncomplaining scouts.[13]

In December, a LRPD team led by Sgt. James R. J. Martin used Hoi Chanh scouts with excellent results. The patrollers discovered a trench as they maneuvered downhill through very thick undergrowth. The scout noted how the trench smelled of sap from newly cut brushes and fresh dirt. As a result, Martin decided to establish an overnight surveillance position and monitor the area. During the night, throngs of Viet Cong porters passed near the patrol position carrying supplies downhill to a large bunker complex. Sergeant Martin stated, "One time a group passed near us carrying a lantern. At any time during the night a cough or the noise from a twig snapping could have brought the VC down on us."

As dawn approached the Viet Cong travel stopped and the team decided to leave and radio for aerial destruction of the area. The scout abruptly motioned them that more Viet Cong were nearby and blocking their escape route. "Our whole team was within ten feet of five VC," Sp4 William E. Gunn commented. Sergeant Martin killed two, and the rest were slain by the other patrol members. Browning Automatic Rifles returned fire, but the team was able to get away and toss smoke grenades for forward air controllers to call in air strikes. Sergeant Martin's team was extracted without further incident.[14]

RELIABLE RECONNAISSANCE

On 20 December 1967, Major General O'Connor activated Company E (Long Range Patrol), 50th Infantry, to give the 9th Infantry Division specialized ground reconnaissance support. The long-range patrol company absorbed the LRPD organization. The new company was designated as "Reliable Reconnaissance," after the division's preferred nickname in Vietnam—the "Old Reliables." The company restructured its six-man patrols to create eight-man teams, an organizational change that provided two balanced patrol elements per team. Some teams were eliminated by this consolidation.

New company volunteers were sent periodically to the MACV Recondo School at Nha Trang. In a bizarre twist of fate, Company E suffered its first loss at that location in Khanh Hoa Province, 300 miles north of the division combat zone. Sp4 Kenneth R. Lancaster was an infantry volunteer who had joined the 9th LRPD on 1 November 1967. During January he was a student at the MACV Recondo School and part of a training patrol advised by Korean liaison officer Lt. Chi Keun Hong and led by experienced Special Forces Sfc. Jason T. Woodworth.

The final patrols of the MACV Recondo School were routinely sent into hostile areas to give students realistic battlefield experience. On 3 January 1968, Sergeant First Class Woodworth's student team 3 was completing its last phase of instruction. That morning the school operations section received a radio transmission from the training patrol, requesting extraction because its position had been compromised by a firefight earlier that morning. At 8:15 P.M. a helicopter hovered at the designated pickup point and all members of the team except Specialist Lancaster and Kozach were able to climb aboard. After waiting for two minutes over the landing zone the aircraft took off.

Specialist Kozach stayed at the clearing and waited for another helicopter, but Specialist Lancaster grabbed the starboard skid in desperation and tried to hang on. The crew did not see him until the aircraft reached a 1,000-foot altitude. Before corrective action could be taken, Lancaster disappeared. An extensive search through the jagged jungle mountains failed to locate him. Kenneth Ray Lancaster of Silver Spring, Maryland, remains the only 9th Infantry Division reconnaissance member from the Vietnam era still missing in action.[15]

Prior to the Tet-68 campaign, Company E patrols were concentrated in Bien Hoa Province, where they routinely scouted the Binh Son rubber plantation and provided area reconnaissance coverage to monitor movements of the 5th VC Division. The company also sent point-reconnaissance patrols into the Mekong Delta. The dense population, lack of concealment, and medical considerations restricted combat patrols in Delta areas to precision strikes with a duration less than twenty-four hours.

One of the most troubling aspects of Mekong Delta operations was the lack of communication stations for distant patrol radio relay. In response, the division's 9th Signal Battalion secured a 2,000-cubic-foot helium-filled balloon from the U.S. Army Concept Team in Vietnam (USACTIV) and used it to hoist radio antennae and increase transmission range. Surprisingly, the signature of the system caused no enemy action against either the balloon or its ground terminal. The large balloon and its elevated radio apparatus enabled the Company E headquarters at Bear Cat to extend signal range to distant teams equipped with ordinary backpack PRC-25 radios. The balloon permitted excellent communications over great distances and provided a good substitute for aerial relays. Unfortunately, high monsoon winds made it impractical during certain seasons.[16]

During January, Reliable Reconnaissance teams began joint operations with Navy SEAL teams to gain training and experience in the Delta environment. The highly selective patrols were designated SEAL-ECHO missions, the suffix being a phonetic spelling of Company E, and the program was extended throughout the year. SEAL-ECHO teams were inserted by Navy patrol boats, Boston whalers, plastic assault boats, and helicopters. The joint teams ambushed sampans, initiated "aquabush" attacks (ambushes that blocked waterways), and seized prisoners. The SEAL-ECHO troops used supporting artillery and airstrikes to destroy larger targets.

Most patrols with the Mobile Riverine Force continued to perform hydrographic and terrain analysis tasks. Combat was only incidental in these laborious missions, and the chores went largely unrewarded by medals and citations of valor. This type of recon work, however, was just as important as any battle patrol assignment. For instance, reconnaissance teams were often landed ahead of airmobile assaults to check predominantly wet tidal areas. The patrollers found that many landing zones reported favorably by helicopter overflights were instead mired deep in mud and completely covered with water at high tide. Recon patrols also assisted riverine shore parties in the nightly movement of artillery barges. The men conducted last-minute reconnaissance of shore conditions, checked for sandbars and other obstacles, and guided barges to selected mooring positions with filtered flashlights.

In February 1968, Maj. Gen. Julian J. Ewell assumed command of the 9th Infantry Division. As a result of the Tet-68 battles, he authorized the Reliable Reconnaissance company to acquire a similar capacity to the 3d Brigade Combined Reconnaissance and Intelligence Platoon. Company E received permission to employ available Provincial Reconnaissance Unit (PRU) personnel from the Central Intelligence Agency's Project Phoenix program. The PRU troops were hardened anticommunist troops dedicated to destroying the Viet Cong infrastructure. The PRU troops generally possessed very high esprit and great knowledge of Viet Cong operating methods.

Company E received nine PRU scouts and "found them to be most highly qualified for reconnaissance missions." The PRU scouts either were integrated into selected patrol teams or operated in independent PRU heavy fire teams. The latter were used like Special Forces roadrunners to move along enemy trails and act either like Viet Cong or innocent peasants. The Viet Cong usually mistook the PRU teams for indigenous comrades. The addition of PRU manpower commencing in early 1968 benefitted Company E operations, but only a few were spared for Reliable Reconnaissance work. Even those scouts were always subject to recall for higher-priority assignments.[17]

From February through the end of April 1968 the Company E patrollers sustained only three combat fatalities. During the same trimester the patrollers killed seventy-four Viet Cong by direct fire. Patrols of this period were typified by a team infiltrated outside Bear Cat in response to reports about the D-251 Infiltration Group. Commencing on 11 April the team, led by co-patrol leaders Sp4 Steven G. Averill and Sp4 Robert J. Wallace, watched enemy troops using the maze of trails for two consecutive days and nights. On the third morning the team leaders decided to ambush one of the small groups as it passed through the area and execute a prisoner snatch.

Specialist Wallace reported, "We were just starting to set up about five yards off a trail and all of a sudden there they were—four VC came down the trail from the west and four more from the east. When they spotted one of our men, we opened up. We usually try to avoid this type of contact but when a VC is looking at you from fifteen meters away, you have to shoot." The patrol killed or wounded their eight opponents, who were serving as scouts for a North Vietnamese infiltration platoon. The patrol members conducted a fighting withdrawal to an emergency landing zone and were safely extracted under the covering fire of gunships.[18]

From May through July 1968, Company E reconnaissance penetrated deeper into the Mekong Delta. For the first time several patrols became involved in heavy fighting inside the Plain of Reeds. During late July and early August, patrols accompanied U.S. Marine advisers and the South Vietnamese 5th Battalion into the rugged U Minh Forest along Vietnam's western coast. Other patrols pushed through waist-deep mud and dense foliage of nipa palms southeast of Tan An and scouted the Viet Cong "Mouse Ears" stronghold located within the twin loops of the Song Vam Co Tay.

The majority of teams were launched from either Tan An, in Dinh Tuong Province southwest of Saigon, or from Dong Tam, in the Mekong Delta. Additionally, two eight-man teams were stationed on Navy river patrol boats to conduct missions along the

Song Dong Nai. One ten-man heavy team patrolled west of Route 15, directly south of Saigon. The seasonal change to moderate rainfall began in early June, but rainfall was still well below expectations. Strong gusty winds, however, hampered helicopter operations and shut down balloon communications.[19]

New patrolling techniques were developed to cope with riverine surveillance. Task Force Starlight combined patrol teams with Vietnamese National Police aboard heavily armed Navy monitors. The joint force intercepted sampans and junks on suspected Viet Cong river supply arteries. During daylight hours the patrol teams provided security on the riverbanks and aloft using helicopters. Targeted boats were searched immediately. Navy Lt. C. Tom Vaught stated, "We have had very little trouble getting the boats over to be checked. When they do try to get by, we just fire a couple of warning shots [from the monitors] and they quickly turn in our direction." After the 8:00 P.M. nightly curfew the patrollers served as standby infantry fire teams equipped with night observation devices.[20]

During July, expert riflemen Staff Sgt. Richard D. Rebidue and Staff Sgt. Aprail Gapol from the Fort Benning Army Marksmanship Training Unit escorted one Company E patrol outside Tan An. Both sergeants were armed with National Match M14 rifles modified to mount commercial Redfield adjustable-range telescopes. The two sergeants occupied night sniping positions. Hours later a group of fifteen Viet Cong approached the darkened trace of Highway 4. The sergeants opened fire at a distance of 400 yards and killed ten Viet Cong before the surprised enemy soldiers could get clear of the slaughtering ground. At daybreak the patrol swept the field and found several loaded rocket-propelled grenade launchers abandoned in the grass.[21]

The 9th Infantry Division organized a division sniper school with the expert riflemen from Fort Benning. The sniper school trained marksmen for special duty throughout the division. The patrollers gained a great advantage from this unique instruction, because sniper employment on combat recon patrols proved very effective in the spacious Delta wastelands. Within a few months, each team possessed at least one sniper-qualified individual.

During the fall of 1968 the Reliable Reconnaissance company continued to launch teams on harassing and interdiction patrols throughout the Mekong Delta. The bulk of patrol assets were concentrated at Dong Tam, although two eight-man teams were retained aboard Navy river patrol boats along the Song Nha Be and one eight-man team served the Mobile Riverine Force exclusively.

Teams supporting the 1st Brigade in Long An Province conducted local strike operations, blocked major infiltration routes, and secured bridges along Highway 4. Despite the generally good weather and lack of heavy rainfall, a shortage of helicopters curtailed long-range patrolling activity in Long An Province until October.

Company E developed new tactics to cope with the flow of enemy supplies traveling through the circuitous waterways from the Rung Sat Special Zone and Go Cong provincial bases into Long An Province. One very effective innovation was the development of the "Parakeet" flight to conduct aerial surveillance and surprise inspection of suspicious boats. The Parakeet flight contained a four-man recon element on a UH-1 Huey helicopter and was named as a play on the larger platoon-sized "Eagle" flight developed by Special Forces. First Lt. Dale L. Dickey stated, "When something is spotted that requires closer inspection, the Huey will land and we jump into action. We move to the edge of the waterway and wave the sampan over. When it beaches, we give it a thorough search." The first Parakeet team consisted of Sgt. Joseph L. Florio, Sgt. Bruce A. Sartwell, Sp4 Ralph D. Harter, and Sp4 Larry D. Hughes.[22]

From August through the end of October, Company E accumulated an impressive record of 202 patrols despite setbacks in securing adequate helicopter support. The Reliable Reconnaissance patrols clashed with enemy troops seventy-one times during ninety days and employed artillery, air strikes, or reinforcing ground units in most of the engagements. The recon teams killed forty-seven Viet Cong by direct fire, captured twenty-six prisoners, and uncovered numerous caches that included a multitude of individual weapons, fifty-eight grenade cases, twelve crates of TNT explosives, and even a giant bench lathe.[23]

The Reliable Reconnaissance Company was headquartered at the main Dong Tam division base throughout the winter and kept several teams under direct headquarters control. One eight-man recon team remained detached on Navy duty at Nha Be, where it provided waterway reconnaissance along the Song Nha Be, using river patrol boats. Six other eight-man teams were evenly divided among the brigades and occupied forward locations. Two recon teams were based with the 1st Brigade at Fire Support Base Moore in Dinh Tuong Province. Two teams supported the 2d Brigade Mobile Riverine Force in Kien Hoa Province and were carried into remote locations by river assault squadrons from Navy Task Force 117. Two recon teams were based with the 3d Brigade forward command post at Tan An in Long An Province.

Reconnaissance efforts in Long An Province were undermined by constant insertion difficulties inside heavily populated districts. Helicopters attempted to infiltrate the teams at dusk or night whenever possible. The majority of these "last-light insertions" resulted in patrols being fired on or engaging the enemy within two hours of insertion. The actions usually necessitated swift team extraction.

The Viet Cong remained hidden in most Mekong Delta areas while division forces conducted sweep operations, and they avoided engaging large allied combat units. Recon teams were inserted with the infantry battalions and stayed behind secretly after the regular troops departed. The patrollers reported that the regions soon became "alive again" with Viet Cong activity. Stay-behind teams interrupted numerous resupply activities, and the Viet Cong reacted by using local guerrilla squads and platoons to search out recon teams—usually by baiting the Americans into opening fire and revealing patrol positions. The guerrillas usually refrained from all-out action and converged only enough firepower to necessitate the recon team's extraction.[24]

Two November patrols typified the success of recon patrols in bringing the otherwise elusive Viet Cong into battle. In the first instance, north of Vinh Long, a Company E reconnaissance team paired up with Troop D of the 3d Squadron, 5th Cavalry. The patrol was flown into enemy base area 470, after radar sightings indicated large movements in an otherwise uninhabited area. The team members saw a suspicious hut with a plastic covering and moved toward the dwelling, calling for anyone inside to surrender. A Viet Cong squad was trapped inside by the surprise airlanding but chose to resist. The team pulled back and radioed for gunships that devastated the structure with rockets. Elements of the 4th Battalion of the 39th Infantry responded to the firing. The infantrymen found ten dead Viet Cong, a large cache of medical equipment, and numerous documents of the 1st VC Regiment inside the demolished building.

On the evening of 29 November another long-range patrol was inserted into the Cam Son secret base of Dinh Tuong Province. The patrollers established an overnight position and observed a large Viet Cong column moving through a tangled patch of nipa and banana trees between Cai Lay and Cai Be. The team immediately radioed their observation and arranged for a dawn extraction by the 3d Squadron of the 17th Cavalry, in order not to alert the enemy to their nocturnal presence. At daybreak, helicopters lifted out the patrol as the 2d Battalion of the 39th Infantry was airmobiled in reaction to the sighting. The resulting action destroyed elements of the VC 261B Main Force Battalion.[25]

During the last three months of Company E's existence, from November 1968 through January 1969, the Reliable Reconnaissance teams conducted 217 patrols and engaged the enemy in 102 separate actions. The company was credited with killing eighty-four Viet Cong by direct fire and capturing eleven prisoners. One large cache was found after a recon team was paired with the division's 65th Infantry Platoon, a combat tracker dog team. Of the 101 recon observations, the division reacted with artillery, air, or ground forces on eighty-four occasions. On 29 December, Company E realized its biggest success indirectly, when two B-52 strategic bombing raids bombed central Giong Trom district in response to patrol information and achieved twenty-five secondary explosions.[26]

RIVERINE AND GO-DEVIL RANGERS

The Department of the Army took action on 1 January 1969 to reorganize the 75th Infantry under the combat arms regimental system as the parent regiment for long-range patrol companies. On 1 February 1969, Major General Ewell activated Company E (Ranger), 75th Infantry, by using the personnel and equipment from Company E, 50th Infantry. The latter unit was then inactivated.

The rangers were known as either "Echo Rangers" (E in conformity with ICAO phonetic alphabet adopted by the U.S. military in 1956) or the "Riverine Rangers," because most operations involved riverine and canal reconnaissance—although the company was only partially assigned to the Mobile Riverine Force. However, the ranger company's overall wet-patrol tactics, regular use of naval or boat infiltration tactics, and Mekong Delta operating arena justified this title for the entire unit.

Ranger Company E was headquartered at Dong Tam and composed of eleven teams (Ranger teams 11, 13, 14, 15, 16, 17, 19, 21, 22, 24, and 29). Patrol size was cut from eight to six men each. Three ranger teams were kept at Dong Tam for division-level missions. Two ranger teams were stationed with the 1st Brigade at Fire Support Base Danger in Dinh Tuong Province. Three ranger teams were devoted to "river raider" patrols with the 2d Brigade Mobile Riverine Force in Kien Hoa Province. Three other ranger teams were based at Tan An in Dinh Tuong Province with the 3d Brigade for recon and Parakeet flight duty.

The Parakeet flights were strengthened into ranger hunter contingents. A full six-man ranger team was assigned to each Parakeet mission instead of the previous four-member element. The Parakeet helicopters ranged over land as well as waterways looking for suitable targets. When the pilot and patrol leader identified an objective, an airmobile raid was conducted immediately. Parakeet tactics depended on rapid insertion, violent action, and swift departure. Two Cobra gunships were added to provide sustaining firepower for the raiding force, especially in case adverse extraction was needed.

From activation until the end of April, ranger Company E took advantage of dry season conditions to harass suspected Viet Cong supply lines throughout the Mekong Delta. The Riverine Rangers conducted 244 patrols and reported 134 observations of enemy activity. The rangers clashed with the Viet Cong during 111 patrols, and employed artillery, aerial, or ground support on eighty-six occasions. Ranger patrols were credited with killing 169 Viet Cong and capturing five prisoners. One of the highlights of the period was the dispatch of ranger team 24 to scour the area where the dredge *Western Eagle* was hit by four 107mm rockets on 3 March. The rangers cleared the vicinity of several Viet Cong rocket positions.[27]

Underlying the ranger claims of mission success was the disturbing undercurrent of declining late-war proficiency affecting all reconnaissance units in Vietnam. High personnel turnover rates and the mandated one-year rotation policy kept stripping the company of experienced recon veterans. The 9th Infantry Division rangers experienced shortages of personnel, like other ranger components in the combat theater, but Company E deficiencies were greatly aggravated by the high percentage of medical impairments. Rangers immobilized by immersion foot and bacterial or fungal infections still had to be carried on the company roster, and this prevented receipt of replacements. The 1st Brigade evaluated its ranger support:

> Ranger activities during the period point out the continuing need for proper training of the patrol members, and better supervision and leadership by ranger officers. Several patrols during the period resulted in almost immediate, real, or imagined contact with the enemy upon insertion—leading to extraction of the teams before contact was developed, before artillery was called in, or before the team attempted to move to a new location.[28]

During May and June, thunderstorms and downpours occasionally restricted helicopter insertions as the weather changed to the rainy season. The Riverine Rangers persisted in their attempts to locate and interdict Viet Cong units in Long An, Dinh Tuong, Go Cong, and Kien Hoa provinces. The recon patrols were largely frustrated by the enemy's secret supply lines and use of small village bands. The three or four teams assigned to each brigade were used on point reconnaissance and Parakeet flights.[29]

The rangers supporting 1st Brigade became so frustrated trying to locate untraceable contraband that teams converted from intelligence-gathering to hunter-killer raids. The hunter-killer tactic employed one ranger team as a hunter element that tried to lock enemy troops into combat. The killer element was composed of two standby ranger teams that maneuvered in the hunter team's support. However, each hunter-killer raider force consumed all three teams normally available to a brigade.

On 31 May 1969, ranger team 22 led by Sgt. Ralph E. Funk was airlifted into the canal-crossed marshland two miles west of Dong Tam. For unknown reasons, the team decided to land near an apparently vacant structure. The Viet Cong squad positioned inside immediately opened fire. Assistant team leader Sgt. Norman Crabb and others engaged the enemy in a five-minute burst of firing before the Viet Cong squad retreated into the nipa palms, still firing their AK47 assault rifles. The rangers found a 60mm mortar and boxes of ammunition inside the structure. A later check of the wooded area revealed that the rangers killed three and another three were hit by strafing from 9th Aviation Battalion helicopters.[30]

On 12 June 1969 the 9th Infantry Division received notification of its selection as the first major U.S. Army formation to leave the Republic of Vietnam. Maj. Gen. Harris W. Hollis was given the mission of reorganizing the 3d Brigade to stay in country, while disengaging the remainder of the division from combat before September.

The 3d Brigade of the 9th Infantry Division was scheduled to remain in Vietnam to safeguard the approaches into Saigon from the southwest. Long An Province was still unsecured and laced with Viet Cong infiltration corridors. The mission of securing the province and its immediate environs was a top MACV priority. To accomplish this mission, the separate 3d Brigade of the 9th Infantry Division—known as the "Go Devil" brigade—was formally established as an independent unit on 26 July 1969. In September the rest of the division departed Vietnam and the Go-Devil Brigade was placed under the operational control of the 25th Infantry Division.

During this transition period, Capt. John E. Conner III's ranger company was transferred to the 3d Brigade and tailored for brigade-level reconnaissance in Long An Province. The ranger exchange from division to brigade status was essentially a logical transaction, but nevertheless caused an inordinate degree of associated confusion at higher Army levels. There were serious misunderstandings between the staffs of MACV, the U.S. Army Pacific, and Pentagon officials over the 3d Brigade's composition and the very retention of ranger assets in view of congressionally mandated troop reduction levels in Vietnam.

In July, when the 9th Infantry Division began phasing out of Vietnam, the foremost military consideration was defending its main Dong Tam base during the redeployment process. The division departure was a relatively rushed affair, and marked by a wind-down euphoria that swept the ranks of most personnel leaving the country. The rangers constituted a dependable source of well-motivated and highly proficient soldiers, and the majority were assigned to protect Dong Tam.

The rangers renamed themselves the "Kudzu Rangers" after the operational code word for the close-in defense of Dong Tam. Two ranger teams were assigned to perform reconnaissance for Task Force Carlson. The task force was a composite contingent raised to sweep the Dong Tam vicinity with one infantry battalion, one air cavalry troop, and one medium artillery battery. The other rangers manned berm positions on the Dong Tam perimeter as ordinary infantry. The ranger company phased its teams out of the Kudzu business by 3 August.

The rangers were reconsolidated at Tan An only to face a bewildering assortment of directives concerning their future viability. Ranger activities were dominated by the larger struggle to finalize structural plans for the reinforced 3d Brigade. Officially, Company E was scheduled to leave Vietnam by 12 August as part of the original division withdrawal deadline. The 3d Brigade staff, anticipating an urgent requirement for future ranger reconnaissance, protested the pending loss of the ranger unit. The Department of the Army, fearing political repercussions, refused to alter the rigid division redeployment schedule to make an exception for the rangers.

U.S. Army Vietnam headquarters took immediate action to circumvent "the political niceties" of this impasse. On 6 July, USARV published General Order 2434 reorganizing the 3d Brigade and creating a provisional brigade ranger company effective 20 July. All personnel and equipment of Company E were transferred into the provisional ranger component. The ranger officers and men smiled at the 10 August order that Company E would proceed through Phase II processing for flight manifesting and baggage customs checks, because Company E was now only a ghost element. However, the division duly logged out the zero-strength company as departing Vietnam on 12 August.[31]

On 23 August 1969 the Army formally inactivated Company E (Ranger), 75th Infantry. The provisional "Go Devil" ranger company at Tan An was, of course, unaffected by this paper ruse. On the following day, 24 August, ranger team 16 executed a successful ambush that killed Viet Cong Col. Hai Tram, the commander of VC Subregion 3 in northwest Long An Province. Pentagon officials authorized a separate brigade ranger company within the month. On 24 September the U.S. Army Pacific reactivated Company E by General Order 705, effective 1 October, and U.S. Army Vietnam headquarters published orders reassigning Company E to the 3d Brigade, 9th Infantry Division.[32]

Thus, on 1 October 1969, the convoluted paper ranger trail came full circle when Company E (Ranger), 75th Infantry, was again activated. The provisional ranger company—which after all was the original Company E—was discontinued and became the new Company E. The only difference was that the rangers no longer called themselves the "Riverine Rangers," but continued their newly acquired provisional slogan as "Go-Devil Rangers"—both informal gestures never officially recognized by the Army. The roundabout scheme's only unfortunate effect was breaking Company E's continuity of service from a lineage standpoint.

The new Company E raised two platoons, each containing three teams, but only ranger teams 11, 17, 21, and 24 were filled. The company reported its continuing personnel quandary:

During this reporting period [November 1969 through January 1970] this unit experienced the loss of 75 percent of our combat experienced field troops to normal DEROS [rotation]. As a result we were forced to expedite a recruiting program at brigade and battalion level to gain combat veteran volunteers to fill the void in our unit. During this void period this unit was only able to field four operational teams, which in turn affected the number of combat missions we were able to perform. Maintenance of unit strength is a constant problem because individuals must be volunteers for the unit.[33]

During its first months of service, the Go-Devil Rangers encountered the usual problems locating dispersed guerrilla forces.

During the wet seasons the Viet Cong usually stopped military activities and harvested rice, and could not be separated from the ordinary villagers. From 12 December 1969 to 12 January 1970 the rangers used Hoi Chanhs on the lead insertion helicopters to spot likely enemy activity and then conducted night ambushes against the 1st NVA Regiment. In the spring, Ranger teams 14 and 22 were added to bring the company up to a six-patrol operating level.

During May and June 1970, elements of the 3d Brigade, 9th Infantry Division, invaded the Parrot's Beak area of Cambodia. The Go-Devil Rangers were left behind to monitor Long An Province as an "economy-of-force" precaution. The rangers covered the brigade's Vietnam operational area by staging a number of small roving ambushes, supplemented by aquabush expeditions using Kenner boats. During the same period, the brigade fought without the benefit of its ranger assets during such battles as the struggle for possession of Chantrea, Cambodia.

Following the return of the 3d Brigade from Cambodia, ranger operations were increasingly integrated into the unattended electronic surveillance and radar system. During June the division developed the tactic of vectoring ranger patrols in reaction to ground radar sightings. The radar-vector missions were designed to reconnoiter the exact nature of as many potential targets as possible. The Go-Devil Rangers relied primarily on the Che Tay ground radar array during this development period, but operations were expanded past July to encompass all regions where radar was installed.

Ranger patrols from February through the end of July 1970 were still comparatively risky ventures. The enemy chose to fight only when it was to his advantage and used the cover of heavily populated districts to otherwise blend with the general population. Every patrol could expect either to encounter a peaceful farming settlement or to be involved in a sudden skirmish. For these reasons, most ranger success was experienced along canals and waterways where point targets—such as sampans and other boat traffic—could be readily identified, or within the uninhabited wastelands of the Plain of Reeds. During the first six months of 1970 the rangers killed ninety-three enemy soldiers by direct fire and captured two prisoners, while suffering two rangers killed and twenty-eight wounded in the same period.[34]

The 9th Infantry Division's 3d Brigade rangers were notified of pending disbandment as part of Increment IV (Keystone Robin) of the U.S. Army redeployment from Vietnam. The Go-Devil Rangers ceased combat activity and relocated to Di An base camp on 15

September. The ranger unit commenced stand-down procedures on the following day, held a final ceremony on 28 September, and was reduced to zero strength ten days later. Company E (Ranger), 75th Infantry, was officially inactivated on 12 October 1970.[35]

No other combat recon units waged reconnaissance and intelligence-gathering operations under circumstances more difficult than those with the 9th Infantry Division in Vietnam. Stealth and surprise, the traditional hallmarks of ranger enterprise, were largely denied in the densely populated, pro-Viet Cong countryside. The division patrollers also suffered disproportionate rates of water-induced diseases that often crippled entire teams.

Despite these hazards, the Reliable Reconnaissance Patrollers, Riverine Rangers, and Go-Devil Rangers manifested sound tactical doctrine and imaginative techniques in adjusting to the alien Mekong Delta environment and applied undeviating pressure against the Viet Cong havens and their supply lanes throughout the division term of service in Vietnam.

7

25TH INFANTRY DIVISION

TROPICAL RANGERS

MACKENZIE'S LERPS

The 25th Infantry Division arrived in Vietnam from Hawaii during March 1966 and occupied Cu Chi in the midst of traditional Viet Cong territory northwest of Saigon. Most division operations were conducted in Hau Nghia, Binh Duong, and Tay Ninh provinces. The division was positioned to bar NVA infiltration corridors and clear Viet Cong–dominated areas between Cambodia and the capital. The division was consequently engaged against such enemy bastions as War Zone C, Filhol and Michelin plantations, Boi Loi and Ho Bo woods, Straight Edge and Renegade woods, the Iron Triangle, the Trapezoid, Nui Ba Den, and the Vietnamese-Cambodian border region.

The division area of operations consisted of flat lowlands dominated by swamps, light forests and rubber plantations, some patches of jungle, and cultivated fields. This type of mixed terrain was advantageous to guerrilla warfare. For example, Viet Cong could hide among the thick hedgerows on the three-foot dikes that often partitioned rice paddies. Small partisan bands also traveled along the maze of area irrigation ditches, canals, and streams that crossed the region, and were undeterred by tidal flooding. The water impeded overland movement but offered approach and escape opportunities for the Viet Cong.

The 25th Infantry Division lacked the ability to conduct sustained long-range foot patrolling. The armored 3d Squadron, 4th Cavalry, conducted ordinary mechanized reconnaissance over roads and open countryside. Additionally, the squadron's air cavalry Troop D

130

rendered aerial reconnaissance. The cavalry troop contained one aero rifle platoon, "the Rifles," but the platoon was a specialized unit for securing downed aircraft and performing immediate reaction reconnaissance for helicopters.

During June 1966, division commander Maj. Gen. Frederick C. Weyand ordered that a provisional Long Range Reconnaissance Patrol (LRRP) contingent be organized, manned, and equipped for the division. Volunteers were interviewed throughout the formation, and three officers and thirty-eight enlisted men were finally selected for the new unit. The new force was known as "Mackenzie's Lerps" because it was assigned to the 4th Cavalry "Mackenzie's Raiders"—a regimental nickname stemming from its ruthlessly proficient commander of the 1870–82 Frontier period, Col. Ranald Slidell Mackenzie. An alternative appellation introduced by minority members referred to the LRRP contingent as the "Bad Hand Lerps." Colonel Mackenzie was known to the Indians as "Bad Hand" because of his Civil War–incurred loss of several fingers, while "bad" in Vietnam-era slang signified dangerously proficient.

On 30 June 1966 the 25th Infantry Division LRRP contingent was declared operationally ready. Mackenzie's Lerps were assigned administratively to the 3d Squadron of the 4th Cavalry, but were operationally controlled by the division intelligence section. The patrol cadre completed three weeks of training at Nha Trang, where Special Forces instructors were establishing the MACV Recondo School. The five-man recon teams trained throughout July and mounted only four combat patrols in three provinces (Hau Nghia, Tay Ninh, and Long Khanh).[1]

Mackenzie's Lerps expanded in size, gained more experience, and broadened operational range from August through October as the division relaxed restrictions on the LRRP operating radius. Teams started patrolling at greater distances outside the scattered division fire support bases. During the trimester, nearly thirty unit patrols reconnoitered hostile territory within Hau Nghia, Tay Ninh, and Long An provinces. The contingent also conducted a ninety-two-hour water infiltration training program, using Special Forces–procured sampans. The advanced training was concluded with two successful river-canal raids.[2]

The overall 25th Infantry Division LRRP mission was to locate Viet Cong activity in the division area of operations as directed by the intelligence section. "Pre-operational" patrols were employed to check out areas prior to division operations. These patrols secured information on enemy troop concentrations, bases, and reinforcement or escape potential. During battlefield operations, the patrols either provided point reconnaissance and anti-ambush duty ahead of the infantry or screened the flanks of infantry or mechanized sweeps.

In February 1967 the 25th Infantry Division invaded War Zone C during Operation GADSEN. Mackenzie's Lerps were employed in a significant combat reconnaissance role, and two long-range patrol teams achieved success of considerable magnitude. On 31 January 1967 the first recon team, led by Sgt. Jerry L. Caldwell, was helicoptered along the Rach Beng Go river. The patrol detected the 271st VC Regiment under circumstances that nearly doomed its six men.

The team tried to avoid contact but had to kill four VC soldiers on the first evening to avoid being annihilated. The patrollers managed to stay hidden throughout the night, but were completely surrounded by enemy reinforcements early on the following morning. Artillery fire temporarily kept the enemy at bay while Sergeant Caldwell radioed for emergency extraction. The team reached its landing zone after daybreak and fought off an enemy platoon. Without waiting for the arrival of gunships, utility helicopter pilot Capt. Gary L. Hatfield bravely landed his aircraft as the door gunners raked the nearby woods and rescued the patrol.

On the morning of 3 February the second recon team, led by LRRP commander Capt. Joseph A. Lacey, found a 70th VC Regiment staging area. From late afternoon until dawn on the following morning, the team counted over 150 Viet Cong soldiers filing past its position in small and widely separated groups. Captain Lacey radioed for air strikes, and the team moved out of the area. Aided by helicopter firepower, the patrollers fought their way over a footbridge and eliminated the enemy sentry force. The team destroyed another Viet Cong squad and reached the rendezvous pickup point safely. Major General Weyand credited both teams for pinpointing major enemy forces and for collecting enough information to allow B-52 bombing raids against the menacing VC troop concentrations.[3]

During March 1967, Maj. Gen. John C. F. Tillson III assumed command of the 25th Infantry Division. He continued to employ LRRP contingent patrols on pre-operational intelligence collection and operational screening assignments. From February through April, Mackenzie's Lerps conducted thirty patrols in Hau Nghia, Binh Duong, and Tay Ninh provinces.[4]

The 25th Infantry Division LRRP contingent also faced its first personnel crisis. Most division soldiers rotated from Vietnam as they concluded their one-year combat tours. More qualified recon troops were desperately needed to replace them. Unit recruitment was based on the following notice:

Join LRRP!

• If you can hide in grass for an hour with 15 VC less than 15 meters from you without giving away your presence, as a LRRP team did recently, call the Leapfrog switchboard. Ask for Delta and then for the LRRP. They are looking for men like you.

• You'll train hard and long. The training will be both physical and mental. You'll learn to detect hidden booby traps, disarm them, and assemble traps yourself.

• You will be specifically trained in one area and cross-trained in several other areas.

• After long days of training and learning to work with a team, you will start your job finding and watching enemy's movements, seeing the enemy without being seen.

• You will become a member of the elite Long Range Reconnaissance Patrol, better known as LRRP.

• LRRP is now looking for men who would like to join the team. Volunteers must be above average in military subjects, proficient in map reading, physically fit, and able to swim.

• Infantrymen with Ranger, Airborne, or Recondo training are preferred. However, men without such training can be accepted.

• Volunteers will be accepted on a two week attachment. If they don't meet the LRRP qualifications, they will be sent back to their units.[5]

The "recent" LRRP team experience cited in the recruiting notice was claimed by Staff Sgt. Billy Ponder's patrol. During April his team was sent into the Boi Loi Woods on a three-day mission to locate suspected VC traffic. The team landed by helicopter in midafternoon. Numerous Viet Cong soldiers in the area forced the patrollers to stay hidden in dense undergrowth. Ponder reported, "We just laid there and watched them. I called back to the base camp for artillery support and a chopper to get us out of the VC-infested area." The patrol withdrew quietly to the landing zone and was extracted. Their allocated seventy-two hours working deep in enemy-held territory was cut 95 percent to four short hours. Ponder summed up the mission: "Our mission was to locate and observe their actions, and we did just that. The men saw what they were sent to see and made a safe return without casualties."[6]

While the majority of the 25th Infantry Division fought northwest of Saigon, the detached 3d "Bronco" Brigade battled through Vietnam's Central Highlands. The brigade LRRP teams were in existence from the spring of 1966 until August 1967. During the course of seven major operations, the Bronco Lerps pushed through primeval jungle and caves west of Pleiku, waded across rice paddies from Qui Nhon to Duc Pho, and patrolled the coastal sands of the South China Sea.

The extreme dangers of Bronco recon duty were highlighted on 30 May 1967, when a five-man patrol was infiltrated to locate the 2d VC Regiment in its remote fastness of interior Quang Ngai Province. One of the team members was a battle-hardened soldier who extended his Vietnam tour to "even the score" for the death of his twenty-two-year-old sister during a mortar attack on Cu Chi. According to a later profile by the 135th Military Intelligence Group, the soldier expressed great "hate for the [Vietnamese] people," "had sworn to kill one Viet Cong for each year of her life," and was up to a "confirmed personal body count of eighteen." His rank was reduced, and he was court-martialed for untoward conduct, but one commander recommended "he should not be eliminated from the service."[7]

Revenge-minded individuals usually made poor soldiers, especially in the reconnaissance business, where objective wisdom and level-headed discretion were routine requirements. Unfortunately, the LRRP teams were so short of manpower that combat-experienced volunteers were sometimes taken without proper regard for their actual motivation. This particular soldier joined the Bronco Lerps in late April 1967, just a month prior to the ill-fated mission.

Brigade radio contact with the five-man team was lost soon after 8:30 P.M. on the night of the insertion. Search teams later found the shattered jungle charnel where the patrollers made their last stand at approximately 3:00 A.M. the next morning. Bodies of two patrol members were found on a hillside along with grenade blast impressions and fragments, as well as expended 5.56mm and 7.62mm brass cartridges. No trace of the other three members was found, but blood trails and thrashed vegetation indicated they were probably wounded or dying and dragged off. The final action was a mystery, but it was conceivable that one of the missing patrol members, motivated by revenge, placed contact above observation as a priority objective and thereby triggered the fatal climax. Joseph Edward Fitzgerald of Northbridge, Massachusetts, John Andrew Jakovac of Detroit, Michigan, and Brian Kent McGar of Ceres, California, remain missing in action.[8]

During May 1967 the monsoon season began in the 25th Infantry

Division area. Reconnaissance activities were curtailed by the heavy rains, but the opportunity was used to absorb and train an influx of new recon volunteers. In August, Maj. Gen. Fillmore K. Mearns succeeded Tillson as division commander. That October, Mearns upgraded combat reconnaissance capability by expanding the LRRP contingent into an enlarged Long Range Patrol Detachment, still known as Mackenzie's Lerps. The attachment to the 3d Squadron, 4th Cavalry, "Mackenzie's Raiders" was solidified, the aerial squadron commander gained the ability to direct the detachment into battle, and patrol combinations were introduced for flexible combat options. These included two-team "ambush groups" and four-team "stay-behind groups."

The detachment comprised a headquarters, mess section, communication section, and two patrol platoons. Each platoon contained a headquarters section and eight six-man teams. About half of the 118 required personnel were obtained by absorbing the former division LRRP contingent. However, fifty-three more volunteers needed to be secured from regular division ranks or the replacement depot. Most urgently needed were infantry sergeants and radio-trained supervisors or operators.[9]

Newly formed teams were trained by existing LRRP cadre and the 4th Cavalry's 3d Squadron artillery forward observation, air liaison, communications, and medical personnel. The team members gained expertise in various patrolling methods by learning helicopter landing, rope ladders, and rappelling; foot-mobile entry and evasion; and small boat handling. The men also rehearsed a technique called "tailgating," where patrollers were dropped from the open rear exits of armored personnel carriers passing down hedgerow-lined jungle avenues.

The most successful patrol techniques in the 25th Infantry Division were found to be stay-behind surveillance missions. The teams arranged these missions by mixing with regular forces and remaining in position after the larger units left the area. Missions lasting three days or more were favored, because the Viet Cong became less vigilant after they believed the Americans were gone. According to the division intelligence section, the least desirable infiltration options were boat or raft insertion, because of their higher visibility and the degree of skill required. Some teams, however, used waterborne methods effectively.

From 18 November to 23 December 1967, division recon teams working with Vietnamese Provincial Reconnaissance Unit (PRU) scouts helped to uncover and explore a massive tunnel complex during Operation ATLANTA. The two tunnel networks extended northwest from the vicinity of the juncture of the Song Thi Tinh and Song Saigon. A few recon-PRU teams traveled for three days and nights while searching over five miles of the subterranean labyrinth. They discovered side tunnels running to either Ben Cat in the east or the Ho Bo Woods in the west. At some points the tunnel system was collapsed because of B-52 bombing, but the PRU scouts would detect another spot to dig through. The upper levels of the tunnel maze were relocated several times in this fashion. The tunnel system was a major VC underground infiltration route through the Iron Triangle.[10]

COBRA LIGHTNING PATROLLERS

On 20 December 1967, Company F (Long Range Patrol), 50th Infantry, was raised from the provisional long-range patrol detachment to officially provide the 25th Infantry Division with a combat patrolling capability. The 118-man binary company included two field platoons composed of seven six-man teams each. The company was now regimentally distinguished from the 4th Cavalry and acquired the new call sign "Cobra Lightning Patrollers." The Lightning was derived from the 25th Infantry Division's nickname "Tropic Lightning," and Cobra was the unit call sign—giving rise to C-number-designated recon teams.

The company's eighty-four recon patrollers were chosen on a strictly voluntary basis. Volunteers were thoroughly screened by the company commander and received several weeks of "shakedown" training before they were finally selected to become team members. The company program was geared to send as many soldiers as possible to the MACV Recondo School at Nha Trang. The company completed training and returned to combat at the outset of Tet-68. Light patrol teams collected military intelligence, while heavy patrol teams acted on this information to disrupt enemy lines of communication or engage targets of opportunity.

During the war there were few instances where the combat reconnaissance components of both sides met on the battlefield. The clash of opposite recon forces, however, could produce furious fighting when important objectives were at stake and each side reinforced. Late on the afternoon of 29 January 1968, a Cobra Lightning patrol was helicoptered into the northern edge of the Ho Bo Woods. Its mission was to find the enemy reported to be moving in that sector and to direct reinforcements into the contact area. At the same time the elite Viet Cong 272d Regiment Reconnaissance Company was serving as the vanguard for communist columns marching toward Saigon—just prior to the start of the major enemy Tet-68 offensive.

At 4:25 P.M. the two recon elements, representing some of the most dedicated soldiers on either side, clashed, and the action escalated rapidly. Machine gun crossfire and automatic rifles riddled the dense jungle as patrollers from different armies tossed grenades and skillfully matched moves with countermoves. The American patrollers radioed for "the Rifles," the aero rifle platoon. The Viet Cong reconnaissance troops called up lead companies of their own forces. The American headquarters told the Rifles to hold on to their positions until more help arrived. The VC headquarters ordered their recon strike force to shield redirection of main columns away from the compromised pathway.

Late-afternoon shadows were falling over the jungle as the Viet Cong slipped around and isolated the patrollers and cavalrymen. An hour later, Major General Mearns sent in the 2d Battalion, 27th Infantry, "Wolfhounds," during a bold twilight air assault. The arrival of powerful American airmobile reinforcements expedited the VC command's persistent instructions to their recon element: hold out and cover the shifting of the main regimental column. The battle was on.

Dug-in enemy gunners riddled the three-company "Wolfhound" relief forces with streams of tracer-lit fire in the deepening evening sky. Capt. Michael Wikon led Company C across the landing field toward the dark tree line as his troops charged through a hail of automatic weapons fire and rocket explosions. The infantrymen returned fire with rifles blazing as they entered the dense undergrowth. The Americans pushed through the woods to reach the beleaguered cavalrymen and patrollers, but progress was interrupted by bursts of well-aimed fire. Platoon leader Staff Sgt. James McCosh recalled, "The VC would wait until you were looking down their gun barrels before they'd shoot."

The Viet Cong reconnaissance troops offered staunch resistance as their patrol squads opened up at lethal ambush ranges, fell back, and fought again in a highly skilled display of delaying ferocity. The VC recon troops were armed with light machine guns, AK47 and SKS assault rifles, and new RPG-2 rocket launchers. Their ammunition, according to one division intelligence report, "seemed limitless." Wolfhound battalion commander Lt. Col. Walter E. Adams reported, "We fought an enemy armed to the teeth in there, and fought all the way through the woods to that platoon."[11]

The 27th Infantry battalion troops finally reached their besieged comrades after advancing 300 yards. Sixty-four Viet Cong recon troops died rather than surrender, and the Americans captured only one prisoner, a VC soldier so badly wounded that he could neither keep fighting nor get away. The recon troops of both armies claimed mission success. The Company F patrollers and Troop D Rifles held their ground successfully until reinforcements arrived. The VC recon company masked the change of direction of their main column and enabled it to reach Tet-68 jump-off positions.[12]

Following the Tet-68 battles, the Cobra Lightning Patrollers became involved in a sustained campaign to weaken Viet Cong regroupment and replenishment attempts northeast of Saigon. Important patrol lessons were learned and relearned during the year as new members processed into the teams. The company's operations were typified by the 5 April 1968 surveillance mission of the five-man recon team Cobra-17, led by Sp4 Gregory R. Kelly. On the first night, the team observed a female Viet Cong nurse carrying a medical aid bag as she met with a squad of VC soldiers farther up the trail. Later that night the team members heard several boat engines from the direction of a nearby canal. At daylight on 6 April the patrol moved to a new location and established another overnight surveillance position. There was American communications wire strewn around the area, but the patrollers disregarded the abandoned lines.

About 6:35 P.M. in the evening, three Viet Cong soldiers approached the team position. The enemy trio were checking the discarded commo-wire circuits and followed the cable until they were directly in front of the team's position. The VC soldiers spotted one of the team's M18 claymore mines and began following the new wire line. The patrollers detonated two claymores and engaged the enemy. Two Viet Cong were killed, but the third sprayed the jungle with automatic rifle fire as he fell wounded. The bullets struck Specialist Kelly in the chest and lower right side and hit another team member in the arm. Assistant team leader Sergeant Hernandez radioed for extraction, and the team was lifted out by helicopter at 7:09 P.M. Specialist Kelly died of his wounds at the 12th Evacuation Hospital. The patrol ultimately paid a high price for ignoring obvious danger signs—such as wires, which habitually attracted enemy attention—in choosing its nocturnal hide-out.[13]

Many Cobra Lightning patrols were "walk-out" ventures that formed part of the roving security around the larger Cu Chi vicinity. Just outside the division main base camp at Cu Chi was Observation Post (OP) Ann-Margret, a wire-entangled outpost guarding the wooden bridge that led to the Filhol Plantation. Night ambush missions were routinely staged from OP Ann-Margret to discourage enemy demolition raids against the bridge. Five-man recon team Cobra-15, led by Staff Sergeant Soetaert, established a night ambush position outside Ann-Margret well after dark on 6 April 1968. The night passed quietly, but the team saw three Viet Cong soldiers on the following morning. Staff Sergeant Soetaert relocated the team. The next night also passed uneventfully, except for sounds of distant rifle shots.

On the morning of 8 April the patrollers organized a river outpost and observed several large sampans. Most looked suspicious, but the patrol did not fire because the boats were flying South Vietnamese flags. A night curfew on friendly canal traffic went into effect at sunset, but more sampans glided past the team position. The Americans shot one boater, who was wearing military suspenders with equipment, and then withdrew to their night defensive position. Everything was quiet until 9:10 P.M., when three rifle grenades suddenly exploded inside the small patrol perimeter. The surprise blasts caused several casualties, and Soetaert moved his wounded men from spot to spot until they succeeded in reaching the Ann-Margret outpost gate at dawn.[14]

The Viet Cong were not immune from making careless mistakes. During May several patrols were staked out along canals and streams to harass Viet Cong infiltration forces. On 3 May two six-man teams were combined into an ambush group and inserted along the canal junction in the Ho Bo Woods. The teams established positions in a wooded area, where several trails led to waterfront boat-beaching locations near the canal intersection. The group divided into a six-man ambush team with two men to each flank and a pair of patrollers watching the rear.

The night was pitch-black. Fog rising from the swampy water obscured even nightscope visibility. At 10:30 P.M., however, right flank assistant patrol leader Sgt. Rodney D. Tavares heard a woman's voice on an approaching sampan. He recalled, "If it hadn't been for that noisy woman, the VC might have slipped right through our ambush patrol." When the sampan reached the middle of the preset kill zone, the patrollers opened fire with automatic weapons and hand grenades. The ammunition-laden sampan exploded violently as the patrollers fell back to an alternate defensive perimeter. During the rest of the night the team heard more sampans and radioed for gunships that strafed and rocketed the canal. At daybreak the patrol found a demolished fourteen-foot sampan near the canal and saw sandals and debris floating in the water. The patrollers booby-trapped the sampan wreckage and moved to another location farther along the canal.[15]

During the day, Company F commander Lt. William Shanaman arrived at the patrol location with an M60 machine gun and more personnel, reinforcing the ambush group into a full stay-behind group. In the evening the twenty soldiers moved into a new position using three staggered movements. The new ambush position was organized into an eleven-man ambush zone with three security troops to each flank and in the rear. At 9:00 P.M. the patrollers heard an explosion that sounded like someone at the previous night's ambush site had struck the booby-trapped sampan.

Later that evening, however, the Cobra Lightning stay-behind group experienced a harrowing action. Right security team leader Staff Sgt. Russell Guy sighted a sampan and alerted the main ambush group to anticipate its arrival, but the sampan never moved farther downstream. The Viet Cong boat crew spotted Guy's position in turn and beached its craft immediately. Sergeant Guy heard the Viet Cong come ashore and move around him. He opened fire into the brush, giving the Americans in the main ambush zone no choice but to commence firing at extended range into other nearby sampans. There were several explosions in the water, however, followed by groaning noises as the American grenades and machine guns found their mark.

Then events took an untoward turn for the Americans. One of the enemy soldiers jumped from his sinking sampan into the canal, swam ashore, and surprised the left flank security position. He fired into the brush with his AK47, wounding two patrollers, and escaped into the night. Sergeant Guy's position on the other side of the main ambush zone was also hit by enemy fire, but succeeded in disengaging without casualties. The Americans regrouped away from the canal, and Lieutenant Shanaman radioed for artillery shellfire to discourage other VC prowlers. Late on the afternoon of 5 May the four teams were extracted from the canal juncture. They claimed destroying seven sampans, either by direct fire or air strikes, and killing up to twenty Viet Cong.[16]

Much of the 25th Infantry Division's operating area was dominated by the granite monolithic slab of Nui Ba Den, "Mountain of the Black Virgin," a huge solitary peak rising abruptly from the vast agricultural plain about fifty miles northwest of Saigon. The sacred mountain marked the legendary spot where a beautiful princess died rather than submit to Chinese conquerors, and its rugged, boulder-strewn slopes offered timeless sanctuary to guerrilla fighters throughout Vietnamese history. During the Second Indochina War, the jumble of giant stones and caverns formed a natural Viet Cong bastion and storage network. The communists held the hillside, but the 3,200-foot summit was crowned by a helicopter-sustained American communications complex. The safety of this mountaintop signal station depended on periodic reconnaissance of the hostile mountainside.

During July a Cobra Lightning patrol led by Sgt. Willard R. Ethridge was given the mission of airlanding on the peak and then moving down the slope for two days to search out enemy positions. The team members were instructed to radio for helicopter extraction once they reached the rice field beneath the mountain, at the conclusion of their forty-eight-hour reconnoitering descent. Throughout the first day the six-man team gingerly threaded its way down steep trails and over mammoth rocks. The perilous downhill trek was complicated by misting clouds that obscured the often-sheer gradient of the enemy-infested slope.

On the second day, as the patrollers neared the bottom of the mountain, the point man spotted a large group of Viet Cong blocking the planned exit path. Sergeant Ethridge realized that slipping past the VC assemblage would be suicidal—"We couldn't get through 'Charlie' so we tried to go back up and around and come down again." The team crept down in another direction. More Viet Cong were sighted around the jungle-covered boulders that overlooked the patrol's alternative route. Sergeant Ethridge directed his men to climb higher and sought a third pathway beyond the enemy camp. The team's final daylight attempt to reach the base of Nui Ba Den on schedule was also deterred by another barricade of enemy troops. The team stayed huddled miserably on the face of the mountain throughout the night.

Further attempts on the third day to get off the slope also met with frustration. Specialist Miller's leg was severely injured by a falling rock. Another man suffered heat exhaustion. Sergeant Ethridge stopped in a rocky gulch and radioed for help. Patrol member Sp4 Joseph Hitchens remembered, "We were out of food and water. When it rained we would catch the water running off the rocks in our canteens. The water was a little dirty, but it was good."

Company F sent two other recon patrols uphill to rescue the trapped team. Both teams were stopped by VC machine gun nests hidden among the narrow cave entrances and rock crevices. Enemy rocket-propelled grenades hurtled down to explode among the American ranks, forcing both teams to withdraw. The Cobra Lightning patrollers reinforced the survivors, assembled a twenty-five-man reaction platoon, and made a fresh assault up the mountain. The commando platoon gained 200 yards in bitter fighting, stopped for the night, and was completely pinned down by enemy fire on the following morning.

The plight of the beleaguered patrol worsened on the fourth day. The team members were weakened by their harrowing ordeal, mountaineering injuries, and lack of sustenance. They knew that American infantry charges had failed to reach them and that the Viet Cong, alerted to the adverse situation, were combing the mountainside. Pfc. Roger F. Van Rensselaer summed up the team's bleak predicament: " 'Charlie' was up above us, down below us, on the right, and on the left.''

The six patrollers were caught on a cliff 1,200 feet above the rice paddies. The terrain prohibited ordinary helicopter extraction, but a medical evacuation aircraft tried to drop a hoist for the injured man. Two Cobra gunships from Troop D of "Mackenzie's Raiders" hovered near the cliffside patrol position and rocketed the area in support of the noon rescue attempt. The enemy remained sheltered by the rocky outcrops and directed close-range fire at every endeavor to lift out Specialist Miller. A Cayuse light observation helicopter piloted by WO Stephen R. Patterson flew Troop D commander Major Fred R. Michelson over the scene. He signaled for more aerial firepower. Two Cobras from the 25th Aviation Battalion, two Huey gunships from the 4th Cavalry squadron, and two Air Force tactical fighter-bombers joined the original Cobras pounding the enemy-held locality.

A second hoist-equipped medical helicopter approached the patrol under darkening storm clouds. The pilot tried to get close enough for the hoist operator to drop the mechanism. Enemy sniper fire hit the aircraft and knocked out its radio system. Further airborne maneuvering was prevented when the threatening clouds erupted into a violent tropical thunderstorm. The torrential afternoon downpour forced all helicopters to return to Tay Ninh. By the time the storm ceased, it was nearing dusk. Major Michelson decided that his only choice was to try a resupply drop to the cornered patrol, hoping they could make it through the night.

The helicopter gunships returned to the mountainside and barraged it with another concentrated dose of rocket and mini-gun fire. Warrant Officer Patterson's Cayuse helicopter arrived with Major Michelson, who leaned out on the skid and swung a bag of food, water, and radio batteries toward the team's granite ledge. The satchel bounced off the rocks, fell over the cliff, and tumbled into the Viet Cong base camp far below. Then Patterson noticed a large boulder that was just wide enough for one skid. He reported, ''I hovered down and put the toe of my right skid on the rock to steady the aircraft because of the bad updrafts. The Lerps handed out the injured man to Major Michelson.''

The small helicopter hung precariously close to the cliff's edge, but the evacuation was completed successfully. Patterson took Miller to Tay Ninh and then brought the small light helicopter back for the other men. Alone this time to save weight, he balanced the tip of the right skid delicately on the rain-slick jutting boulder. The aircraft rotor blades swung dangerously close to nearby trees and other rocks. Private Van Rensselaer and Sgt. Ralph J. Hosey leaped from the ledge to the skid and into the tiny chopper. Patterson said, ''Every time they jumped on the aircraft, it would lurch, and I'd cut down a few small trees with my rotor.''

Nightfall enveloped Nui Ba Den, but Patterson decided to pilot his craft back for the remaining three patrollers. Sergeant Ethridge radioed that the team still possessed one smoke grenade. Patterson advised them to save it, in case he could not complete another successful lift-out. Patterson flew close to the darkened mountain and hunted for the right landing spot. At one point he flew right over the Viet Cong base camp and was sprayed with automatic rifle fire. Finally, he found the ledge and perched his Cayuse on the same hazardous, slippery stone overhanging the flatland 1,000 feet beneath.

The men donned their equipment and rucksacks for the final try. As agreed, Ethridge and Hitchens jumped on first. Pfc. Merilan Henry volunteered to go last, but the tiny helicopter looked full and unsteady. In fact, Patterson was struggling to recover the aircraft from a lurch caused by the added weight. Henry stated, ''I couldn't wait. I just dove in. All I could do was throw my feet on, with the rest of my body hanging over the side. I had my right hand up on the pilot's chair, and the team leader was holding on to my left hand.'' Henry dangled from the side as Patterson gently steered the helicopter away from the steep slope and into Tay Ninh. What appeared impossible was accomplished not once, but three times by the gallant pilot. The personal valor and professional bonding between long-range patrollers and aviators constituted one of the finest legacies of the Vietnam conflict.[17]

In August 1968, Maj. Gen. Ellis W. Williamson took over the 25th Infantry Division. He redirected Company F operations toward gathering information about, and then harassing, the Viet Cong ''Third Offensive'' outside Tay Ninh. The VC attacks were broken, and Cobra Lightning teams resumed normal patrolling patterns in the territory around Trang Bang, inside the Ho Bo Woods and Boi Loi Woods, and along the upper Saigon River. Special emphasis was placed on the Viet Cong–occupied "Mushroom" river bend, and virtually every patrol in this region made significant contact or observations. For example, on 16 November, team Cobra-15, led by Staff Sgt. David H. Ridell, discovered a hidden rice cache in the Mushroom along the riverbank. Most of the five tons of rice were lifted out in nets slung underneath Chinook cargo helicopters, but 2,700 pounds had to be dumped in the river before nightfall.[18]

On 5 November 1968 a patrol-related skirmish led to serious aircraft losses. Just before noon a recon team ambushed a solitary boat as it plied one of the canals traversing the Ho Bo Woods. The Troop D aero rifle platoon of Mackenzie's Raiders was inserted as a precautionary measure while the patrol was safely extracted. When the helicopters returned to lift out the Rifles—now two miles west of Bau Dieu village—the Viet Cong launched a surprise attack. The helicopters were hit by close-range machine gun fire and salvos of rocket-propelled grenades. Two of the five helicopters burst into flames on the landing zone and were destroyed. The other three helicopters sustained heavy damage, and two managed to gain some altitude but then crashed. Only one crippled aircraft, flown by a wounded crew, was able to return to base.[19]

During December 1968, fewer patrols were sent into the Mushroom, but intense recon activity took place along other parts of the Saigon River and inside the Boi Loi and Ho Bo Woods. On 15 December a failed prisoner snatch mission outside Cu Chi led to a serious reverse. Eleven-man recon team 14, led by Staff Sergeant Byrd (with Captain Dawson as assistant team leader), was temporarily separated while posting security farther up a trail and retrieving claymore mines from their previous location. A rocket-propelled grenade suddenly exploded among the patrollers bringing in the mines, wounding several and triggering three claymores that wounded more men. Seven patrollers were wounded in the Viet Cong onslaught, but the team repelled the VC attacks until finally extracted by helicopters. During January 1969, reconnaissance was confined south of the Mushroom and east of Bao Don, within the Boi Loi Woods.[20]

TROPICAL RANGERS

At the beginning of 1969 the Army Department reorganized the 75th Infantry as the parent regiment for various infantry patrol units, and the Cobra Lightning Patrollers were transformed into ranger Company F of that infantry regiment. On 1 February 1969, division commander General Williamson activated Company F (Ranger),

75th Infantry, from the assets of deactivated Company F, 50th Infantry, for 25th Infantry Division reconnaissance.

Ranger Company F provided each brigade with teams to collect
military intelligence and, if the opportunity arose, to inflict casualties on or capture enemy personnel. Each of the three field platoons initially contained three or four eight-man teams. Ranger
teams 11–14 supported the 1st Brigade covering Tay Ninh Province.
Ranger teams 21–23 supported the 2d Brigade in Hau Nghia Province, and Ranger teams 31–33 assisted the 3d Brigade, also in Hau
Nghia Province. At least one sniper-qualified individual was assigned to each team.

The rangers were known as either "Fox Rangers" (derived from
F for "Foxtrot" in the ICAO phonetic alphabet adopted by the U.S.
military in 1956) or the "Tropical Rangers," from the 25th Infantry
Division's nickname "Tropic Lightning." Ranger teams reached
objective areas by foot patrol, helicopter airlift, naval or boat insertion, or armored personnel carrier. A common ranger mode of
entry into populated sectors involved blending with a larger infantry force and then remaining behind in surreptitious positions.

During spring 1969 the Tropical Rangers became involved in the
division counteroffensive against NVA/VC encroachments toward
Saigon. The rangers reported and disrupted enemy logistical lines
supporting the Viet Cong thrust at the capital, and patrols encountered sporadic enemy portage units along the Saigon River and near
the Cambodian border. Throughout June the rangers secured information and timely intelligence that helped to defeat a renewed
enemy push against Tay Ninh city.

In September 1969, Maj. Gen. Harris W. Hollis assumed command of the 25th Infantry Division. Beginning in October, he
switched ranger employment from military intelligence collection
to raiding enemy targets. The rangers were placed under the supervision of the division operations section and converted into an
infantry raider force. Major General Hollis explained:

> Rangers in this division were used offensively as opposed to the more
> conventional and passive role—that of gathering intelligence. We
> also employed the rangers on rescue missions, with sniper teams,
> with ambush patrols, on reconnaissance missions, and in combined
> operations with the U.S. Navy and [South] Vietnamese forces, and
> on nighttime helicopter raids to secure prisoners.[21]

Each of the three ranger field platoons directly supported one
maneuver brigade. The division operations staff monitored overall

utilization, with the advice and assistance of the ranger company commander, but the brigade commanders planned and controlled their ranger platoon missions. Ranger operating methods were redirected toward ambush and combat reconnaissance exploitation. Air rescue missions were performed with sniper teams. Ranger snatch missions used helicopter raids to capture prisoners. Rangers also responded to helicopter "sniff" missions that tried to pinpoint enemy presence with mechanical detectors capable of measuring human-emitted chemical particles.

A typical mission was executed on 10 October 1969. Ranger commander Capt. William D. Watson inserted teams 11, 12, and 23 east of Trang Bang, near Cau Truong Chua stream, to search for a reported North Vietnamese mortar unit. Staff Sgt. Kenneth D. Cecil led the seven-man ranger team 12 into the densely populated farming region by mixing with a Vietnamese-American Combined Reconnaissance and Intelligence Platoon (CRIP). The ranger team remained hidden in stay-behind positions after the CRIP departed.

Staff Sergeant Cecil established a five-man ambush position among the dense hedgerows and situated a two-man observation post fifteen yards away. During midafternoon, Cecil spotted a lone Viet Cong soldier. He told one of the observation teams to engage the suspect, but his men could not see the targeted VC soldier in the dense underbrush. Sergeant Cecil decided to personally crawl through the shrubbery and get the VC himself, but the noise of his movement attracted the Viet Cong's attention. The enemy rifleman spotted the team leader, but Cecil fired first. The VC was wounded but managed to turn and disappear into the jungle undergrowth.

A short time later, the team members heard ten rifle shots, sequenced like signaling reports, southwest of their position. Staff Sergeant Cecil dispatched three men to investigate the firing. The trio found the wounded Viet Cong crawling across a field. They started to go after him but refrained from further movement when they suddenly heard more signal shots from another direction and a Vietnamese woman shouting in the distance. The three rangers left the wounded enemy soldier and went back to report the situation to Sergeant Cecil at the ambush position.

Cecil realized that the team position was now compromised. At 4:30 P.M. he withdrew the team to a new location in the darkening forest. Rain started pouring a few minutes after the patrollers settled into their new ambush site. Just before 5:00 P.M., Specialist Hix, peering beyond his rain-drenched machine gun, saw a North Vietnamese scout ambling into range. He opened fire, and the NVA soldier fell. Almost immediately, the team came under fire from several directions as enemy weapons opened up, wounding Kit Carson scout Trinh Van Lon. A group of North Vietnamese infantrymen stormed out of the rainy jungle, but the rangers fired selectively to conserve ammunition. They killed four more NVA soldiers, and the enemy charge faltered.

Ranger radioman Specialist Zellner radioed for artillery fire on the enemy target, but was told that the proximity of two other ranger teams precluded the use of explosive rounds. The only artillery support they received consisted of white phosphorous airbursts that exploded overhead with little effect. The headquarters had placed armed helicopters on standby back at base, in order to make up for the artillery deficiency, but these aircraft missions were scrubbed by the tropical rainstorm. Fortunately for the small ranger team, the NVA withdrew rather than continue the fight, and the weather cleared before enemy reinforcements could arrive. At that point, aerial gunship runs were used to discourage further maneuvering against the rangers.

Staff Sergeant Cecil carefully moved back to the original kill zone and, under the cover of circling helicopters, stripped the dead NVA scout of his AK47 rifle and three ammunition magazines and identification papers. The team then boarded a helicopter and returned to Fire Support Base Pershing, where the recovered papers were analyzed. As a result, ranger team 12 was credited with gaining new information on the whereabouts of the 268th VC Regiment's mortar battalion.[22]

From November 1969 through the end of April 1970, most of the Tropical Ranger teams under Capt. Paul C. Schierholz were employed in direct support of the 3d Brigade. These combat reconnaissance efforts were directed against the enemy An Ninh infiltration corridor. The ranger company performed about ninety patrols monthly, and worked target sectors at Nui Ba Den, north of Cu Chi, outside Tri Tam, and within both the Straight Edge Woods and the Renegade Woods. The rangers reported killing nearly a hundred enemy troops by direct fire, but body counts were largely meaningless in the combat reconnaissance trade. More important, the rangers disclosed the absence of enemy troops in certain areas and obtained essential intelligence from four captives, enabling 3d Brigade to operate more effectively.[23]

The most serious ranger incident during the An Ninh corridor reconnaissance campaign occurred in response to division intelligence assessments sent to 3d Brigade at the end of March. The intelligence summaries indicated that sizable Viet Cong elements

were slipping back into the Renegade Woods. The woods constituted a well-known VC refitting area and were covered by vine-
choked double-canopy jungle. Helicopter insertion was extremely
difficult, because the few open fields consisted of high elephant
grass divided by hedgerows and containing either brush or deadwood.

On the morning of 2 April 1970 the 3d Brigade commander, Col.
Olin E. Smith, directed Captain Schierholz to send two ranger teams
into the Renegade Woods and scout out the situation. Within an
hour a thirteen-man recon strike force, composed of ranger teams
38 and 39, was assembled for the mission. First Lt. Philip J. Norton
commanded the assembled force and was seconded by Sfc. Alvin W.
Floyd and Sfc. Colin K. Hall. The rangers were taken into the
region by Huey helicopters from Mackenzie's Raiders. The mission
aircraft commander decided to air-assault the rangers into two large
bomb craters that appeared to offer some degree of initial protection.

At 8:35 A.M. the rangers landed in the cratered landing zone,
near a bend in the South Vam Co Dong river, and proceeded toward
the tree line in the direction of Ap Ben Dinh, a ruined village. The
column was approaching the forest when it was suddenly raked by
an enemy light machine gun. The bullets wounded Sgt. Fred B.
Stuckey, severed the handset cord to Lieutenant Norton's radio, and
blasted Sp4 Donald E. Purdy's M16 rifle out of his hands. Stuckey
and Purdy were able to silence the machine gun nest by throwing
hand grenades.

The experienced rangers realized that a machine gun indicated
the presence of a larger force. Lieutenant Norton secured suppressive fire against the woods from Cobra helicopters overhead. He
then began maneuvering team 39 forward, behind the aerial strafing
runs, while covered by automatic weapons fire from Sgt. First Class
Floyd's team 38. The rangers advanced to the eastern edge of the
woods, where they ran into more determined opposition. At this
point Pfc. Steven Perez's usually reliable M79 grenade launcher,
the only one carried by the force, malfunctioned after firing a single
shot. Perez had 249 rounds left, so he turned his M79 into a "light
mortar substitute" by firing up into the air, but the weapon lost the
firepower advantages of aimed, direct fire.

Ranger team 38 followed at a distance and reached the largest
bomb crater, which was thrirty feet across and fifteen feet deep.
the latter ranger team was hit near this position by a deluge of
rockets and machine gun fire. The enemy fire killed Sergeant First
Class Floyd and Sgt. Michael F. Thomas, and mortally wounded

Sp4 Donald W. Tinney. The blast that killed Floyd also destroyed his radio, putting the rangers temporarily out of communication and cut off from outside assistance.

Lieutenant Norton directed his first team back to the large crater, where the rangers could be consolidated for a defensive stand. The retreat was made possible by the individual heroism of two sergeants. Sergeant First Class Hall coolly destroyed one menacing enemy machine gun with hand grenades and accurate rifle fire. Sgt. Charles P. Avery eliminated the enemy rocket crew before they could cause more immediate damage, but was severely wounded in the process.

Lieutenant Norton dragged the dying Tinney into the bomb crater. By salvaging the handset and wire from the ruined radio on Floyd's body, the rangers were able to make their remaining radio set operable again. Norton called for medical evacuation aircraft and reaction troops. Headquarters advised them that no reaction force could be spared, and that the Cobra gunships were now out of ammunition and returning to the base. Fortunately, the light observation helicopters—also out of ammunition—refused to leave and continued to buzz the NVA lines with "dry gun-runs." This valiant tactic temporarily kept the enemy from mass-assulting the ranger position.

The rangers realigned themselves to cover all sides of the crater in expectation of enemy charges. The patrol warded off continual probes. They initially had the firepower of two M60 machine guns, but Pfc. Kenneth J. Langland's M60 machine gun jammed after firing 850 rounds. Machine gunner Pfc. Raymond L. Allmon then expended the rest of the M60 ammunition, including a belt taken off Thomas's body, and then used his .45 automatic pistol. By 9:20 A.M. every ranger was almost out of individual ammunition, and many were experiencing weapon malfunctions.

The rangers realized their own position was now untenable and prepared for the inevitable enemy overrun. Both teams were surrounded and under fire from all directions. Their casualties already totaled two dead, one dying, and six wounded. Yet the rangers calmly continued to man their positions around the rim of the crater and countered further enemy advances. Sergeant Stuckey personally killed one enemy grenadier who had slithered through the upturned earth to within grenade-throwing range.

Realizing the desperate ranger circumstances, WO1 James Tonelli and Capt. Philip Tocco bodly flew their UH-1H Huey helicopter onto the fire-swept field. The pilot frantically signaled Norton to get his men aboard. The rangers scrambled for the helicopter as it was racked with enemy hits. Crew chief Sp5 Charles E. Lowe kept the enemy at bay by sweeping the trees with sustained aircraft machine gun fire. Door gunner Pfc. Richard K. Adams, himself a former Tropical Ranger, leaped off the helicopter and dragged Tinney on board. The damaged aircraft, overloaded with fifteen people, lifted off "with maximum torque and severe vertical vibration" and somehow managed to clear all the trees. Later the shattered helicopter was examined by Bell Aircraft Company technicians, who "expressed utter amazement that it was still able to fly."[24]

The 25th Infantry Division airmobiled the 2d Battalion of the 27th Infantry "Wolfhounds" onto the battlefield, where it linked up with the mechanized 2d Battalion, 22d Infantry. The infantrymen discovered that ranger teams 38 and 39 had inadvertently encountered strongly entrenched forces of the 27 1st VC Regiment. Captain Schierholz observed, "At the time [of the initial encounter] the forces available for immediate commitment in support of the ranger teams proved to be inadequate. Employment of ranger teams to react to intelligence reports allows rapid exploitation of enemy sightings. However, the size and nature of the team makes it necessary to be able to 'pile on' quickly should contact with a large unit be initiated. A light [aviation] fire team should be on immediate standby along with a minimum of one rifle company ready to reinforce."[25]

During the spring the rangers were assigned to train selected Vietnamese units as part of a division-wide project instituted by MACV as the "Progress Together Campaign." The Tropical Rangers' portion of the program consisted of working with the 4th Battalion of the 49th Regiment from the 25th ARVN Division. The training increased South Vietnamese proficiency and allowed soldiers from both armies to gain better insights into different military methods, but imposed additional burdens on scarce ranger resources and detracted from overall mission capability. The tasking of elite ranger personnel to train straight infantry units, instead of other Vietnamese rangers, also caused concern about headquarters' cognizance of ranger capability.

Maj. Gen. Edward Bautz Jr. assumed command of the 25th Infantry Division in April and sent division forces across the Vietnamese border on 6 May 1970, with the objective of destroying North Vietnamese sanctuaries inside Cambodia. The rangers were ideally suited to perform combat reconnaissance in Cambodia, but the division employed aerial helicopter recon (with its 3d Squadrons of both 4th Cavalry and 17th Cavalry) instead of foot patrolling.

This was not a satisfactory solution, because ground teams could find many locations not observable from the air.

During the Cambodian incursion, some Company F patrols were fielded in the vicinity of the Rach Beng Go river, along the Cambodian border, but most ranger teams stayed on "economy-of-force" assignments inside South Vietnam. For example, ranger patrols in enemy secret base areas 353 and 354, which straddled the frontier, were kept primarily on the Vietnamese side of the border. The ranger Third Field Platoon remained entirely ihn Hau Nghia, Tay Ninh, and Binh Dutong provinces rendering support to the 3d Brigade.[26]

On 28 June 1970, General Bautz overhauled ranger utilization and reoriented ranger operational techniques. He discarded most of their raiding functions and reemphasized acquistion of information through stealth, avoidance of contact, and passive surveillance. Ranger combat reaction to targets of opportunity became a secondary function, performed by direct action mission teams. The ranger platoons were shifted from brigade control and consolidated directly under division command. Electronic warfare measures increasingly dictated field ranger employment. The rangers planted unattended ground sensors and responed to radar target acquisition.[27]

The Nature of the redirected recon campaign was typified by ranger operations from August to October, when eighty-five patrols killed only four enemy soldiers directly and took four prisoners, but succeeded in gathering "superior information confirming or denying presence of enemy activity." Ground surveillance devices or airborne personnel detectors ("sniffers") became increasingly relied on to monitor NVA/VC movement in dangerous outer areas. Data from the sensor fields was correlated by the division intelligence staff and ranger teams were dispatched accordingly.[28]

In November 1970 the 25th Infantry Division was alerted that it would be redeployed from Vietnam by the end of the year, except for one bridge. On 8 November 1970 the 25th Infantry Division's 2d Brigade at Xuan Loc was reorganized as the separate brigade that would remain in Vietnam. The brigade represented a third of the former division strength, and a smaller ranger company was tailored as the brigade's residual ranger element. From 14 to 18 November the Tropical Rangers were halved from an authorized strength of 123 to a final configuration of sixty-two rangers.[29]

The independent 2d Brigade's area of operations encompassed Bien Hoa and southern Long Khanh and northern Phuoc Tuy provinces, including part of the vital Long Binh logistical complex.

Actual ranger field service focused on surveillance and interdiction of enemy lines of communication in the region. The teams found and destroyed numerous enemy storage depots around Xuan Loc. The rangers also operated against the Viet Cong "shadow supply system" along Highway 1. The success of the final ranger campaign was perhaps best reflected by the unusually quiet 1971 Tet holidays—a traditional Viet Cong attack period that was remarkably free of significant enemy offensive activity.

During February the 25th Infantry Division's 2d Brigade rangers were alerted of pending disbandment as part of Increment VI (Keystone Robin-Charlie) of the U.S. Army redeployment from Vietnam. The Tropical Rangers ceased combat activity and commenced formal stand-down procedures on 5 March. The final company formation and awards ceremony was held on the following day. Company F (Ranger), 75th Infantry, was reduced to zero strength and officially inactivated on 15 March 1971.

During the Second Indochina War, Mackenzie's Lerps, the Cobra Lightning Patrollers, and the Tropical Rangers fulfilled a vital role in reconnoitering and protecting one of the most dangerous upcountry slices of Vietnam territory. The 25th Infantry Division combat patrol and ranger elements fought a cunning and dangerous adversary and mastered a variety of airmobile strike, waterborne raiding, mechanized infiltration, rice-land security, and foot-patrol reconnaissance roles. The rangers also adjusted to diverse roles that shifted their tasks between combat recon, raider, and intelligence surveillance.[30]

8

101ST AIRBORNE DIVISION

AIRBORNE EAGLE RANGERS

THE RECONNAISSANCE NOMADS

During early 1965 the United States rushed major forces into Vietnam to forestall insurgent victory. This emergency national response included the 1st Brigade of the 101st Airborne Division, a reinforced parachute-infantry strike unit composed of prime troops chosen from all available division resources. On 29 July 1965 the 1st Brigade arrived at the central Vietnamese port of Cam Ranh Bay, where it provided security and became acclimatized before mounting combat expeditions throughout South Vietnam.[1]

The separate 1st Brigade was outfitted as a standard unit and received no special deviation from regular authorizations, except for new radio equipment, before going to Vietnam. Unit leaders had to adjust their own organizations to the demands of jungle warfare. The brigade's opening clashes—especially at the An Khe, while clearing out the 1st Cavalry Division's future overseas base— demonstrated the need for more ground reconnaissance. The press of uninterrupted field assignments, however, precluded internal reorganization until the brigade reached restaging areas at Phan Rang and Bien Hoa during November.

The operating efficiency of the three line battalions was upgraded by transforming the ordinary headquarters jeep recon and antitank platoons—which proved useless in Vietnam except for occasional roadrunning and convoy escort—into combat recon elements. In this manner the 502d Infantry's 2d Battalion raised the "Recondos," the 327th Infantry's 2d Battalion formed the "Hawks," and 327th Infantry's 1st Battalion created the "Tiger Force." Averaging

153

about sixty members, these recon forces were used as small teams for special missions or as combined rifle contingents that infiltrated into targeted areas and reduced the ambush vulnerability of advancing battalions.[2]

The Tiger Force exemplified this new type of combat reconnaissance. Acting on the advice of executive officer and Korean war raider veteran Maj. David H. Hackworth, battalion commander Lt. Col. Joe Rogers "parked the jeeps" of his AT and recon platoons and raised a reconnaissance-and-maneuver unit to extend the reach of the battalion. Commanded by Lt. James A. Gardner, the Tiger Force was so named after one of its platoons' original radio call signs. One of the force lieutenants, Dennis Foley, recalled:

> Everyone in Vietnam was feeling their way through the first year of US troop experience, and the missions, organization, and deployment of the Tigers had to be very flexible. There was no common mission that we stuck with. We organized into long range patrol teams and saturated areas way the hell and gone away from the US units; we worked as one- and two-platoon ambush; and we walked trails with 15-man patrols carrying as many as eight M60 machine guns, hoping to obliterate VC ambushes. We were given all the new experimental and classified equipment to test out. We got some of the first Starlight scopes, chemical man-pack personnel detectors called People Sniffers, and other nifty goodies.[3]

The Tiger Force participated in heavy fighting during its first year of existence, highlighted by the spring 1966 battles in the Tuy Hoa rice bowl. The Tigers led the way into the battle of My Canh 2, where Lieutenant Gardner was killed at the head of his troops storming bunkers on 7 February. On 4 March another major action erupted at My Phu after one of the battalion's rifle platoons bumped into an NVA battalion digging in for a planned assault on the main American fire base. In this chance encounter the U.S. battalion quickly wrapped around the enemy and the Tiger Force was inserted—by executing the brigade's first night helicopter assault in Vietnam.[4]

The Tiger Force was also involved in extensive patrolling while trying to locate the Viet Cong and develop contacts for larger operations. This activity included one daring nocturnal amphibious raid along the coastal foothills south of Phan Rang. The Tigers sailed in a South Vietnamese Navy junk, planning to offload into sampans and paddle ashore. When the Tigers started transferring from the junk to the sampans, however, the machine guns and light mortar baseplates fell through the flimsy bottoms of the sampans and sank them. The Tigers stayed on the junk as its crew tried to land them on shore, but the strong surf dashed the boat on the beach and hurled the recon troops unceremoniously into the sand. The Tiger platoon managed to set up an inland observation post and ambushed a small patrol at first light, but the clamor in landing had compromised mission secrecy.

While the Hawks, Recondos, and Tiger Force were pioneering battalion reaction tactics, 1st Brigade commander Brig. Gen. James S. Timothy authorized the brigade headquarters to form its own long-range reconnaissance patrol (LRRP) platoon. In December 1965 the 1st Brigade LRRP Platoon was organized at Bear Cat-Bien Hoa and divided into nine six-man teams. Each team had a leader, two scouts, a medical specialist (usually an additional scout who could administer advanced first aid), and two radiomen (one of whom was also trained in artillery forward observer duties). The members later became known as the "Reconnaissance Nomads," a title bestowed for their widespread geographical activities in Vietnam.

In January 1966, Brig. Gen. Willard Pearson took over the brigade. For the next two months the airborne LRRP Platoon was employed in the Tuy Hoa sector as part of Operation HARRISON. The long-range reconnaissance patrols used night helicopter missions and expanded their range during searches for the 95th NVA Regiment. Recon teams on patrol avoided telltale aircraft overflights and made four radio contacts daily. Aircraft were sent out whenever two sequential patrol signals were missed, but most of these cases resulted from the failure of radio signals to transmit over normal distances in tropical terrain.

Alertness was a patrolling commandment. Sp4 Patrick Kinsler was in front of one team when he spotted Viet Cong only twenty yards ahead on the same trail. The enemy saw him also, but Kinsler fired a fraction of a second first, killing two Viet Cong. A return bullet drilled the barrel of Kinsler's weapon and knocked it out of his hands. The platoon sergeant, Master Sgt. Lloyd L. Smith, explained, "Our targets were ones of opportunity because of our element of surprise. If Charlie sees us, we zap him. We have to." Staff Sgt. John A. Dietrich summed up patrol spirit: "We're closer than brothers and we know what the other guy can do. No one complains because we're a small unit and prefer to fight that way."[5]

The hazards of long-range patrolling in the rugged coastal mountains was manifested during a mission led by Staff Sgt. Lawrence C. Smith. At daybreak on 26 February, Sergeant Smith sent two experienced scouts forward to check the next ridge 300 yards away and return. The senior scout was Sgt. Donald S. Newton, a rugged NCO with ruddy blond hair who always carried a shotgun, a .45 pistol, and a personally engraved nine-inch hunting knife in a leather sheath. Pfc. Francis D. Wills was a black scout who carried an M16 rifle. Neither man came back.

An hour later, Corp. David Dever and Pfc. Desmond Hanakahi thought they heard movement in the draw between the two ridges. Corporal Dever believed the sounds were Smith and Wills trying to relocate the patrol position. Dever went downhill to find them but was unable to detect anyone in the dense foliage below. He rejoined the patrol with a negative report, and Sergeant Smith radioed that both scouts were missing. The patrol waited on the hillside another five hours before being extracted, and the brigade launched two search teams twice daily for three days.

On 11 March 1966 the mystery was apparently resolved after South Vietnamese Lt. Tran Hua Tien, the intelligence officer for Tuy Hoa district, contacted an informer in Phu Sen village. The villager related that ten days earlier two Americans, one white and the other black, had dug an overnight foxhole near the village and were unaware of partisans watching them. On the following morning an observation aircraft flew overhead and the Americans tried to signal it with three red smoke grenades. The partisans realized that both men were in trouble and attacked. The black soldier was slain after killing three partisans, and the white soldier was captured after he was wounded in the arm and ran out of ammunition. The partisans stripped the black soldier's body and tossed it into the river, and used the white captive in a propaganda march through Thanh Hoi village. The inhabitants were assembled and the prisoner was accused of being a Viet Kich (People's Action Team member). The captive was also paraded through Phung Ha village and seen by the widow of a VC-murdered hamlet chief. She reported that the communists redressed the prisoner in a plain khaki uniform and moved him across the river into Heiu Xuong district.[6]

The airborne brigade stayed in Phu Yen Province until early April. During Operation FILLMORE the 1st Brigade LRRP Platoon was backed up by specified infantry reaction companies for the first time. The use of entire infantry companies to respond immediately to team intelligence marked a significant tactical innovation for future ranger development. The brigade moved farther south along the coast to Phan Thiet and began Operation AUSTIN to search out a suspected Viet Cong redoubt astride the boundary of II and III Corps Tactical Zones. At dusk on 11 April the 1st Brigade LRRP

Platoon teams were inserted to secure small fields for battalion air assaults on the following day. The teams accomplished this path-finder task and then were redirected to explore ahead and develop intelligence leads for the regular infantry. The patrols alternated in searching the drought-stricken region for over a month.

The sustained patrolling during Operation AUSTIN was unusu-ally arduous because the torrid heat and dry streams caused extreme water shortages. Teams carried extra canteens, but patrol duration was curbed to replenish water supplies. One rather humorous in-cident alleviated the otherwise frustrating "walks in the sun." A 1st Brigade LRRP Platoon reconnaissance team was attempting to locate a reported Viet Ccng headquarters when it stumbled across an enemy training camp and surprised the class in session. The paratroopers recovered the lecture placards and sent them back for translation. The subject of the class was "Beware of American Long Range Patrols." The story became proverbial throughout the Vietnam war and was repeated endlessly in various forms by dif-ferent recon units claiming credit. However, the original happen-stance was first reported in Operation AUSTIN.[7]

Following the conclusion of Operation AUSTIN the 1st Brigade LRRP Platoon was given a respite from active operations. Empha-sis was placed on training, absorbing lessons learned, and infusing new replacements. The Reconnaissance Nomads were soon moved again, this time to the west, and assisted Operation HAWTHORNE in Kontum Province in the tri-border area near Cambodia. Snipers equipped with Winchester Model 70 rifles were attached to the patrols. The teams confirmed the presence of the entrenched 24th NVA Regiment on mountains overlooking the Dak Tan Kan valley. The ensuing battle involved pounding the ridges with waves of B-52 bombers, followed by heavy ground fighting as two battalions assaulted the enemy fortifications.

The Reconnaissance Nomads were switched to patrol Phu Yen Province through the remainder of the year. Constant rainstorms and flooded mountain streams hampered team effectiveness, be-cause of high foot and ankle injury rates suffered by the patrol-lers, and the recon platoon returned to Phan Rang in February 1967. The 1st Brigade was given a new commander, Brig. Gen. Salve H. Matheson, and Capt. Robert Friedland's 1st Brigade LRRP Platoon was rested to absorb and train replacements. During this "rest break" the platoon executed a seaborne commando landing from clandestine military junks of the South Vietnamese Navy's Coastal Group 28.[8]

The 1st Brigade LRRP Platoon returned to combat in Operation

FARRAGUT, and reconfirmed its appellation as the Reconnaissance Nomads by scattering patrols across Binh Thuan, Ninh Thuan, and Lam Dong provinces. The patrols traveled for extended distances through suspected Viet Cong strongholds while attempting to uncover secret base camps. During these patrols, the recon teams were often followed closely by enemy tracking parties. The patrollers set hasty ambushes at irregular intervals behind them and succeeded in surprising and discouraging some of their trail-following adversaries.

On 30 March 1967 the Reconnaissance Nomads regrouped in central Vietnam's Khanh Hoa Province and commenced Operation SUMMERALL. One six-man team participating in this endeavor made a crucial contact. The team was moving in split-fashion, with three pairs of scouts, through heavy jungle near Khanh Duong. Sgt. Jimmy L. Cody and Sp5 Virgil D. Polk moved cautiously through the dense foliage while the other two pairs advanced to either side. Cody and Polk followed a trail of broken branches and matted leaves left behind by a slowly walking enemy soldier. They followed the obvious track until they unexpectedly entered a jungle clearing and surprised a cluster of enemy troops.

Specialists Cody and Polk had walked inadvertently into a Viet Cong district command meeting. Not bothering to count, the paratroopers opened fire on full automatic. The enemy scattered in bewilderment. Specialist Polk later reported, "Everyone was running. One Viet Cong pushed me aside as he fled for the jungle." The reconnaissance team pulled back and reconsolidated in a small overnight position. On the following day the patrollers guided an infantry reaction force to the site. The surrounding area was searched and a Viet Cong suspect was seized. He stated that nine Viet Cong were killed during the night by a "two-man army."[9]

On 29 April, following the conclusion of Operation SUMMERALL, the Reconnaissance Nomads moved into far northern Quang Ngai Province. On two occasions in June the 1st Brigade LRRP Platoon conducted airmobile raids to capture identified enemy personnel in the Song Ve valley. On 11 June, Lt. Daniel McIsac led the thirty-three-man platoon in a carefully planned raid on a known Viet Cong village. The platoon studied aerial photographs of the hamlet until they knew the location of every thatched-roof hut, narrow alley, and surrounding rice paddy. The helicopters flew over the jungle at treetop level and landed the raiders in the village only minutes before dusk. "It was a difficult mission," platoon sergeant Master Sgt. Lloyd Smith recalled. "We couldn't fire unless we were fired upon."

The entire village population was rounded up in twelve minutes, but Viet Cong sentinels in the hills soon recovered from the aerial surprise assault and began firing at the village. Sgt. Ronald H. Weems saw several muzzle flashes and poured machine gun fire into a nearby ravine as helicopters returned to extract the patrollers and their captives. McIsac's raid was a successful prisoner snatch mission that netted a high-ranking Viet Cong political action officer, along with fifteen other detainees and numerous documents. One detained female was the fiancée of a South Vietnamese soldier and pleaded that she had been kidnapped, while visiting relatives, and forced to undergo political indoctrination by an officer who wanted to use her as a spy.[10]

During the first part of July 1967 the entire 1st Brigade LRRP Platoon occupied blocking positions to protect engineers opening Route 1 between Dien Truong and Sa Huynh. The platoon returned to reconnaissance work in Quang Tin and Quang Ngai provinces through the end of August. During the following month, MACV commander General Westmoreland ordered 1st Brigade commander General Matheson to return the recon platoon to Phan Rang, where it would form the cadre for a field force patrol company: Company E (Long Range Patrol), 20th Infantry (Airborne). The transfer of the Reconnaissance Nomads reduced the 1st Brigade LRRP Platoon to practically zero strength, and it was never fully rebuilt.

THE SCREAMING EAGLE PATROLLERS

The absorption of the 1st Brigade LRRP Platoon into a new fieldforce long-range patrol company created a dilemma for the remainder of the 101st Airborne Division in the United States. In August 1967 the division was stationed at Fort Campbell, Kentucky, but preparing to deploy to Vietnam. That month the commander, Maj. Gen. Olinto M. Barsanti, ordered that a new provisional Long Range Patrol Company be raised by transferring the staff out of the Fort Campbell Recondo School.

The Fort Campbell Recondo School was thus converted into a fifty-member provisional recon unit and sent to the Army ranger camp at Eglin Air Force Base, Florida. They received intensive training in advanced patrolling, forward observation, aircraft techniques, and report procedures. Four teams were then sent ahead to Vietnam for combat experience. On 3 December the first six-man team arrived in Nui Dat for Australian Special Air Service instruction. On 10 December the other three teams arrived in the Mekong

Delta for swamp-conditioning patrols with the 9th Infantry Division. Later that month, the rest of reconnaissance company arrived in Vietnam.[11]

On 10 January 1968 the Army Department authorized General Barsanti to officially activate a parachutist-capable 118-man recon company for the 101st Airborne Division. As a result, Company F (Long Range Patrol), 58th Infantry (Airborne), was raised at Bien Hoa airbase. Company commander Capt. Peter Fitts used the half-strength provisional Long Range Patrol Company—known as the "Screaming Eagle Patrollers" from the "Screaming Eagles" nickname of the 101st Airborne Division—as the basis for the new organization.

For many reasons, Company F was a "hard-luck" outfit. This was not the fault of its original planners, who acted to create a solid reconnaissance foundation for the division months before it departed the United States. Unforeseen events, however, combined to work against the new company. The previous gutting of the 1st Brigade LRRP Platoon required the company to reach authorized strength by taking volunteers from the replacement pool and division ranks. The new members lacked training in patrol methods and prevented Company F's initial use as a recon unit.

The company was dispatched from Bien Hoa to the outlying provincial capital of Song Be and provided ordinary rifle security. A few ambush points were established around the city perimeter, but lack of helicopter support mandated close-in outposts that could be reached easily by reaction elements. The company suffered its first casualties when enemy mortar rounds killed one soldier and wounded two others. On 21 January, Captain Fitts was instructed to begin phasing the company back into Bien Hoa, where it would be airlifted to rejoin the division in northern South Vietnam.

By 28 January 1968, half the company was staging at Bien Hoa while the remainder was still occupying defensive positions around Song Be. The major Viet Cong Tet-68 offensive interrupted further movement plans. Company F became embroiled in heavy fighting at both transit locations of Bien Hoa and Song Be. The Viet Cong onslaught at Song Be succeeded in overrunning another unit's quad .50-caliber machine gun. Company F soldiers led a valiant counterattack that repelled the enemy and recovered the weapon.

In the midst of these battles, assistant division commander General Clay took two teams north with him to help establish a temporary forward base at Gia Le for the division. The teams accompanied General Clay in surveying the area. Shortly after the Tet emergency ended, the company was airlifted to northern I Corps

Tactical Zone and reassembled. Just when it appeared that the company might start active recon training, General Barsanti assigned luckless Company F to secure the new 101st Airborne Division base camp at Camp Eagle, outside the city of Hue.

For the next two months, Captain Fitts's unit guarded the rapidly developing division installation under dismal conditions. The company's morale sagged as they performed daily sweeps of the frequently mined Camp Eagle connector road to Route 1. The miserable weather, inadequate facilities, and bleak security responsibilities postponed reconnaissance training. Personal skills for mastering patrol doctrine and team reaction drill could be rehearsed only on a piecemeal basis.

Cold monsoon rains lashed the company area constantly. While other patrol units in Vietnam gained pride from the combat accomplishments of their recon team leaders, the most respected man in Company F was Staff Sgt. Richard Burnell. He alone displayed enough ingenuity at waterproofing his bunker quarters to stay dry, while all other live-in bunkers were washed away or turned into soggy mudholes.

During May 1968, Company F's status finally improved. General Barsanti released the company from its defensive role and placed it under division intelligence section control. On 4 May, Lt. John W. Gay Jr. led the first six-man recon patrol of Company F into the mountainous jungle northwest of Fire Support Base Birmingham. The patrol was extracted two hours later after killing three North Vietnamese soldiers. The unit sent more teams on long-range patrols to collect military intelligence on NVA activity, gain information about terrain conditions, and interdict enemy forces as opportunities allowed. Teams ventured farther west until they were patrolling as far as the A Shau Valley on the Laotian border.

During its existence, the Company F "Screaming Eagle Patrollers" successfully performed 124 long-range patrols, sighted the enemy on fifty-four occasions, and killed a total of sixty-two NVA/VC troops by body count. A much larger but undetermined number of enemy personnel were killed by air strikes and artillery fire directed by the teams. The company provided valuable information on enemy movements, trail networks, bunker complexes, caches, and rocket-firing positions.[12]

The company's fortunes were at their highest in midsummer. In June, General Barsanti boosted reconnaissance prowess by arranging to attach a platoon from the South Vietnamese 1st Division's elite *Hǎc-Báo* ("Black Panther") strike company. The Vietnamese troops completed a week-long familiarization program in American patrol techniques and signals. Six teams, each composed of four U.S. and two Vietnamese scouts, were sent into the field.

One of the first mixed long-range reconnaissance teams was led by Staff Sgt. James M. Johnson. The team members were inserted near the Song Be river and reconnoitered the tropical foliage along the river until they discovered a well-used trail hidden under the dense jungle canopy. The team followed the trail and found smaller trails branching to the river's edge. Each trail ended next to a large tree overhanging the river, where several rafts constructed of bamboo logs were pulled up along the bank. The team recorded the position of the "NVA river port" on their maps and then climbed uphill as the trail snaked up a steep incline.

Staff Sergeant Johnson led the difficult trek by grasping vines and boulders as a handhold. Despite the dense foliage, he spotted a hut perched on top of the hill. The dwelling overlooked the trail, and the team stopped for a few moments to observe the dwelling. The patrollers heard only the squawking of birds and the rustling of branches as a monkey leaped through the trees. The patrol continued and reached the empty hut. A quick search revealed a lower level dug underneath the structure, complete with firing ports that dominated the trail beneath. The patrol later found another similarly constructed hut. Near the top of the mountain they found an empty North Vietnamese Army base with thirty more huts. The team exited the camp when they found damp enemy uniforms draped over the vines.

Sergeant Johnson radioed that they had found a hastily evacuated NVA base camp, and then returned with two other troops from another direction while the rest of the team watched the rear. Johnson watched a group of enemy troops, who abruptly spotted him and began firing. The team retreated as the North Vietnamese rapidly reinforced and began looking for the intruders. Johnson radioed for extraction and air support. Within a few minutes two gunships arrived overhead and pinned the NVA troops down with rockets and miniguns. When Air Force fighter-bombers appeared overhead, Johnson called for an air strike. "I had them lay napalm on both sides of the trial. We could hear the enemy screaming and feel the searing heat as we headed to our pickup point." The team was lifted out by extraction helicopters as aircraft continued to pummel the burning camp.[13]

Soon after "Contact" Johnson's successful patrol, Company F's luck turned for the worse. The first inauspicious event was the sudden cancellation of the Vietnamese-American patrol experiment on 19 July, after the Vietnamese division commander demanded the return of his *Hắc-Báo* reconnaissance members. The second and worse occurrence, as far as troop superstitions were concerned, was the untimely injury of new commander Capt. James G. Shepard. He arrived in Company F on 23 July, stepped on an antipersonnel mine, and was medically evacuated home within three days. Capt. Kenneth R. Eklund was then assigned to command the company.

The Screaming Eagle Patrollers of Company F kept an average of three five-man patrols simultaneously in the field. Unless compromised by enemy activity, each team patrolled for seventy-two hours and ideally covered a 25,000-square-yard area. Maj. Gen. Melvin Zais, the new 101st Airborne Division commander in July 1968, began restructuring the formation in accordance with its new Army role as an air cavalry division. General Zais decided to use the Vietnam-proven airmobile reconnaissance doctrine of the 1st Air Cavalry Division, and he consolidated reconnaissance assets under the operational wing of the 2d Squadron, 17th Cavalry, instead of the intelligence section.

On 3 October 1968, Company F was transferred from control of the division intelligence staff and became part of the air cavalry squadron. The tactical employment of the company was altered to more active combat scouting instead of "passive" intelligence-gathering. Field raiding and combat strike commitments increased. Captain Eklund was soon deploying five, and as many as eight, teams on reconnaissance assignments at any one time. Casualties mounted, and within weeks the company suffered a battlefield catastrophe.

On 19 November 1968 a twelve-man team sprang an ambush on ten North Vietnamese troops and killed nine of them. One managed to escape. The team searched the bodies, confiscated weapons and documents, and moved a short distance away to prepare for helicopter extraction. Unfortunately, the lone enemy escapee returned with reinforcements. The patrol's point man was moving toward the pickup zone when he was caught in a sudden burst of automatic weapons fire. The outnumbered team returned fire and formed a hasty defensive perimeter. During the firefight, North Vietnamese soldiers exploded a directional-mine charge against the packed circle of defenders, killing four and wounding seven.

Every man in the team was now a casualty, and annihilation appeared imminent. They desperately radioed for assistance. Two other recon teams as well as an aero rifle platoon of the 17th Cavalry's 2d Squadron responded to the distress call. The rescue effort retrieved the survivors of the beleaguered team, but not before thirteen additional Americans were severely wounded.

The undesirable consequences of the Black November mission, as it came to be known, were profound. The incident could not have come at a worse time. First, it occurred just as most of the original company members were preparing to rotate home at the end of their year in Vietnam. Second, the incident happened soon after Company F was transferred to the 17th Cavalry. The squadron cavalrymen used the terminology "troop" instead of "company," and began calling the unit F Troop. The soldiers of Company F, 58th Infantry, considered this title humiliating, because "F Troop" was a screw-up outfit featured in a 1967 situation comedy series on ABC television with the same title.

AIRBORNE EAGLE RANGERS

At the beginning of 1969 the Department of the Army reorganized the 75th Infantry under the combat arms regimental system to become the parent regiment for long-range patrol companies that were retitled to share a common ranger heritage. Accordingly, during the first week of February 1969, General Zais received an Army Department message ordering the activation of Company L (Airborne Ranger), 75th Infantry, from the assets of Company F, 58th Infantry. Company L was activated with paperwork retroactive to 1 February, and the actual Camp Eagle ceremony formally transforming Company F into ranger Company L was held on 13 February 1969.[14]

The rangers were known as either "Lima Rangers" (L in conformity with ICAO phonetic alphabet adopted by the U.S. military in 1956) or the "Airborne Eagle Rangers," a term that combined their distinguishing paratrooper qualification with the division's "Screaming Eagle" nickname. The ranger company was always kept as a parachutist unit, although by this stage of the war the 101st Airborne Division was removed from "jump status" and declared an airmobile formation. Ranger teams within the company were designated after countries, cities, and automobiles.

The ranger company's mission was to give the division a long-range reconnaissance, surveillance, and target acquisition patrol capability. The company was assigned to the 2d Squadron of the 17th Cavalry, but missions and utility methods were assigned by the intelligence section based on brigade requirements. As a result, many early ranger patrols involved exploratory probes ahead of rifle company airmobile assaults.

Ranger integration with the 2d Squadron of the 17th Cavalry guaranteed responsive aerial support. A gunship was in immediate support of each team on patrol. Unfortunately, after the gunship expended its ammunition and departed, the rangers often experienced long delays before another gunship arrived. When available, a pair of gunships were always welcome. Ranger First Lt. Kevin J. Henry remembered, "There have been times when Cobras have spotted one of our ambushes from the air and remained in the area waiting for us to call if we need help. It's a great feeling when you're way the hell out there with a strong possibility of enemy troops all around, and you look up and see a couple of Cobra [gunships] flying overhead."

In May 1969, Maj. Gen. John M. Wright Jr. assumed command of the 101st Airborne Division. He instituted additional division incentives to increase the flow of ranger volunteers. The official division recruiting pitch for the Airborne Eagle Rangers emphasized the "great personal satisfaction that a Ranger gets out of his job." The seasoned professionals were more likely to volunteer because of more practical military reasons, as Sgt. First Class José Mendoza explained: "I just feel safer. In a line unit there is just too much noise and I like the idea of knowing where the enemy is instead of the other way around."[15]

General Wright established a divisional "Reconnaissance Zone" across the western mountains and valleys adjacent to the Laotian border. The zone was designed as a buffer between enemy-held portions of Laos and populated regions of coastal Vietnam. The division used screening and airmobile raids to deter North Vietnamese infiltration through this zone. The rangers operated almost exclusively in the Reconnaissance Zone.

The rangers tried to use natural landing zones instead of sites created by explosive charges or engineers, because the enemy covered the more likely touchdown points with lookout teams. Suitable ordinary fields, however, were often covered by elephant grass eight to twelve feet high. The helicopters sometimes failed to descend to a safe exiting height during insertions over grassy areas, causing some rangers to jump unwittingly eighteen or twenty feet to the ground. These accidents resulted in serious injuries until pilots gained experience in avoiding unsatisfactory locations. Unfortunately, the army's annual individual rotation problem caused inevitable repetition of the same problems, which had to be "relearned" continually every year.[16]

The rangers also discovered that operations in any one specific area of the Reconnaissance Zone could never exceed a two-week period. Once initial teams were employed, the enemy rapidly became aware that small patrols were probing the area because of the greater degree of air traffic and radio signals. When the North Vietnamese sensed recon intrusion, they used counter-raider groups to seek out ranger locations. To avoid jeopardizing its teams, Company L instituted precautionary measures and alternated randomly between different areas with territorial recon periods limited to a maximum of two weeks.

Monsoon conditions from November through January hampered ranger operations by interfering with communications and decreasing the availability of air support. Thick clouds covering the higher elevations often made ranger infiltration and extractions impossible. Monsoon patrols carried enough rations and ammunition for ten days, in case inclement weather precluded scheduled lift-out, but added weight lessened ground mobility.

During November, ranger Company L added Kit Carson scouts (turncoat NVA soldiers) for the first time on ranger teams. Kit Carson scout advantages were initially offset by the poor weather. For example, in November the rangers conducted thirty-eight patrols but made only sixteen sightings. Ranger observations declined again in December, when thirty-one patrols spotted enemy troops on only seven occasions. Rainstorms with low cloud ceilings and dense fog suspended operations altogether in the A Shau Valley.

During January 1970, ranger Company L concentrated its patrols mostly in the Khe Sanh plain and the Da Krong Valley. On 11 January a six-man team ambushed a North Vietnamese squad with claymore mines but was immediately engaged by a larger enemy force in a savage firefight. Both the patrol leader and the assistant patrol leader were killed, but the other four team members managed to fight their way back to an emergency jungle pickup point in the dense jungle. They experienced a narrow escape when a pair of brazen pilots, flying light observation helicopters through misting rain, lifted the survivors out two at a time by McGuire rigs through the towering trees.[17]

The northeast monsoon and its accompanying rainy weather prevented regular airmobile insertions of ranger teams into the borderland of the Reconnaissance Zone. The North Vietnamese Army took advantage of the situation to infiltrate large units into the mountains east of the Laotian border. The NVA engineers and soldiers constructed a number of well-stocked ammunition depots and major supply centers in the rugged rain forest. More units were deployed for future strikes on allied regional garrisons.

During May 1970, Maj. Gen. John J. Hennessey assumed command of the 101st Airborne Division. He increased the tempo of ranger operations in an effort to determine the extent of fresh NVA force buildup within northern South Vietnam. His orders for heightened surveillance required the air cavalry squadron to fly teams from Capt. James D. Stowers's ranger Company L repeatedly into forbidding landing sites near suspected enemy mountain encampments. Some paratrooper ranger teams were launched deep into the jungles of the Ruong Ruong Valley. Other teams scouted the primeval tropical forest that covered the three forks of the Song Bo river. The remaining ranger patrols were dispatched through the Khe Sanh plain near the Demilitarized Zone.

The Company L ranger patrolling offensive went so far into enemy-controlled territory that it became routine practice to position radio relay teams, equipped with special ground antenna stations for long-distance communications, for teams inserted farther afield. Radio relay teams performed vital but extremely perilous work, because they occupied fixed locations and surrendered the ranger advantages of mobility. High casualties were occasionally suffered on such duty. On 11 May, for example, an entire radio relay team was annihilated when a North Vietnamese company overran its signal transmitting point and killed the six rangers in hand-to-hand combat.

The Company L airborne rangers pushed through some of the most desolate tropical wilderness in Southeast Asia and reported on the locations and movements of veteran NVA formations. These patrols took unusual chances and sometimes smashed into battle-hardened NVA guards, but the Airborne Eagle Rangers exerted relentless pressure in their endeavor to collect information that might map out the enemy dispositions.

The month of July 1970 was dominated by fierce skirmishing. On 6 July 1970, eleven-man heavy ranger team Ferrari was launched into the thick jungle on the northern rim of Tennessee Valley. Shortly after insertion the team bumped into a large enemy force and was immediately embroiled in a desperate fight for survival. Repeated strafing runs by helicopter gunships enabled the team members to reach an emergency extraction area. Close aerial support enabled team Ferrari to be lifted out under heavy fire, with six wounded members, and an entire North Vietnamese platoon was decimated in exchange.

On 17 July 1970, ranger team Renault detected a major enemy unit displacement. Two days later, team Corvair found newly installed blue communication wires in the same area and summoned a cavalry helicopter "pink team" of one gunship and one observation helicopter. The aerial team received heavy ground fire, but the rangers escaped North Vietnamese entrapment attempts and reached friendly lines safely. Ranger teams Austin and Mustang also made valuable observations of enemy activity during the month.[18]

Company L was authorized only 118 rangers to wage this war of extended reconnaissance. This number was clearly insufficient, given the large expanse of remote countryside that required coverage. In addition, actual unit strength averaged well less than a hundred members at any one time. General Hennessey was anxious to stretch the ability of his rangers and began setting up an array of sophisticated electronic sensor equipment now available to the division. The rangers planted strings of sensor devices under the supervision of the intelligence section. These unattended ground monitors indicated enemy activity, acquired targets, and provided advance warning near observation bases. Ranger tactics increasingly relied on responding to information collected by surveillance devices and ground radar.

The electronics program was somewhat hampered by dependence on Air Force aerial-relay aircraft for transmission of the more remote sensor read-out data within the Reconnaissance Zone. The Air Force never provided continuous aerial monitoring on a twenty-four-hour basis over unattended sensors. However, Air Force aerial-relay aircraft always flew on station over actual ranger patrols. There was no satisfactory substitute for this support, because ranger communication through ground FM relay points was always marginal at best. When informed that the Air Force was failing to constantly overfly remote electronic sensors, Company L commander Capt. Robert A. Guy countered forcefully, "The Air Force air relay center should be commended for their great support in this unit's operation."[19]

The 101st Airborne Division generally fielded excellent patrols throughout its wartime service, but ranger expertise diminished in the late war period. Reconnaissance proficiency was gradually eroded by the less-trained nature of newer troops, discouragement over missions that often produced good information but no follow-up for lack of allied support, the cumulative and shattering impact of the Vietnam rotation policy on small unit cohesion, and the sheer difficulty of operating continuously in the same, predictable regions that compromised ranger stealth.

One shocking manifestation of this decline occurred on 25 August 1970. A ranger team was setting up its overnight position in Thua Thien Province when a North Vietnamese soldier walked straight into the perimeter and opened fire with his AK47. He killed one ranger and seriously wounded another. Before the shocked rangers could react, the enemy soldier escaped back into the jungle. The patrol was immediately extracted and the team leader dismissed from the ranger company.

Later that same month, ranger teams Japan I and Japan II executed a ladder roll-out. The roll-out was a ranger "stay-behind" technique that used one helicopter to simultaneously insert a replacement team and lift out a ground team. The new team descended on rope ladders from the cabin of the hovering helicopter, while the other team boarded the aircraft using ropes dropped from the other side. The roll-out was supposed to be a well-rehearsed fast exchange of ranger teams. The Japan teams were inexperienced in the procedure because of insufficient rehearsal before entering combat. The helicopter was kept hovering over a dangerous landing zone for nearly ten minutes, and the insertion was ultimately compromised to enemy trail watchers.

On 29 August, for ultimately unknown reasons, ranger team Kenya attempted to land on perhaps the worst possible terrain feature, an artificially cut landing zone on the highest hill in the area. No preparatory fire from gunships was used. North Vietnamese sentries were assigned to the obvious clearing and apparently watched the helicopter approaching from a considerable distance. They leisurely set up a machine gun and shot the aircraft down over the landing zone. Every crew member and ranger was either killed or wounded (four dead, six injured), and team Kenya was wiped out.

In yet another example, on 24 September, ranger team Dallas was inserted to probe the jungle southwest of Fire Support Base Pike. The team leader sent two scouts ahead but gave them no hand radio. During the afternoon the scouts encountered other troops wearing standard U.S. Army-pattern camouflage. Both rangers were momentarily surprised, and one was killed when the enemy opened fire first. The survivor could not communicate with the rest of the patrol farther back. The enemy force disappeared into the jungle, and the scout was able to reach the rest of the team. As a consequence of these incidents, the Company L ranger training program was completely overhauled and hand-held ARCR-10 and URC-68 radios were distributed to all teams.[20]

Command emphasis and rehearsal of patrol basics soon returned Company L teams to high ranger standards. The ranger reconnoitering campaign continued from August until the advent of the rainy monsoon season in December. The rangers conducted intensive patrolling surveillance within the forested, jagged ridges of the Ruong Ruong Valley, sent deep penetration patrols into the elephant grass bottomlands of the A Shau Valley, and reconnoitered the jungle-covered Spear Valley.

Ranger team New Zealand confirmed the presence of the long-sought Chi Thieu Sapper Battalion in the Tennessee Valley on 28 August. Other ranger teams found the 5th NVA Regiment as it tried to move secretly into the Spear Valley. Expert North Vietnamese counter-raiders became a more frequent menace to the patrols. On 16 November, ranger team Bills suffered two rangers killed in action, but pinpointed the 803d NVA Regiment moving against the fire support bases of Ripcord and Kathryn.[21]

Tropical storms and monsoon downpours interrupted most ranger expeditions from mid-November through January 1971. In February, as favorable weather returned, Maj. Gen. Thomas M. Tarpley became the new division commander. The South Vietnamese invasion of Laos during Operation LAM SON 719 renewed the crucial importance of ranger reconnaissance in the Reconnaissance Zone, because it became imperative to prevent undetected enemy movements against allied lines of communication leading into Laos. The rangers used far-ranging trail reconnaissance and helicopter overflights throughout the Reconnaissance Zone. Seven ranger teams also combed the Ruong Ruong Valley and masked the relocation of a paratrooper battalion moving to support the Laotian incursion.

In March 1971 the rangers concentrated on harassing North Vietnamese troops that overran Fire Support Base Ripcord. During April the rangers shifted emphasis to the A Shau Valley. On the afternoon of 23 April 1971, six-man ranger team Cubs, led by Sp4 Marvin A. Duren, was inserted into the eastern rim of the A Shau Valley to establish a ground radio relay for rangers raiding an enemy-held bridge on Route 548.[22]

Unfortunately, the same area that ranger team Cubs entered had been used for a false insertion several days previously—drawing enemy attention to the area. This factor was overlooked by the division operations staff when they assigned the team mission. Team Cubs was immediately engaged by North Vietnamese troops, and Specialist Duren was wounded twice before his rangers could escape the firing. The rangers carried Duren to a field along the nearby ridge spur of Hill 809 and radioed for a medical evacuation helicopter.

The first helicopters to reach the rangers were not medical aircraft but two 17th Cavalry helicopters alerted by the distress call.

They carried ranger team leader Staff Sgt. William R. Vodden to replace Duren. Both helicopters were shot down over the landing zone. Capt. Lewis J. Speidel's helicopter, carrying Vodden on board, was raked with enemy automatic weapons fire and crashed on the ridge. Captain Speidel was badly burned, aircraft commander Capt. William Cullum was killed, and both crew chief Pfc. Clarence D. Allen and right door gunner Sp4 Brian H. Plahn were critically wounded. The other helicopter also sustained heavy fire, but its pilot managed a forced landing on the valley floor some distance away, where the crew were rescued almost immediately.

Staff Sergeant Vodden leaped from the shattered helicopter and assumed command of the ranger team. He turned back to see Specialist Plahn stumbling across the field before collapsing not far from the wreck. Vodden directed the other rangers to give him covering fire and then raced out into the tall grass. He reached Plahn and asked about the rest of the crew, but the wounded aviator mumbled they were all dead. As Vodden stood back up he was shot in the leg and tumbled down the ridge.

The evacuation helicopter from the 326th Medical Battalion, piloted by WO1 Frederic Behrens, arrived on the landing zone shortly afterward but was unopposed by enemy fire. The rangers put Duren and Plahn aboard, and Warrant Officer Behrens flew them to the 85th Evacuation Hospital. He then headed back to the beleaguered team and attempted an emergency night extraction. At 8:00 P.M., Behrens landed the helicopter on the darkened ridge and five rangers clambered on board. Suddenly a fusillade of enemy automatic weapons fire tore through the engine and cabin, killing crew chief Sp5 Michael Brunner and ranger Sp4 Johnnie R. Sly instantly. The bullet-riddled helicopter sank to the ground, and its 800 pounds of aviation fuel threatened to explode. The survivors scrambled to get away from the aircraft, reached the tree line, and set up a tight circular perimeter.

At dawn on 24 April, Cobra gunships appeared overhead and began raking the forest around the landing zone with concentrated machine gun fire. The strafing ripped into the stranded Americans and mortally wounded assistant crew chief Sp4 David P. Medina. The men realized that the Cobra fire was directed at the trees and staying clear of the wrecked helicopters. Leaving Medina for dead, they dashed into the field closer to the medical helicopter. The group was split, however, when aircraft commander Lt. Roger Madison and rangers Sgt. Fred W. Karnes and Sp4 Steven N. MacAlpine attempted to retrieve the radio. The trio were pinned down in a separate area of the field for the duration of the day.

That afternoon, Company L commander Capt. David H. Ohle led a six-man ranger rescue team to reach the site of the downed helicopters, as part of a reinforcing element from the 17th Cavalry's Troop D. The reaction force was enveloped by intense fire as it climbed the ridge, and further maneuvering was halted. During the firefight, North Vietnamese snipers climbed the trees and began shooting into the isolated Americans trapped on the landing zone. Medical aidman Sp5 Robert F. Speer was killed, ranger Pfc. Issako F. Malo was shot through the hip, and Warrant Officer Behrens was struck in the left arm and both legs. Another ranger, Pfc. James A. Champion, managed to cross the fire-swept area and reach the wreckage of the first downed helicopter. He found Captain Speidel and Private Allen both wounded and remained with them to ward off enemy soldiers in the gathering twilight.

As darkness descended on 24 April, the enemy fire diminished and the paratrooper reaction unit withdrew from the ridge to establish overnight defenses. Taking advantage of the darkened conditions, Lieutenant Madison and his two rangers dashed from the field where they had been pinned all day, dodged a hail of bullets as they ran through the woods, and linked up with the reaction force. They briefed Captain Ohle about the situation of the remaining Americans as they knew it.

Back on the landing zone, Warrant Officer Behrens and ranger Private Malo were badly wounded and unable to walk. They painfully dragged themselves toward the western slope of the landing zone but became separated because Behrens was slower and weak from loss of blood. Malo crawled on ahead to get help but was never seen again. Warrant Officer Behrens rested through the night. At dawn he started moving back to his helicopter wreck.

At daybreak on 25 April, Private Champion was still guarding Captain Speidel and Private Allen at the first wreck. The wounded aviators were suffering and in dire need of water by this time. Champion told Allen that he would try to get water for them. Those were his last words. Private Champion moved toward the edge of the ridge and was never seen again.

By noon, Captain Ohle's rangers broke through the enemy resistance and advanced across the landing zone to capture Hill 809. The reaction force found Warrant Officer Behrens, badly injured but alive, between two fallen trees some distance northwest of his aircraft. Another reaction team ranger, Sp4 David W. Rothwell, found Staff Sergeant Vodden immobilized with a fractured leg on the slope of the ridge where he first fell. The rangers then checked Speidel's crashed helicopter and recovered the two wounded aviators. The five dead were also removed. Rangers James Albert Champion of Houston, Texas, and Issako Faatoese Malo of Pago Pago, American Samoa, were declared missing in action.[23]

Company L shifted its focus of operations back to the Ruong Ruong Valley in May and June. In mid-July 1971, General Tarpley received instructions from XXIV Corps to begin planning for 101st Airborne Division redeployment back to the United States. While the staff sections started drafting stand-down procedures, the ranger company kept teams active on combat reconnaissance. The rangers expected to cease or reduce operations at any time, but still performed an average of twenty reconnaissance missions per month from July through October. Many of these missions involved covering the withdrawal of division battalions from forward fire bases and other camps.[24]

On 2 September 1971, ranger team Julia was inserted by helicopter in the mountainous triple-canopy jungle near the Rao Trang river. The five-man patrol contained team leader Sergeant Wyatt, assistant team leader Sergeant Thibodeaux, scouts Sp4 Knibbs and Byers, and Lieutenant Montano, who was along for combat patrol familiarization. The rangers spotted a camouflaged trail cut with machetes about a week before and followed it past an abandoned enemy sleeping area. The trail crossed several rocky, leech-filled streams. Team attempts to transmit by voice on radio failed because all FM frequencies were jammed by loud Vietnamese music and song recordings.

In the afternoon, Sergeant Wyatt thought he heard movement and moved the team fifty yards through dense underbrush to the east. Later the rangers returned to the trail and discovered fresh footprints of a squad-sized unit. The team continued to follow the pathway and found two old sawed-off tree stumps with a table board and teacup. The patrol also noticed that the trees to either side of the trail were torn by gashes indicating the portage of heavy equipment.

On the second day the rangers investigated another hidden trail in thick jungle shrubbery that was interspersed with bamboo thickets and banana palms. The team then set up overnight positions. An hour after midnight the men heard five mortar rounds being fired about a mile away. Team Julia spent the third day of its mission moving slowly northwest through the sloping tropical forest covered by seventy-foot-high hardwoods. Throughout the patrol, whenever the team attempted to transmit using voice mode, the enemy jammed their radio frequencies with blaring Vietnamese music.

During the fourth day the patrollers discovered a third hard-packed reddish clay trail last traveled within the week. While investigating this trail the rangers found a discarded North Vietnamese poncho and tree branches marked by carved arrows underneath X-slashes. On the last morning of the patrol, Sergeant Wyatt led his men away from the trail network to a predetermined pickup point. The selected area was covered by lush jungle, but enemy jamming prevented radio discussion of alternatives with platoon headquarters. The rangers spent most of the day cutting a small clearing. That afternoon helicopters arrived over the preplanned site and hoisted the team out using ropes. The five-day expedition of team Julia provided valuable information on previously unknown enemy traffic routes and exemplified division ranger reconnaissance missions.[25]

The northeast monsoon arrived in the late fall of 1971 and blanketed the western mountains and valleys of the Reconnaissance Zone with low clouds and torrential rains. The normally shallow highland streams were turned into raging torrents that could be negotiated only by using long ropes tied to overhanging trees. Ranger teams disdained carrying the once-customary nylon ropes on monsoon missions, because the latter were now considered too heavy and cumbersome. The lack of long ropes forced patrollers to tie individual sling-ropes together into one safety line. Individuals could cross the rope combination without wearing heavy equipment, but knotted field-expedient lines caused trouble hauling rucksacks and radios across rain-swollen streams.[26]

The monsoons curtailed ranger activities. However, a temporary spell of good weather during two weeks in November enabled the rangers to verify helicopter sightings of a significant enemy logistical complex in the Da Krong Valley. These proved to be the last ranger missions of Company L in Vietnam. On 24 November 1971 the Airborne Eagle Rangers received stand-down orders to cease combat operations and turn in equipment to the division redeployment center. Many of the company's eighty-eight personnel were reassigned to bolster the 1st Cavalry Division rangers still fighting in Vietnam. On 25 December 1971, Company L (Airborne Ranger), 75th Infantry, was officially inactivated.[27]

During the Vietnam conflict the 101st Airborne Division Reconnaissance Nomads, Screaming Eagle Patrollers, and Airborne Eagle Rangers operated in the forefront of the reconnaissance effort. The original brigade and battalion combat recon elements generated many patrolling tactics that later became Army-wide principles of small unit maneuver. The 1st Brigade LRRP Platoon's exploratory surveillance and intelligence collection significantly enhanced combat reconnaissance techniques. The field force absorption of such an excellent platoon was perhaps inevitable, but it interrupted the division's combat recon progress and caused a setback in patrolling performance.

The advent of the Company L rangers signified a return to a normal level of division reconnaissance capability. The Airborne Eagle Rangers endured harsh tropical conditions, great personnel turbulence, and high unit casualties during their prolonged reconnoitering campaign in the borderland Reconnaissance Zone. The paratrooper ranger teams confronted some of the strongest enemy infiltration units while gathering valuable intelligence and performed their important ranger mission with a high degree of effectiveness.

9

173D AIRBORNE BRIGADE

NOVEMBER RANGERS

AIRBORNE CAVALRY RECONNAISSANCE

In May 1965 the 173d Airborne Brigade deployed as the first major Army maneuver unit to enter Vietnam. The paratrooper brigade served in Southeast Asia over six years and pioneered many important combat reconnaissance techniques. During the war, the brigade's provisional cavalry platoon of long-range patrollers evolved into Company N (Airborne Ranger) of the 75th Infantry. The wartime paratrooper rangers of Company N, formed in the latter period of brigade service and the last to receive black berets, chose the appropriate field name "November Rangers."

The 173d Airborne Brigade initially relied on its motorized jeep and aero-scout components of Troop E (Airborne), 17th Cavalry, for reconnaissance. The paratrooper unit had participated in antiguerrilla exercises on Okinawa, but it did not perform ranger-style reconnoitering. Instead of gathering intelligence by stealth and foot patrolling, the cavalry scouts were organized to fight in an "airborne pocket" and perform the traditional role of mounted scouts in road reconnaissance. The unit was not trained in conducting the type of long-range infantry patrols needed in Vietnam.

On 5 May 1965 the 173d Airborne Brigade, commanded by Brig. Gen. Ellis W. Williamson, arrived in Vietnam and Troop E commenced routine reconnaissance activities of a light cavalry nature. The cavalry troop secured field artillery positions, escorted motorized convoys, and screened battalion movements. The first foot cavalry patrols were not ranger-type activities but only "dismounted patrols" supplementing the jeep-riding "mounted patrols" being used to clear roads and accompany convoys.

Almost a year later, on 25 April 1966, brigade commander Brig. Gen. Paul F. Smith organized a provisional brigade Long Range Reconnaissance Patrol (LRRP) Platoon and added the unit to Troop E of the 17th Cavalry. The provisional platoon cadre was selected from brigade volunteers with combat experience and jungle warfare knowledge. The patrols used helicopter insertion or overland foot infiltration to perform advance scouting or stay-behind surveillance. The long-range patrol teams primarily observed enemy activity, although they were equipped to execute small ambushes or call in radio-directed artillery and aerial firepower on targets of opportunity.[1]

The brigade LRRP Platoon's mission was "to scout fifteen to twenty kilometers forward of the CP [command post], thereby obtaining and relaying information of military intelligence concerning terrain, enemy strength, etc. to the commander." The platoon was commanded by a captain and contained a lieutenant executive, an intelligence sergeant, a senior communications sergeant, two radio-telephone operators, and a medical corpsman at headquarters.

Patrols were coded with temporary designations such as predatory fish species. Each of the nine patrols consisted of a patrol leader and his assistant, a radioman, one senior scout, and two additional scouts. The small size of these teams meant that calling in a fire mission or taking a prisoner was the exception rather than the rule. When it was decided to initiate such actions, meticulous on-the-spot planning had to be done despite intense time pressures that intensified the risk and danger to the team.[2]

Operation TOLEDO, fought near Gia Ray in Phuoc Tuy Province, demonstrated how brigade long-range patrols performed surveillance. On 12 August 1966, recon teams Kelly and Elaine were deployed into the enemy Mao Tao secret base area. On the third afternoon of their mission, both teams were extracted after experiencing negative contact. Their lack of sightings revealed the enemy's absence from the area. Three days later another trio of long-range patrols were inserted north of Nui Chua Chan to observe an area previously swept by armor and engineers. In this area, patrol teams Shark, Barracuda, and Bass spotted enemy trail parties and called in artillery fire. On 20 August the teams were airlifted from their positions after team Bass became compromised in a firefight and was pursued to an emergency pickup zone, alerting the enemy to American presence.[3]

During November 1966, as part of Operation WACO, the brigade

LRRP Platoon gained preliminary intelligence about enemy infiltration routes north of the Dong Nai river in upper Bien Hoa Province. Several six-man teams were helicoptered close to War Zone D and clashed with enemy elements. The teams captured prisoners and documents disclosing that the war zone's western approaches were guarded by the Viet Cong 800-D Battalion. The Viet Cong, however, eluded larger brigade sweeps reacting to this patrol information.[4]

The brigade's reconnaissance prowess matured under the stewardship of Brig. Gen. John R. Deane Jr., who took over the 173d Airborne Brigade in December 1966. In the following month, the brigade invaded the Iron Triangle in Operation CEDAR FALLS and Brigadier General Deane diversified the scope of recon patrolling. The brigade LRRP Platoon, commanded by Capt. Allan B. Phillips, was sent aloft in helicopters over the bombed-out forest and landed periodically to make damage assessments. On 12 and 13 January 1967 the teams switched to tunnel searching. During the next two days the patrols scouted the treacherous root-clogged tidal tributaries of the Saigon River. One recon patrol found and destroyed a supply cache containing 265 hundred-pound bags of polished and paddy rice.

On 16 January, after another day of exploring tunnels, Captain Phillips's platoon was directed to establish night ambushes along a marshy canal footbridge near the small village of Ap Nhat. The first eleven-man ambush patrol was led by Sgt. Michael J. Howard and occupied positions covering the bridge approaches on both sides of the canal. At 7:19 P.M. the ambushers killed a Viet Cong walking toward the bridge. The Americans saw several lights blinking, indicating that a larger enemy force was nearby signaling their intention to cross.

At 8:15 P.M. in pitch darkness another Viet Cong walked toward the bridge. The Americans failed to spot the enemy soldier until he reached the middle of the team's hundred-yard ambush zone. The patrollers opened fire at point-blank range, but the Viet Cong managed to pull out a hand grenade that exploded as he fell across it. The explosion sparked a barrage of enemy rifle fire that tore through the dense shrubbery and fatally wounded Sp4 William E. Collins on the other side of the canal.

Sergeant Howard's men threw grenades at the enemy, instead of firing rifles, to prevent disclosing their positions with muzzle flashes. After the return fire abated, the patrollers carried Collins back across the canal and evacuated him by medical helicopter. The patrol then resumed their original ambush position. Incredibly, despite all this activity, two more Viet Cong ambled into the ambush zone at 10:37 P.M. Detecting something wrong, both enemy soldiers stopped and exchanged a few words directly in front of Specialist McDonald's M60 machine gun. McDonald attempted to fire his weapon, but it jammed. Nearby, Sergeant Howard tried to open fire with his M16, but his rifle also malfunctioned, because it had become muddied in the canal when he retrieved Collins. Sergeant Bolen saw the trouble and opened fire. He killed one Viet Cong instantly and wounded the other, whom he then tracked to the water's edge and "finished the job." There were no other contacts for the duration of the night.[5]

The next evening, Hawaiian Sgt. Harold Kaiama positioned a reinforced twelve-man night ambush team in the same canal vicinity but north of the footbridge. He brought a starlight scope to prevent the mishaps that had plagued the previous ambush venture. However, there were still problems. A misunderstanding caused the assistant patrol leader, Staff Sergeant Vigo, to abandon his planned rear security position and establish another ambush site farther down the canal. The mistake was realized only after the paratroopers set up their machine guns and claymore mines, and silence precautions mandated no further change in the ambush layout.

At 8:30 P.M., Sergeant Vigo and Specialist Smith sighted a squad of Viet Cong and opened fire when the enemy soldiers reached the canal bank. The Viet Cong were stunned and unable to determine the direction of fire. In the confusion one enemy soldier was killed and a second wounded man dropped out of sight behind the dike. Later that night, Sergeant Kaiama used his starlight scope to spot more Viet Cong in front of the bridge. He signaled his machine gunner, Specialist Miller, who immediately opened fire and killed two leading enemy soldiers. Hours afterward, Sergeant Kaiama sighted a third group of Viet Cong. He directed grenadiers Rosson and Dapello to fire six volleys of M79 grenade fire into their ranks. The patrol checked the impact area on the following morning and found four dead Viet Cong in the impact area.[6]

The two ambush experiences of the brigade long-range recon platoon in Operation CEDAR FALLS taught important lessons. Both were extremely fortunate situations, because the enemy was trying to leave the Iron Triangle in small bands, intent on avoiding entanglement in actions that might impede their escape. The patrol cordon caught the vanguards of some of these groups, but apparently each Viet Cong contingent anxiously sought other ways across the canal. Under other circumstances—where the enemy was willing to maneuver against a blocking force or dislodge a patrol element—the reconnaissance teams might have paid dearly for calling medical helicopters in the midst of ambush duty, having inoperable weapons, failing to ensure that rear security was properly posted, or engaging in nightly returns to the same area.

The long-range patrollers were parachutist-qualified, but did not perform combat jumps in Vietnam because helicopters offered more precise and less dangerous infiltration alternatives. Recon teams did not participate in the one brigade combat jump of the war—executed near Katum during Operation JUNCTION CITY on 22 February 1967—because pathfinders were used to perform drop zone reconnaissance and security for the mission. However, some recon-qualified personnel were attached to the 2d Battalion, 503d Infantry (Airborne), during the combat parachute assault on an individual voluntary basis.

In June 1967, General Deane shifted the 173d Airborne Brigade northward into the Central Highlands to assist the 4th Infantry Division fighting Operation GREELEY. Capt. Thomas H. Baird was now the LRRP Platoon leader. During the early weeks of brigade participation the LRRP Platoon teams discovered numerous NVA shelters, bunkers, and weapon storage points in the high mountain ranges of the Vietnamese tri-border front.

On 17 August a long-range patrol under Staff Sgt. Charles J. Holland was infiltrated to conduct a trail surveillance mission. There was no contact on the first day and no sign of recent enemy activity. On the following day the patrol established an observation point at a trail intersection. Shortly after noon the team saw several groups of black-uniformed enemy soldiers moving along the main path. Staff Sergeant Holland immediately arranged for the radioman to call an artillery fire mission through the long-range radio relay. Suddenly team rear security man Sp4 Robert E. Brooks hand-signaled the other patrol members that he heard movement to their rear.

Almost at once, a heavy volume of enemy fire erupted from three directions. Specialist Brooks was wounded and knocked down by the initial burst of automatic fire. Scout Sp4 James Gowen was wounded in the right side of his head. Staff Sergeant Holland grabbed Sgt. Chester A. McDonald, pointed to the bottom of the hill, and told him to get the team out of there. The patrol members scrambled downhill as Holland returned fire with his M16 and yelled, "Keep going! I'll cover the rear!" The team reached a marshy area at the bottom of the hill, where Holland soon rejoined

This painting of Rogers' Rangers by Frederick Remington shows the original combat reconnaissance unit of American Provincials in action during the French and Indian War. Company O (Arctic Ranger), 75th Infantry, would duplicate these winter scouting techniques during the Vietnam era. *(War Department)*

Mule skinners attached to the 475th Infantry (Long Range Penetration, Special), the successor regiment to Merrill's Marauders, cross a swift Burmese river during the offensive toward Si-u on 17 November 1944. The 475th was later redesignated as the 75th Infantry and became the parent regiment for all ranger companies during the Vietnam war. *(U.S. Army)*

A Company D (Airborne LRP), 17th Infantry, recon patrol led by Sfc. Vance Simonis, second from left, follows point man Sp4 Arthur Kruesi, left, while reconnoitering the Fulda-Hanau Corridor of Germany in 1963. The patrollers are wearing French camouflage parachutist uniforms and mountain rucksacks and are armed with M14 rifles.
(V Corps Signal Office)

The Army ranger course was taught by the Fort Benning-based ranger department and designed to produce patrolling experts who could lead, endure, and succeed—regardless of the odds or enemy, weather, and terrain obstacles. These students receive instruction in the Florida ranger camp's swamp phase in 1965. *(Ranger Department Information Office)*

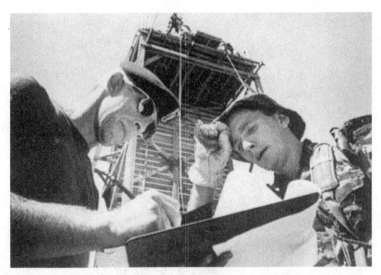

An instructor of the MACV Recondo School at Nha Trang, Vietnam, checks a student who has just completed his descent from the forty-foot rappelling tower in 1968. The Special Forces-run recondo school functioned as a combat theater academy specializing in Vietnam-specific reconnaissance practices. *(Gordon Gahan)*

Enemy weapons, typified by the Soviet/Chinese 7.62mm assault rifle AK47 with bayonet extended (right) and North Vietnamese Army B-40 rocket-propelled grenade launcher (left), were commonly encountered by rangers such as these members of Company C (Airborne Ranger), 75th Infantry, at An Khe in June 1970. *(U.S. Army)*

The M18A1 "claymore" antipersonnel mine projected 700 steel balls in an arc of about 60 degrees. The claymore mine could be command-detonated or rigged to numerous remote firing and mechanical ambush devices, and its lethality made it a staple of ranger ambushes throughout the Vietnam conflict. *(U.S. Army)*

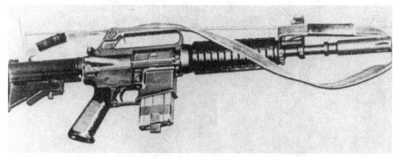

The CAR-15 or Colt Commando, also known as the XM177E2 5.56 submachine gun, was favored by many rangers because of its light weight and compact size. The telescoping stock, improved flash hider, and revised handguard features represented improvements over the M16 rifle. Note the tape used to ensure quick ejection of ammunition magazines. *(Author's Collection)*

Helicoptered patrol insertions were subject to flight hazards, exemplified by the 1 June 1970 crash of this 192d Aviation Company UH-1C helicopter during a ranger insertion south of the Dalat, Vietnam. The ranger team of Company C (Airborne Ranger), 75th Infantry, was required to secure the downed gunship. *(Author's Collection)*

Rangers of Company N (Airborne Ranger), 75th Infantry, rehearse extraction techniques using helicopter-dropped ropes with McGuire rigs—named in honor of Project Delta Sgt. Maj. Charles T. McGuire. These kinds of extractions were used as a last alternative, usually only when a team was in trouble and could not reach the normal pickup zone. *(Author's Collection)*

Lt. John Howard of the Airborne LRRP Platoon, 1st Brigade, 101st Airborne Division, camouflages his face with soot prior to a mission in the Tuy Hoa sector as part of Operation HARRISON on 27 February 1966. Most recon patrollers commonly wore tiger-stripe camouflage uniforms and various types of "jungle hats." *(U.S. Army)*

Sgt. Philip Chassion of the Airborne LRRP Platoon, 1st Brigade, 101st Airborne Division, conducts a final patrol briefing for his recon team preparatory to being inserted on a mission during Operation HARRISON on 27 February 1966. The patrols avoided telltale aircraft overflights and made four radio contacts daily. *(U.S. Army)*

A 4th Infantry Division recondo-hawkeye patrol tracks enemy movement in western Pleiku Province near the Cambodian border in 1967. In December the provisional division recon assets were formalized as Company E (LRP), 58th Infantry (Long Range Patrol). *(Army News Features)*

The provisional 1st Infantry Division Long Range Patrol Detachment (LRPD) scouts for enemy infiltration corridors around Loc Ninh in 1967. The detachment formed the basis of the "Danger Forward Reconnaissance" patrollers of Company F (LRP), 52d Infantry, that December. *(U.S. Army)*

Above: Sgt. Donald Newton was on a LRRP patrol from the 1st Brigade, 101st Airborne Division, and never returned from searching a ridge west of Tuy Hoa on 26 February 1966. He was last reported as a VC captive being paraded through several villages.

Left, top to bottom: Pfc. Joseph Fitzgerald, Sgt. John Jakovac, and Pfc. Brian McGar remain missing in action after their Task Force Oregon LRRP patrol was annihilated northeast of Special Forces Camp Ha Thanh on 31 May 1967. *(MACV CICV Det)*

Ranger sniper Sp4 Richard Guth of Company F (Ranger), 75th Infantry, holds his M14 rifle prior to the ill-fated ranger insertion into the Renegade Woods on 2 April 1970. *(Author's Collection)*

Pfc. Raymond Allmon of Company F (Ranger), 75th Infantry, charges forward with his M60 machine gun and ammunition carrier boxes during the action in the Renegade Woods on 2 April 1970. Sp4 Donald Tinney, at extreme left, was mortally wounded shortly after this picture was taken. *(Author's Collection)*

A recon team leader of Company F (LRP), 58th Infantry, gives directions during a patrol skirmish in the western mountains of Thua Thien Province in 1968. The 101st Airborne Division patrollers uncovered major North Vietnamese troop movements in this area. *(Rockoff)*

A member of Company G (Ranger), 75th Infantry, uncovers enemy 82mm mortar rounds during patrol operations in Quang Tin Province in 1969. The Americal Rangers served the 23d Infantry Division (Americal) in Vietnam. *(I MR MACOI Release)*

A combat recon patrol of Company E (Long Range Patrol), 50th Infantry, wades through typical swampland while conducting 1968 search operations in the Mekong Delta. The patrollers engaged in many riverine and waterborne operations. *(U.S. Army)*

The only National Guard infantry unit to serve in Vietnam was Company D (Ranger), 151st Infantry. This well-trained unit gained considerable fame in Vietnam. Here Sp4 Walter Hasty, second from left, is interviewed by a reporter at the Bien Hoa air base just after his patrol's return from the field. *(U.S. Army)*

Lieutenant Grange, center, and other decorated members of Company L (Airborne Ranger), 75th Infantry, are reviewed after achieving major successes in the western Reconnaissance Zone. The unit did not discontinue operations until November 1971 and—when linked with other divisional LRRP units—served the longest in Vietnam. *(Author's Collection)*

A member of the elite 173d Airborne Brigade's Company N (Airborne Ranger), 75th Infantry, cautiously moves through tropical terrain in Binh Dinh Province during Operation WASHINGTON GREEN in 1970. The rangers maintained constant surveillance of a rugged region near the coast. *(U.S. Army)*

A team of Company H (Airmobile Ranger), 75th Infantry, pushes deep through a rainy forest as it follows the Serges Jungle Highway enemy infiltration corridor in 1969. The ranger company reconnoitered as part of the 1st Cavalry Division screen along the Vietnamese-Cambodian border region. *(USARV 10)*

Ranger team 52 (R) was surprised by devastating enemy machine gun fire from a bunker (B) at the edge of this forest clearing southeast of O'Rang, Cambodia, on 17 June 1970. Team leader Staff Sgt. Deverton Cochrane of Company H (Airmobile Ranger), 75th Infantry, remains missing in action after this encounter. *(MACV 28 Jun 70 MIA Board Exhibit T)*

The Vietnamese ranger pride is exhibited by this honor guard of the prestigious 55th ARVN Ranger Battalion assembled in full uniforms at Cat Lai, near Saigon, in July 1967. The South Vietnamese rangers were used as light infantry and reconnaissance strike forces and rendered valuable service during the war. *(William Dupuis)*

A Vietnamese ranger commander grimacing in pain—having lost his right hand below the wrist—nevertheless insisted on personally lifting out his battalion survivors following a 1963 battle against the Viet Cong. His U.S. Army adviser captain sits beside him.
(Steven Stibbens)

A recon team of Company F (Ranger), 75th Infantry, returns in a Royal Thai Victory Flight C-123 aircraft under the watchful eye of Thai loadmaster Staff Sgt. Viwai Kuanniyom in April 1969. The victory flights brought Thai recon troops and their 46th Special Forces Company Detachment A-41 (Ranger) advisers into Vietnam, where they worked occasionally with U.S. rangers. *(U.S. Air Force)*

Thai ranger students patrol through the swamps near Chantaburi during RTA Special Warfare Center ranger course #21, conducted by 46th Special Forces Company Detachment A-41 (Ranger) advisers in September 1969. This detachment was the only dual-qualified Special Forces/ranger unit in the Vietnam war. *(John Olson)*

Paratroopers of Company O (Arctic Ranger), 75th Infantry, board aircraft for the 4 March 1971 jump onto the seven-foot-thick polar ice cap located about 130 miles north-north-east of Point Barrow, Alaska. The Arctic Rangers conducted a series of combined winter exercises that demonstrated their winter warfare excel-lence. *(Lyman Woodman)*

Arctic Rangers of Company O, 75th Infantry, watch fuel-carrying CH-47 Chinook helicopters arrive at their overnight bivouac on the frozen Beaufort Sea in March 1971. Temperatures on the polar ice cap reg-istered minus 38 degrees, and wind chill factors plummeted effective temperatures to minus 70 degrees. *(USARAL Photo Section)*

them. The enemy was still firing but ceased movement temporarily while trying to develop the situation.

Staff Sergeant Holland told the radioman to call for help. The radioman replied that he had left the radio because it had been put on the ground with the long antenna up, and the heavy crossfire prevented him from retrieving it. About the same time, Specialist Brooks, who was separated and moved downhill farther to the east, saw his comrades and ran over to them. Staff Sergeant Holland stated that he would remain behind to divert the enemy pursuit force and calmly ordered Sergeant McDonald to lead the team out of the area.

The team fled across the open grassy field, and Staff Sergeant Holland was last seen charging back up the hill, firing toward the enemy at the original patrol position. This solitary counterattack enabled the rest of the team to reach another ridge. Sergeant McDonald and his men hid in the brush and tried unsuccessfully to contact several helicopters using emergency panels and mirrors. McDonald finally set off a smoke grenade to attract the attention of pilots flying overhead. The team was picked up within forty-five minutes of the initial encounter.

The next day a parachute rifle company was deployed to the skirmish site and found Holland's body with part of his equipment hacked off. Judging from the numerous wounds inflicted and the shattered vegetation around his body, it was determined that he made a vigorous last stand before being killed in hand-to-hand combat. Holland had realized that his isolated team was without radio communications, had two wounded individuals, and was twenty miles from friendly elements. In the finest tradition of a team leader, he deliberately sacrificed his own life to save the remainder of the team members and to regain or destroy the equipment they had lost.[7]

THE COCHISE RAIDERS

In September 1967, Brig. Gen. Leo H. Schweiter took over the 173d Airborne Brigade and was alerted to prepare his brigade for movement to a battleground. At the same time, MACV commander Gen. William C. Westmoreland ordered the brigade's patrol reconnaissance members transferred to form a detached reconnaissance company for II Field Force Vietnam. The brigade assembled 229 handpicked paratroopers for the new unit (designated long-range patrol Company F, 51st Infantry) and detached them from brigade jurisdiction in October.[8]

During the sanguinary battle of Dak To in November 1967, the 173d Airborne Brigade was forced to rely almost exclusively on Special Forces reconnaissance assistance in the rugged mountains of Kontum Province near the Cambodian border. Troop E remained a brigade reaction force responsible for command post security and convoy escort. One cavalry platoon was helicoptered into action but failed in its attempt to destroy a clandestine enemy radio site. The brigade had not yet fully rebuilt its LRRP Platoon, but on 4 November it was airlifted into Dak To.[9]

On 12 November the LRRP platoon initiated operations and performed eight missions that killed a total of five NVA soldiers. In the reconnaissance business, however, contacts and body counts were no indicator of success. The platoon apparently collected enough valuable intelligence for the brigade, through negative activity reports as well as confirmed sightings, that it was awarded the Presidential Unit Citation for this action.[10]

After the battle of Dak To, General Schweiter revitalized brigade long-range reconnaissance. The Army authorized him to create the 74th Infantry Detachment (Airborne Long Range Patrol) to render specialized brigade reconnaissance. The unit was arranged similar to the former brigade LRRP Platoon with two officers and fifty-nine enlisted men, but several weeks were needed to rebuild reconnaissance capability. The detachment was authorized effective 20 December 1967 but not actually activated until 5 February 1968.[11]

The 74th Infantry Detachment became known as the Cochise Raiders because Brig. Gen. Richard J. Allen—who took over the 173d Airborne Brigade in March 1968—used it almost exclusively in support of Operation COCHISE. The detachment headquarters was relocated to Landing Zone English near Bong Son, within flying distance of the entire operational area. The Cochise Raiders initially used mixed teams that contained U.S. brigade volunteers and South Vietnamese from the 22d Division at Ba Gi. The teams were lettered from team A upward, although some sequences were skipped. Additionally, team C was not immediately reconstituted after its near-destruction on 1 May 1968. Likewise, team R was virtually destroyed six days later on 7 May and never replaced.[12]

Reconnaissance for 173d Airborne Brigade operational areas in the Tuy Hoa-Phu Hiep and An Khe areas was undertaken by attaching Company E (Long Range Patrol), 20th Infantry, from I Field Force Vietnam. This freed the 74th Infantry Detachment to concentrate on Operation COCHISE, a long-standing counterinsurgency campaign in northern Binh Dinh Province. The Cochise

Raiders performed an average of twenty-three patrols monthly during its existence. The patrols engaged in trail-watching, bomb- or artillery-damage assessment, and prisoner snatches. The duration of the patrols were commonly forty-eight to seventy-two hours, but some sorties lasted four or five days. The Cochise Raiders were also reinforced by Special Forces–led indigenous reconnaissance teams operating out of Camps Ha Tay and Vinh Thanh. Their main opponent was the widely scattered 3d NVA "Yellow Star" Division.

Information gained by the Cochise Raider reconnaissance teams was exploited by brigade reaction platoons or, if larger targets were located, by company- or battalion-sized airmobile assaults. Promising observation missions were stretched out by slipping in a new patrol while the same helicopters lifted out the previous ground team. The procedure inserted fresh patrols with less chance of detection, reduced aviation requirements, and made better use of scarce landing zones. In some cases the replacement stay-behind patrols detected and ambushed enemy scavengers who frequented extraction sites.[13]

Operation COCHISE took place in the Vietnamese coastal zone, and sudden offshore gales could hamper patrol activity. The stormy weather, however, sometimes provided team salvation. On 19 October 1968, team F of the 74th Infantry Detachment was caught by approaching typhoon weather twenty miles north of Bong Son, in the enemy mountain fastness of the northern An Lao Valley. Despite heavy rainsqualls, team leader Sgt. Peter G. Mossman detected enemy noises coming from behind his patrol and set up a hasty ambush. The rear security man, Sp4 Chase Riley, waited for three Viet Cong to round a bend and opened fire, killing one and causing the others to flee back down the trail.

The patrollers quickly searched the body and continued forward another 200 yards. Sergeant Mossman halted his team again to listen to the jungle. This time they heard noisier movement behind them, including a lot of talking and dogs barking. The team members realized that a larger enemy group was trying to track them using dogs. Mossman tried to radio friendly forces, but distance and weather prevented contact. He knew his team was deep in a jungle valley under the gathering storm clouds of a coastal typhoon and unable to signal for help. Mossman knew that the recon team had to evade the North Vietnamese by moving ahead faster and reaching high ground for transmission purposes.

Led by dogs, the North Vietnamese force pursued the recon members for three harrowing hours. Finally, the paratroopers climbed the crest of a ridge and transmitted their predicament by radio to an element of the Americal Division. The receiving station officer advised the patrol members to maintain their escape and evasion course, because the impending typhoon had grounded all helicopters. The message was relayed to the 173d Airborne Brigade, where the intelligence section learned that enemy trackers were chasing the recon team. The commander of the 61st Aviation Company (Assault Helicopter) recognized the emergency situation and sent two utility and two armed helicopters on a rescue mission to save the endangered team.

Radio contact was secured with Sergeant Mossman, and the team was instructed to commence evading to an open field abut 500 yards away. By now lowering clouds were masking the steep hillsides and sheets of rain were periodically washing out the horizon. Mossman recalled, "When we got to the pickup zone, the NVA were practically breathing down our necks. They couldn't see us though, because the visibility was down to about twenty-five meters. We couldn't see the choppers either, but we could hear them, so we just kept signaling with a strobe light and just hoped."

The crew of the command helicopter swept low over the broken mountain range but could not locate the team in the swirling rain clouds. The two gunships departed the formation and went back to base because the low ceiling prevented effective suppressive fire. The second lift helicopter, piloted by Warrant Officer Sam M. Kyle, began scouring the treetops. Kyle related, "I made the decision to stay and try to get them out because I figured this was their only chance because the weather wouldn't clear up for a couple of days, so I just kept circling lower and lower until I finally spotted their [strobe] light."

The recon team members were positioned beside large clumps of bushes in the dense eight-foot-high elephant grass. They scanned the misting fog, but the fading drone of three helicopters lowered any hopes for rapid extraction. The beating roar of one helicopter, however, suddenly became louder and the grass around them began swirling violently. They looked up to see the belly of a Huey helicopter looming through the misting rain. Warrant Officer Kyle fought to keep the wobbling helicopter steady in the rainstorm as the recon patrollers clambered quickly aboard. The rescue highlighted the indomitable link forged between ground recon and aviation, where mutual assistance often prevailed despite the most adverse conditions.[14]

The 74th Infantry Detachment experimented with different operational techniques to enhance patrol results. During October the

Cochise Raiders formed their first "hunter-killer" teams. These were small and highly airmobile patrols designed to seek out and ambush the enemy in a campaign of sustained harassment. Unfortunately, the advent of the northeast monsoon and rapid turnover of helicopter crews prohibited the desired level of joint patrol-aviator training on extraction methods. Several unfavorable combat situations resulted when ground teams were lifted out under fire, in extremely poor weather, by helicopter crews unskilled in extraction methods.

Cochise Raider commander Capt. John B. Buczacki could never afford the ideal luxury of having every man a certified graduate of the MACV Recondo School. Demands for long-range patrol replacements required crash-training courses, although rigorous standards of physical fitness and specialized patrol preparation were not relaxed. Brigade reconnaissance replacements received accelerated training in map reading, weapons use, rope rappelling, adjustment of artillery or aerial firepower, and helicopter employment techniques related to a patrol environment. Only the most promising volunteers were accepted for training, but the final graduation rate was still low for replacement purposes. Of the fifty-six trainees accepted in September, a total of thirty-four received qualifying certificates that October.[15]

High cumulative field losses claimed more irreplaceable team leaders. On the morning of 13 November 1968, reconnaissance team D, led by Staff Sgt. Laszlo Rabel, established a defensive perimeter on the sheer side of a forested mountain overlooking the Nuoi Luong river. Scout Pfc. Arthur F. Bell heard sounds of enemy movement and looked toward Sgt. Cameron T. McAllister, who nodded as they both carefully rotated their rifles toward the noise. Sp4 Paul L. Desmond, the radioman, was on rest break under a poncho with the PRC-25 handset held near his ear. Sp4 Stephen Fryer shook him and whispered, "Movement to the front! Stay quiet!"

The jungle then became very quiet. McAllister asked Fryer if he saw anything. Specialist Fryer held up one finger and whispered, "I think he went back down." After waiting a moment, Staff Sergeant Rabel and McAllister decided to check out the rugged jungle drop-off to their front. Rabel stood up and was bending under a tree limb to lower himself down the steep slope. A grenade bounced into their positions and struck a rock. The clustered men had no time to react, but Rabel immediately jumped on the grenade and smothered the explosion. He was mortally wounded, and he rolled downhill. The other four members fired claymore mines, succeeded in extracting the fallen sergeant and breaking contact, and reached a pickup point.[16]

The valor of the 74th Infantry Detachment leaders was almost legendary, but no amount of bravery could compete against the monsoon weather as it worsened in the weeks ahead. The detachment scaled down its reconnaissance effort and used the opportunity to retrain and receive new members. By the time the weather cleared, the Cochise Raiders were transformed into a ranger company.

THE NOVEMBER RANGERS

On 1 January 1969 the Department of the Army reorganized the 75th Infantry under the combat arms regimental system to give a common parent regiment, with ranger heritage, for the long-range patrol units. The transition to ranger status in the 173d Airborne Brigade happened under the tenure of Brig. Gen. John W. Barnes, and Capt. Richard D. James's Company N (Airborne Ranger), 75th Infantry, was activated on 1 February 1969 by transforming the 74th Infantry Detachment into a ranger company tailored for brigade reconnaissance support. The rangers were known as the "November Rangers" in conformity with N of the ICAO phonetic alphabet adopted by the U.S. military in 1956.

There was some confusion in the 173d Airborne Brigade over utilizing the 75th Infantry as the ranger regimental title, because the brigade also contained another 75th Infantry—a combat tracker dog platoon. Both units were organized into teams. However, they were distinguished by the fact that the two tracker teams were labeled teams One and Two, whereas Company N teams were designated by international phonetic letter codes, such as team Alpha. I Field Force Vietnam also used the brigade to render personnel and equipment support for the corps-level ranger company (Company C), and this added more complications and confusion in paperwork regarding ranger Companies C and N.[17]

The phonetic labels also varied slightly from the pure letter identifications used previously by the Cochise Raiders. The new code was supposedly imposed as a deliberate attempt to erase the stigma of destroyed teams and their consequently "unlucky letters." For example, ranger team Romeo would be completely distinguished from recon team R already lost in action. The ranger company retained identical sixty-one-member detachment operating levels, but all team members were Americans.

Company N became fully operational on 9 February 1969, and

its twelve teams were immediately deployed to forestall the projected enemy Tet-69 offensive in Binh Dinh Province. General Barnes anticipated that ranger patrol saturation would screen enemy buildups and allow him to counter NVA/VC movements with regular brigade forces. The company's twelve ranger teams were instructed to use artillery and aerial firepower against enemy targets and were infiltrated into the An Lao, An Lo, Suoi Ca, and 506 valleys; the Highland Fishhook; the Crow's Foot; and the Nui Ba and Tiger mountains.

The brigade Tet-69 campaign lasted from 9 February through 26 March 1969 and marked the first independent employment of a ranger company in screening operations during the Vietnam war. The rangers, often serving on back-to-back patrols, conducted over one hundred reconnaissance missions, sixty-five of which lasted from seventy-two to ninety-six hours, and accounted for 134 separate sightings of enemy personnel. The intelligence-gathering aspects of this assignment deliberately drove down body count statistics. While only thirty-four NVA troops were killed by direct ranger contact, a much larger number of enemy troops were killed by ranger-sponsored indirect fire and reaction elements. Most important, the ranger screen ultimately prevented enemy mass assaults on urban localities within Binh Dinh province during the 1969 Tet holiday period.[18]

The preemptive ranger patrols were typified by the 21 February 1969 experience of team Juliet. The team members located a well-used trail and followed it twenty-five yards until they reached an enemy base camp built into the caverns of a rocky overhang. The point man, hearing voices and chopping noises, went further to investigate and killed an enemy soldier walking toward the team. The patrol leader spotted five North Vietnamese troops dressed in green fatigues running away to the south. Team Juliet withdrew from the cave complex and radioed for helicopter rocketing of the hillside. Following the intense aerial bombardment, the team reentered the shattered complex and found numerous foxholes ("spider holes") and timber bunkers. The bunkers were covered by three feet of dirt, connected to caves, and largely impervious to air strikes. Ranger team Juliet captured documents and weapons abandoned in the fortified compound and prepared for afternoon extraction.

The helicopter lift-out of team Juliet at 2:25 P.M. was marred by rain-slick conditions that caused one patrol member to fall from the skids of the first extraction ship. Fifteen minutes later, another helicopter crew found the fallen man on the thickly forested slope and retrieved him. The patrol leader stayed on the ground to look for the fallen paratrooper and was unaware that the injured man was already found. The team leader, searching through the brush for another landing zone, killed two North Vietnamese troops who chanced to see him and tried to intercept. The sergeant finally reached another open grassy area, used a cut-down emergency panel to signal a forward observation aircraft, and was rescued by helicopter at 4:40 P.M. [19]

Ranger Company N remained in northern Binh Dinh Province throughout its wartime service in Vietnam. The company performed essentially the same task during a host of different brigade operations. Teams were sent into the rugged mountains and interior river valleys to maintain a roving picket line of patrols. The patrols monitored NVA/VC activities and watched for enemy movements directed against the populated coastal lowlands. The patrols were flexibly arranged on the periphery of the brigade zone and relied on various sources of intelligence—aircraft observations, intelligence interrogations, radio intercepts, etc.—to place the teams most advantageously.

In November 1969, ranger coverage was found to be insufficient at the outset of Operation WASHINGTON GREEN. The brigade permanently strengthened Company N (Ranger) from platoon to full company size. The recruiting of new ranger personnel was performed at Phu Tai and Cha Rang by taxing infantry battalions for additional personnel, and the company was expanded to newly authorized levels of 128 rangers. Company N reported, "Factors considered are GT [general testing] of 100 or higher, no physical or mental impairments, high weapons qualification scores, and voluntary request for the ranger company. All prospective personnel are interviewed prior to acceptance. Past experience has proven that it is generally better to recruit new personnel coming into the brigade than personnel from the battalions. [Veteran] personnel from the battalions have picked up habits, both good and bad, that are not normal to ranger operations. Also, the battalions will not release a good man." [20]

The rangers maximized team potential with new equipment. For example, Company N received an experimental system that upgraded their ability to fire electrically detonated claymore mines—the staple of ranger ambushes in Vietnam—through the use of Remote Firing Devices. These devices (boxes) were pre-positioned and concealed along ambush zones and linked into multiple claymore mines that could be fired by rangers with hand-held firing devices from distances up to a thousand yards away. The rangers improved this system by using Personal Seismic Detectors in conjunction with the Remote Firing Devices. Another refinement involved rigging concussion grenades in the center of remotely-triggered ambush zones so that a few stunned enemy soldiers were left alive for capture.[21]

Another November Ranger technique involved the use of pre-planned artillery fire on the ambush zone, triggered by ranger radio signals. The combination of shell bursts and claymore mine detonations effectively confused enemy troops, who sometimes believed that they were under artillery instead of ranger fire. Late in the war experimental Army mechanical mines were issued to the rangers. These provided a means of covering back-trails and non-observable areas near ranger ambush sites. The rangers connected them to trip wires laid across likely pathways and were able to detonate daisy-chains of claymore mines or grenades.[22]

During emergency extractions, Special Forces–style McGuire extraction rigs were preferred but proved difficult for some aircrews to install properly. Rangers tried to radio their requirements in advance, but in some cases helicopters were forced to leave, return to base, and re-rig correctly before the patrols could be lifted out. Rope ladders could be quickly rigged and easily dropped by all helicopter crews, but they were difficult to scale and took a lot of time to climb. In some instances, however, rangers were forced to link into rope ladders that were then hoisted out. One tragic helicopter mishap occurred after an inexperienced aircrew wasted excessive time while attempting to lift out four Company N rangers by rope ladder. The helicopter lost emergency power and crashed.[23]

Ranger Company N commander Capt. John P. Lawton stated that his unit owed its success to its team leaders:

Team leaders who trained hard and expected their teams to put out 100 percent [effort] and they got that 100 percent. When back on the LZ they concentrated on 'break contact' drills and physical conditioning, as in some instances they had to run two or three miles to get to an extraction LZ. Probably the most decorated man in the unit, if not in Vietnam, was a Chinese-Hawaiian NCO named Patrick Tadina. One of the team leaders was David Dolby, who had won the Medal of Honor in a previous tour with the Cav. Dolby was a character in the company and was well known for carrying an M60 machine gun slung over his shoulder on a rope, rather than an M16 rifle. Finally, but not by any means last, there were sergeants like Maddog Cupids, Matos, and the rest. All were ideal combat leaders who were smart, fearless in combat, and cared dearly for their teams.[24]

On 12 November 1969, Sgt. Santos A. Matos's ranger team finished reconnoitering and placed claymore mines along an ambush site. Shortly afterward, two unarmed North Vietnamese officers walked into view. Sergeant Matos motioned the team to give him covering fire while he attempted a prisoner capture. As Sergeant Matos stepped onto the trail and seized one of the enemy officers, five rifle-carrying NVA soldiers appeared on a second trail leading into the ambush zone. Sergeant Matos fearlessly held the captive by one arm while he used the other hand to level and open fire with his M16—scattering the approaching squad. The team immediately left the area and successfully extracted the high-ranking prisoner. Ranger commander Captain Lawton remarked:

> What amazed everyone is that Matos chose to put a headlock on the prisoner when he discovered VC/NVA coming down another trail and took his other hand, leveled his M16, and fired up that patrol. He then broke contact and dragged the prisoner out. In any other situation of that sort, we all felt a soldier might have shot the prisoner and ran. Matos's action was fearless and compassionate.
>
> The prisoner was so grateful to Matos for sparing his life, as well as being thankful for the medical treatment and overall consideration he received, that he volunteered to lead us [Company N] to a long-sought enemy hospital complex. The brigade put a rifle company on standby and in we went. The General asked how long I thought it would take to blow a hole in the jungle and create a one-ship LZ so he could put a rifle company into the area. I told him we'd take in rucksacks full of C4 [explosives] and det[onating] cord and have him an LZ in an hour. We did locate the hospital but we were discovered, had to break contact, and withdraw. I selected another site for the LZ and three and a half days later, reinforced with engineers, we lowered in and accomplished the mission.[25]

Operation WASHINGTON GREEN lasted through December 1970. During this period the brigade was commanded in turn by Brig. Gen. Hubert S. Cunningham, who took over in August 1969, and Brig. Gen. Ray Ochs from August 1970 forward. Both generals were staunch believers in airborne esprit and believed that special ranger privileges might undermine paratrooper camaraderie. For these reasons ranger black berets were banned, despite their common use by other ranger outfits.

The expansion of Company N still provided too few ranger patrols to effectively maintain the screen. For this reason, ranger pickets were supplemented by reconnaissance raider teams from

Company E of the 503d Infantry's 3d Battalion. One example of this patrol reinforcement occurred on the evening of 27 August 1970, when two raider teams were inserted by helicopter at the entrance of the Soui Ca river valley. The two teams moved into surveillance positions overlooking the Soui Ca before dark. Throughout the night the team members counted over 200 enemy troops advancing along the trails in groups ranging from four soldiers to entire companies.

The two raider teams remained hidden throughout the following day while the leaders devised a joint ambush scheme for the next night. The sergeants decided to create mutually supplemental ambush zones about 300 yards apart. The first ambush was designed to snare a small enemy contingent and cause it to flee into the other team's kill zone farther down the trail. If a larger enemy force appeared, both ambushes could be sprung simultaneously.

At nightfall, both teams split up and established separate ambush positions closer to the main trail. Fifty Viet Cong appeared on the hillside path after dark, and both ambushes were simultaneously triggered with claymore mines. The raiders threw hand grenades into the smoke and scrambled back through the underbrush to gain better positions farther up the slope. The forest suddenly erupted in gunfire from all directions. The raiders sustained automatic weapons fire from more enemy troops counterattacking along the trail, as well as from Viet Cong flank troops who were traveling parallel to the trail but higher on the ridge line. It quickly became apparent that the Americans were isolated and outnumbered.

One recon team was equipped with an M60 machine gun. The gunner brazenly charged the enemy lines with his weapon blazing and enabled the team to escape through the nearest enemy defenders. The other team was not as fortunate. Without a machine gun and handicapped by two men wounded in the initial crossfire, the team was forced to stay where it was. The seasoned recon troops coolly refrained from firing their M16 rifles, lest the muzzle flashes reveal their individual positions in the night-shrouded tangle of jungle. Instead, they tossed dozens of grenades that succeeded in keeping the enemy temporarily at bay. Their radio distress calls also brought prompt aerial support. Helicopter gunships, already hovering on station in case of trouble, appeared overhead and began raking the nearby hedgerows. Air Force Shadow and Stringer aircraft also provided aerial support.

The 173d Airborne Brigade responded by helicoptering a reaction infantry platoon to the battle scene. These reinforcements linked up with the first recon team and fought toward the trapped band. The beleaguered raiders were rescued because the enemy force disappeared into the jungle rather than become pinned into positions subject to aerial retaliation. The raiders claimed victory because sweeps of the trail at first light revealed twelve enemy dead, along with "beaucoup" blood trails and drag marks in the nearby undergrowth.[26]

In actuality, the recon teams narrowly averted catastrophe. They sacrificed topside security in their zeal to create a clever double ambush, and they posted no one to safeguard higher elevations. The team leaders arranged an improper ambush plan that displayed scant regard for flank or rear protection, and suffered a sharp reverse. Furthermore, in the resulting firefight there was no defensive cohesion. Indeed, one team with superior weapons abandoned the other—although the confusion of night fighting probably contributed to this fragmentation.

The 173d Airborne Brigade raiders of Company E quickly canceled this adverse episode when eight paratroopers of recon team 3 ambushed an enemy company just before dawn on 1 October. Twenty-three North Vietnamese were cut down by the initial claymore blasts, and two wounded prisoners were seized. Although both prisoners later died of their wounds, the action gave the brigade its biggest single victory of Operation WASHINGTON GREEN Phase V. Only nine days later the same recon team executed one of the most successful vengeance ambuscades of the Vietnam war.

The groundwork for this lethal retaliation mission commenced shortly after the death of Lt. Col. John J. Clark, commanding the 503d Infantry's 3d Battalion, on 2 June 1970. The brigade intelligence section initiated a persistent search for the high-ranking Viet Cong officials responsible. These military intelligence experts carefully nurtured Vietnamese village informants. In the fall, a villager from the Hoai An district provided the crucial information. The long-sought killers, who included the deputy Viet Cong commander for Binh Dinh Province, were scheduled to hold a rare field policy meeting on 10 October.

Reacting to this information, recon team 3 of raider Company E prepared ambush positions outside Fire Support Base Orange. At five minutes to noon, a Viet Cong platoon armed with American pistols, carbines, M79 grenade launchers, and M16s moved into the area. Five Viet Cong soldiers then left the platoon and walked 200 yards farther, straight into the raider trap. The recon troops sprang the ambush with claymore mines, killing the VC province executive, a company commander, and two other officers. A communications liaison master sergeant was captured. One of the dead Viet Cong officers possessed a citation describing his actions in killing Lieutenant Colonel Clark. The VC escort platoon fled the area when the firing erupted, although the ambush position was constructed to deal with this expected enemy threat.

The vengeance mission of 10 October 1970 was a salutary example of a skillfully administered ambush task. The 173d Airborne Brigade maximized the military intelligence gathering efforts of the 172d Military Intelligence Detachment to obtain precise targeting data and then utilized the superior ambush discipline of a professional combat reconnaissance team to complete the assignment.[27]

In January 1971, after twenty months of pacification security, the 173d Airborne Brigade returned to flexible combat operations in Operation GREENE LIGHTNING. The ranger screen remained in place. An important aspect of screening duty was providing ground damage assessment of air strike and artillery results. For example, on 21 January a scout helicopter was fired on over the Tiger mountains and heavy artillery bombarded the reported location. Thickened fuel drums, rigged as flame bombs by the brigade's 51st Chemical Detachment, were also dropped from helicopters over the dense mountain jungle. In midafternoon, ranger teams Delta and Mike were airlanded to appraise damage results.

The thirteen rangers moved through the jungle toward the mountain subjected to artillery shelling. Almost immediately, the rangers noticed the acrid odor of burning powder. They soon uncovered a burning structure to the left of their march route. Team Mike Sgt. Gary Bushinger and team Delta Sp4 James Wagner investigated the charred ruins and discovered a bunker complex entrance protected by compacted sandbags. Several enemy soldiers were seen running past the trees, and Sp4 Stephen Joley succeeded in killing one of them. Sergeant Bushinger spotted three more escaping up the hill and opened fire, dropping two and causing the third to retreat back into the bunker complex. The rangers left a two-man security team near the bunker and checked out the hillside, where they discovered one of the dead enemy was a female nurse. The trapped bunker personnel were persuaded to surrender, and four pounds of documents were found hidden inside two M60 ammo cans.

The rangers swept the area debris thoroughly and secured more prisoners, who were brought to the extraction site. The Hawaiian radioman, Sp4 Jimmy Akuna of Honolulu, called in a "dust-off" helicopter for those prisoners suffering facial and hand burns from the bombardment. The rangers confirmed the destruction of a North

Vietnamese battlefield dispensary and obtained valuable intelligence information.[28]

The ranger screen was flexible enough to permit withdrawal of teams for special missions of a higher priority. These special contingencies included any type of prisoner rescue attempt, coded BRIGHTLIGHT missions. During Operation GREENE LIGHTNING information was received that six U.S. captives were being held in an enemy prison compound west of Kron River. On 19 February 1971, BRIGHTLIGHT TIGER commenced when Capt. Richard M. Tanaka led four eight-man ranger teams to attempt to liberate the Kron River prison inmates. The rangers were issued bolt cutters, demolition charges, and protective masks. Shortly after 7:00 A.M., ranger teams Charlie and Delta were inserted in deep jungle north of the objective, uncovered several food storage sheds, and took up assigned blocking positions near a small stream.

Helicopters sprayed the jungle objective with a fifteen-minute dose of riot-control chemical agents. The gas concentration was designed to render enemy personnel temporarily combat-ineffective. The rangers of teams Kilo and Oscar rappelled through the triple-canopy jungle wearing lightweight protective masks. They carried only mission-essential equipment and depended on pre-packaged bundles of rations, poncho liners, and extra ammunition being lowered later through the trees. The gas clouded the base of the objective area for two hours with a dense white blanket of chemical mist but did not adversely affect search operations. The teams' rangers used cloverleaf patrols to cover the entire area but found no trace of the prison compound. Brightlight Tiger was another frustrating example of attempted prisoner recovery operations, where the rangers might have achieved success if given accurate prison information.[29]

The overall surveillance nature of the ranger screen made it a defensive instrument, but tactically the screen was maintained through aggressive, offensive patrolling. Unrelenting pressure was applied against enemy way stations and reinforcement avenues to hinder North Vietnamese mobility. On 28 February, Staff Sgt. Kirk Cheney led a ranger foray composed of Mike and India teams. The strike was aimed at a hidden trail network in the Nui Mieu Mountains. The rangers split into two groups, leaving five men to watch the trail while six advanced up the thickly wooded slope. As the rangers moved slowly toward the top of the hill, they heard voices behind them in a ravine. The rangers reversed direction in the dense underbrush and quietly slipped around a group of enemy soldiers who were carelessly chatting and smoking cigarettes while they rested and cleaned weapons.

One of the NVA soldiers suddenly climbed out of the ravine and spotted point man Sp4 Edward Welsh approaching. Specialist Welsh screamed, "Now!" and the rangers opened fire. Three enemy soldiers fell dead in the first volley. The rest of the surprised squad ran from the ravine into the jungle. The rangers followed, dodging grenades and yelling in Vietnamese for the enemy to "Chieu Hoi." The North Vietnamese troops tossed two more fragmentation grenades, which landed near the rangers but failed to explode. The rangers responded with a fusillade of grenade and rifle fire that killed the remaining enemy soldiers and eradicted the trail rest area.[30]

The ranger screen proved a valuable deterrent in stifling enemy attacks on friendly bases. In April 1971, during Operation GREENE SURE, Sgt. Jerry Curtain led a ranger team to provide advanced warning of enemy movement near Fire Support Base Pony. The team was moving down a ridge in a sudden cloudburst when point man Sergeant Barnes saw an enemy observation post. The position was wedged between large boulders and covered by a tarp for protection against the rain. The rangers opened fire, killing the North Vietnamese forward observation officer. His companion quickly fired one magazine from his AK47 rifle and then escaped through the maze of boulders. The rangers received credit for stopping a mortar attack on the American base.[31]

In rare instances, the ranger screen was temporarily suspended in order to establish blocking forces. Normally, regular infantry was used to seal off a battlefield and prevent enemy reinforcement. During the latter years of the war, however, commanders preferred rangers because of their greater dependability and military expertise. On 2 April 1971, for example, the 173d Airborne Brigade became locked in a week of intense combat against entrenched North Vietnamese regulars on Nui Cung Chap. The November Rangers were ordered to cordon off the battlefield with a patrol picket line and prevent enemy reinforcements from reaching elements of the 2d NVA Regiment defending the summit.

On the late afternoon of April 6, Company N was air-assaulted into the western periphery of the Suoi Ca Valley. Ranger team Lima was surrounded almost immediately by enemy forces and nearly overrun. The steady radio liaison work of ranger Sp4 Michael Bowers, who called in a ring of artillery fire throughout the morning darkness, saved the team from annihilation. At sunrise on the following morning, Staff Sgt. Juan S. Borja linked up ranger teams

Kilo and Oscar and destroyed an unsuspecting column of North Vietnamese rocket troops. Staff Sgt. Walter Solgalow's team Tango annihilated a second enemy column with mechanical ambush devices and captured two wounded prisoners. Platoon Sergeant Roger Brown's Team Echo was helicoptered in reaction to team Tango's contact and uncovered a forward enemy command post. On April 9, as the battle of Nui Cung Chap terminated, teams Echo and Tango destroyed a North Vietnamese way-station complex.[32]

In recognition of their heroic action in the Battle of Nui Cung Chap, the parachutist rangers of the 173d Airborne Brigade finally received their coveted black berets. The unofficial black ranger beret was already emblematic of the 75th Infantry and the ranger department, but it was denied the airborne rangers over two years past their creation. They were the last rangers in Vietnam to receive black berets, primarily because of brigade senior officer opposition to further distinctions between unit paratroopers.

The last commander of the 173d Airborne Brigade, Brig. Gen. Jack MacFarlane, overturned this policy after the heavy April fighting. He assembled the rangers in formation and announced that "the rangers of N Company have performed with excellence in a very difficult and risky job." He then personally fitted the first black beret on company guidon bearer Pfc. George L. Miller. When the rest of the formation donned black berets in unison, they achieved consistency in uniform apparel among all six ranger companies remaining in Vietnam.[33]

The dangers inherent in maintaining the Company N ranger screen were very real. The screen was composed of small patrols that probed known enemy strongholds and infiltration routes, in very rugged mountain jungle terrain, at considerable distance from friendly installations. The screen was maintained in one general area—the four northern districts of Binh Dinh Province—for over three years. Under normal wartime conditions, this length of time would have enabled any unit to gain intimate familiarity with the terrain characteristics. The North Vietnamese and Viet Cong enjoyed this advantage. On the American side, annual soldier rotation and patrol interchange between areas prevented this same level of knowledge.

The paratrooper rangers of Company N exhibited remarkable professionalism and calm courage in patrolling remote enemy sanctuaries. Every ranger understood that insertions into known trouble spots could trip a hornets' nest and pit them against vastly superior enemy numbers. The valiant November Ranger teams persisted in scouting these areas, however, until the very end of the war.

During the afternoon of 29 May 1971, ranger team Bravo, now led by Staff Sergeant Solgalow, was helicoptered into the dangerous Suoi Ca Valley to observe hostile troop movements. The six rangers marched southwest over 150 yards through the thick jungle, chose a suitable static listening post, and established all-around security. As the rangers crouched motionless in the thick tropical foliage, they began hearing Vietnamese talking not far away.

Sergeant Solgalow decided to investigate. The rangers dropped their rucksacks, except for Sp4 Mike Hines, who backpacked the team's PRC-77 radio at all times, and walked warily toward the sound of the voices. Point man Sgt. Terry Ziegenbein was moving with special caution when three enemy soldiers suddenly stepped into view, almost face to face. Sergeant Ziegenbein automatically fired his M16 rifle's full thirty-round magazine into the startled trio, killing all three instantly at point-blank range. No sooner had Sergeant Ziegenbein decided this one-sided exchange than the entire team came under concentrated machine gun fire from the high ground to their front.

The rangers hastened behind a small embankment and tossed grenades in the direction of the enemy weapon. Further attempts to withdraw were met by more enemy fire. The rangers radioed for assistance, and a reaction company from the 2d Battalion of the 503d Infantry (Airborne) was sent in response. The rescue attempt by the regular paratroopers faltered only a hundred yards from the entrapped ranger position. The new skirmish, however, momentarily alleviated the tempo of enemy fire directed against the rangers. They took advantage of the lull by scrambling back to their ammunition-laden rucksacks. Ranger commander Maj. William Shippey circled the contact area in a command helicopter as daylight faded overhead. He notified the ranger team that the relief company had taken severe casualties and was pinned down, and further advances were unlikely before morning.

The surrounded rangers stayed hidden as darkness enveloped the jungle. Fortunately, nightfall was accompanied by torrential rains that hampered enemy search parties trying to find the rangers. Groups of North Vietnamese soldiers equipped with flashlights and electric lanterns thrashed constantly throughout the dense shrubbery. Ranger Pfc. Chris Simmons recalled, "At times, they were only a foot away from my head." Toward dawn the enemy troops called off their futile search.

The battle between the relief company and the North Vietnamese force resumed in full intensity at first light. The rangers had inadvertently stumbled across a major enemy force. Ordinary linkup seemed impossible. The infantry company was unable to maneuver forward without incurring unacceptable casualties, because ranger proximity to the enemy positions prevented customary artillery and air support. With each passing hour, the danger of further enemy reinforcement threatened to ensnare the small ranger band. Ranger team Bravo was ordered to get out at once—regardless of losses.

The rangers slithered past the North Vietnamese firing positions toward the edge of the base camp. Specialist Hines radioed their intention to dash across the open ground toward the American positions now in front of them. This vital radio coordination ensured that on signal their fellow paratroopers would cease firing. The first three rangers then raced across the small clearing and reached friendly battle lines before the enemy could react. The next three rangers waited for a while longer before running across the field. The enemy was surprised by the second group and shifted fire late, but still managed to hit Sp4 Don Bizadi with four rounds. When Bizadi fell wounded, team leader Solgalow dropped beside him. He applied emergency first aid despite the withering fire and dragged Bizadi the rest of the distance to safety.[34]

This was one of the last actions of the Vietnam war for Company N, but it demonstrated the willing risk that teams undertook to preserve the ranger screen. In July the 173d Airborne Brigade was ordered to begin preparing to return to the United States. The ranger observance of Binh Dinh Province was finally relaxed and then terminated, but the 22d ARVN Division reconnaissance unit, trained by Company N, proved very capable in monitoring the sector after the American departure. On 25 August 1971 the ranger company was solemnly inactivated and the brigade colors were furled for Vietnam departure. Company N (Airborne Ranger), 75th Infantry, was distinguished as one of the only paratrooper-qualified ranger companies serving a larger parachutist command in the Vietnam war.[35]

The airborne patrollers and November Rangers who served the 173d Airborne Brigade became masters in infiltration, and their small teams performed daring ambushes and prisoner snatches at great distances inside tightly controlled NVA/VC territory. The success of the ranger company, however, was handicapped whenever higher commanders wanted their talents used as fighting units. While equipped to fight, the rangers had the primary mission of reconnaissance. Team assignments to light infantry tasks inevitably diminished intelligence-gathering capability.

10

II CORPS TACTICAL ZONE

I FIELD FORCE RANGERS

CENTRAL HIGHLAND RECONNAISSANCE

During the Second Indochina War, South Vietnam was divided into four corps tactical zones for military operations. Within the period of United States wartime involvement, the northernmost region of the country (I CTZ), near the Demilitarized Zone, was initially a Marine responsibility. The southernmost region (IV CTZ), comprising the Mekong Delta, remained primarily a jurisdiction of the Army of the Republic of Vietnam. This arrangement meant that U.S. Army forces principally operated in central South Vietnam (II CTZ) and the capital region (III CTZ).

On 15 March 1966 the Army created the I and II Field Force Vietnam to exercise operational control over the II and III Corps Tactical Zones, respectively. The field force concept was adopted instead of a normal corps headquarters for three basic reasons. First, adding another corps designation into an existing South Vietnamese corps zone would have caused confusion. Secondly, the field force organization was flexibly designed for pacification and advisory responsibilities beyond normal corps tactical functions. Finally, field force organizations could add more required subordinate units, including other corps.[1]

Corps-level reconnaissance for I and II Field Force Vietnam was performed by Special Forces–led indigenous warriors organized into "unconventional warfare projects" to cover remote areas. Special Forces Detachment B-50 Project Omega at Ban Me Thuot served I Field Force Vietnam and used Sedang, Jeh, and Rhade Montagnard tribal volunteers as well as Cham and Chinese ethnic minorities. Special Forces Detachment B-56 Project Sigma supported II Field Force Vietnam. MACV commander General Westmoreland decided that the highly proficient Special Forces recon experts and their native irregulars would be better utilized in a strategic reconnaissance role, serving MACV Studies and Observation Group (MACV-SOG) on clandestine missions across the border into Laos and Cambodia.[2]

On 22 June 1967, Joint Chiefs of Staff chairman Gen. Earle G. Wheeler authorized two regular infantry long-range patrol companies for the field forces. He informed General Westmoreland that the Army planned to activate both units in November, but that neither company would be ready for Vietnam service until at least September 1968. Westmoreland expressed strong dissatisfaction with this arrangement, because the field force reconnaissance units would arrive too late to immediately substitute for Projects Omega and Sigma—scheduled for November 1967 absorption into MACV-SOG.[3]

General Westmoreland requested to form both patrol companies in Vietnam, where they could be organized much quicker by using available personnel and equipment. On 12 September 1967, Army chief of staff Gen. Harold K. Johnson approved Westmoreland's suggestion. Following this decision the U.S. Army Pacific issued activation orders for the companies, but restricted their formation assets to "locally available resources" within the Vietnam theater.[4]

On 25 September 1967, Company E (Long Range Patrol), 20th Infantry (Airborne), was activated and assigned to I Field Force Vietnam, commanded by Lt. Gen. William B. Rosson. He ordered the unit formed at Phan Rang with a nucleus of combat veterans, and these were secured by absorbing the 1st Brigade LRRP Platoon of the 101st Airborne Division. Additional personnel were obtained by diverting soldiers in the "Vietnam replacement pipeline" scheduled to join the 18th Military Police Brigade. Two Air Force forward air controllers with observation aircraft were also permanently attached.[5]

Company E was commanded by Maj. Danridge M. Malone and provided long-range reconnaissance, surveillance, and target acquisition on a corps-level basis. Company members were known as "Typhoon Patrollers" after the signal code word Typhoon favored by I Field Force Vietnam headquarters. Teams were numbered in accordance with platoon assignment. For example, team 47 represented the seventh team of the Fourth Platoon. Priority MACV assignments kept the unit at full capacity, a Vietnam rarity, so that nearly six months later the company commander still reported that "factors in personnel strength affecting the unit performance have been limited to rank rather than personnel shortage."[6]

On 15 October 1967, Company E was placed under operational control of the 4th Infantry Division. A week later the company relocated from coastal Phan Rang in Ninh Thuan Province to the division's base at Camp Enari in far western Pleiku Province. The company trained through December and phased its four patrol platoons through ten-day preparatory courses, followed by sequential attendance at the MACV Recondo School at two-week intervals. The platoons concluded their training with a one-week field combat exercise in the rugged Central Highlands outside Special Forces Camp Plei Do Lim. The first platoon completed its program and was declared ready on 1 December, and the entire company was declared combat-operational on 23 December.[7]

Company E was designed to field two active patrol platoons while the other two platoons trained and prepared for further missions on a rotating basis. Active platoons were deployed to mission support sites, such as forward fire bases and Special Forces camps. Each platoon normally employed three six-man recon teams at a time, because commitments beyond this limit overtaxed available resources and undermined operational effectiveness. The company kept operations and signal personnel, along with a base radio station from the communications platoon, at each outlying mission support site.

The Typhoon Patrollers were destined to become one of the finest patrol units in Vietnam. Several factors accounted for this reputation. First, the former "Reconnaissance Nomads" of the 101st Airborne Division's 1st Brigade provided a combat-experienced cadre. The company also benefited greatly from the diversion of military police replacements to its ranks, because many of the arriving MPs had dog-handling knowledge and knew the scouting advantages of canine assistance. Finally, the company profited from its solid recondo school training and continuing Special Forces working relationship that even included the acquisition of indigenous scouts.

The original 101st Airborne Division 1st Brigade LRRP Platoon had formed the basis for Company F, and on 3 December 1967 the Typhoon Patrollers sent its First Platoon to assist the 1st Brigade in reconnoitering support. Unfortunately, the lack of helicopters prevented the patrol unit from operating as intended. The brigade had also grown used to operating without its patrol platoon and simply employed the supplemental recon troops as an extra rifle platoon.

The First Platoon of Company F battled through the Bao Loc vicinity in a regular infantry capacity. On 19 December both the platoon leader and a squad (team leader) sergeant were killed by enemy fire during a jungle firefight. From 26 December until 5 January the Second Platoon was rotated to Bao Loc, but it was also misused as ordinary infantry. Company E commander Maj. William H. O'Connor expressed his dismay: "The primary lesson during operation [at] Bao Loc was that it is uneconomical and a waste of valuable assets to employ personnel trained for long range patrol work in a rifle platoon configuration."[8]

During December 1967 the Special Forces supported the Typhoon in Operation KLAMATH FALLS by filling the gap—caused when the recon company attached platoons to the 101st Airborne Division—and sending a Special Forces-led indigenous company from the native II CTZ (Pleiku) Mike Force to Camp Tan Rai, where it served as a standby force for Typhoon patrols. Fifteen Montagnard tribal warriors were integrated into Company E to give it an intrinsic native scouting capability. The operation sealed a unique bond between Special Forces and Company E that lasted throughout the conflict.[9]

On 18 December, Company E returned the favor by attaching Fourth Platoon to the II CTZ (Pleiku) Mike Force for reaction support. The Typhoon Patrollers reconnoitered the mountains and beaches southwest of Qui Nhon in an attempt to locate a Viet Cong battalion suspected of targeting the Phu Tai ammunition storage area. The teams reported several sightings but detected no significant enemy activity. During this operation the platoon rehearsed beach landings with rubber boats. One planned amphibious raid was canceled at the last minute because of worsening seas. The combined Special Forces and Typhoon Patroller activity disrupted the enemy plans against Phu Tai, and the operation was terminated at the end of the month.

On 30 December the Third Platoon entered action in support of the 4th Infantry Division near Cambodia. The company's establishment of a mission support site at Fire Support Base Oasis, west of Pleiku, meant that its platoons were engaged across the width of II Corps Tactical Zone, from the coastal mountain spurs to the remote mountain borderlands. The Third Platoon sent recon teams into the mountains and Plei Trap Valley northwest of Special Forces Camp Plei Djereng. Skirmishes flared between patrols and NVA trail parties, but no large-scale movement of enemy forces was uncovered. One team was inserted onto a jungle ridge where extraction proved almost impossible, but it was finally lifted out, under fire, in a daring helicopter night rescue.[10]

Company E continued this intense pace of combat recon through

January 1968, by which time it had accomplished seventy-eight patrols, observing enemy activity on thirty-one. The danger of these Central Highland expeditions was evidenced by the necessity to perform fourteen emergency team extractions within the same first two months. During this time the company developed an excellent reputation for recon prowess. The recon platoons demonstrated their ability to combine regular and irregular patrolling techniques, as well as to employ scout dogs as an adjunct to normal patrolling activity.[11]

During February 1968 one Typhoon Patrol team was operating with its German shepherd scout dog, Nick, in the jungle west of Pleiku. The patrol was moving through a dense forest near Fire Support Base Oasis when Nick suddenly stopped and perked up his ears. Team pointman Dave Seidel stated, "I didn't hear anything but Nick had never been wrong before, so we ducked into the brush." The patrol members soon heard voices coming through the woods, and moments later four North Vietnamese troops strolled into view. The team opened fire, killing two and wounding the other pair of NVA soldiers. During the clash, Nick—already a veteran of several encounters—remained alert and ready to warn the paratroopers if more enemy soldiers were nearby. The team swept their hasty ambush zone, collected the prisoners, and continued farther into the thick shrubbery.

After the team had moved only a short distance, the dog again gave warning. Patrol member Sp4 Jeffrey Dick reported, "We thought there were more of them in the area, and when Nick started acting jumpy, we were sure of it." This time the patrol was almost outflanked by a much larger enemy element. Gunships were radioed to bolster the patrol's firepower. The team, which was now low on ammunition after several days in the jungle, was extracted by helicopters. "I'm not sure how many times Nick has kept us out of trouble," said Specialist Seidel, "but when it comes to spotting Charlie before he sees us, this dog's the best thing we've got going for us."[12]

TYPHOON PATROLLERS

In March 1968, Maj. Gen. William R. Peers assumed command of I Field Force Vietnam. He kept Company E dispersed on a wide variety of duties. Every month the unit fielded fifty combat reconnaissance patrols that spanned central Vietnam, from the coastal rice-producing districts to the western wilderness. In addition, twelve members taught helicopter rappelling techniques to 4th In-

fantry Division combat engineers, who were learning how to con-
struct landing zones in jungle terrain. Another six-man mobile
training team taught recon courses for the South Vietnamese 22d
and 23d Divisions at Ban Me Thuot and De Duc. Finally, the company became responsible for the ARVN long-range patrol course
at the Duc My Ranger Training Center, in Khanh Hoa Province.[13]

Company E heightened its reconnaissance coordination with
Special Forces. This bonding was strengthened during Operation
BATH (12 March to 5 April 1968) when teams from the First and
Fourth Platoons complemented the Special Forces–led native contingents of the 2d Mobile Strike Force Command (MSFC). The
recon teams swept the mountain jungles around An Khe on scouting
expeditions that lasted up to seven days at a time. Special Forces
Eagle Flight teams reacted flexibly to patrol observations and struck
with increased lethality. The Special Forces reported that "the two
platoons allotted to this operation worked well with MSFC elements and performed in a highly professional manner," making
"this operation most satisfactory."[14]

During May 1968 the weather in central Vietnam changed from
the northeast to the southwest monsoon, and by early June the
region was shrouded by low clouds, dense morning fogs and rainy
drizzle, and afternoon thunderstorms. The weather, however, was
not the only adversity that threatened Company E operations. On
28 July the company instructors attached to the Duc My ARVN
Ranger Training Center incurred the wrath of the South Vietnamese
high command for graduating only twenty-two students out of the
121 Vietnamese soldiers who started the course. The company was
also accused of selecting twenty-nine superior Vietnamese rangers
from the center and adding them to its own ranks.

During fall 1968 the South Vietnamese high command, upset
over the July failure of a hundred recon students at Duc My, insisted
that all unsatisfactory soldiers be retested in November and credited
for completing the course. On 2 December the ARVN Joint General
Staff lodged a formal protest over the demanding course requirements and renewed accusations that the American instructors from
Company E were "skimming top graduates" for its own unit, while
unfairly penalizing other Vietnamese students. Using this excuse,
the senior Vietnamese command relieved Company E from further
duty at the Ranger Training Center. The relief was actually wel-
comed by the Typhoon Patrollers, because it freed experienced
noncommissioned officers for field assignments.

Company E covered a vast amount of territory to help I Field
Force Vietnam keep apprised of the current enemy situation. There

were too few allied formations to cover the territory, and this situation necessitated extensive patrolling efforts. During the six months from February through the end of July, the Typhoon Patrollers completed 300 patrols and made almost as many separate sightings of enemy personnel (306 patrols and 262 observations). They also claimed killing 117 enemy soldiers by direct fire. American casualties during the six months totaled five killed and thirty-three wounded.[15]

During the fall of 1968, Lieutenant General Peers ordered Company E to concentrate its reconnaissance support for 4th Infantry Division along the tri-border front of western Kontum province. The missions were typified by Sgt. Pete Lazcano's team, landed by helicopter on the summit of a heavily forested mountain to watch for possible enemy infiltration. The patrol descended the steep slope by zigzagging along pathways and passed numerous abandoned enemy bunkers and foxholes. Sergeant Lazcano reported, "I was forced to keep the team on trails as we made our way down the mountain—which is something we don't like to do—but the vegetation was so thick we had no choice."

The team reached lower ground and detected more recent signs of enemy activity, such as punji stakes made of freshly cut bamboo. The patrollers spent the night at the base of the mountain. On the following morning the team members continued traveling through the dense foliage until they reached a hard-packed, heavily traveled trail leading up a nearby ridge. Sergeant Lazcano attempted to make a communications check, but the radio failed to transmit from the low valley. Within five minutes a North Vietnamese trail-watcher group began walking up and down the path. The patrol waited for the enemy to pass and then moved to more open ground on the hillside. Sergeant Lazcano wanted to regain radio contact before conducting any ambush.

The team repositioned itself on the slope, and assistant team leader Sgt. Steven H. Hightower heard movement again. He saw two enemy soldiers appear in the field behind them and signaled Sergeant Lazcano, who detonated the team's hastily implanted claymore mines. Radioman Specialist Marr and the team's Kit Carson scout tossed grenades, and the enemy pursuit stopped. The team checked the bodies and climbed farther uphill, killing two more NVA troops who suddenly appeared in front of them. Once the Typhoon Patrollers reached the mountaintop they successfully radioed for assistance and were extracted by helicopter.[16]

On 10 October 1968 the Company E headquarters was transferred from 4th Infantry Division control and attached to the 173d

Airborne Brigade, but the platoons remained split between the two commands. One important company requirement involved reconnaissance along Highway 19, the main allied resupply lane from the central South China Sea ports into the highland city of Pleiku. The twisting highway threaded through forested mountains that offered excellent VC ambush opportunities. Recon team 13 was reconnoitering the mountains along a vital highway pass when the patrol and its supporting helicopters came under heavy automatic weapons fire. The team defended its position so staunchly that the VC became unsure of the size of the American force and temporarily withdrew. The team was later retrieved safely, in spite of a sudden deluge of mortar and rifle fire that swept the extraction site.

On 11 December 1968, Company E recombined its platoons for the first time in a year as the unit was reconsolidated at An Khe. Field activity was suspended and the company spent two weeks reconditioning teams and training personnel. The company resumed direct platoon control, and "morale improved immeasurably as a direct result of the revised concept." In January the company was alerted that it would be converted to ranger status. In the final six months of Company E service, from August 1968 through the end of January 1969, the Typhoon Patrollers amassed an enviable record of 320 patrols with 232 sightings of NVA/VC personnel, at the cost of two patrollers killed and thirty-nine wounded. These patrols were accomplished across rugged terrain under adverse weather accentuated by late-November typhoons Mamie, Nina, and Ora.[17]

CHARLIE RANGERS

In January 1969 the Army reorganized the 75th Infantry under the combat arms regimental system as the parent regiment for the various infantry patrol companies. On 1 February, Company C (Airborne Ranger), 75th Infantry, was officially activated by incorporating the Typhoon Patrollers into the new ranger outfit. The rangers were known as "Charlie Rangers" in conformity with C in the ICAO phonetic alphabet adopted by the U.S. military in 1956. Company C continued to operate as a unified component under the operational control of I Field Force Vietnam.[18]

From 4 to 22 February 1969, three Charlie Ranger field platoons rendered reconnaissance support for the Republic of Korea 9th Division in the Ha Roi region. Two field platoons supported the Phu Bon Province advisory campaign along the northern provincial boundary from 26 February through 8 March. Company C then concentrated its ranger teams in support of the 4th Infantry Division by reconnoitering major infiltration routes in the southwestern HINES area of operations, a mission that lasted until 28 March. Throughout the first part of the year the rangers also posted one or two platoons on recon-security duty along ambush-prone sections of Highway 19, primarily from An Khe to the Mang Yang Pass.

During March 1969, Lt. Gen. Charles A. Corcoran assumed command of I Field Force Vietnam. Ranger capability was enhanced during the same month by the receipt of the first six National Match M14 rifles with telescopic sights. Training of selected marksmen commenced immediately, and snipers were assigned to several teams. Another major task of Company C was constructing basic and refresher training facilities at its An Khe base camp. The instruction area and range enabled the company to conduct a three-week course for all non-recondo-graduate patrollers during April. The course emphasized physical conditioning, radio skills, map reading, advanced first aid, and patrol-related helicopter techniques. The company then used the area as a pre-recondo course for newly assigned volunteers preparatory to their entering the Nha Trang MACV Recondo School.[19]

In late April 1969 the Charlie Rangers shifted support to the 173d Airborne Brigade's Operation WASHINGTON GREEN in northern Binh Dinh Province. Ranger Company C assisted ranger Company N by conducting surveillance of enemy infiltration routes that passed through the western provincial mountains toward the heavily populated coastline. In one typical encounter, on the morning of 8 May, ranger team 11 ambushed a North Vietnamese squad near Vinh Thanh. The rangers used claymore mines, automatic rifles, and CS-gas grenades to kill six of the infiltrating soldiers and wound the rest. The team was extracted without further incident.[20]

Most Charlie Ranger assets remained in Binh Dinh Province in a screening role, but at the end of April one field platoon was dispatched on a week-long expedition into the Ia Drang Valley near the Cambodian border. This sortie was followed by a two-platoon expedition to help the Republic of Korea (ROK) 9th Division scout the To Hop-Ba Cum region in late May. The rangers also kept two field platoons with the ROK Capital Division on diversionary and surveillance operations through mid-July. On 21 July the ranger company received an entirely new assignment in the southernmost portion of I Field Force Vietnam territory, where it was attached to Task Force South operating against Viet Cong strongholds along the boundary of II and III Corps Tactical Zones.[21]

Maj. Bill V. Holt's ranger Company C served as the combat

patrol arm of Task Force South until 25 March 1970. The rangers operated in an ideal reconnaissance setting that contained vast wilderness operational areas, largely without population or allied troop density. Flexible patrol arrangements were combined with imaginative methods of team insertion, radio deception, and nocturnal employment. The company worked in eight-day operational cycles and used every ninth day for "recurring refresher training." The ranger teams rehearsed basic patrolling principles, as well as newly discovered techniques varying from night ambush to boat infiltration. Ranger proficiency flourished under these conditions, and MACV expressed singular satisfaction with Company C results.[22]

The Viet Cong had taken advantage of the "no-man's-land" of Binh Thuan and Binh Tuy provinces straddling the allied military jurisdictional boundary between II and III Corps Tactical Zones, to reinforce the Military Region Six headquarters. The Charlie Rangers performed a monthly average of twenty-seven patrols in this rough area and reaped a rich harvest of military intelligence despite heavy afternoon and evening rainstorms.[23]

Staff Sgt. Hendrick Greeneword's ranger team 23 performed a typical mission in this area. On 14 September 1969 the patrol was helicoptered into the rugged jungle on a three-day reconnaissance mission to locate and identify reported communist elements moving from southeastern Lam Dong Province across the II-III CTZ boundary into northern Binh Tuy Province. The rangers established an overnight position and saw several distant campfires during an otherwise uneventful evening.

On the following afternoon the team discovered a well-used trail along a wooded knoll, littered with cigarettes, small plastic bags, and a beer bottle. Staff Sergeant Greeneword was discussing ambush possibilities with his senior scout when they spotted fifty well-armed North Vietnamese infantrymen marching up a gully from a nearby stream. Within minutes, the rangers saw another group of fifty enemy soldiers. The NVA force wore light gray and khaki uniforms with green pith helmets and carried at least one RPD machine gun.

The team leader radioed the sighting to the field platoon leader, Lt. Richard Grimes, who was orbiting the area in an O-1 Bird Dog aircraft. Lieutenant Grimes ordered the rangers to continue observing the situation, to use air strikes only if compromised, and to wait for the arrival of airmobile infantry being dispatched to their location. Sergeant Greeneword realized that helicopter gunships were in the air. He also knew that premature employment of the gunships would only disperse the enemy company—probably without inflicting serious casualties—and alert it to probable ranger proximity. This could easily lead to an overrun situation against the small team.

The team 23 patrollers remained hidden in the thick shrubbery and watched breathlessly as the NVA company continued to move within thirty feet of their position. The enemy soldiers were talking and were obviously unaware of the American presence. The North Vietnamese stopped and rested in a grassy clearing on the other side of some fifty-foot-high trees. Fortunately, the hardwoods had a width of three feet across and were embedded in dense foliage. An NVA leader wearing silver lapel insignia issued directives. His soldiers cleared their weapons and inserted new magazines, and each chambered a round. Then they cut twigs from the underbrush, coming within inches of some individual rangers, and spread ponchos or plastic sheets in obvious preparation for an overnight halt.

Helicopters and F-100 fighter-bombers were now circling the hills, but refrained from attacking because of the nearness of the rangers to the hundred North Vietnamese troops. The airmobile reaction force passed overhead with nine utility and four Cobra helicopters. As the droning helicopters approached, the rangers watched the enemy soldiers become very quiet and then start to run en masse toward the stream. Staff Sergeant Greeneword radioed immediately for aerial firepower against the formation fleeing the area. The helicopters dived and delivered a barrage of rockets and machine gun fire that tore through the enemy personnel.

Several North Vietnamese ran in circles through the devastating aerial bombardment, and some fled back toward the ranger-occupied hill. As the terror-stricken NVA soldiers raced up the slope, ranger team 23 opened fire with its M60 machine gun, grenade launchers, and rifles. When the smoke cleared, fifty-eight crumpled North Vietnamese bodies and dozens of discarded weapons lay scattered over the shattered hillside. Numerous blood trails led farther downhill and into the jungle, but the rangers did not count all the dead. They hurriedly surveyed the carnage and collected papers before a threatening afternoon thunderstorm canceled overhead air cover. The team members also ripped off the silver insignia and grabbed a packet of documents from the dead leader, revealing the unit was a component of the 240th NVA Battalion. The rangers accomplished exactly what they were assigned to do, and suffered no casualties.[24]

The burden of dangerous ranger work fell heaviest on the shoulders of the increasingly young team leaders who propelled the patrols into action and were ultimately responsible for the lives of their men on the battlefield. Their gallant service was typified by team leader Sp4 Keith M. Parr, who commanded a ranger patrol searching the military boundary zone southwest of Phan Thiet. Shortly after insertion, the team reached an enemy base surrounded by mechanical alarm devices. The alerted North Vietnamese charged the rangers, forcing them into an open field, and brought up a machine gun that kept the Americans pinned down. Specialist Parr realized that his team members could not break contact until the crew-served weapon was silenced. He advanced through a hail of enemy fire and killed the crew with rifle fire, but was mortally wounded in the process. Despite great pain from multiple wounds that ultimately proved fatal, Parr radioed air strikes until the team was extracted. The gallant action by the dying patrol leader was later recognized by a posthumous Silver Star—although a much higher decoration might have been bestowed in a regular line unit. Valiant acts, however, were so commonplace in ranger ranks that they were routinely "above and beyond the call of duty."[25]

On 19 November 1969, six-man ranger team 16 under Sgt. Ronald O. Lesley was infiltrated into lower Binh Thuan Province. The rangers established ambush positions along a trail network. Two groups of eight Viet Cong came from different directions on the trail and stopped in the middle of the kill zone. The team's Kit Carson scout overheard one member ask if there were any Americans in the area. The sixteen VC continued to converse until the team detonated its claymore mines, threw hand grenades, and opened fire with automatic weapons. Eight enemy were killed, two fell wounded in the pathway, and the rest fled.

Sergeant Lesley and his senior scout disregarded enemy sniper fire and crawled out onto the trail. They captured two prisoners, a document case, and a rucksack. Sergeant Lesley also retrieved the senior scout, who had been mortally wounded by the enemy rifle fire. A reaction force from the 2d Squadron, 1st Cavalry, arrived to extract the rangers. One of the prisoners was Hoang Hong, a senior captain in charge of the Binh Thuan Province communist Armed Security Subsection. The other prisoner was Nguyen Van Tien, who was the combined subsection chief of the Security Section. Among the documents was the entire Viet Cong 1969–70 winter-spring campaign plan of the Thuan Thanh current affairs section, including protective measures for Viet Cong internal cadre personnel.[26]

Sergeant Lesley's ranger team 16 was typically young and tough. Sp4 Mike Maattala described the men as "a strange tableau—a combination of youth, eccentricity, and professionalism. Only one man is over 22 and that is the Kit Carson scout, Do Van Bay, who is 27. A few of the men wore embroidered sweat bands. AK47 rounds strung on shoe laces hung from the necks of others. Most of them wore black leather gloves with the finger[tip]s cut off, to protect their hands from the hot barrel of a weapon while still providing their fingers with the proper touch. . . . Bay came to the rangers right after he Chieu Hoi'd from the Viet Cong." Team grenadier Don Norton stated, "You can't ever relax out there. You might feel tired and sluggish until the adrenalin starts flowing, but you never realize until you get back into camp how beat you are. You just don't have time to be tired in the woods." Sp4 Calvin Davis, a black ranger who banded his Afro with camouflaged parachute silk, described individual expertise simply: "Everyone knows his lines."[27]

The numerous ambush situations led Company C to anticipate an opportunity to use stay-behind infiltration tactics. One team was usually kept in reserve for such a contingency. On 14 December 1969, north of Phan Thiet, ranger team 36 executed a clean ambush without opposition. On that day, team 33 was on special standby and monitored the contact development by radio. The team boarded the helicopter sent to extract the ambush element and was surreptitiously inserted on a stay-behind mission. Two days later, team 33 killed a trio of careless enemy soldiers who were not expecting Americans in the area. The rangers found papers on one of their victims identifying him as the executive officer of the 200-C Sapper Battalion, a unit previously unreported in the area.[28]

On 1 February 1970 the company was split when two platoons moved into Tuyen Duc Province. The unit was rejoined 6 March, however, after the discovery of numerous team sightings in the main Binh Thuan operational area that led to Operation HANCOCK MACE. The Charlie Rangers scouted ahead of Task Force South, but action was only light and scattered as the enemy eluded ground pursuit.

On 29 March 1970 the ranger company moved to Pleiku city and was placed under the control of the aerial 7th Squadron of the 7th Cavalry. The Charlie Rangers conducted thirty-two patrols in the far western border stretches of the central highland plateau. On 19 April the company was attached to the separate 3d Battalion, 506th Infantry, and relocated to An Khe, where it was targeted against the North Vietnamese 95 Regiment in the Mang Yang Pass region of interior Binh Dinh Province.[29]

Company C did not enjoy a high measure of success during the last two assignments. The rapid redeployments into Pleiku and An

Khe provided insufficient time for acquainting teams with new terrain and enemy situations prior to their tactical employment. The unit was often unable to gain adequate information before inserting patrols. Sometimes the rangers lacked current charts and aerial photographs. The adjustment problems hindered ranger effectiveness and were exacerbated by poor logistical response. Supply and equipment shortages were occasioned by the company's absence from supporting headquarters and by often transient tenant relationships with a multitude of different commands.

Ranger difficulties were complicated by air cavalry squadron and infantry battalion commanders who were unfamiliar with ranger employment. They did not understand ranger limitations or focus on mission priority. As a result, the Charlie Rangers performed routine pathfinder work on landing zones or guarded unit flanks as well as performing long-range reconnaissance.[30]

As happened with other late-war ranger companies, the psychological toll of seemingly interminable Vietnam operations—coupled with the incessant curse of the one-year combat rotation policy—eroded Company C performance. The malady was apparent in the number of casualties incurred in previously routine matters, like sweeping areas after contact. Rangers were killed checking their own kill zones after ambushes. To reduce this danger, the rangers began taping small bags of persistent-agent CS (gas) powder to the front of their claymore mines. The mines spewed both pellets and gas to render targeted soldiers temporarily ineffective and were supplemented by gas grenades. The method was not foolproof, and one team was shocked after "dead" Viet Cong "incapacitated" by gas agents bushwhacked their attackers. Air-dropped fifty-five-gallon drums of CS-gas enabled the startled rangers to break contact. Major Holt reported in mid-June:

Many enlisted personnel after eight or ten months of small team ranger operations are no longer motivated or capable of continuing field work, even though their previous performance was outstanding. A great deal of tension is placed on team members during operations because of the small number (six men) of personnel on the team, and the continuous requirement for team alertness twenty-four hours a day. After a period varying in length of from four to ten months— depending on the individual's ability to operate under continuous pressure—many feel they can no longer stand the strain. Those individuals who have demonstrated outstanding ability are either given a long rest or reassigned to a rear area job if there is a suitable vacancy.[31]

Company C was placed under operational control of the 4th Infantry Division on 4 May 1970, a day prior to the formation's invasion of Cambodia's Ratanaktri Province—coded Operation BINH TAY I. The late attachment and strict MACV prohibitions against cross-border ground reconnaissance ahead of the operation (to maintain "surprise") precluded ranger reconnaissance of objective areas selected for the opening attack. The lack of adequate ranger preparation forced the 4th Infantry Division to conduct what was essentially a "blind strike" into Cambodia and almost proved fatal to the operation. Failure to scout the landing zones exposed descending helicopters, crowded with assault troops, to an unexpected storm of enemy automatic weapons and rocket fire.

For example, helicopters carrying the 1st Battalion, 14th Infantry, came under such fierce antiaircraft fire over both primary and alternate landing zones that they were forced to abandon landing attempts and return to Vietnam. A surprise volume of flak also blocked the insertion of the 3d Battalion, 506th Infantry. Three major attempts were made on 5 May to insert this battalion. Finally, two open fields were found left unguarded by enemy antiaircraft weapons.

Unfortunately, the unexpected return of so many helicopters from aborted airmobile assaults jammed the Camp Plei Djereng runway. The helicopter-packed airstrip prevented Air Force cargo aircraft from delivering additional aviation fuel. Without the extra fuel, three further combat air assaults scheduled for invasion day had to be canceled. This left the entire division in the unfavorable position of having only a single battalion (3d Battalion, 506th Infantry) on Cambodian soil by the conclusion of D-Day, 5 May.[32]

Three days later, on 8 May, the Charlie Rangers uncovered NVA documents in enemy base area 702 that revealed the reasons for this fierce reception. The captured papers verified that allied intelligence had seriously underestimated the military potential of North Vietnamese Army units in the invasion sector. Prior to the Cambodian invasion, MACV believed that enemy base area 702 contained only 1,500 troops of the B-3 Front headquarters, scattered among a number of "T" communications-liaison stations and "Q" supply depots. These rear-echelon troops were considered unprepared and unwilling to offer much resistance. As a result, the allied high command felt no need to send rangers across the border to reconnoiter selected landing zones.[33]

The documents showed that the enemy was well aware of allied plans and intent on defending possible helicopter landing fields. Advance ranger infiltration might have discovered this as well as the exact magnitude of defense at each selected landing zone. Ranger Company C was used instead to reconnoiter base area 702 in the wake of the main infantry assault. The ranger record in Operation BINH TAY I was rather lackluster as a result; thirty patrol observations of enemy personnel, five NVA soldiers killed by direct fire, and fifteen weapons captured.[34]

The ranger fighting episodes inside Cambodia were often fierce and sometimes adverse. For example, at noon on 14 May, Sgt. Steen B. Foster's ranger team 44 ambushed a dozen enemy soldiers along a high-speed trail. The team members ventured out onto the trail to check the four bodies and came under accurate but sporadic sniper fire. Radio communication was severed with the radio relay site for twenty minutes. The team was finally able to call for helicopter gunship support. By this time an enemy machine gun was brought forward, and its fire hit radioman Pfc. Nathaniel R. Allsopp, Pfc. James L. Loisel, and Kit Carson scout Dong Van Hoa. The patrol detonated its flank and rear claymore mines in an effort to suppress the increasing volume of enemy fire.

Sergeant Foster ran from the dense foliage to aid Loisel and was hit immediately in the left shoulder. He continued to fire his weapon with his right hand. Within minutes, both men were killed by a volley of automatic fire. The Vietnamese scout also died. By this time, Private Allsopp was the only wounded patrol member still alive. When he was hit again, this time in the neck, Sp4 Tommy Allen and Sp4 Henry Van Utrecht braved the enemy crossfire and dragged him to cover. Specialist Allen eased Private Allsopp out of his rucksack and checked the PRC-25 radio inside. The radio was completely destroyed by enemy bullets. Utrecht and Allen then pulled Foster's body back and found the URC-68 emergency radio in his rucksack. The survivors regained communications and were extracted by helicopter.[35]

On 24 May 1970 the Charlie Rangers were pulled completely out of Cambodia and released from 4th Infantry Division control. Four days later the company was rushed to Dalat to reconnoiter a North Vietnamese Army thrust toward the Vietnamese city. The rangers covered the Dalat area but made only seven sightings. The otherwise unproductive mission was highlighted by the discovery of an enemy medical cache containing 2,350 pounds of food, 200 pounds of hospital supplies, and fifty pounds of equipment.

The Charlie Rangers remained in the Dalat area less than a month before being sent south to rejoin Task Force South at Phan Thiet. New ranger commander Maj. Donald L. Hudson summed up the trimester of May, June, and July 1970 as involving a dizzy pattern of operations in Binh Thuan, Lam Dong, Tuyen Duc, Pleiku, and Binh Dinh provinces. There were sixty-five days of tactical operations, because a full twenty-seven days were devoted to major movements. Each move necessitated adjustment with novel terrain, unfamiliar aviation resources, and fresh superior commands.[36]

Unexpected hazards caused more team emergencies. On 1 June 1970 a flight of four 192d Aviation Company Huey helicopters was inserting a Charlie Ranger team south of Dalat. WO1 Stephen T. Rowe was flying his UH-1C gunship as the trail aircraft in the formation. About five minutes into the flight, and at an altitude of 600 feet, the helicopter crew heard a loud "pop" from the engine compartment, which was followed by a violent yaw to the port. Warrant Officer Rowe suspected an engine failure and initiated autorotation as caution lights began illuminating prior to shutting off. He radioed the accompanying aircraft that he was going down and chose an open hilltop field.

Rowe, believing the aircraft might overshoot the field and go into the trees, flared it to slow his forward motion. Crew chief Sp4 Joseph M. Jenkins and door gunner Pfc. Donald C. Starr threw out most of the machine gun ammunition boxes as copilot WO1 Steven L. Alford jettisoned the rocket pods. The aircraft dropped rapidly and landed hard, nosing over as its main rotor blades struck the ground. The helicopter turned on its side and skidded thirty feet from the point of impact. The ranger team was immediately landed to secure the crash site and treat Private Starr's injuries. Technicians later found that the engine failure was caused by a creeping rupture in the fourth-stage compressor disk. The incident exemplified the common accidents that curtailed or endangered many heliborne ranger missions.[37]

On 26 July 1970, ranger Company C was transported by cargo aircraft to Landing Zone English outside Bong Son and was returned to 173d Airborne Division jurisdiction. The rangers supported Operation WASHINGTON GREEN in coastal Binh Dinh Province with small unit ambushes, limited raids, and pathfinder assistance for heliborne operations. During August the Charlie Rangers attempted to locate and destroy the troublesome Viet Cong Khanh Hoa provincial battalion.

Ranger scouting was deterred by Korean Army insistence that the territory was within their jurisdiction and not an American sector. The brigade reported ruefully that "as we had learned with the Tuy Hoa operation, the ROKs were reluctant to give up any of their territory." As it turned out, the requirement for this operation became secondary to events in secret base area 226 in the Central

Highlands, where the 173d Airborne Brigade discovered a large communist headquarters complex. On 17 August, the 2d Brigade of the 4th Infantry Division moved into the region and the Charlie Rangers were attached for reconnoitering assistance.[38]

In mid-November 1970, ranger Company C was attached to the 17th Aviation Group, and it remained under aviation or 173d Airborne Brigade control for most of the duration of its Vietnam service. At the end of April 1971 the Charlie Rangers were reassigned to the Second Regional Assistance Command, following the inactivation of I Field Force Vietnam in Vietnam. Later that year, on 15 August, the ranger company was reduced to a brigade-strength ranger company of three officers and sixty-nine enlisted men.[39]

The I Field Force Vietnam rangers were notified of pending disbandment as part of Increment IX (Keystone Oriole-Charlie) of the U.S. Army redeployment from Vietnam. Company C (Airborne Ranger), 75th Infantry, commenced final stand-down on 15 October 1971 and was reduced to zero strength by 24 October. On the following day the ranger company was officially inactivated.

The Typhoon Patrollers and Charlie Rangers performed admirably during the Vietnam conflict. The I Field Force rangers probably confronted and identified more enemy units, conducted a wider range of ranger-type combat and training functions using both conventional and special warfare techniques, and served in more jurisdictions than any other ranger component. Company C saturated fourteen provinces in two Corps Tactical Zones with ranger patrols, performing crucial reconnaissance for U.S. Army, South Vietnamese, and South Korean forces. Most important, the remarkable wartime record of ranger Company C vividly demonstrated the high degree of flexible success achieved by a corps-level ranger endeavor.

11

III CORPS TACTICAL ZONE

II FIELD FORCE RANGERS

HURRICANE PATROLLERS

The most demanding allied assignment in South Vietnam was defending the country's political heartland, a 10,000-mile swath of hilly jungle, forested plains, and populous farmland known militarily as the III Corps Tactical Zone. The area also contained Saigon, the national capital and command center, as well as much of the country's industrial wealth and logistical hubs. United States commitment to South Vietnamese security hinged on the protection of this region, and Army tactical responsibility rested with II Field Force Vietnam.

II Field Force Vietnam, nominally a corps-sized command, was actually a field army. The command experienced intelligence-gathering weaknesses that were disclosed by the perseverance of viable Viet Cong and North Vietnamese Army forces within striking distance of Saigon. These military intelligence deficiencies were aggravated by the lack of a ground reconnaissance patrol outfit devoted exclusively to field force requirements.[1]

During August 1966 the Special Forces organized an expedient ground recon element, Detachment B-56 (Project Sigma), to render corps-level reconnaissance and intelligence collection. Sigma was one of several "Greek-letter" special reconnaissance projects in Vietnam. The element performed its tasks with unconventional warfare patrols and generally produced reliable information on enemy locations, movements, and intentions. Project Sigma became operational in October, but was inherently limited by its mixed

native irregular composition—Chinese and Cambodian merce-
naries led by Special Forces officers and sergeants.

This arrangement lasted about a year before being reshuffled by
General Westmoreland in the fall of 1967. He alerted II Field Force
Vietnam commander Lt. Gen. Frederick C. Weyand that the Project Sigma commandos would be transferred in November to
MACV's special cross-border-raiding outfit. In the absence of
Sigma, General Weyand expected to retain the 173d Airborne Brigade (with its superb long-range reconnaissance platoon) as a field
force "fire brigade." These hopes were dashed when the airborne
brigade was alerted to move north in October. General Weyand
complained that no adequate combat reconnaissance substitute existed if both Project Sigma and the 173d Airborne Brigade LRRP
Platoon were removed from his jurisdiction.[2]

General Westmoreland realized the importance of keeping exclusive long-range reconnaissance capability under II Field Force
Vietnam. Early detection of VC and NVA movements in the area
surrounding Saigon demanded top-priority attention, and the relocation of patrol assets farther north and west could not be allowed
to expose the territory around the capital. He ordered the Special
Forces to create B-36 Project Rapid Fire as a transient special warfare unit for field force employment. Project Rapid Fire would be
used to perform reconnaissance until a regular infantry patrol company could be formed for field force retention. The new patrol
company was built by stripping all personnel from the LRRP platoon of the 173d Airborne Brigade before it departed III Corps
Tactical Zone.[3]

On 25 September 1967 the II Field Force Vietnam finally gained
its own independent ground reconnaissance when Company F
(Long Range Patrol), 51st Infantry (Airborne), was activated. The
incipient company was immediately assigned to II Field Force
Vietnam with the mission, upon completion of training, of providing long-range reconnaissance and intelligence appraisals directly
to the operations staff at field force level.[4]

Company F, commanded by Maj. William C. Maus, was formed
by battle-experienced personnel and equipment derived from the
173d Airborne Brigade LRRP Platoon. Additional manpower was
needed, however, to fill the organization to its required 230-man
authorization level. The additional personnel were gained by diverting soldiers in the replacement stream for the 199th Infantry
Brigade. Recon personnel of the company were known as the
"Hurricane Patrollers" after the signal code word "Hurricane"
favored by the II Field Force Vietnam headquarters.[5]

To provide Company F with an optimum training period, the company was formed in accordance with a carefully arranged schedule that deliberately prevented its premature commitment to battle. General Weyand refrained from deploying the Hurricane Patrollers on operations until the teams were declared fully prepared for combat. The orderly development program was made possible by using Special Forces Project Rapid Fire as an immediate combat recon substitute.

The carefully phased II Field Force long-range patrol training program for Company F started on 8 October 1967. Each patrol member was sent through two weeks of reconnaissance training at the Special Forces–run MACV Recondo School in Nha Trang. The academy was forced to suspend regular classes until the end of November, in order to offer special instructional phases for company personnel. The recondo course ensured a solid foundation of recondo-qualified reconnaissance personnel in the new patrol company.

After the Hurricane Patrollers completed recondo schooling, they were sent back to Company F at Long Binh. Company F was placed under the helicopter-equipped "Red Horse" 3d Squadron, 17th Cavalry, for aerial support, and conducted practical exercises in hostile areas of Gia Dinh Province. The manpower priorities that were accorded to Company F caused inconveniences in other units. The 173d and 199th brigades were most seriously affected by the action. To partially offset this adverse impact, Company F patrolled principally in support of the 199th Infantry Brigade.

On 2 December 1967, Company F was declared combat-ready and became fully operational. Within a week, on 8 December, the Hurricane Patrollers were formally paired up with the "Silver Spur" Troop A of the 17th Cavalry "Red Horse" squadron. The combination gave the patrollers responsive helicopter support as well as backup contingents of aero-riflemen. The amalgamated unit provided II Field Force Vietnam with a highly flexible air-ground reconnaissance battalion. The force provided support to the 199th Infantry Brigade and the newly arriving 3d Brigade, 101st Airborne Division, through January.[6]

On 31 January 1968, Viet Cong forces began their major Tet-68 offensive by attacking targets throughout the III Corps Tactical Zone. Enemy infiltration and sapper battalions demolished parts of Saigon, struck vital military installations surrounding the capital area, and besieged several outlying government posts in the field force area. In response, the Silver Spur–Hurricane Patrollers reinforced the 199th Infantry Brigade and penetrated enemy staging areas in the "Catcher's Mitt" region north of Bien Hoa base.

Company F patrols saturated the Catcher's Mitt during a sustained reconnaissance campaign that lasted until the end of March. The recon teams battled through the NVA/VC stronghold in a series of daring ambush raids and interdiction missions. The Hurricane Patrollers—supported admirably by the Silver Spur aerial cavalrymen—cut supply lines, uncovered weapons caches, and bushwhacked assembly areas. The saturation patrolling disrupted enemy plans to direct a sustained offensive against Bien Hoa and its key air base and was instrumental in hindering enemy regroupment efforts.

Throughout spring 1968 the Hurricane Patrollers and their integral air cavalry assets were employed to provide combat reconnaissance in a wide operational arc around the capital military district. For example, the long-range company reconnoitered lower Tay Ninh Province in Operation WILDERNESS until 10 April, scouted the region northeast of Long Binh until 22 April, and then moved south of Duc Hoa on the Oriental River front of the Song Vam Co Dong. Toward the end of the month the company returned to the Catcher's Mitt.

During these operations, Company F maintained its desired operating level of twenty-eight six-man patrols. The patrollers introduced a wide range of deception techniques to enhance team results. For instance, patrol-directed artillery fire was adjusted by relaying information through observation aircraft. The practice deceived the enemy into thinking that aircraft spotters rather than ground teams were making shellfire corrections. The Viet Cong often remained unaware of patrol presence in the vicinity.

In another example, false helicopter insertions ("deceptive touchdowns") were supplemented by deceptive extractions. This artifice was used by teams calling for extraction after they were observed by the enemy. Helicopter gunships arrived over the patrol positions and expended their ammunition in aerial strafing runs. The team members then set off smoke grenades and utility helicopters landed. The aircraft stayed for a minute before lifting off empty with cargo doors closed. The tactic often convinced the enemy that the team had departed and enabled the patrollers to retaliate effectively against VC patrol-monitoring parties that had relaxed their vigilance.

From May until mid-July 1968 the Hurricane Patrollers participated in Operation TOAN THANG and conducted advance reconnaissance for two brigades. Company F supported the 3d Brigade of the 101st Airborne Division until 24 May and then shifted to work with the 199th Infantry Brigade. The missions usually involved watching suspected enemy trails for VC cart, bicycle, or foot traffic. Most team missions were conducted northeast of Saigon either in the vicinity of Phuoc Vinh or around Long Binh.

The magnitude of the field force surveillance effort was reflected by Company F accomplishments from April through June. The Hurricane Patrollers fielded 250 patrols that reported 284 separate observations of enemy personnel and became engaged in combat on 115 occasions. The company claimed forty-eight NVA/VC soldiers killed by direct fire and captured four prisoners. Unfortunately, twenty-nine patrol members were wounded in patrol clashes during the same trimester. The company suffered increasing personnel shortages caused by annual rotation from Vietnam, leaves and reassignments, hospitalization as a result of injuries or disease, and convalescence from wounds. As a result, Company F was forced to reduce team size from six to five men each.[7]

On 18 July 1968 the Hurricane Patrollers received a new assignment. Company F and its air cavalry troops were assigned to a reconnaissance task force that also included the South Vietnamese 36th Ranger Battalion and aerial Troop D from the 17th Cavalry "Red Horse" squadron. The joint "field force recon regiment" performed reconnaissance-in-force operations that screened the vital Long Binh—Bien Hoa military installation east of Saigon. The concept combined the American and Vietnamese patrol units in cooperative ventures that received sustained airlift and aerial fire support. The ad hoc regiment participated in sixty missions that established over 300 ambush positions. Only thirteen Viet Cong soldiers were snared by the accelerated activity, but the regiment kept enemy units from directly threatening the allied logistical complex.

During August 1968, Maj. Gen. Walter T. Kerwin Jr. assumed command of II Field Force Vietnam. General Kerwin continued using the Hurricane Patrollers as an integral component of the field force reconnaissance regiment protecting Long Binh and Bien Hoa. He bolstered the regiment with the Special Forces 1st Battalion of the 3d Mobile Strike Force Command, as well as the 11th Armored Cavalry's tank Company D and mechanized Troop E.

Commencing on August 11 the Hurricane Patrollers were withdrawn on a separate expedition to monitor the infiltration corridor that extended from Cambodia through the Pineapple plantation area west of Saigon. The marshy wasteland and canal-laced rice fields presented an extremely difficult patrolling environment, because much of the land was constantly inundated by the tidal fluctuations of the Vam Co Dong river. Many patrols were able to move only short distances through the boggy soil. The most dramatic episode occurred when one team became isolated by rising water in a sudden storm that almost prevented helicopter rescue. The patrollers were saved from drowning by aircraft crews who defied the worsening weather.

The waterway reconnaissance campaign along the Song Vam Co was concentrated against Viet Cong boats and sampans plying the canal networks. The unsuitable terrain and proximity to active North Vietnamese bases along the border made the interdiction endeavor especially dangerous. The Hurricane Patrollers suffered increased casualties from August through October: three members were killed and forty-eight wounded. The company sent out 241 patrols that spotted NVA/VC troops in 193 cases and killed 125 enemy soldiers in exchange. The company completed the waterway recon mission southwest of Cu Chi at the end of the first week in November.[8]

Maj. George W. Heckman's Company F returned to Long Binh, where it rested, reequipped, and underwent its Annual General Inspection on 12 November. On the following day the company was relocated northeast of Bien Hoa to reconnoiter War Zone D for the operations section of II Field Force Vietnam. Teams were used to perform a variety of missions during the War Zone D reconnaissance campaign. Some teams tracked enemy movements in the vicinity of Rang Rang, while other teams interrupted the services of the North Vietnamese Army 81st Rear Service Group. The Company F operations officer, Capt. Dennis Foley, remarked:

> We rarely ran any recon patrols. They were almost all combat patrols. The teams were given missions to raid, ambush, kill, capture, or destroy something when they left the LRP pad. Recon was only secondary. The company was under the operational control of the Field Force G-3 [operations] staff and not the G-2 [intelligence]. They were shooters, not lookers.[9]

The Hurricane Patrollers refrained from engaging larger targets directly, but identified NVA logistical activities for air strikes and B-52 bombing sorties. The advantages of patrol-generated aerial warfare were confirmed by 81st Rear Service Group records captured in mid-November. One logbook recorded that the strategic bombers forced group personnel to "live underground" and "greatly hampered resupply activities" out of "fear and madness." The patrollers later found material that further verified the impact of the heavy bombing raids. The communist high command decentralized the 81st Group by breaking it up into the D40-A and D60-B Transportation Battalions.

On 23 December 1968, Major Heckman reconsolidated Company F south of Rang Rang. The Hurricane Patrollers were scheduled to be replaced by Company D (Long Range Patrol), 151st Infantry—an Indiana National Guard unit arriving from the United States at the end of the month. The Army officially inactivated Company F three days later, but the unit actually continued to function. On the day following Company F's "inactivation," General Kerwin announced the unit would be perpetuated as the provisional II Field Force Vietnam Long Range Patrol Company (Airborne).[10]

The provisional long-range patrol company concentrated on two distinct objectives. The first mission was releasing its operational area in an orderly transitional program to the corps-level National Guard patrol company. To complete the transition, the provisional field force company undertook a carefully phased training program designed to acquaint the Indiana Rangers with their operational environment within III Corps Tactical Zone.[11]

The familiarization program gave the Indiana Rangers practical combat reconnaissance exercises. The provisional company instructed its successor unit in patrolling techniques peculiar to the capital-area battlefield. The courses also acquainted the Indiana Rangers with the aircraft pilots, forward observers, and artillerymen who would be supporting them.

The field training agenda was the most critical portion of this program. A comprehensive set of patrols was used to teach, correct, and appraise individual performances. In the first phase the recon members participated in seventy-two-hour introductory patrols within "safe areas." Each six-man training patrol was led by an experienced sergeant in charge of three novice National Guardsmen and three combat veterans.

Following the conclusion of the three-day combined patrols, the next patrols were still led by experienced sergeants but the other members were National Guardsmen. These advanced training patrols were actually a final test in hostile territory. The Regular Army team leaders relinquished their command and resorted to an observer role as the Indiana guardsman mastered local conditions. The teams were declared operational as soon as they completed their final patrols and were "passed" by accompanying NCO graders.

In addition to engaging in the transitional training of the Indiana

National Guard, the provisional field force patrol company was also preparing to divide into two new ranger companies. The veteran patrollers were placed into parachutist and nonparachutist sections and the teams realigned accordingly. In late December the personnel began transferring to either the 1st Brigade of the 5th Infantry Division or the 3d Brigade of the 82d Airborne Division. Paratroopers were assigned to the latter organization.

On 15 February 1969 the Provisional II Field Force Long Range Patrol Company (Airborne) was discontinued. During its last three months of service, from November through January, Company F and its successor provisional company accomplished 208 patrols that made eight-two sightings of enemy activity and became involved in sixty-two contacts. The company captured seven North Vietnamese soldiers and killed twenty-seven by direct fire, and in exchange suffered six patrollers killed and thirty-five wounded. Of much greater significance, the Hurricane Patrollers directed one of the most successful patrol-directed aerial onslaughts of the war, accomplished the groundwork necessary to prepare another patrol company for corps-level Vietnam duty, and built two completely new ranger companies. [12]

INDIANA RANGERS

Company D (Long Range Patrol) of the 151st Infantry was the only Army National Guard infantry unit to serve in Vietnam. The company was called into federal service on 13 May 1968 and was composed of Indiana National Guardsmen primarily from the Indianapolis, Greenfield, and Evansville area. The company commander was initially Capt. Kenneth W. Hemsel, who was promoted to major just prior to the unit's overseas deployment and replaced by his brother, Capt. Robert E. Hemsel.

Company D volunteered for Vietnam duty, and the Army agreed to exclude it from "infusion" of outside personnel in order to maintain unit integrity. The Indiana guardsmen completed an extensive six-month preparatory training program sponsored by the U.S. Army Infantry School at Fort Benning, Georgia. Personnel received specialized individual instruction and became airborne-qualified. The ranger school also provided extra training. Most personnel went through the Army School of the Americas in the Panama Canal Zone and were qualified as jungle experts. The superior training and high standards shaped Company D into an exceptionally battle-worthy long-range patrol company.

The Joint Chiefs of Staff tentatively planned for the company to join XXIV Corps, formed in I Corps Tactical Zone during mid-August 1968, to give the command a separate reconnaissance capability. These plans were changed when politically mandated limits were placed on the Army, restricting the number of troops stationed in Vietnam. The addition of the Indiana National Guard company would cause Army forces to surpass their newly authorized personnel strength level. General Westmoreland, now the Army chief of staff, decided to go ahead with plans to deploy Company D because "commitment of a National Guard unit of this [well-trained] caliber to the effort in Vietnam was expected to promote and enhance the overall reserve component program."[13]

As a result, MACV commander General Abrams was directed to "furnish trade-off spaces prior to deployment of the Indiana National Guard LRP [Long Range Patrol] company in order to prevent over-strength at a time when USARV [U.S. Army Vietnam] was approaching its authorized space ceiling." This directive meant that a Regular Army unit would have to be "traded off" to accommodate the arrival of Company D, 151st Infantry. General Abrams canceled the reconnaissance requirement for XXIV Corps, deactivated the patrol company already serving II Field Force Vietnam, and redirected the new company to take its place.[14]

Company D was flown to Vietnam at the end of December 1968. The Indiana Rangers were based at Camp Atterbury East, a former Hawk missile battery site outside Camp Frenzell-Jones in Long Binh. The company underwent a week-long Vietnam familiarization course with the 199th Infantry Brigade and received four more weeks of intensive training from the provisional II Field Force Vietnam Long Range Patrol Company (formerly Company F, 51st Infantry). The Indiana National Guard teams were declared operationally ready by the end of their third patrol, and all patrols passed muster by 23 January. On 1 February, Company D's parenthetical designator (Long Range Patrol) was changed to (Ranger). Captain Hemsel stated, "We're ready to get to work. We've been training long and hard and morale is high."[15]

General Abrams was not so pleased with the unit. He had been forced to ax a combat-experienced patrol company to make room for it, the National Guard company did not conform to the MACV-prescribed organization slated for a corps-level ranger unit, and rigid restrictions on personnel changes prevented him from putting combat-experienced leaders at critical levels within the unit. General Abrams was well aware of the unit's political sensitivity and sent a message to General Kerwin on 10 January stating, "This unit will not be infused" and "All actions which result in the removal of original members from the unit will be fully documented and made a matter of record to preclude misunderstandings on the part of the individuals concerned. Any contemplated reassignment of key officers and NCOs will be cleared with this headquarters.''[16]

The contemplated reassignment primarily concerned General Kerwin's dissatisfaction with Company D's command situation. He felt that Captain Robert Hemsel—a freshly promoted, combat-inexperienced former sales manager with the International Harvester Company in Indianapolis—was hardly qualified to lead a corps-level patrol company on the battlefield. General Kerwin wanted the company overhauled and former Company F commander Major Heckman placed in charge. MACV summarized the situation:

When D Co, 151st Inf was activated, the CO [commander] and XO [executive officer] were brothers. Prior to overseas deployment, CPT [Captain] Himsel [sic] was removed from command for unknown reasons and LT [Lieutenant] Himsel was promoted and placed in command. The original commander was sent to RVN [Republic of Vietnam] as an individual replacement and is currently assigned as Assistant S3 [operations officer], 3d Bde, 4th Inf Div.

It is the desire of the CG [Commanding General], II FFV [Field Force Vietnam] to place Maj. Heckman in command of D Co in view of his experience in LRP operations. In consideration of the relative inexperience of the officers and men of this National Guard unit, it is considered to be sound judgment to interpose no objection to this assignment.

There are political considerations concerning the proposed change of command. Co D is a National Guard unit which volunteered for duty in RVN [Republic of Vietnam]. Placing a Regular Army officer in command could cause emotional (political) problems. There are a few RA [Regular Army] enlisted men in the unit; however, all of the officers are NG [National Guard]. Because the unit will not be infused, it is unlikely that many other RA personnel will be assigned other than to replace those NG members who become casualties. If the lack of experienced personnel contribute to heavy casualties, this command may be subject to criticism. The principal concern should be the military situation and the desire of this command to provide Company D with the best possible experienced leadership.[17]

General Abrams received guidance from General Westmoreland that a dual arrangement could be worked out to satellite the provisional company nucleus with the Indiana company, effectively placing Major Heckman in charge with Captain Hemsel as his executive—while retaining the captain as commander of his own unit. Westmoreland also stated that Regular Army soldiers would be infused as normal operations demanded. Indiana guardsmen who voluntarily transferred or became incapacitated would be replaced as MACV desired. The infusion process was expected to commence within three months and then accelerate. As soon as the number of National Guardsmen dropped to 50 percent of unit total strength, he intended to assert full MACV control. Westmoreland pointed out that Company D was scheduled to return to the United States at the beginning of December and would be supplanted by a Regular Army ranger company at that time.

General Westmoreland's guidance was put into effect. On 8 February 1969 the Indiana Rangers began long-range saturation patrols into southern War Zone D and the Viet Cong U-1 secret base area in Bien Hoa Province. On the last day of the month a patrol became embroiled in fierce combat with a large VC force northwest of Bien Hoa. The team suffered three wounded in a fierce firefight and radioed for emergency medical extraction. The Air Force 38th Aerospace Rescue and Recovery Squadron's Detachment 6 dispatched a helicopter with para-rescue technician Master Sgt. David D. Rhody to the skirmish site. Enemy fire riddled the HH-43 Pedro helicopter with twenty-four hits and forced it back to the base.

Master Sergeant Rhody volunteered to go back to the trapped patrol with another HH-43 Pedro. In the interim, an Army Cobra gunship suppressed the enemy fire enough to land a quick reaction force of eight patrollers. The soldiers formed a forty-yard perimeter around the wounded men for additional protection. The hovering Pedro helicopter lowered Rhody to the ground, and he hoisted up two litter patients to the waiting aircraft. More enemy automatic weapons began firing, and Rhody waved the pilot off. He remained with the isolated team and rendered life-sustaining medical treatment for the third wounded man. Another rescue helicopter returned and was pierced by five bullets. The crew picked up the technician and injured patroller. Rhody's valor enabled the wounded men to reach waiting hospital surgeons, an action later recognized by the Silver Star.[18]

Lt. Gen. Julian J. Ewell assumed command of II Field Force Vietnam in April 1969. He continued using Company D patrols in a primary screening capacity that provided early warning of enemy movements against the massive Army Long Binh–Bien Hoa logistical center. The company usually kept eight to eleven patrols in the field at any one time and averaged ninety-five patrols per month.

Most team sorties were of a short-duration nature, but missions could last up to four days.[19]

One of the most bizarre patrols occurred in April when an overnight patrol position in the jungle of Long Khanh Province suffered an "elephant overrun." About 6:00 P.M., Sp4 Loren Dixon was observing the perimeter of his team position when he noticed a large gray mass in the underbrush about twenty-five feet away. Suddenly the pachyderm turned and came into full view as it began churning full speed toward the men. Dixon screamed, "Elephant!" as it charged directly at Lt. Eric T. Ellis and Sp4 H. C. Cross. The two men dove to either side of the massive animal and immediately fired twenty-round M16 magazines at it. The elephant thundered forward undaunted. As the rest of the patrol scrambled for their lives, the beast headed straight for Sp4 Ken Bucy. Bucy was a former football halfback in high school and tried to sidestep the charging animal, but he completed only one sidestep before being tackled by an elephant trunk. Lieutenant Ellis remembered, "She had him coiled in her trunk and lifted him way up over her head. Then she flung him to the ground and lifted her foot right above his head when we opened up with the sixteens and a machine gun." The elephant crumpled to its knees. Then a baby elephant darted from the other side of the camp and the huge mother pachyderm groped to her feet and lumbered after the infant, disappearing into the brush.[20]

During its first six months of Vietnam combat patrol operations, from February through July, Company D fielded 573 patrols in southern War Zone D and eastern Bien Hoa Province. The Indiana Rangers primarily contested the Viet Cong Dong Nai Regiment of communist Subregion 5. The patrols reported 134 separate observations of enemy personnel and became involved in ninety-four actual contact situations. In these clashes the Indiana Rangers killed seventy-six NVA/VC soldiers by direct fire and inflicted many more casualties through tactical air strikes and artillery fire.[21]

The Indiana Rangers called their field actions "baseball games," because the "individual team members worked together like the fingers of an outfielder's mitt." Patrol baseball games started when the team was inserted and ended at the debriefing that followed every extraction. Reflecting the more democratic nature of National Guard units, the team leaders made their decisions after gaining mutual approval from other members. As team leader Sgt. Dave Waters reported, "But it is a must that all team members agree. If one member feels insecure in an ambush setup, then we move to another site."

Five-man recon team 42, led by Sgt. Dave Waters, performed a typical September ambush along a small path. At 8:00 A.M., point man Sp4 Mike Slabaugh spotted three Viet Cong carrying packs as they walked down the trail. The enemy trio suddenly spotted the patrol, and the team countered by detonating their claymore mines. The team radioman reported the ambush to the company tactical operations center (TOC) located at Camp Atterbury East. Within the TOC a wall siren blared and the loudspeaker announced, "Contact!" The TOC personnel crowded around the radio to listen to the stream of team reports as two Cobra gunships, armed for immediate response, lifted off their pads and sped northward.

The Cobras reached the contact area within minutes, radioed for smoke to pinpoint the team's location, and then strafed the vicinity with mini-guns. At 8:20 A.M. the recon members searched the kill zone. They found no bodies, although Sergeant Waters was "certain at least one of the three was seriously injured." The patrollers retrieved a pair of sandals and a discarded rucksack containing rice, soybeans, canned fish, clothing, a hammock, and AK47 ammunition. Extraction helicopters landed the team back at the helipad at 8:46 A.M., and the team was debriefed before the hour ended.[22]

In August and September the Indiana Ranger operational area was awash in torrential rains of the southwest monsoon season. The adverse conditions forced the company to reduce the number of fielded teams to five at any one time. The patrols received most of their artillery support from batteries at Phuoc Vinh, Bien Hoa, and Xuan Loc, although Spooky and Shadow aircraft supported the reconnaissance campaign as weather permitted. The company continued to provide a continuous flow of military intelligence information on enemy locations and activities as it located jungle trails and ambushed small groups of enemy soldiers.

The Indiana patrol experiences were typified by a late-year surveillance patrol inserted into the jungle fringes of War Zone D near the Dong Nai river. During the night, a group of Viet Cong appeared along the darkened trail. Team leader Sgt. Dave Mallory waited tensely as he scanned the approaching enemy. He remembered previous patrols and instructional advice, as Lt. Chuck Babcock related: "Don't initiate [contact] unless you know what you're getting into. Look at the lead men. If they were smoking and joking, blow them away. If alert with weapons on the ready, let them pass. They're probably the point for a bigger unit close behind." Sergeant Mallory could see the column of ten enemy troops was quietly disciplined and fully alert. He decided that the group was probably a lead element and signaled his men not to open fire.

Mallory then radioed the sighting and arranged for artillery shellfire farther down the trail. This characteristic observation team accomplished its mission, and gave early warning to II Field Force Vietnam about the enemy movement south toward Long Binh.[23]

From 5 September to 26 October 1969 the size of the Company D reconnaissance zone was reduced sharply. The company mission was readjusted to provide close-in patrolling for the Bien Hoa Tactical Command. By the end of October, National Guard membership in Company D dropped below 60 percent, and the remaining Indiana guardsmen were within a few weeks of rotating home. Maj. Kenneth Hemsel reassumed command, while Lieutenant General Ewell prepared to use the Regular Army members as the basis for a ranger company of the 75th Infantry.[24]

DELTA RANGERS

On 20 November 1969 the Army National Guard Company D (Ranger), 151st Infantry, departed Vietnam for demobilization in Indiana. In its stead, Lieutenant General Ewell formed Company D (Ranger), 75th Infantry, with a cadre of Regular Army personnel, and appointed Maj. Richard W. Drisko as the commander. The rangers referred to themselves as the "Delta Rangers" in conformity with the letter "D" of the ICAO phonetic alphabet adopted by the U.S. military in 1956. On 1 December the new ranger company was placed under the operational control of the aerial 3d Squadron, 17th Cavalry.

Intensive ranger training was conducted to prepare the new unit for combat reconnaissance operations. Each of the field platoons completed a seven-day preparatory program that included instruction on communications, map reading, tracking, prisoner snatches, demolitions, ambush techniques, sensor emplacement, and familiarization with rappelling, rope ladders, and McGuire rigs. Four rangers were sent to the sniper school and graduated on 28 January 1970, giving the company sharpshooter capability for special countermeasure patrols.

Ranger Company D was given the mission of providing corps-level ranger support to II Field Force Vietnam by collecting intelligence, interdicting supply routes, locating and destroying encampments, and uncovering cache sites. The ranger surveillance zone was expanded to encompass the former Indiana Ranger area of operations, as well as the northeastern portion of the Catcher's Mitt and western War Zone D in Bien Hoa and Long Khanh provinces. The Delta Rangers concentrated on ambush patrols but also performed point, area, and route reconnaissance with elements as small as three men.

On 2 December 1969 a Delta Ranger ambush killed a transportation executive officer of the communist Subregion 5 who was carrying the enemy payroll, capturing 30,500 Vietnamese piasters. In early January 1970 a nine-man combined ambush group, composed of ranger teams 14 and 15, killed eleven North Vietnamese soldiers from the 274th Regiment of the 5th VC Division and fixed its location for higher headquarters analysis.[25]

The North Vietnamese and Viet Cong instituted increased precautions against ranger tactics by assigning more trail-watchers to landing fields, mining or booby-trapping routes that they no longer intended to use, and forming counter-raider teams. These enemy teams consisted of four soldiers who were highly skilled in tracking patrols and heavily armed with light machine guns and rocket-propelled grenades.

On 8 February 1970, ranger Company D was released from the 3d Squadron, 17th Cavalry, and placed under the operational control of the 199th Infantry Brigade. The Delta Rangers continued operating in southwestern War Zone D and the eastern Catcher's Mitt area. On 18 March, ranger Company D returned to direct II Field Force Vietnam control; it was employed to sweep the Nhon Trach district and train recon members of the South Vietnamese 18th Division.[26]

At the end of March 1970 the Delta Rangers ceased operations and commenced stand-down procedures. Company D (Ranger), 75th Infantry, was reduced to zero strength by the afternoon of 4 April and was officially inactivated on 10 April 1970. During the unit's Vietnam service the Delta Rangers performed 458 patrols that reported seventy separate sightings of enemy activity and clashed with NVA/VC forces on sixty-five occasions. The rangers killed eighty-eight enemy soldiers by direct fire and captured three, while suffering two killed and twenty-four wounded rangers in exchange. Of supreme importance, the ranger company unmasked changing enemy unit displacements and supply channels aimed against the main allied bases outside Saigon.[27]

II Field Force Vietnam was well served by a succession of highly proficient combat reconnaissance units. The requirements to safeguard the allied capital area placed a tremendous burden on corps-responsive teams to provide accurate and timely information. Fortunately, the patrolling expertise and professional ranger spirit of the Hurricane Patrollers, Indiana Rangers, and Delta Rangers enabled them to render excellent recon support in South Vietnam's most crucial region. In many cases, however, their reconnaissance specialty was sacrificed by higher commanders who utilized the units as a "special field force reserve" of light infantry strike forces.

12

BRIGADE RANGERS

REDCATCHER RANGERS

Saigon, the capital of the Republic of Vietnam, was the power center of the South Vietnamese government and the main headquarters for the American-Vietnamese war effort. The immediate city environs included numerous complexes that provided direction and support for the country's entire defense. These included essential command and control installations, air terminals, logistical bases, deepwater ports, and communications compounds at Saigon, Tan Son Nhut, Bien Hoa, Long Binh, Newport, and Nha Be. Successful Viet Cong or North Vietnamese penetration into this area, even by sapper attacks or rocket fire, could produce significant and even catastrophic allied political and military difficulties.

Military Assistance Command Vietnam depended on a wide ring of United States and Vietnamese formations to deter major enemy approaches toward the Saigon vicinity. However, the close-in protection of the capital area was always one of General Westmoreland's chief concerns. During December 1966 he used the arriving 199th Infantry Brigade to bolster the inner defenses. The brigade had acquired the nickname "Redcatchers," a symbolic anticommunist appellation, from its first commander while training in Georgia. General Westmoreland now positioned the brigade at Long Binh to "catch Reds" east of Saigon, and it remained in this location for most of its wartime service.

Despite the magnitude of the 199th Infantry Brigade's security assignment, as well as the heightened awareness of the need for patrolling by this stage of the conflict, the brigade had been sent to Vietnam without any long-range patrol assets. The infantry battalions raised ad hoc recon platoons, but the requirement for well-trained separate long-range patrollers remained apparent. Brigade commander Brig. Gen. Robert C. Forbes complained persistently that he lacked enough infantry reconnaissance capability to safeguard the area properly.

Finally, in September 1967, the regional II Field Force Vietnam commander, General Rosson, alerted General Forbes that a long-range patrol company (Company F, 51st Infantry) would be raised at Long Binh. Rosson insisted on maintaining control of this valuable resource directly, but entrusted Forbes with the major responsibility for manning and supplying the outfit while it was being built. This arrangement was mutually satisfactory, because it ensured that the reconnaissance company would be raised at Long Binh and have a close operating connection with the brigade.

At the conclusion of Company F's training, a number of selected personnel were transferred to form the brigade's own reconnaissance unit. As a result, on 20 December 1967, the 71st Infantry Detachment (Long Range Patrol) was activated by sixty-one recon troops chosen by General Forbes from the ranks of Company F. The timing could not have been more fortuitous. Within a month the contingent was fully operational and acquainted with its Long Binh sector. On 31 January 1968 the Viet Cong initiated their all-out Tet-68 offensive against Saigon.

One hour before midnight an outpost patrol gave the brigade its initial warning of this assault when it reported Viet Cong irregulars moving into attack positions outside Long Binh post itself. The report propelled the Redcatchers into a maelstrom of continuous fighting and emergency reaction tasks throughout the eastern Saigon defensive zone. For six months the reconnaissance detachment performed important surveillance and ambush work in the Bien Hoa and Long Binh locality.

During late April 1968 a typical ambush was performed by Sergeant Carter's recon team that surprised twenty Viet Cong infiltrators approaching a portion of Long Binh known as Camp Frenzell-Jones. Sergeant Carter waited until eight of the enemy soldiers were within a few yards of his ambush site and detonated claymore mines. The resulting blasts killed a few VC and stunned the rest. As the smoke cleared, Sgt. James R. McElwee aimed his rifle at the disorganized intruders. Suddenly fellow team member Sp4 Dennis Cameron shouted a warning, and McElwee turned around to see a Viet Cong soldier ready to fire at him. Sergeant McElwee quickly detonated another hidden claymore mine situated to cover the team's rear. The explosion instantly knocked the menacing soldier backward into the air. McElwee reported, "I grabbed a weapon and fired at three other VC coming up the trail. I got two of them." He credited the automatic response drill and team discipline gained by constant ambush rehearsal for saving the team from becoming surrounded and suffering casualties.[1]

The Tet campaign was concluded by the end of May 1968, and the 199th Infantry Division was relocated southwest of Saigon, into the extensive marshlands commonly called the "Pineapple" plantation. The flat, swampy region offered an ideal Viet Cong approach corridor to Saigon, and General Westmoreland believed that the brigade's presence would hamper this well-known enemy route into the capital. The 71st Infantry Detachment was based at "Horseshoe Bend" and conducted regular patrols into the bomb-scarred rice paddies, elephant grass clearings, and stretches of succulent fruit thickets and nipa palms.

The patrollers highlighted the "light, swift, and accurate" trademark of the brigade. For over a year the reconnaissance patrols watched scores of footbridges, embankment pathways, and other guerrilla travel avenues across the paddy landscape. The recon teams also operated effectively from Navy patrol boats that scoured the Song Vam Co Dong and landed ambush parties along the mud flats and reed-covered shores. During this time the brigade recon framework was enhanced and the detachment was expanded and transformed into a ranger company.

On 15 January 1969, 1st Lt. Robert Eason Jr. took over the 71st Infantry Detachment with an assigned priority to reorganize it into a brigade-level ranger company by the end of the month. In conformity with this schedule, on 1 February, brigade commander Brig. Gen. Frederic E. Davis activated Company M (Ranger), 75th Infantry. The ranger structure gave the separate 199th Infantry Brigade a reinforced combat reconnaissance and surveillance capability, and Capt. James E. Lewis became the new commander on 27 February. Known as either "Mike Rangers" (M in conformity with ICAO phonetic alphabet adopted by the U.S. military in 1956) or the "Redcatcher Rangers" (after the brigade nickname), the company members were formed into phonetically lettered teams, such as team Alpha, and paired closely with Troop D, 17th Cavalry.[2]

On 14 June 1969, 1st Lt. Ronald D. Harper assumed command of ranger Company M. On the following day the brigade moved into a new operational area northeast of Saigon and resettled at Fire Support Base Blackhorse in Long Khanh Province. The region was geographically different from the old swamp terrain, but brigade leaders considered the sparsely populated rubber plantations and vast jungles ideal for full ranger utilization. The rangers found the change initially unsettling because they were "on unfamiliar ground facing a more hardened, professional soldier [adversary] than they had ever faced before."[3]

The majority of combat operations in Long Khanh Province invariably encountered elements of two large, well-trained, and highly disciplined organizations—the 274th VC Regiment and the 33d NVA Regiment. For many soldiers, facing disciplined and aggressive enemy soldiers was an unpleasant task compared to fighting the unskilled peasant guerrillas in the old Pineapple zone. Other soldiers liked the new area better, noting the relative absence of booby traps and mine contraptions that had caused such high casualties during plantation patrols.

The rangers were soon unleashed in an ambitious extended reconnaissance campaign to locate NVA and VC hiding places, resupply points, and infiltration routes. The Redcatcher Ranger teams were sent into the gloomy rain forests northeast of Trang Bom, north of Dinh Quan, and along the heavily vegetated Lga Nga and Dong Nai rivers. The ranger scouts grappled with the enemy in a series of sharp clashes. From these opening skirmishes, the rangers learned that their opponents were highly elusive but willing to stand and fight when cornered or occupying good positions. However, the ranger company gained confidence as its incessant raiding began to unbalance NVA and VC attempts to safeguard previously uncontested supply lines and caches.

The unswerving pace of this prolonged ranger operation was demonstrated in September 1969, when Sgt. David Reeser's ranger team Bravo was dispatched on a long-range mission into the jungle near the Dong Nai river. On the second day his patrol discovered an enemy base area in the lush tropical forest and counted a dozen camouflaged bunkers before moving 300 yards away. Sergeant Reeser prepared to call for artillery against the campsite and ordered Sp4 Lou Garland to climb a high tree and observe marking rounds for artillery firing adjustments.

Suddenly Specialist Garland hastened down the tree trunk, jumped to the jungle floor, and ran over to the clustered team members. He reported seeing at least twenty North Vietnamese soldiers moving swiftly in their direction. With little time to spare, the rangers hastily rigged a claymore mine and moved back into a sheltered embankment covered by dense foliage. They detonated the claymore directly into the advancing soldiers, and this opening blast was followed by a grenade explosion, in the midst of the enemy platoon, that Garland scored with his M79.

The startled enemy troops fell back into the jungle, set up machine guns, and started maneuvering against the ranger defenders. Sergeant Reeser radioed for air support, and OV-10 Bronco observation aircraft, along with F-100 fighter-bombers, appeared overhead. Reeser tossed smoke grenades to signal the planes. Once identification was confirmed, he directed the Bronco forward air controllers by radio. The Broncos flew close to the ground and received heavy fire, but pinpointed enemy reinforcements rushing toward the battlefield. F-100s dropped 500-pound bombs and Cobra gunships rocketed the surrounding terrain, and this aerial onslaught sealed off the skirmish site.

The firefight between the rangers and the already-engaged enemy platoon lasted three hours. During this time, Reeser was forced to use all the team smoke grenades to contact the aircraft on their firing passes. He then flashed an orange panel to signal the gunships. In the meantime, ranger Specialist Arrell spotted and killed a North Vietnamese soldier who was slithering close by with a full bag of grenades. The climax of the action was reached when the isolated team nearly ran out of ammunition. A light observation helicopter skimmed the trees and dropped a fresh case of M16 ammunition, enabling the rangers to replenish their rifle magazines and hold out in their small perimeter. Staunch infantry resistance and aerial suppressive fire finally caused the enemy to flee, and the team was extracted.[4]

During mid-November, a reinforced two-team ranger patrol moving north of the Dong Nai river initiated a small ambush that almost caused disaster. The lead rangers saw an enemy squad but failed to wait and ascertain its purpose. Instead they ambushed the enemy soldiers, who, as it turned out, were scouts for an entire company of the 33d NVA Regiment. The hasty ambush provoked a violent skirmish, in which one ranger team leader was killed and another ranger seriously wounded, before emergency extraction could be accomplished.[5]

On 18 November 1969, Capt. Hugh J. Turner III took over ranger Company M. As a consequence of the recently botched ambush, he directed that his sergeants and experienced rangers conduct a thorough critique of the action. The review reemphasized the fact that enemy units habitually employed five to seven men moving fifty or seventy yards in front of their main contingents. Team leaders were cautioned to use patience and sound judgment before initiating a surprise attack. The company rehearsed the correct positioning of ambushes, so that individuals could observe a good length of suspected enemy paths.

The persistent ranger reconnaissance campaign continued relentlessly, as sustained pressure was applied on the network of supply lines used by the two enemy regiments. By 6 February 1970, when Lt. Deems C. Watkins assumed command of the company, the rangers had interdicted so many enemy resupply trails that the 274th VC Regiment was reduced to eating bananas and roots. The 33d NVA Regiment withdrew from Long Khanh Province altogether, and ranger company patrols were ordered to continue tracking it east into Binh Tuy Province.

The expanded reconnaissance campaign forced the rangers to arrange long-distance communications. For example, in late March 1970, one team was placed on a remote mountaintop and set up a radio-relay point for two weeks. This duty was extremely hazardous, because it involved transmitting signals from a static location. Mobile long-range patrols also became more dangerous as scattered forays were launched deep into North Vietnamese strongholds. In one incident, troops of the 33d NVA regiment ambushed Troop D of the 17th Cavalry near Vo Xu on 1 April. Brigade commander Brig. Gen. William R. Bond landed his helicopter to organize a search party during the action and was killed by a sniper.[6]

On 25 April 1970, Capt. John W. Perkins took over ranger Company M. During mid-July he shifted the ranger forward mission site to Fire Support Base Mace, near Gia Ray in Binh Tuy Province. The ranger teams prepared to go deeper in pursuit of the evasive North Vietnamese. Instead, they were informed that their exemplary reconnaissance pursuit campaign was about to end. The brigade had received higher orders that it was scheduled for redeployment from Vietnam as part of the Army's Keystone Robin Increment IV program.

On 9 September the ranger company ceased active combat operations, and the last four ranger teams were extracted by helicopter from the field for reconsolidation at Fire Support Base Mace. The veteran Redcatcher Rangers were moved by truck convoy to Camp Frenzell-Jones in Long Binh and started stand-down procedures. Company M (Ranger), 75th Infantry, was reduced to zero strength on 14 September and officially inactivated effective 12 October 1970.[7]

The 199th Infantry Brigade combat reconnaissance record was a model of effective scouting progression that produced one of the most successful ranger endeavors of the Vietnam conflict. The Redcatcher patrollers and rangers were adjusted from close-in installation defense around Long Binh, to short-range swamp patrol monitoring assignments in the Pineapple plantation, and finally to independent long-range ranger patrols on a sustained reconnaissance campaign in enemy-dominated territory. This proper groundwork enabled Company M to achieve good results during its relentless tracking of two formidable enemy regiments.

FROM ALL-AMERICAN TO ARCTIC RANGERS

The 82d Airborne Division was one of the premier combat divisions in the United States and configured for rapid global response contingencies. During the Vietnam conflict the division was part of the Army Strategic Forces, reserved for domestic and European-Middle East emergencies, and this posture initially excluded it from Vietnam duty. The sudden onslaught of the communist Tet-68 offensive, however, caused General Westmoreland to seek urgent release of a divisional brigade as a temporary emergency reinforcement for his embattled forces. The 3d Brigade was accordingly airlifted from Fort Bragg, North Carolina, to the Hue-Phu Bai region of northern South Vietnam under command of Col. (later Brig. Gen.) Alexander R. Bolling Jr.

The separate airborne brigade included no standard ground patrolling component. This condition would have been intolerable by the midpoint of the war, except that the speedy assembly of the brigade precluded any chance of orderly alteration in its stateside composition. Upon reaching Vietnam, however, Colonel Bolling authorized his three battalion commanders to form ad hoc reconnaissance-security elements as they required.

The 1st Battalion, 508th Infantry, formed a sixty-man "Delta Company" by dismounting the jeep reconnaissance platoon; the 2d Battalion, 505th Infantry, organized a "Strike Force" of forty men using its recon and antitank platoons; and the 1st Battalion, 505th Infantry, raised two "Combined Platoons" by cross-attaching its recon and antitank platoons. This battalion provisional reconnaissance never substituted adequately for a brigade-level recon unit capable of executing long-range patrols.[8]

The experience of the 1st Battalion, 508th Infantry, typified the field-expedient patrol approach. The recon element was formed in June by Lt. Roger Watson and Sfc. William "Rock" Spring. At this time the battalion was located along Route 547 southwest of the recaptured strongpoint of Hue and tasked to interdict fleeing North Vietnamese troops believed to be escaping along the Perfume River. Lieutenant Watson had served his first Vietnam tour as a sergeant with Special Forces, and he petitioned the line companies to obtain troops who wanted to be with a small, cohesive airborne-qualified force. He zealously avoided using the "leg" (nonparachutist) replacements who were now filling the unit and were believed to be lowering the high morale normally associated with airborne esprit.

The battalion spent most of summer 1968 reconnoitering the hills west of Hue without major enemy contact. One sharp clash did develop southwest of former Landing Zone Birmingham, in the midst of mountainous triple-canopy jungle cloaked by low clouds. Battalion recon assets were misused by being kept in defensive positions, guarding the mortars and howitzers on a ridge. After Lieutenant Watson pleaded for permission to run patrols, his reconnaissance troops were allowed farther out on observation and listening missions. The men traded fire with snipers and found numerous blood trails, indicating moderate success in close-in recon, but never searched out "body count" statistics.

During late October 1968 the 3d Brigade relocated to the Saigon area to provide additional security, especially in the densely populated urban suburbs and farming communities of Hoc Mon and Tan Binh districts. This part of western Gia Dinh Province, although prosperous, was considered a hotbed of rebel discontent and sympathetic to the Viet Cong. The brigade's new responsibility, guarding part of the sensitive capital region, caused a higher command interest in allocating proper reconnaissance assets. On 15 December the 78th Infantry Detachment (Airborne Long Range Patrol) was activated under the command of Lt. William E. Jones and stationed at Camp Red Ball, northeast of Saigon.

Brigade foot reconnaissance proved extremely difficult, because the communists were reluctant to wage open warfare in the region following heavy losses in the Tet-68 offensive. Most enemy activity was carried out using subversive methods targeted against governmental and pacification projects. Recon patrols were also hampered by cleverly hidden booby traps and other "terror weapons." Most patrollers found it extremely difficult to adjust from the mountain upland of northern Vietnam to the muddy conditions of the south.

One patrol, scouting along the Nha Be river to interdict river traffic, conducted a village search that found a woman in possession of U.S. government documents. The woman was in her fifties and ran a small store out of her home. The documents—which listed the names, identification numbers, and other personal data on most officers and NCOs assigned to MACV headquarters—were stored under her bed in a homemade suitcase constructed out of flattened Ballantine beer cans. Intelligence officials later found out that she was a leading Viet Cong spy and tax collector.

The recon patrollers returned to a spot near her village and set up a night ambush along the Nha Be river. They detected a large amount of flotsam, bathed in moonlight, drifting slowly downstream. No one was observed on or near the tangled mass of branches and vegetation, but the troops fired machine guns and grenade launchers in front of the floating debris and then into the middle of it. There was no effect from all this shooting until an M79 grenade round caused a tremendous detonation, followed by secondary explosions. The patrol was credited with destroying a major VC ammunition resupply packet.

Another recon patrol led by Staff Sgt. Malcolm M. Budd conducted five successful night operations during January 1969. On the final mission, Staff Sergeant Budd's team detected a Viet Cong squad attempting to cross a collapsed bridge over the Song Saigon. The patrollers killed three enemy soldiers before the rest fled from the scene. Gunships flew into action from nearby Tan Son Nhut airfield, and a reaction force recovered important documents from the fallen trio on the demolished structure.[9]

On 1 February 1969 the separate airborne brigade activated Company O (Airborne Ranger), 75th Infantry, to expand its long-range patrolling and surveillance capability. The 78th Infantry Detachment was accordingly deactivated and its members were absorbed into the new company. The remaining personnel needed to fill the sixty-one-man authorized unit were secured by levying the provisional II Field Force long-range patrol company, still stationed at nearby Long Binh. However, the brigade's strength averaged less than fifty troops throughout its wartime service. The rangers referred to themselves as the "All-American Rangers" after the division shoulder sleeve insignia (AA) title.

On 1 March 1969, following a month-long training period, ranger Company O was declared fully operational and Capt. Peter A. Donald assumed command. The ranger teams were deployed along the fringes of the brigade area of operations to cover the outlying farming neighborhoods and river-canal junctions. The patrols were routine, and the brigade reported in June, "Primarily they have provided intelligence of a negative nature, in that very little activity has been noted in their area of operations."[10]

The All-American Rangers patrolled the outer Saigon area throughout the summer. Their proficiency increased with experience, and the ranger teams began uncovering valuable information on a main-force Viet Cong regiment and H-5 Water Sapper Battalion. From May through the end of July, the rangers accounted for only six enemy soldiers killed by direct fire. The "low body count" resulted from the rangers' professional restraint from firing on possible civilians, and the Viet Cong tendency to disperse into solitary or three-man elements while moving around or through the brigade area.[11]

Ranger Company O contributed significantly to area stability operations. The teams restored security by patrolling suspected VC avenues and foiled rocket attacks from the west against Tan Son Nhut airfield and Saigon. The rangers experienced considerable problems trying to reach crowded urban and agricultural localities without being detected. The 1st Battalion, 508th Infantry, inserted its attached ranger teams into the Hercules area of operations by conducting company-sized airmobile operations and then bringing in rangers on resupply helicopters. The rangers remained surreptitiously in stay-behind ambush positions after the infantry company departed the area aboard other helicopters.

On 29 July 1969, Capt. Patrick H. Downing took command of ranger Company O. The rangers became heavily involved in supporting the brigade "surveillance task force" screening the Capital Military District Command. The task force was actually an elaborate battlefield surveillance system composed of electronic ground sensor devices, radar towers, and night observation points. The rangers responded rapidly to sightings and readings on the surveillance line and greatly assisted in deterring enemy advances toward Saigon.

The All-American rangers remained headquartered at Camp Red Ball, but in the fall, teams were deployed farther out into the Iron Triangle and the Phu Hoa districts. These expanded operations were terminated shortly after the ranger company was alerted for standdown on 17 September. The teams were then reconsolidated at Phu Loi and reduced to zero strength. Company O (Airborne Ranger), 75th Infantry, was officially inactivated on 20 November 1969, just prior to the brigade's departure from Vietnam in December. During their short tenure of Vietnam service, the airborne brigade rangers executed a difficult assignment within a heavily populated area and pioneered many important advances in ranger-responsive electronic warfare techniques.[12]

Company O was destined to serve again during the Vietnam era, but its second life was spent in a climate far removed from any previous tropical environment. The reactivation of the ranger company was triggered by the 1968 discovery of immense oil fields along Alaska's northern coast at Prudhoe Bay. Petroleum engineers identified the major find as the largest in North America, and development of the new fields assumed strategic priority for the oil-reliant United States during 1969. The military command in Alaska adjusted war plans to include Prudhoe Bay security, but its geographical isolation on the arctic shoreline posed extreme difficulties for even air-delivered troops.

The U.S. Army Alaska (USARAL) commander, Maj. Gen. James F. Hollingsworth, needed a strike force that would respond swiftly, even under adverse winter conditions, if the Prudhoe Bay oil reserves were threatened. He knew that ice and snow conditions might prevent the immediate landing of troop-filled aircraft, but decided that key facilities could be temporarily safeguarded by air-dropping an elite combat spearhead until larger reinforcements arrived. As a result, Hollingsworth insisted on a full company of rangers capable of parachuting into the frozen Alaskan northland and executing a wide range of reaction and antisabotage missions.

Under General Hollingsworth's direction, Company O (Arctic Ranger), 75th Infantry, was reconstituted at Fort Richardson on 4 August 1970—less than a year after the original Company O had been closed out in Southeast Asia. The new separate company was directly subordinated to U.S. Army Alaska, with the mission "to provide long range reconnaissance, surveillance, and target acquisition patrol capability to USARAL." Known as Arctic Rangers, they wore the gold-starred, growling polar bear head patch of USARAL as their shoulder sleeve insignia.[13]

The first ranger commander, Maj. George A. Ferguson Jr., worked feverishly to build his company into one of the finest winter fighting units in the Army. He was authorized 216 soldiers, and formed the company as rapidly as qualified soldiers could be recruited. Ranger Company O was organized into three special long-distance patrol platoons. Each platoon was designed to operate a remote base camp and was fully equipped with long-range communications and over-snow terrain apparatus, to include snow machines that replaced dog teams. In addition, every platoon contained eight patrols, consisting of five men each, who were qualified in cross-country skiing and snowshoe travel.

Another important facet of Major Ferguson's task was supplementing the Alaskan Army National Guard Eskimo Scouts with a full-time Regular Army ranger presence. The Eskimo Scouts were known as the "Eyes and Ears of the North" and had existed as a unique National Guard component since 1949, although the force traced its natural heritage to the rugged Eskimo, Indian, Aleut, and prospector volunteers who composed the Alaskan Scouts of World War II fame. Organized into scout battalions, the modern natives relied on centuries of arctic hunting mastery to perform surveillance and reconnaissance across western Alaska's barren tundra and offshore islands near the Soviet Union.

The Eskimo Scouts watched for and provided early warning of enemy infiltration by patrolling vast stretches of the otherwise unprotected Alaskan coast, as well as islands such as St. Lawrence and Little Diomede in the Bering Strait. Soviet military activity became more aggressive in this region during the late 1960s, and the importance of scouting and observation missions increased. Aircraft overflights and detections of surfaced submarines were reported frequently. These reports were underscored by sightings of suspicious persons (some wearing wet suits) and the recovery of rubber rafts and chemical masks on secluded beaches. Pentagon officials dampened the public alarm by describing the culprits as ivory poachers engaged in illegal walrus hunts, but secretly issued orders to heighten watchfulness through more vigorous patrolling.[14]

The Eskimo Scouts, however, were largely neglected during the Vietnam buildup years, and their modern specialty training was deficient. The situation was further eroded by the Army's practice of placing non-Eskimo officers in scout contingents. The native force totaled roughly 1,500 men, who were drawn from ninety small impoverished settlements almost totally reliant on government assistance. The Eskimos either hunted caribou and other game from nomadic encampments or occupied tiny fishing hamlets that were connected by plane whenever adjacent inlets froze into natural runways. Eskimo Scout service relieved the boredom of long winters and doubled many family incomes, but the isolated native lifestyle handicapped both National Guard supervision and sporadic Special Forces advisory visits.

General Hollingsworth realized that the renewed importance of the Eskimo Scouts demanded better measures. He also shared Major Ferguson's confidence that close ranger-scout cooperation would create mutual advantages. The rangers could offer prolonged instruction in modern snow vehicle, radio, and advanced night vision utilization. In turn, the rangers would benefit greatly from the scouts' demonstrated proficiency in arctic survival and wilderness patrolling.

The Eskimo livelihood of hunting and fishing demanded that any ranger-scout training occur during winter months. The rangers prepared by sending eighty members through the USARAL Unit Leaders Course at Fort Greely, Alaska during November. Two rangers, James P. Anderson and John H. Taylor, became the course officer and NCO honor graduates, respectively. The company was then fielded for the first time as a complete unit, and participated with

Canadian forces in ACID TEST III from 5 to 12 December 1970. The rangers deployed satisfactorily and succeeded in infiltrating the main "aggressor" camp. At the end of the test, Company O was declared operational for commitment anywhere within Alaska.[15]

The Arctic Rangers next embarked on a series of brutal combined winter exercises with the Eskimo Scouts code-named ACE BAND. The true nature of arctic warfare rapidly became apparent as temperatures routinely plummeted to 30 degrees below zero, cracking metal and tearing off skin in contact with icy M16 rifle barrels. The aurora borealis atmospheric phenomena canceled signal transmissions, and radio batteries lasted only five minutes. Savage wind gusts blasted marchers on snowshoes as they struggled across miles of trackless white tundra, and sudden snow blizzards forced ski-mounted patrollers to link themselves by rope behind straining snowmobiles ("snow machines"). ACE BAND became a supreme test of human endurance, and the rangers often depended on the contents of their twenty-eight ahkios—runnerless fiberglass sleds—packed with a five-man tent, stove, extra radio batteries, and rations. The rangers often subsisted on proven native fare such as dried fish strips and body-warming chunks of whale blubber, known as *muktuk*.

The rangers persisted in accomplishing their "dynamic arctic training," and slowly they became familiar with many aspects of northern country and weather conditions. During January 1971, Company O conducted the first basic airborne course in the history of U.S. Army Alaska and qualified fifty-seven of its non-jumper personnel in parachuting. On 18 February the Arctic Rangers demonstrated this parachute capability by executing a winter jump over frozen Lake Clunie at Fort Richardson. This was a training prelude to the daring March ranger para-drop over the frozen Beaufort Sea, the first military parachute operation on the polar ice cap.

On 4 March 1971, following a twenty-four-hour weather delay, four C130 Hercules aircraft of the Alaskan Air Command lifted off from Elmendorf Air Force Base. They parachuted 135 rangers onto the seven-foot-thick ice sheet about 130 miles north-northeast of Point Barrow, Alaska. The rangers set up camp and bivouacked overnight before being flown by CH-47 helicopter to the Point Barrow Navy Research Center airfield. The true ranger assignment, to protect northern oilfields, was masked by Defense Department cover stories concerning the sixteen daily winter commercial flights scheduled between Alaska and Europe. Press releases announced that "the main purpose of this unusual training is to develop a small force of men able to serve in search, rescue, first aid, and recovery actions at 'the top of the world' in the event they are ever needed in conjunction with an emergency occurring along trans-polar airline routes."[16]

The company followed its celebrated polar ice cap jump by conducting an abbreviated ranger course at Fort Richardson. This unit program followed infantry school ranger instruction as closely as possible. The course lasted three weeks, and students received extensive training in patrolling, map reading, communications skills, and a variety of subjects oriented toward arctic-style warfare. At the conclusion of the ranger course, the company dispatched a hundred rangers to St. Lawrence Island for anti-Soviet combat surveillance commencing 30 March.

The rangers on St. Lawrence Island were only forty-seven miles from Soviet territory. They were reinforced by selected personnel of the 1st Scout Battalion, 297th Infantry, and 38th Special Forces Group. Eskimo scouts accompanied the ranger teams, but high winds and dense fogs prevented systematic patrolling. Aircraft maintenance problems forced an early ranger withdrawal on 8 April, but the maneuver still stands as one of the few combatant incidents that occurred, outside the Dominican Republic and Korea, during the Vietnam period.

On 25 June 1971 the Arctic Rangers moved to Eklutna Mountain and rehearsed mountain climbing, erection of suspension bridges, and the traversing of glacial obstacles. This practice was followed by July river navigation exercises at Clear Water Lake and advanced mountain training at Black Rapids. This additional ranger training was soon put to the test. On 28 August 1971 a woman in Palmer, Alaska, notified the Air Force Rescue Coordination Center that she had seen flashes from a signal mirror atop Pioneer Peak. Major Ferguson was alerted that two sheep hunters had scaled the summit from the east side and become trapped on the sheer western face. Both were stranded at the 6,400-foot level and unable to descend. The mountain topography also barred the men from returning by their original route.

On the early morning of 29 August a ranger mountaineering team was airlanded on a ledge at the 3,500-foot level of Pioneer Peak. The rescue party began a long and difficult ascent to reach the hunters, but the steep rocks proved more treacherous than expected. Attempts to scale the mountain were suspended at 10:00 P.M. after alpine expert Staff Sgt. Ronald Thompson fell and suffered a broken leg. A short time later, Lt. James Little and Sgt. First Class Gary Patterson boarded a helicopter to extract Thompson and make another attempt to rescue the hunting pair before nightfall. A radio message reached their helicopter that Thompson was being treated on a wooden outcrop and would not be ready for immediate lift-out. The lieutenant then directed the helicopter pilot to survey the hunters' exact predicament on the mountain wall.

The helicopter crew spent fifteen minutes moving back and forth along the mountainside before spotting the hunters. Their serious plight was quickly manifested, but the helicopter pilot could not move closer than fifteen feet for fear of striking a rocky overhang with the main rotor blade. Little and Patterson prepared climbing ropes, and the sergeant opened the port door to throw the rope to the hunters. During the first two tries, the rotor wash blew the rope out of reach, but on the third attempt one of the hunters succeeded in grabbing the line and securing himself. The helicopter lowered him into the valley and then returned to retrieve the second hunter from the cliff. The flight finally picked up Thompson and flew him directly to the hospital at Fort Richardson.[17]

On 29 October 1971, Maj. Edward O. Yaugo, a ranger-qualified officer and a veteran of two Vietnam battle tours, took command of the Arctic Rangers from Major Ferguson. The rangers spent the next month serving as aggressor forces near Akiak village during Operation ACE CARD BETHEL. On 29 November a ranger rescue mission was dispatched to locate an Air Force doctor who never returned from a hunting expedition. The rangers searched unsuccessfully for five days in spite of heavy snowstorms. The rangers returned to the area in June 1972, after the deep snow melted, and found the doctor's body at the base of a 300-foot cliff where he had fallen to his death from a narrow sheep trail.

During 1972 the Arctic Rangers continued their proficiency training throughout Alaska. On 25 March the company conducted another para-drop onto the polar ice cap, 103 miles north of Point Barrow. The company also conducted mountaineering exercises at Bear Mountain outside Sitka. Ranger expertise was highlighted in July when a selected twenty-four-man party traversed the sixty-five-mile-wide Harding Ice Field, one of the largest ice fields in the world. During their arduous four-day hike, the rucksack-laden rangers encountered numerous ice hazards, a large glacier bear, and near-disastrous white-out conditions. The Arctic Rangers spent the next month pinpointing and recovering bodies from the wreckage of an Air National Guard C-54 that had crashed in August 1969.

One of the last ranger company exercises, held at King Salmon from 9 to 18 August 1972, was dominated by miserable rainy weather, swarms of insects, and a pesky brown bear. The bear finally became such a nuisance around the mess tent that the rangers summoned a biologist to drug it and remove it from the area. The bear continued its antics aboard the returning CH-47 helicopter when it began to revive and panicked the aviation crew chief. The bear later managed to relocate the ranger field area, but this time it made a conscious effort to avoid being seen near the mess tent. The bear deliberately side-stepped or negotiated all trip wires and demonstrated such tactical prowess in avoiding detection that it was designated an "honorary ranger bear."[18]

General Hollingsworth had departed Alaska in January 1972 to take over the post of senior adviser to the South Vietnamese III Corps region. His new position placed him in charge of the former operating area of the original Company O. In the meantime, the arctic rangers lost their champion and were slated for elimination in his absence. Strength reductions throughout the Alaskan Command finalized this decision, and Company O (Arctic Rangers), 75th Infantry, was deactivated on 29 September 1972. The Arctic Rangers existed for just over two years, but during this interval they forged an indelible mark on the diverse record of United States Army ranger service.

RED DEVIL RANGERS

The last ranger company in letter sequence served the last major combat unit to enter Vietnam. The mechanized 1st Brigade of the 5th Infantry Division arrived in northern South Vietnam in July 1968 as part of the final Army deployment into the combat theater. The mobile infantry force, equipped with armored personnel carriers and supported by tanks and motorized equipment, was based at Quang Tri and assigned a wide sector of responsibility along the Demilitarized Zone.

Known as the "Red Devil Brigade," the mechanized unit conducted cordon and search missions around villages, performed search and clear expeditions on the Khe Sanh Plains, made road-clearing expeditions to secure Highway 9 to the Laotian border, and staged interdiction strikes against Highway 926. The brigade was also responsible for guarding the rice harvests and denying unchecked enemy access to the agriculture-rich coastline. Extended foot reconnaissance was needed in many of these tasks, but the brigade was not authorized a separate ground-patrolling capability until 15 December 1968, when it activated the 79th Infantry Detachment (Long Range Patrol).

The detachment never reached operational status. The Army authorized the conversion of the detachment, still in training, to a regular brigade-level ranger company. On 1 February 1969, Company P (Ranger), 75th Infantry, was activated to provide long-range reconnaissance, surveillance, and target acquisition for the 1st Brigade, 5th Infantry Division (Mechanized). Commonly known as the "Red Devil Rangers," they garnered additional personnel from the provisional II Field Force Vietnam Long Range Patrol Company. This process was completed in March, and Company P was declared combat-ready.

During the spring of 1969 the Red Devil Rangers began active patrolling throughout the brigade's operational area. The ranger company fielded an average of twenty-five six-man patrols per month. Roughly a third of these were performed within the brigade's normal area, and two-thirds were extended patrols sent into the far "Reconnaissance Zone" that abutted the border with Laos. Most teams were delivered and taken out by helicopter. However, taking advantage of brigade assets, roughly 15 percent of all patrols used either mechanized (armored personnel carrier) or armored (tank) infiltration.[19]

One reconnaissance patrol was following a stream when point man Sp4 Mike D. Rich heard voices to his left and motioned for the team to stop. The team decided to double around and hit the enemy position from its blind side, but Sgt. George Padrick spotted three North Vietnamese soldiers bathing in the stream a mere twenty-five yards away. Specialist Rich recalled, "One of them turned around and we were staring directly at each other and then they all started for shore to get their weapons. One burst from my M16 and all three tumbled dead into the water." The patrol then received fire from several directions and withdrew to an extraction point.[20]

Teams inserted into the Reconnaissance Zone were assigned six-kilometer squares known as "patrol boxes." The patrol boxes were chosen according to brigade operating requirements, current intelligence appraisals, and previous ranger experience in the same area. Patrol duration within the Reconnaissance Zone was ideally five days. During the first four days and three nights the teams were to reconnoiter signs of activity. Patrols were positioned along infiltration routes chosen for enemy use and proximity to pickup zones, in case fast extraction was required. On the last day the teams selected a final ambush position and radioed for extraction after executing a deliberate contact, a tactic that conserved scarce helicopter resources. Covering gunships and other aircraft were used both to lift out the team and to deliver punishing aerial fire against the enemy.

During May 1969 a typical patrol led by Sp4 Tom Snow was on

the first day of its mission when the patrollers spotted two North Vietnamese soldiers. Specialist Snow reported, "We knew they were setting up overnight in the bunker to conduct sightings the next day. They were recon NVA. They were at the ready, and knew what they were doing, watching every inch of the ground." The rangers quickly set up claymore mines around the nearby unoccupied bunker and camouflaged them in expectation of the scouts' return. The ranger leader reasoned that the North Vietnamese were probably no different from Americans in relaxing when they reached their campground. As predicted, the two scouts returned, and the rangers watched intently as they proceeded closer to the bunker. The North Vietnamese temporarily relaxed their vigilance near the entrance, and at that instant the rangers detonated the mines. Both men were killed, and the rangers recovered important documents, letters, and wallets from the fallen soldiers.[21]

One of the most successful Red Devil Ranger missions was an assassination mission that targeted communist guerrilla leader Nguyen Quyet. The XXIV Corps Intelligence Collection Division's Ground Reconnaissance Branch considered Quyet "the most wanted Viet Cong guerrilla leader in Quang Tri Province." The Special Forces had tried to kill Quyet for the past six years. A heavy sniper team from Company P was inserted on a ridge in the Ba Long Valley, eight miles southwest of Quang Tri. The team established a sniper position and waited.

The senior marksman recalled, "I saw movement in the trees and then saw a man walking briskly down the creek bank toward the east. He was carrying an M16 rifle and was walking hunched over with his cap pulled low on his head and his collar turned up. I stayed down and waited until he was about twenty meters away and then I opened fire." The body was identified as Quyet because the little finger of his right hand was missing. The dead communist leader was displayed in his operational village of Nhu Le. The previously undefeated guerrilla band, lacking Quyet's leadership and shaken by his obvious mortality, ceased effective operations in the Quang Tri area.[22]

The war on the northern fringes of South Vietnam continued unabated into 1970. During the spring, Capt. Luke B. Ferguson's Red Devil Rangers resorted to more deceptive infiltration techniques to confuse their battle-hardened North Vietnamese adversaries. False insertions were made with six torso mannequins ("dummy rangers") dressed in camouflaged tunics with camouflage-painted faces. The dummy rangers were placed behind the closed doors of a helicopter and braced with sandbags. One real ranger rode between the six dummy rangers and shook them to produce lively motion. When the helicopter landed, the ranger pulled the six dummies down and concealed himself on the floor. The method fooled all but the closest observers into thinking that the ranger team made an actual insertion.

The Reconnaissance Zone remained the most dangerous arena of ranger activity. The Red Devil Rangers alleviated some of the risk by executing long flights deep into the zone and then patrolling close to the intended extraction sites. In spite of these precautions, North Vietnamese surprise attacks sometimes prevented clean breakaways. To lessen the chances of being trapped, ranger teams carried bountiful CS-gas grenades and 40mm grenadier cartridges that dispersed enough riot gas to daze and distract the enemy, thus covering a short retreat. The ranger company also kept a helicopter, loaded with ten E-158 fifty-pound canisters of gas, on stand-by. This helicopter thoroughly doused the point target with gas concentrations, followed immediately by armed gunship strafing runs, enabling the team to be lifted out by armed extraction helicopters.

On 12 June 1970 the mechanized brigade was alerted that it would return to the United States and rejoin its parent 5th Division as part of Increment IX (Keystone Oriole-Bravo) of the U.S. Army withdrawal from Vietnam. The last ranger missions were scrubbed early because of Tropical Storm Kim. The Red Devil Rangers began standdown procedures on 23 July, and all personnel were transferred out of the unit by 5 August. Company P (Ranger), 75th Infantry, was officially inactivated on 31 August 1971.[23]

Army mechanized divisions were not normally authorized ranger companies. A ranger component was added to a mechanized command during the Vietnam conflict because the brigade's role encompassed many extended security assignments. The ranger company was also unique because it utilized both helicopter and armored personnel carrier insertions on a frequent basis. This blend of patrolling with aerial and mechanized assets rapidly displaced across plains and mountains produced a reconnaissance environment that matched postwar conventional or "European battlefield" expectations. Company P provided a practical basis for further Army development of wide-ranging ranger special missions and tactics in a mobile environment.

13

RANGER ADVISERS

VIETNAM: DEVELOPMENT AND DEFENSE (1960–1965)

The South Vietnamese Army Rangers, known as the Biêt-Dông-Quân or BDQ, were created in 1960 as a counter-guerrilla force of light companies that could track the elusive Viet Cong and strike them in their jungle hideouts. The ranger units were also intended as an elite backup force for outlying districts.

Special Forces Col. William Ewald's training teams were rushed to Vietnam during May 1960 to select three training sites and get training underway by June. Ranger courses were established by Capt. Mel Slade at Da Nang, by Capt. Ray Call at Nha Trang, and by Capt. Ken Beard at Song Mao. The first training was conducted with old French ammunition, for lack of American materiel. The erratic fragmentation grenades caused the scariest incidents—a previous Special Forces adviser, Capt. Harry G. Cramer, had already been killed by one at Nha Trang in October 1957. The defective French blasting caps were considered safer because they would not detonate.[1]

Song Mao was considered the best training site, and the students rapidly progressed under Special Forces tutelage, although not without weird incidents. During the weapons training the ranger students were learning how to disassemble and reassemble their M1 rifles blindfolded. A snake happened to crawl across some of the disassembly mats and students groping for rifle parts latched onto the reptile. Captain Beard recalled that this was the fastest he ever saw rangers move while reacting to a hostile situation. The blindfolds came off in a hurry, and the blindfold portion of the class had to be dropped.

251

The Special Forces–directed "aggressor force" at the Nha Trang training site moved into the field and established automatic rifle positions for ranger patrol practice. One night a herd of cattle migrated close to one of the listening posts. The Vietnamese soldier challenged the movement but received no response. Realizing that Viet Cong might be in the area, he opened up with his Browning Automatic Rifle at close range. The soldier fired high, however, and missed the entire herd. This incident convinced the Special Forces sergeants that ranger units were definitely needed by the ARVN command.

The original Nha Trang course became the South Vietnamese Ranger Training Center at Duc My (just outside Nha Trang), and Special Forces turned over training assistance responsibilities to Regular Army advisory teams. During the next four years, Vietnamese ranger companies were trained and scattered into the countryside. One ranger battalion headquarters was raised as an administrative entity in each corps zone. Most ranger companies were stationed around the capital and in the Mekong Delta on antipartisan duty.

During the summer of 1963 there were eighty-six Vietnamese ranger companies. The original 10th, 20th, 30th, and 31st ARVN Ranger Battalions, serving I–IV CTZ respectively, were renumbered consistently with their corps assignments as the 11th, 21st, 31st, and 41st ARVN Ranger Battalions. The new 22d ARVN Ranger Battalion was assembled at Duc My to give a second administrative headquarters for II CTZ, and the 32nd and 33rd ARVN Ranger Battalions were raised for the same purpose around Saigon. More than half of all ranger companies were still concentrated in the capital area. The mid-1963 dispositions of the Vietnamese ranger companies are displayed in Appendix F.

By August 1964 the advisory teams totaled only thirty-five officers and nineteen sergeants for the entire ranger force. They expressed disapproval of the tendency of Vietnamese corps commanders to use the rangers as personal reserves, regular infantry, or "palace guards." The rangers had been conceived as light counterinsurgency units able to conduct patrols, ambushes, and other jungle patrolling tasks. Unfortunately, as the battlefield fortunes of South Vietnam declined, the rangers were pressed into action as "fire brigades" for regular Vietnamese formations.

U.S. Army officers and ranger advisers performed exceptionally heroic service in these confrontations. On 10 July 1964, one aviation officer, Maj. Edwin C. Riley, saved the pinned 30th ARVN Ranger Battalion from destruction by repeatedly flying low-level firing passes with his UH-1B gunship close over enemy positions. During 30-31 July 1964, Master Sgt. Calvin J. Bowlin took over the advisory duties for a battalion after it was ambushed and the senior adviser killed. Master Sergeant Bowlin moved through the open rice fields under heavy enemy fire and retrieved the battalion radio. He put the radio back into operating condition and called for air strikes, and then restored the Vietnamese defensive position by directing helicopter gunship support to within twenty-five yards of his own position.[2]

By 1965 the absorption of the ranger companies into ranger battalions was complete. The American advisers imagined the light combat battalions would be elite and the troops would stalk the VC through jungle and swamp, in either search or reaction roles. Instead, after a few sanguinary battles, the Vietnamese corps commanders became extremely reluctant to employ them in the field, where they might be annihilated. General Westmoreland insisted on better performance from the ARVN Ranger Command, but its commander, Gen. Pham Xuan Nhuan, had no authority over the dispersed battalions. The operational employment of the rangers remained with the corps, divisions, and regiments that they served.

The American ranger advisory teams were technically under MACV and reported to the South Vietnamese Ranger Command, but they enjoyed a high degree of independence. Each ranger battalion advisory team ideally contained five ranger-qualified members: a battalion adviser (captain), an assistant battalion adviser (lieutenant), a light weapons infantry adviser (sergeant first class), a junior light weapons infantry adviser (staff sergeant), and a radio operator (specialist fourth class). The advisory teams totaled forty-two officers and thirty-six sergeants at the start of 1965, and reached fifty-four officers and sixty-four sergeants a year later.

On 29 March 1965, one advisory team experienced a particularly harrowing experience when their Vietnamese ranger battalion stumbled into a Viet Cong main force battalion and was quickly surrounded. The rangers tried to fight their way out and attacked the enemy lines five times to no avail. Outside South Vietnamese Army attempts to break through to the isolated rangers also proved futile. The surrounded rangers were engaged for forty hours without resupply of food, water, or ammunition. A resupply helicopter was shot down on the afternoon of 30 March, and its four American crew members joined the encircled ranger battalion. During the day the battered ranger battalion was directed to try to fight its way out of the enemy entrapment.

The Vietnamese rangers fled in confusion, and Capt. Francis D.

Lynch and 1st Lt. Alison A. Bartholomew led six other Americans out as a separate group. The small party was slowed by one sergeant who had been wounded twice in the foot and leg, but whom they refused to abandon. An hour after midnight on 31 March, large numbers of Viet Cong passed through the jungle close to the Americans and began searching the shrubbery. The encircled advisers remained hidden in the dense foliage. The Viet Cong probed through the dense vegetation for two hours, coming to within five feet of the motionless advisers, but never found them.

Captain Lynch believed that the Viet Cong were going to finish the area search when daylight arrived, so the group decided to keep moving and try to reach friendly lines. The eight advisers organized themselves into patrol formation, as they remembered from their individual escape and evasion courses in stateside ranger and other military schools. The patrol contained a point element, a main element (including the wounded NCO), and a rear security element. During hours of darkness the advisers kept the distance between them at one to three yards, and during daylight the patrol lengthened to cover fifty yards of ground. The advisers maintained special vigilance during rest breaks and whenever crossing streams or trails.

The patrollers deliberately selected the most rugged terrain possible, and moved through thick jungle most of the day. The Americans finally passed the Viet Cong outer lines and once passed a platoon bivouac only twenty yards away. The eight advisers crawled or lay silently for over fifteen hours prior to reaching a clearing in the forest. The patrollers secured the field and signaled search helicopters, and were finally evacuated out of the area at 3:15 P.M. on 31 March. Captain Lynch remarked:

The success of our escape and evasion can be attributed to two main factors. First, the discipline instilled in the American soldier in his military training and second, the expert escape training we had received. Of the eight Americans, three of us attended the basic infantry officer course, which included an escape and evasion course, and two were graduates of the ranger course. All others except one artillery officer attended basic training conducted by graduates of the infantry school.[3]

On some occasions, the Vietnamese rangers served with the spirited determination that was expected by MACV. On 6 April 1965 the 44th ARVN Ranger Battalion was serving as a reserve element for a search and destroy operation against two Viet Cong battalions within Chuong Thien Province. The lead South Vietnamese infantry battalion, accompanied by a line of armored personnel carriers, was halted by intense enemy fire, and the ranger reserve was committed to battle.

The 44th ARVN Ranger Battalion conducted a midmorning helicopter assault into the landing zone just behind their fellow pinned infantrymen and stranded armored personnel carriers. The rangers immediately charged the enemy positions. The entrenched, well-camouflaged Viet Cong delivered machine gun fire against the rangers crossing the field, but the rangers continued to charge regardless of their sustained losses. The rangers reached the enemy earthworks and drove the insurgents back in hand-to-hand fighting. The rangers then continued their drive by maneuvering to take the main VC defensive lines along a canal. The ranger executive officer and an Army ranger adviser were killed during the battle, and three helicopters were shot down. The 44th ARVN Ranger Battalion concluded the battle victoriously by collapsing the Viet Cong left flank and causing the enemy to flee the battleground.[4]

Another successful ranger mission took place on 11 November 1965. The 52d ARVN Ranger Battalion was sent by truck to relieve a besieged hamlet in Phuoc Tuy Province near the Van Kiep training center. American ranger advisers Major Charley Price, Captain Frank Adams, Captain Husnian, Lieutenant Hinshaw, Staff Sgt. Barsons, and Sergeant Cook accompanied the battalion. While the battalion trucks were still moving toward their destination, the South Vietnamese sector headquarters obtained information about an ambush along the roadway. The information was radioed to the rangers, and the advisers stopped the trucks. They directed the rangers to divide into two columns that advanced on either side of the main road. One company proceeded along the rice paddies and the other element moved through dense woods.

The rangers hit the flank of the Viet Cong ambush force near Kim Hai hamlet and attacked. The VC ambushers withdrew and the rangers consolidated their positions. Another Viet Cong group managed to overrun the trucks, which were guarded by a small security element. The rangers counterattacked and recovered their vehicles, although three were destroyed by helicopters to prevent enemy capture during the midst of the fighting. The ranger battalion lost seventeen killed and nine wounded in the engagement, and killed several hundred of the enemy through a combination of ground fire and air strikes.

VIETNAM: THE MAIN WAR PERIOD (1966-1968)

The successful combat examples of 1965 did not diminish the overall ineffectiveness of the widely scattered Vietnamese ranger battalions. The rangers were supposed to be part of the elite Vietnamese forces, but their advisory evaluations were consistently poor. Ranger desertion rates were very high. General Westmoreland considered the rangers substandard, and he threatened to withdraw his advisers if ranger battalion performance did not improve. He even considered forming the twenty ranger battalions into separate light ranger divisions for better Vietnamese Army control and logistical support.[5]

During March 1966, as a result of political upheavals, the ARVN Ranger Command boss, Gen. Pham Xuan Nhuan, was sent to take over the 1st ARVN Division at Hue. The new ARVN Ranger Command officer became Col. Tran Van Hai, who became director of the South Vietnamese National Police two years later. The ARVN Ranger Command, however, was helpless to improve the handling of individual ranger battalions. Those units continued to work directly for various corps, division, and regimental commanders, who used them as they pleased.

A few Vietnamese ranger battalions consistently performed above expectations. The 42d ARVN Ranger Battalion received two United States Presidential Unit Citations during the time it was commanded by Major Luu Trong Kiet. On 16 October 1964 the battalion won honors in a successful battle against the Viet Cong at Phuoc Long in Bac Lieu Province. On 17 May 1966 the same battalion was airmobiled into action against the Viet Cong Soc Trang Provincial Battalion at Vinh Chau in the mangrove swamps of Ba Xuyen Province. The ranger advance was struck by Viet Cong automatic weapons fire, but the rangers countered and deployed against the enemy's well-prepared defensive positions. Two ranger companies attacked the VC flank but made scant progress in heavy fighting. Ranger commander Maj. Luu Trong Kiet sent in his remaining two companies and launched a battalion frontal assault. The rangers cleared three staggered lines of entrenchments and defeated the Viet Cong in close combat. Unfortunately, Major Kiet was later killed in another ranger battle outside Vi Thanh, in Chuong Thien Province, on 8 December 1967.[6]

During 1966 the 11th ARVN Ranger Battalion performed typical security duty for the Lam Dong sector, where it broke up a Viet Cong tax collection ring by systematically eliminating communist checkpoints along Route 20. At the beginning of 1967 the ranger battalion was reassigned to the Central Highlands, where it protected over 10,000 Montagnards being moved into the Plei Rongol relocation center west of Pleiku. The rangers guarded the encampment with roving daylight patrols through the adjacent hills. During the night the rangers established lurking ambuscades and swept nearby Route 19B for enemy mines.

The ranger advisers considered battalion commander Capt. Nguyen Kim Bien typical of the professional long-term officers who commanded some of the best Vietnamese ranger units. Captain Bien had graduated in 1953 from the National Military Academy at Dalat, campaigned with the French against the Viet Minh, and battled the Viet Cong for ten years before heading the ARVN Ranger Training Center's training committee. Captain Bien was thoroughly conversant in English and graduated from the United States Army Infantry School at Fort Benning as well as from a counterinsurgency course on Okinawa. He described his pride with the 11th ARVN Battalion simply: "This is a good battalion with good soldiers."[7]

By mid-1967 the American ranger advisory teams totaled fifty-three officers and seventy-nine sergeants. During the year, ranger advisers Capt. Bernard Muller-Thym and Sfc. James Fox escorted a ranger patrol through the Mekong Delta swamps near Sa Dec. A grenade booby trap wounded the point scout, and the advisers rigged up a mat of grass to allow a medical helicopter to land in the marshy quagmire. The patrol continued deeper into the swamp. Two Viet Cong suddenly emerged from an earthen bunker and threw several grenades.

The grenades exploded harmlessly at a distance from the patrol, and the rangers fired carbines and heaved grenades to silence the enemy position. Captain Muller-Thym led a squad into the destroyed fortification entrance, where they found a wounded Viet Cong female in her teens. The rangers often faced female soldiers in the Delta region, and Captain Muller-Thym was not surprised. He sent the captive to Can Tho for treatment and interrogation.[8]

Three ranger battalions confronted the 275th VC Regiment northeast of Xuan Loc during another 1967 battle. Acting on a tip from a Hoi Chanh deserter, the 52nd ARVN Ranger Battalion probed the dense jungle as the 35th and 43d ARVN Ranger Battalions took positions on either flank. The 52d suddenly ran into a reinforced enemy company entrenched in four-foot trenches and bunkers. Before nightfall, the close action included desperate hand-to-hand fighting. The ranger advisers radioed air strikes that enabled the hard-pressed Vietnamese rangers to disengage.

The enemy withdrew during the night, and the area was searched on the following day. The advisers found two dead rangers more than 700 yards inside the enemy perimeter, where they had fought through almost to the enemy command post before being cut down by enemy fire. Another ranger was hit in the arm and leg, and was isolated from his unit by the ferocity of the battle. Counted as a deserter initially, the ranger returned later—after walking three days through the tropical forest while carrying a wounded comrade on his back.[9]

Heavy fighting continued throughout 1968 and prohibited many ranger battalions from reconditioning on regular schedules. During May 1968 the 11th ARVN Ranger Battalion, under Lieutenant Colonel An, was sent to clear the area west of the Central Highlands airfield at Dalat, and advanced toward a ridge west of the airfield. The ranger skirmish line began receiving fire against their right front from enemy forces located on a second, higher ridge extending farther to the west. The battalion commander, upon receiving fire, maneuvered his first and second companies to the right, where they received more fire from the first ridge.

The battalion commander requested artillery. American artillery supported the rangers, but no Army forward observer was with the Vietnamese unit to coordinate supporting fire. The Vietnamese rangers had to wait forty-five minutes before receiving a smoke marking round that fell over three miles past the reported enemy positions. The supporting fire was finally adjusted correctly, and the lead ranger company assaulted the ridge. The soldiers gained the top of the hill but were immediately counterattacked in hand-to-hand combat. The rangers repulsed the enemy and dug in under fire. The second company tried to maneuver around the attacking enemy troops but was pinned down by heavy automatic weapons and grenade fire.

Colonel An asked his ranger adviser to have two Special Forces-advised Mike Force strike companies move to the northwest into blocking positions. The adviser directed the Special Forces to have the position occupied by nightfall, but received word that the native irregulars were not permitted to move without permission from their Vietnamese provincial commander. The ranger battalion then coordinated with the 2d Battalion of the 44th Regiment to make a deeper sweep behind the enemy lines. The 11th ARVN Ranger Battalion conducted a night attack at 9:00 P.M. and charged uphill in pitch-black conditions. This offensive maneuver completely surprised the enemy and constituted one of the first Vietnamese ranger night assaults.

The fighting was costly but the enemy was driven off the high ground. Casualties increased when a helicopter, attempting to evacuate wounded rangers, collided with the trees and crashed. Enemy mortar fire also wounded Colonel An and his adviser. The enemy dead were identified as being from the 240th NVA Battalion, who had been wearing newly issued NVA uniforms and pith helmets that showed little wear. The rangers lost twenty killed, thirty-two wounded, and nineteen missing. The advisers reported the success, with the tactical observation that the planned attack should have been along the ridges instead of across them.[10]

South Vietnamese combat reconnaissance instruction was a responsibility of the Ranger Training Command. Each ARVN division reconnaissance company contained a Long Range Reconnaissance Patrol (LRRP) platoon. South Vietnamese military doctrine stressed the observation role, and the use of recon teams in any combat role was prohibited. Unfortunately, the rigid application of this mandate robbed the teams of flexibility and excluded valuable intelligence sources. Combat reconnaissance involving capture of prisoners, for example, was prohibited. Some reconnaissance units became merely command post guards and never engaged in patrolling activities.

South Vietnamese reconnaissance units and teams were trained either in the Duc My Ranger Training Center's LRRP course or in the Australian-sponsored LRP course of the Van Kiep National Training Center. At Duc My the South Vietnamese ranger cadre taught a basic five-week patrolling course for 150 students. Emphasis was placed on reconnaissance techniques and physical fitness. Each session included three short field exercises, which were never conducted in areas of known or suspected enemy activity. Lt. Col. James C. Burris, the senior MACV adviser to the ranger training center, stated, "Every effort is made to avoid even the possibility of any enemy contact, even though the trainees are being prepared for combat. The course could have been greatly enhanced by the addition of a five- or six-day operational problem designed for infiltration into actual, likely, or suspected enemy occupied terrain. Such a change in the POI [program of instruction] could have served a great service to the local district chief and his forces by assisting him in gathering intelligence in such areas."[11]

The Van Kiep course was caught by the Australian Army Training Team in Vietnam and started in June 1968. This eight-week course for eighty students was divided into two phases. The Australians included combat reconnaissance tactics in addition to passive observation. Six weeks of formal instruction was given in patrolling and ambushes, followed by two weeks of field combat exercises inside Phuoc Tuy Province.

Attendance at the patrolling courses was based on quotas assigned to each corps tactical zone. Some units repeatedly sent unqualified soldiers, and attrition rates in both schools averaged half of each class. Most students were dismissed because of insufficient motivation, poor physical condition, or inability to comprehend written instructions. Lieutenant Colonel Burris blamed the attrition problem on lack of entrance standards: "Results of this system have been large numbers of trainee drop-outs and considerable time and effort wasted on unqualified and poorly motivated people. The [Vietnamese] Joint General Staff should establish specific medical, physical fitness, and military knowledge requirements, which could easily be standardized from one corps area to another. For example, if a candidate is required to complete a one-mile run in seven minutes or less, then he should be tested on this requirement before being sent to the training center for LRRP training."[12]

Upon completion of the LRRP or LRP courses, recon units received additional instruction during reconnaissance company unit training, a separate five-week program given at all national training centers. The greatest problems in Vietnamese reconnaissance units involved their misuse by higher commands and the personnel stagnation. Once assigned, the officers, sergeants, and common soldiers languished on perpetual duty with their outfits, and any zeal for hazardous patrolling, even if it was available, was sapped of vitality.

VIETNAM: FINAL ADVISORY CAMPAIGN (1969–1972)

The 1969 situation of the 3d ARVN Ranger Group, commanded by Lt. Col. Phan Van Phuc, typified Vietnamese ranger experiences in the Saigon region. The 1,971-member group was fully armed with modern U.S. M16 rifles and other weapons, but battlefield results were poor. Only 103 enemy soldiers were killed during the year, averaging only eight Viet Cong per month. During the year only one enemy soldier rallied to the ranger group despite strenuous propaganda broadcasts by loudspeaker. In exchange the ranger group suffered seventy killed in action, including twelve shot accidentally by American helicopters, and two hundred eighty-three wounded.[13]

The lackluster ranger group performance, however, was part of larger problems that concerned the entire Vietnamese soldiering establishment. There was hardly any meaningful logistical support by higher authorities, who would not cooperate with the ranger staff or the American advisers. In many skirmishes the rangers had actually run out of ammunition, medical supplies were "barely adequate," and none of the authorized 1,422 protective armor vests was available.[14]

Communications and transport problems affected ranger capability. Batteries had short duration in tropical conditions, but were essential to provide the communications link for artillery and air support. Yet battery stocks were low. The 3d ARVN Ranger Group reported that strictly rationed annual stocks of PRC-25 batteries dwindled to zero balances as early as October 1969, despite priority requests from American advisory and Vietnamese supply channels. Fuel shortages idled trucks while the Vietnamese rangers executed long road marches in the torrid heat that exhausted them before patrol sectors were reached. Every three months the entire group was allocated only eighty liters of gasoline and fifteen liters of diesel fuel for its eighty-two trucks.

One ranger adviser complained in disgust that the Vietnamese rangers were often clouded in the dust of buses and sedans transporting American officers, soldiers, and visitors between Long Binh and Tan Son Nhut airport. Maj. Nguyen Van Biet, commander of the 3d ARVN Ranger Group service company, was amazed to learn that MACV kept a grand fleet of air-conditioned limousines, the 9th Transportation Company (Sedan Car), at Long Binh. In the meantime, Major Biet could not find enough fuel to transport potable water into ranger Camp Phan Hanh on the edge of the same installation.

The rangers also lacked decent housing for their families. The 3d ARVN Ranger Group barracks and its family quarters were located at Camp Phan Hanh in Long Binh, but the group command post was located miles distant, at Newport bridge just outside old Saigon. Phan Hanh was a shanty town comprising eleven rows of wooden shacks and twelve rows of tin- and iron-sheet roofed buildings. The ranger advisers managed to hook up the dilapidated structures to electricity and some water, thanks to promises and favors, from a nearby U.S. artillery battalion. There was still not enough water and it had to be procured from Bien Hoa and Trang Bom.

American ranger advisers tried to upgrade the town's deficient condition, but were informed by the 20th Engineer Brigade that the Vietnamese rangers could build their own town. This remedy forced the rangers to buy lumber and undertake work construction projects whenever they returned from patrolling and extended field duty. Both American advisers and Vietnamese rangers toiled under the scorching tropical sun to pour concrete and hoist timbers. The advisers exchanged more favors to borrow tools and wiring from the engineer brigade, and paid for many sundry items—like light bulbs—out of their own pockets.

Throughout 1969 this adviser-inspired building program ensured that most family quarters received some renovation, a needed maternity hospital was constructed, and that the ranger camp contained a dependents' dispensary. Following all this work, however, the Phan Hanh ranger settlement still contained only ninety houses for the 31st ARVN Ranger Battalion's 148 families and another ninety houses for the 219 families of the 52d ARVN Ranger Battalion. The 36th ARVN Ranger Battalion was scarcely better off at its Hoang Hoa Tham dependent quarters, where 103 houses existed for its 145 families.[15]

The 3d ARVN Ranger Group camps and life-style reflected a petty "company town" operation, dominated by profiteering, dubious enterprises, and illicit favors. The group contained its own commissary store, opened during September 1967, where items such as cigarettes, sugar, milk, and canned food were sold on a rationed basis to the group servicemen. Monthly soldiering rations consisted of two pouches of ruby cigarettes and two pouches of 3-M cigarettes, three kilograms of sugar, and one can of milk for single rangers and five cans for married rangers. Other commissary foodstuffs were more expensive and limited to beef soup, chicken soup, spaghetti, noodles, white beans, pork, creamed corn, orange juice, jam, and Leyna toothpaste. The unit purchased its installation supplies from the same store, and the cost was further deducted from ranger salaries.[16]

Guided by their advisers, the Vietnamese rangers organized a Phan Hanh social club where Boy Youth Groups and Girl Youth Groups could associate. Colonel Le Quang Hien, the Vietnamese inspector general, lamented of the ranger group's children that, "The two schools only meet 25 percent of the educational requirements. In the future, children of servicemen may fall into the military if no additional schools are built."[17]

The 3d ARVN Ranger Group staff manifested concern over the lack of security from VC terror incidents, against both Newport bridge and their families at Phan Hanh. The Vietnamese displayed heightened concern about the safety of their families after the Viet Cong Tet-68 attack on Saigon. The American ranger advisers understood the importance of this protection, especially when the battalions were on far-ranging operations, but they found the problem another matter beyond their control.

The group sent repeated requests to the Vietnamese Joint General Staff seeking permission to raise three ranger reconnaissance companies "for the defense of the group headquarters" in both field (Newport bridge) and home (Phan Hanh) locations. The Vietnamese Joint Chiefs of Staff responded not by authorizing the reorganization, but by ordering more group work. The 3d ARVN Ranger Group received orders to conduct a massive "civilian proselytizing" effort in the Saigon area during 1969. This political warfare campaign was part of the Vi-dan ("For the People") campaign and was conducted throughout the Bien Hoa, Long Binh, and Saigon vicinities. As statistical proof of success, the rangers reported the distribution of medical drugs to 3,982 men, gift donations to another 9,364 men, and haircuts for 488 children. The recon companies were not allowed.[18]

The poor government care of wounded and injured rangers was another alarming discovery to the ranger advisers. They organized group response to bolster the often-callous official care. During 1968 the advisers and the rangers made forty visits to give personal gifts and comfort to sick and wounded ranger comrades at the Cong Hoa General Hospital. The advisers also tried to aid impoverished relatives of war victims, who were desperately in need of assistance. The Americans disbursed cash "death gratuity" payments and secured extra funding from U.S. civil assistance sources. The Vietnamese inspector general stated that the 3d ARVN Ranger Group's servicemen "displayed a high sense of discipline and endurance of hardship."[19]

Considering the hardships of military service, the Vietnamese rangers performed surprisingly well. The valor and dedication of the Army ranger advisers was also evinced by their actions. During early April 1970 the 23d ARVN Ranger Battalion was airlifted into western Kontum Province to confront North Vietnamese forces besieging the Special Forces border surveillance outpost at Camp Dak Seang. On the morning of 4 April the rangers marched through the tropical rain forest and secured the top of Hill 763. The battalion dug into defensive positions on the crest of the ridge and cleared a helicopter landing site in the double-canopy jungle on the northern edge of the perimeter.

The 28th North Vietnamese Army Regiment was entrenched on Hill 1043, a westerly mountain that overlooked the ranger-occupied hill. That afternoon a sudden mortar barrage struck the ranger lines, and the first twenty rounds scored direct hits on the battalion command post. The ranger battalion commander and the assistant senior adviser were killed immediately, and the battalion senior adviser and heavy weapons adviser Staff Sgt. Robert L. Dikes were among those seriously wounded. Sfc. Gary L. Littrell, the only unwounded advisory team member, took over as senior ranger adviser.

The ranger battalion reorganized and strengthened its defensive positions despite the sporadic mortar fire that continued until nightfall. After dark, Sergeant Littrell helped to move Staff Sergeant Dikes and the other wounded to the helicopter landing site. He placed the wounded in a protected bunker and used signal flares and a strobe light to mark the landing site for an emergency medical evacuation helicopter.

The lighted landing site attracted considerable enemy fire. However, the American ranger adviser stayed there, in spite of the fusillade, in an attempt to bring in the dust-off helicopter. The intense NVA automatic weapons fire prevented the helicopter from landing, and Littrell returned the wounded soldiers to the medical bunker of the inner perimeter. Sergeant First Class Littrell then went back to the landing zone and used its lights as a reference point for directing the overhead fighter-bombers and helicopter gunships.

Shortly after sunrise on 5 April, another enemy mortar bombardment struck the ranger perimeter. Littrell moved through the position administering first aid to the newly wounded, and he carried many of them to the medical bunker. At 10:00 A.M. he moved the more seriously wounded soldiers to covered positions near the landing zone. A resupply helicopter tried to reach the fire-swept ridge. Ranger replacement adviser Sp5 Raymond Dieterle, aboard the lowering aircraft, looked down to see Sergeant First Class Littrell guiding the helicopter on its final approach. Littrell was alternately standing and waving to the helicopter, and then dropping down to fire his M16 rifle and suppress the enemy fire.

As soon as he was sure that the helicopter was going to land, Littrell ran back to the edge of the landing zone and reappeared carrying wounded personnel. Sergeant Littrell personally loaded the three wounded American advisers and some Vietnamese rangers aboard the helicopter. Specialist Dieterle unloaded ammunition and supplies from the other side. The helicopter was partially obscured from the enemy fire by the smoking hilltop, and was able to lift off as mortar rounds began exploding once more across the ridgetop positions.

Specialist Dieterle dived into a foxhole bunker and used a field phone to call the command post and inform them that he had arrived safely. Sergeant First Class Littrell was in the main command post bunker and did not immediately realize that Dieterle had landed from the helicopter. As soon as Littrell heard the call, he ran out the main bunker door and yelled to battalion operations officer Lt. Nguyen Ngoc Khoan, "I'll go get him!"

Specialist Dieterle watched from his own bunker door as Sergeant First Class Littrell came within view, head down and dodging, but not stopping until he was beside him and said, "Welcome, D., where the hell have you been? Come on, hurry up, and keep your head down." The two ranger advisers ran back to the main command post, where Littrell briefed the newcomer on the isolated battalion's situation.

For the remainder of the day the ranger advisers moved from position to position along the perimeter front. They continuously called for air strikes and adjusted the fire from gunships and artillery. Sergeant First Class Littrell repeatedly stood up to get a better view of the enemy lines. Once a bullet struck Littrell's radio set out of his hands, but the sergeant obtained another nearby radio and continued to direct supporting fire into the enemy-held forest. During a lull in the fire direction task, Littrell encouraged the Vietnamese ranger defenders in fluent Vietnamese. Capt. Nguyen Cong Bao, the commander of the battalion's 2d Company, was pleasantly surprised to hear the American speaking Vietnamese, and it lifted the morale of his troops.

During late afternoon the North Vietnamese soldiers commenced probing attacks against the ranger defenses. That night Specialist Dieterle stayed on the perimeter and radioed artillery fire that disheartened and broke up several North Vietnamese probing efforts. Small groups of NVA sappers intensified pressure throughout the night and increased the frequency and size of their probes. Sergeant First Class Littrell spent the night on the landing zone, where he adjusted effective aerial support that discouraged larger NVA assaults. The enemy fired more volleys into the landing zone whenever they spotted illumination beams from his hand-held strobe light crossing and brightening parts of the overhead forest canopy.

On the morning of 6 April the Vietnamese rangers repulsed a major North Vietnamese charge. Throughout the following two days, the North Vietnamese continued to pour heavy weapons and mortar fire on the beleaguered battalion. The ranger advisers moved around the perimeter, redistributed ammunition, cared for the wounded, and directed the improvement of defense positions.

At 6:30 P.M. on 7 April the NVA bombarded the battalion lines with a firestorm of mortar and rocket explosions. During this heavy barrage the Vietnamese rangers heard and spotted enemy soldiers massing for an assault in the forest. Sergeant First Class Littrell ran through the mortar blasts and reached a position at the expected danger point, where he called in close helicopter strikes against the forming enemy ranks. A nearby rocket erupted in the location of 1st Company and wounded its commander, Capt. Tran Mung. Littrell moved the injured officer to the relative safety of the medical station.

A half hour later the North Vietnamese infantrymen conducted a human-wave assault that nearly breached the ranger positions. The Vietnamese rangers, low on ammunition and fatigued from three days and nights of continuous shelling, managed to repulse the main enemy attack in close combat on the perimeter edges. The advisers braved enemy fire to direct orbiting helicopters closer in support of the beleaguered ranger defenders. The gunships raked additional groups of enemy soldiers emerging from the woods and prevented them from reinforcing points of heaviest action.

On several occasions the rangers were in imminent danger of being overrun, but they managed to hold out throughout the night. By the morning of 8 April the battalion had depleted almost all its remaining munitions. At 10:30 A.M., higher headquarters ordered the rangers to withdraw from Hill 743 and conduct an escape through hostile jungle, crossing the Dak Poko river, to reach the 22nd ARVN Ranger Battalion. The advisers organized the unit for the march, dispensed the few remaining grenades and rifle magazines, and prepared the dead and wounded for litter bearers.

The descent from the ridge started at 11:00 A.M. The dazed executive officer ignored his American advisers and mistakenly led the ranger columns down the wrong spur of the hill. The course of movement appeared at first to steer the rangers away from the NVA lines, but it actually took them closer to Hill 1043. After proceeding about 500 yards in the wrong direction, lead elements of the battalion reached the bottom of the ridge and passed through a large abandoned bunker complex.

The battalion executive officer ordered a five-minute "teabreak." Sergeant First Class Littrell turned to Specialist Dieterle and grinned, "D., this is just like a Sunday stroll, baby." Just then the disoriented Vietnamese ranger formation was smothered by mortar fire. Littrell radioed Lieutenant Kenneth D. Hicks (22d ARVN Ranger Battalion adviser) for support. Littrell stated, "I think we're on the wrong finger of the hill. Fire a couple of shots to give us our bearings. We're getting hit by mortars." Lieutenant Hicks directed the artillery fire as requested, and the offending enemy mortar emplacements were silenced.

The two ranger advisers then radioed about four promised gunships that were supposed to cover the withdrawal, but they were informed that no armed helicopters were available in the area. The executive officer was standing beside the radio and heard the negative reply. He panicked, and attempts by Sergeant First Class Littrell to restrain him from running were unsuccessful. The other Vietnamese rangers, seeing their acting commander running away, started to flee the area and left the dead and wounded behind.

Littrell said to Dieterle, "Come on, partner, let's hat up," and both advisers slowly regrouped the dispersed rangers and regained control over the situation. The ranger column point element was reconsolidated and turned in the right direction. The next several hours involved scattered fighting as the ranger column weaved back and forth in the dense jungle to avoid North Vietnamese infantry units.

The ranger advisers repeatedly asked for mortar fire within fifty yards of their end element to cover the retreat. This last-resort tactic prevented the North Vietnamese pursuers from overrunning the rear guard. On one occasion, Sergeant First Class Littrell directed 500-pound bombs almost on top of their lines to stop the advancing North Vietnamese. The bombs exploded so close that both advisers were knocked to the ground.

The rangers fought past two NVA ambushes, and the American advisers again saved the columns from piecemeal destruction. They constantly radioed for more helicopter gunships and ensured that the Vietnamese rangers stayed in organized columns. During the last ambush, Sergeant First Class Littrell stopped to assist three wounded Vietnamese rangers. He carried the most seriously wounded man on his back. The other two rangers, believing that Littrell enjoyed blessed fortune, grabbed onto his web gear and would not let go. Littrell dragged them along as he led the survivors of the 23d ARVN Ranger Battalion across the Dak Poko and to final safety. The battalion suffered over 218 casualties and nineteen missing in action. Sergeant First Class Littrell and Specialist Dieterle exhibited the finest ranger attributes of determination and valor during the engagement.[20]

During the Cambodian invasion of 1970 the Vietnamese rangers were again hurled into action. During late April the South Vietnamese mounted a major operation, TOAN THANG 42, against 9th NVA Division storage depots and staging areas located in the flat countryside and low marshes of the "Angel's Wing"—a shoulder of Cambodia that jutted into III CTZ. The experiences of Lieutenant Colonel Phuc's Ranger Task Force 333 (based on the 3d ARVN

Ranger Group) typified the incessant demands made on Vietnamese ranger forces.

Task Force 333, composed of the 36th and 52d ARVN Ranger Battalions (and later the group's third ranger battalion), moved from Saigon and crossed into Cambodia on 29 April. Within two hours after entering Cambodia the rangers became engaged with North Vietnamese Army regulars. For the next eight hours, the rangers attacked aggressively, but received little support from the armored 5th Cavalry Regiment in the task force. The regiment displayed reluctance to join the battle with its fourteen M41 tanks, and this failure hindered infantry effectiveness. The rangers finally won the field when the NVA slipped away.

After 2 May 1970, Task Force 333 became the temporary corps reserve. During this stage of the operation, however, the 52d ARVN Ranger Battalion was continually committed to action and suffered heavy losses. Unit strength dropped from 510 to 390 personnel, but more ranger replacements were received and prevented the battalion from becoming combat-ineffective. At this time, the task force's new organized ready-reaction unit (3d ARVN Ranger Reconnaissance Company) was inserted for the first time and conducted valuable forward scouting duties.

By the end of the first week in May, the enemy became disorganized and tried to elude the South Vietnamese attackers. On 10 May the daily rains of the annual monsoon season began. Task force accomplishments were hindered by weather and the enemy tendency to scatter instead of fight. The rangers conducted slow and methodical searches of numerous bunker complexes. The task force advanced west of Svay Rieng, Cambodia, zigzagged back into Vietnam, and moved forward again to Krek, Cambodia. The rangers attacked along Highway 7 to seize the Chup Rubber Plantation. Two more ARVN ranger battalions reinforced this maneuver.

Enemy resistance was sporadic until the last major battle on 21 June, when a North Vietnamese Army battalion made an all-out night assault against the task force headquarters. During the entire operation the rangers were characterized by their ability to achieve surprise and their aggressive zeal in closing with the enemy. Relations between the ranger task force and its Army ranger advisers were considered excellent. Seven Army ranger advisors accompanied the task force headquarters, and teams of three advisers (a captain, lieutenant, and senior light weapons NCO) were assigned to each battalion. The American losses in TOAN THANG 42 were limited to the wounding of the assistant senior adviser to the 52d ARVN Ranger Battalion, on 17 May, and the normal rotation of the same team's staff sergeant weapons NCO—who departed Vietnam 15 May.

The battle for Nui Bai Voi, fought 27 September to 20 November 1970, rendered an example of the unique difficulties confronting ranger operations in the Mekong Delta. Lt. Col. James E. Witek, senior adviser to the ARVN MR (Military Region) 4 Ranger Command, was the principal adviser during this action. Nui Bai Voi was a craggy mountain fortress held by Viet Cong troops, and the 42d and 44th ARVN Ranger Battalions were ordered to seize the bastion and clear it. Both ranger battalions were accustomed to airmobile operations across the open marshlands, and attacks against mountains and cave systems was a new combat experience.

The South Vietnamese senior command, the 9th ARVN Division, issued a plan of attack to the rangers that did not allow sufficient time for the initial assault battalion to reach its jump-off positions at the base of the mountain. The night approach to Nui Bai Voi required three of the four ranger companies in the lead 44th ARVN Ranger Battalion to struggle six miles through waist- and sometimes chest-deep swamp water. Once they were assembled at the base of the mountain, the rangers had to hack their way through a thick tangle of jungle. The delays occasioned by this laborious trek made it impossible to coordinate the opening mountain assault with preparatory artillery barrages and air strikes.

The 44th ARVN Ranger Battalion stormed the northern side of Nui Bai Voi under cover of darkness. The main point of enemy resistance was a large cavern about one-third up the northeastern rocky slope. A full Viet Cong weapons platoon occupied the cave with orders to hold it at all costs. The VC defenders lashed the advancing rangers with a deluge of fire from automatic weapons, heavy machine guns, and 57mm recoilless rifles. Cobra helicopters made repeated strafing runs against this strongpoint, but air support was marred by the premature release of a 250-pound bomb from one of the Vietnamese aircraft. The explosion ripped through the ranger lines and caused serious casualties.

The ruggedness of the mountain wall also hindered the forward scaling companies. To get around the cave, the rangers required climbing equipment. After daylight, helicopters airdropped 120-foot lengths of nylon rope and gloves, along with some pitons and mountain hammers, and the ascent continued. Two ranger companies were finally able to gain a foothold on the northern portion of the mountain and, moving under the cover of darkness on the second night, were able to seize the summit. The loss of eighty-one rangers during the opening stage of the attack, however, caused the commander to become very reluctant to engage in further fighting, and he relaxed the searching and clearing of caves. This inactivity emboldened the Viet Cong snipers and mortar observers, and the battalion suffered additional losses.

On 21 October 1970 the battalion was relieved by the 42d ARVN Ranger Battalion, which took over search and clearing operations among the innumerable caves and crevasses along the mountainside. Capt. George A. Crocker was the battalion adviser. The main northeastern mountain cave remained in enemy hands, and Captain Crocker arranged daylight raids and nonilluminated night assaults against the large cave complex. During these forays, Crocker realized the defensibility of this natural fortification.

The concave configuration of the mountain around the cave entrance formed a barrier against friendly fire from above while enabling its occupants to fire at climbers below. In addition, the main entrance was linked into small entrances and holes in the surrounding rocks. When Crocker and his rangers penetrated the entrance, they found not one main tunnel leading to the inner chamber but twelve small tunnels. Each separate tunnel was covered in turn by successive claymore mines, B-40 rocket positions, and machine gun nests. The cavern was pitch-black inside, and to turn on a flashlight invited certain death.

As a result, Captain Crocker advised against any suicidal attempts to reach the inside recesses of the cavern. On 10 November, after a successful ambush raid killed two enemy soldiers leaving the cave, Crocker began setting up mechanical ambushes near the cave entrances. These booby traps intercepted enemy movements back and forth through the rocks and were very successful in besieging the northeastern position.

Captain Crocker also considered using antiriot gas against the defenders. The soundness of this idea was manifested after the rangers began blasting the main cave with 106mm recoilless rifles and troops on the opposite side of the mountain smelled gunpowder wafting through. The northerly winds across Nui Bai Voi provided favorable draft to draw CS II gas throughout the mountain. The battalion commander ruled against the tactic, however, because his battalion possessed only fifty-three gas masks. The steadfast two-month ranger campaign on the mountain, although ultimately unsuccessful in clearing the entire objective, was a good indication of Vietnamese ranger assignments in the IV Corps Tactical Zone of Vietnam.[21]

During 1970, Gen. Do Ke Giai, fired from the 18th ARVN Division, took over the ARVN Ranger Command. In October 1971 the regular ranger force became stabilized at seven groups and twenty-one battalions, providing a three-battalion group for each corps as well as for Saigon capital defense. This was the composition that the Army ranger advisers had recommended for five years. There were also thirty-seven Border Defense Ranger battalions, but those units were not mobile field ranger battalions. Border rangers were raised by converting Montagnard tribal warriors and other ethnic minorities from the discontinued Special Forces–run civilian irregular defense group program. The natives were given token national citizenship, but resented the central government and Vietnamese control, and the border rangers became the least-capable segment of the Vietnamese ranger program.[22]

Battlefield demands on the Vietnamese rangers increased, even as American ranger advisory participation was being phased out. In northern South Vietnam, the 1st ARVN Ranger Group participated in several major battles during 1972. The group was composed of the 21st, 37th, and 39th ARVN Ranger Battalions. Senior ranger adviser Lt. Col. Robert L. Merrick assumed his duties at Hill 55 on 20 May, and within three days two ranger battalions were air-assaulted into action along the My Chanh river line. After five days of bitter fighting, both battalions were nearly annihilated when their trenches were overrun by NVA tank-escorted infantrymen. Ranger group commander Lieutenant Colonel Dao pleaded for assistance, and Colonel Merrick was able to arrange naval firepower and air strikes against the tanks. This "in extremis" fire support saved about half the rangers in the battle.

Following this debacle, on 6 June, Lieutenant Colonel Dao was replaced by Lt. Col. Tran Kim Dai. The new ranger group leader was an outstanding officer of great integrity and devotion to duty. The two battalions decimated on the My Chanh river line were rebuilt, and in late June the 1st ARVN Ranger Group began probing operations in the mountains north and west of Hue around Camp Evans and Fire Base Rakkasan. The group was progressively reinforced during these expeditions until it reached the size of a brigade with attached artillery and armor.

During September 1972, Colonel Dai's ranger group fought alongside the Vietnamese Marine Division as part of the advance to capture the citadel of Quang Tri. The rangers fought with great distinction in this campaign and defended the Marine right flank from Trieu Phong to the coast during the battle's climax. There the rangers destroyed the better part of two North Vietnamese regiments. One of the bravest and most innovative ranger battalion commanders proved to be Major Thiet of the 39th ARVN Ranger

Battalion. Following the Quang Tri operation, the 1st Ranger Group absorbed replacements and relocated into security positions around Camp Evans to retrain. In late October the group moved to Quang Ngai Province as the mobile reserve for the 2d ARVN Division, and American ranger advisers were withdrawn from the group at the beginning of December. By the end of March 1973, all Army ranger advisers were withdrawn from Vietnam.

THAILAND: ADVISORY DUTY

The Royal Thai Army demonstrated excellent qualities of professional ranger service during the Vietnam conflict. The Royal Thai Army (RTA) Airborne Ranger School was established at Camp Erawan, an encampment at Lopburi originally set aside by Prime Minister Pibulsongkhram and taken over by the Thai police in 1950. The police originally used the camp for special weapons and parachute training. In 1952 the Royal Thai Army assumed control over Camp Erawan and incorporated it into the infantry center as the Special Operations School. During the next year, U.S. military advisers arrived in Thailand on temporary duty and transformed the school into the Student Airborne and Ranger Battalion. The advisers also recommended the formation of a ranger battalion for extended field operations.

On 4 June 1954 the RTA Field Ranger Battalion was organized under the command of Lt. Col. Thienchai Sirisumphan. The three-company battalion was stationed at Camp Pawai and attached to the Thai infantry center. The first missions of the unit were conducting combat and reconnaissance patrols for the First Army Area in southern Thailand. During early 1955 the battalion was reorganized with United States military assistance program funding and added a fourth company. From 15 May until 15 September the battalion entered combat along the Thai border, where it provided infiltration and distant patrolling assistance to both Thai border police and Malayan security forces fighting the communist insurgency along the frontier.

Commencing in 1957, the RTA Field Ranger Battalion received advanced unit unconventional training from Okinawa-based Special Forces mobile training teams. The 509 Thai battalion personnel completed a five-month course in survival and commando, airborne, and jungle operations at the Special Operations School before starting three-year tours with the battalion. The battalion was directly responsible to the commander in chief of the Thai armed forces and provided him with a forty-two-man personal bodyguard.

The RTA Field Ranger Battalion prepared its troops for country-wide employment by assigning each ranger company a specific area of Thailand. The company was parachuted every four months into the region for a month-long familiarization operation. The U.S. Pacific Command noted, "Overall, the rangers are rated among the best-trained and efficient troops in the Thai Army. They are considered to be more at home in the jungle than in garrison." During 1963 the unit became the nucleus of the first Thai Special Forces Group.[23]

On 3 November 1962 another Thai unit, known as the Student Airborne and Ranger Battalion, was reorganized into a combination operational and schooling component. This element was designated officially as the 1st Airborne (Ranger) Battalion. The battalion's personnel and equipment were redistributed to enable it to fight as well as train parachute and ranger students. However, this adaptation left the battalion seriously understrength for both assignments.

On 23 April 1965 the American ranger advisers assisted the Royal Thai Army in bringing the battalion up to full operational capability. The unit acquired a dual-role configuration and contained 737 Thai rangers. In 1966 the 1st Airborne (Ranger) Battalion was transferred to the newly established RTA Special Warfare Center (the old special operations school) at Camps Erawan and Narai in Lopburi Province.[24]

The Royal Thai Army Special Warfare Center was formalized in conjunction with the arrival of the first permanent Army Special Forces advisory contingent (Company D of the 1st Special Forces Group) during October 1966. The company was later designated as the separate 46th Special Forces Company and eventually reinforced to the size of a small Special Forces group. The Special Forces unit was collocated at the center and assigned to advise the center commander, his instructional staff, and the operational units. The center included a headquarters and academic department, a research and development division, and the 1st RTA Special Forces Group and the 1st Airborne (Ranger) Battalion, along with a psychological operations company and the quartermaster aerial resupply company. During 1969 the 2d Special RTA Special Forces Group was also activated there.

On 26 November 1966 the first Thailand-based Special Forces ranger adviser was wounded in action while coordinating a classified Thai patrolling mission inside Vietnam. He was flying aboard a Thai C-123 Provider that was hit by Viet Cong medium machine guns shortly after taking off from the jungle airstrip at Dua Tieng, about forty-five miles northwest of Saigon. The bullets tore away the left flap and part of the port engine and severed the wing hydraulic lines.

Thai pilot Lt. Anavil Phakdeechitt closed the side window to prevent fire from entering the cockpit as Air Force instructor pilot Capt. Richard A. Nagel took control of the crippled plane and guided it back toward the runway. The Special Forces ranger battled the intense fire that erupted in the cargo compartment, despite fumes and intense heat. The flaming liquid poured from the ceiling and burned out a ten-foot section of the fuselage, and except for his efforts it might have destroyed the flight control cables. The plane dragged over the treetops and skidded 200 feet across a rice paddy before stopping on the edge of the runway. The Special Forces ranger adviser, who was a temporary duty sergeant from the Florida Ranger Committee, was severely burned but credited with saving the control cables—an act later recognized with the Distinguished Flying Cross.

In September 1967 the Thai Army Volunteer "Queen's Cobra" Regiment, commanded by Col. Sanan Yuttasarnprasit, landed at Newport in Saigon and moved to Bear Cat, where it operated along the rim of the swampy Rung Sat Special Zone. On 25 June 1968, Special Forces advisers from Thailand arrived with the long-range patrol company of the Royal Thai Army expeditionary forces. On the following month, twenty-six members of the Royal Thai Army Volunteer Force long-range patrol company attended the MACV Recondo School at Nha Trang along with their Special Forces ranger instructors.

On 25 June 1968 a midair helicopter collision during an airmobile operation killed sixteen Thais, including Lt. Col. Sujinta Mongcolcumnuelkhet and Maj. Suphon Sittimongkol. A Special Forces liaison sergeant was also killed in the mishap. Thailand's military responsibilities in Vietnam expanded, and on 9 August the Thai Army force assumed responsibility for local security missions around the Bear Cat and Binh Son plantation.

The Royal Thai Army Volunteer Force continued to perform security for allied installations near Bear Cat, Long Thanh, and Binh Son. Patrol operations were light and scattered. The enemy shelled Thai forces around Binh Son on 15 and 28 November 1968, and the Special Forces–advised Thai reconnaissance company was deployed to search the Binh Son region. During early 1969 the Special Forces advisers and the reconnaissance element performed extended patrolling around Bear Cat camp, the Long Thanh Special Forces training center of MACV-SOG, and a bridge over the Song La Buong. In January 1969 the second increment of the Royal Thai Army Volunteer Force arrived in Vietnam.

Special Forces–escorted Thai ranger patrols were shifted to the southern portion of the Duc Tu district of Bien Hoa Province. On 12 August 1969 the third Thai volunteer increment finished replacing the first Thai contingent in Vietnam. During August 1969, Marine advisers with the Vietnamese Marine Corps joined with Special Forces advisers and the RTA recon unit and performed reconnaissance of the Tan Go–Ong Cua vicinity within the Rung Sat Special Zone swamps. The Thai reconnaissance troops interdicted enemy infiltration routes through Long Thanh and Nhon Trach districts for the duration of their Vietnam service.

The 46th Special Forces Company Operations Detachment A-41 (Ranger) was the ranger advisory team for the RTA Special Warfare Center in Thailand, and was the only formally designated Special Forces ranger unit of the Vietnam war. Some detachment sergeants were assigned directly from the Fort Benning ranger department, where they had served as lane instructors. Later in the war, selected members of the Special Forces detachment were committed to temporary duty in Laos and Cambodia, along with other Special Forces troops serving in Thailand, on classified assignments, including long range patrols.

The ten-week Thai ranger course was conducted in three phases. The first phase lasted five weeks and was conducted in the Lopburi area. The training consisted of classroom instruction, demonstrations, and practical exercises. The initial program encompassed physical training, hand-to-hand combat, confidence testing, map reading, compass utilization, river-crossing techniques, and rappelling. A twelve-mile forced march conducted with full combat gear completed this phase.

The second, three-week, mountain phase was conducted in the rugged and forested Kanchanaburi area of western Thailand. The field training rotated students through patrol planning and leadership excercises, where they were observed by Thai instructors and Special Forces advisers. The third and final phase of the course, two weeks in duration, took place in the swamps of coastal Thailand near Sattahip and Chantaburi. Students learned survival and rubber boat handling as well as more difficult patrolling techniques.

One of the greatest Special Forces detachment ranger problems was maintaining the remotely situated mountain camp. The site was located within ten miles of the hostile Burmese border and was over twenty miles from the nearest railhead and market town. The dense forests and bamboo clusters were crossed by woodcutter trails, but these became impassable during the rainy season. Flooding streams and mud often prevented vehicular traffic, and Special Forces advisers routinely hired logging trucks to pull their jeeps and utility vehicles out of the mire. Commencing in 1970 the Special Forces relocated the mountain camp to the Ban Ta Kilen area near the River Kwai.

The Special Forces advisers were the first rangers committed to Vietnam to establish the Vietnamese ranger training center and the first ranger courses. Special Forces advisers were also the last American rangers to depart Southeast Asia—leaving in April 1974 when Detachment A-41 (Ranger) was inactivated at the Royal Thai Army ranger school. Throughout the Vietnam conflict, Special Forces and Regular Army ranger advisers worked in close and mutually productive harmony to achieve stronger allied ranger and combat reconnaissance within the Southeast Asian combat theater. This tradition of close Special Forces and ranger comradeship continues to be maintained by the United States Army Special Operations Command (Airborne).

14

IMPROVING RANGER STANDARDS

THE WARTIME ARMY RANGER SCHOOL

The Army ranger course was taught by the ranger department of the U.S. Army Infantry School at Fort Benning, Georgia. The ranger course was designed to produce soldiers who possessed the "ranger imprint" of "pride, confidence, self-determination, and the ability to lead, endure, and succeed—regardless of the odds, or obstacles of the enemy, weather, and terrain." This objective remained constant throughout the Vietnam conflict, although the course was adjusted periodically to conform to battlefield demands. The ranger department also monitored the Army-wide physical fitness program, developed patrol doctrine, evaluated parachute and reconnaissance equipment, and trained selected units in advanced patrolling prior to overseas deployment.[1]

The ranger school was staffed by 300 carefully selected cadre who divided the course into three roughly equal phases. Prior to the Vietnam buildup, the 923 hours of ranger training focused on the patrol as a tool for teaching basic infantry tactics and small-unit leadership skills up to platoon level. The Fort Benning ranger committees introduced patrolling for either temporary recon ventures or elements trapped behind enemy lines. The outlying Florida swamp and northern Georgia mountain camps reinforced patrol tactics by offering specialized water and mountaineering instruction.[2]

During mid-1965, ranger director Col. I. A. Edwards completely revised the curriculum to fit wartime requirements. The ranger course became a performance-based field learning experience that instilled the skills, physical stamina, and mental confidence re-

277

quired to lead extended reconnaissance patrols into enemy territory. The ranger class of 8 July–7 September 1965 was first to complete the extended 1,149-hour course of instruction. During 1966, combat intelligence, airmobile operations, and helicopter rappelling classes were added to ranger training requirements. Colonel Edwards also revamped the ranger committee's main demonstration of ranger tactics during the Vietnam era, Infantry School Scenario 8004, "Rangers in Action."[3]

The ranger course was demanding, dangerous, and extremely difficult. The tough ranger entrance requirements assured physically hardy students, but endurance was strengthened with combat-conditioning exercises that included hand-to-hand fighting and cross-country running. Safety standards were also assisted by pairing students into two-man buddy teams for course duration. Unfortunately, almost every class was marred by fatalities or serious injuries caused by parachute or hiking accidents, crossing of treacherous mountain streams or turbulent tidal swamps, exposure to frozen and torrid weather extremes, or severe lightning storms that exploded suddenly over patrols in the Florida panhandle.[4]

The ranger course was geared to teaching progressively more difficult patrol techniques. Lane instructors in each phase accompanied the patrols and imparted ranger skills in navigating over rough terrain regardless of weather and light conditions. The lane instructors started each patrol by choosing a student leader, giving him a battle situation, and then demanding a workable plan for accomplishing the mission. At the conclusion of each mission, the student leader was graded on how well he achieved patrol objectives. Whenever patrols became lost, the lane instructors attempted to guide the student leader into finding his location or, in hopeless cases, declared him a casualty and picked a replacement. In an effort to prevent aimless wandering, which wasted training time, the lane instructors usually ensured that the new student leader understood his exact location and gave the patrol a fresh start.

The first phase of ranger training was held at Fort Benning. Students had all insignia and rank privileges removed and spent twenty-two days learning patrol basics, as well as a smattering of survival tactics. The latter were tested during Escape and Evasion (E&E) Problems 8630 and 8635. Patrols were encouraged to break apart while eluding "aggressor" search parties, and this resulted in the inevitable scattering and disorientation of many students. Invariably, the ranger committee had to scour remote post areas for lost rangers. The searches gave beneficial experience to Fort Benning's seven infantry scout dog platoons, but frequently delayed firing clearances on Fort Benning's Carkner, Ninninger, and Arkman ranges—much to the chagrin of division and brigade commanders readying units for Vietnam deployment.[5]

The second phase of the ranger course was taught by the mountain ranger committee at Dahlonega, Georgia. This phase subjected the ranger students to twenty days of climbing and airmobile experience under grueling conditions in the rugged Blue Ridge Mountains. This area of northern Georgia had been seized from the Cherokees following the nation's first gold rush there in the late 1820s, and a federal mint was operated at Dahlonega until the Civil War. The surrounding territory, conveniently still under government control and inclusive of mountain ranger Camp Frank Merrill, northwest of Dahlonega, was ideal for Vietnam-oriented ranger training because the summits of the Chattahoochee National Forest reached 2,000 to 5,000 feet, matching Vietnam elevations, and the narrow valleys and wooded ridges bore striking resemblance to Vietnam's central highlands. Regional conifers and deciduous trees substituted for tropical hardwoods, dense underbrush for bamboo thickets, and small bottomland corn pastures for Vietnamese upland rice fields.

Mountain camp instruction concentrated on normal long-range patrol employment in a conventional warfare environment. The forested slopes were broken by cliffs, rocky outcrops, and overhanging ledges that were ideal for teaching basic mountaineering and cross-terrain maneuver. Ranger students were introduced to rock climbing and various rope-crossing expedients for negotiating rapids and steep mountains. Training patrols staggered over hills strewn with deadwood, deep gullies, and other obstacles that gave ample opportunity for rehearsing individual patrolling expertise.

After mid-1965 the wartime ranger course replaced previously short-duration mountain patrols with an extended seven-day problem. This taught students how to properly pace patrols on longer missions. The continuous daylight and nocturnal practice built ranger confidence and reinforced principles of patrol stealth and field sanitation that covered routes from enemy observation and pursuit. Ranger students learned to trust their compasses and avoid the deceptive web of unmapped logging trails that duplicated treecutter pathways of interior Vietnam.

At the end of the second phase, the ranger students returned to Fort Benning and received a day of instruction in counter-guerrilla operations. This respite helped transition the students from conventional mountain patrolling to the irregular warfare taught in the final Florida phase. Airborne-qualified students then boarded either

CV-2 or C-123 aircraft and executed a night parachute insertion into the Florida swampland. Among the many hazards was the chance of landing in the Gulf of Mexico or Choctawhatchee Bay. Non-parachutist members were transported to Florida by truck, but reached the actual camp only after completing a long forced march.

The Florida phase lasted eighteen days at Eglin Air Force Base and encompassed small boat handling, helicopter infiltration, and anti-guerrilla operations across the marshes and flooded woodland of East Bay Swamp. The operational area even included "hostile natives", who lived and traveled through the region. The students established patrol bases, secured roads, explored tunnels, and encountered other Vietnam-type problems. Past August 1965, each ranger class received thirty support missions from the 1st Air Commando Wing, which provided simulated air strikes, para-drop, loudspeaker, illumination, and convoy escort sorties.

The Florida phase culminated in a two-week long-range patrol that taught students how to survive and engage in combat over extended distances inside enemy-dominated territory. Patrol members were expected to perform a multitude of tasks despite the stress of fatigue and hunger. Patrols through tidal swamp channels burdened students with waterlogged ropes and weapons, and the semi-daze caused by lack of sufficient sleep or food soon had tired radiomen answering radio checks by exclaiming, "I'm awake! I'm awake!" Careless patrollers engaged in numerous futile tunnel checks, but thorough searchers often uncovered extra rations. By the end of the problem some students were even hallucinating phone booths inside cypress trees, but this final swamp patrol built individual confidence and a keen understanding of soldier endurance.

The Florida experience taught some of the most valuable ranger lessons, but a longstanding Army–Air Force dispute over Eglin base leasing terms jeopardized the camp's existence during most of the Vietnam conflict. Wartime competition for available training and air space caused further Air Force restrictions. On 26 August 1965 the ranger department recommended relocating to Fort Stewart, Georgia. The possibility of switching the Florida site to Georgia had been considered periodically since December 1953, but was always declined because of its fewer small boat and Air Force support opportunities. Now the rangers pointed out the administrative advantages of conducting the counter-guerrilla phase without the trouble of a host-tenant agreement.[6]

On 26 May 1966 the Army and Air Force chiefs of staff decided to move the Florida ranger camp to Fort Stewart, but the timing was held in abeyance. Former ranger commandants like Brig. Gen.

John Corley protested vigorously during this delay, describing Fort Stewart as "hopeless terrain" and saying that "all it is good for is what it was initially purchased for during World War II, an antiair-craft range." The issue was finally resolved in 1970, when reduced Vietnam demands (and fewer Air Force requirements) enabled the Joint Chiefs of Staff to agree that Eglin Air Force Base should be retained as a center for special warfare and ranger requirements. As a result, the rangers trained in Florida "snake country" throughout the Vietnam conflict.[7]

A far more serious ranger school problem involved the substance of the course and its role in the Vietnam war. During 1966, Gen. Ralph E. Haines Jr. chaired a panel reviewing ways to bolster the battle proficiency of fresh Army officers, especially the proverbial "unprepared lieutenants" at the forefront of skirmishing actions in Southeast Asia. The Haines Board concluded that Ranger instruction would improve the ability of officers to act decisively and independently on the battlefield. On 16 August 1966, Army chief of staff Gen. Harold K. Johnson began implementing the Haines Board recommendations that all newly commissioned Regular Army officers attend mandatory ranger training.[8]

The ranger department recognized the Army-wide need for better junior officers, but feared that involuntary course attendance would dilute the elitism crucial to the school's production of quality ranger graduates. The ranger staff also realized that drastic school expansion might undermine its instructional program. The ten ranger classes of 1965 graduated 1,042 rangers from 1,458 original students, and the ten 1966 ranger classes graduated 1,089 rangers from 1,320 enrolled students. The Army's existing output of about 1,000 new rangers per year, however, was insufficient to meet wartime ranger advisory and recon requirements—much less to provide ranger-qualified junior leader "stiffening" for regular formations.[9]

General Johnson insisted on trebling Army ranger production, especially among the crucial junior officer ranks. In early 1967 the size of ranger classes was nearly doubled, closer scheduling was arranged, and a week was sliced from the Benning phase. These expedient measures expanded the annual ranger program from ten 130-man classes to fourteen eight-week 220-man classes, spaced at three-week intervals. The process also sacrificed the cherished hallmark of ranger volunteerism, once an inherent cornerstone of ranger philosophy. Commencing in June 1967 all newly appointed Regular Army officers began compulsory attendance. Voluntary priorities were reserved for non-RA junior infantry, armor, artillery, and engineer officers assigned to Vietnam. Infantry noncommissioned officers being programmed for assignment as rifle platoon sergeants and rifle squad leaders were also placed high on the Army's list of desired attenders, but field NCO shortages prevented many from attending.[10]

Strenuous ranger entrance standards combed out physically unfit students before enrollment, but "board case incompletions" became more frequent. Some disgruntled Regular Army officers balked at their forced participation by refusing to exert the willpower needed during more arduous problems. Deliberate course failures were reported in the first two classes that graduated thirty-three of forty-one and ninety-nine of 128 newly commissioned Regular Army lieutenants, respectively. Continental Army Command (CONARC) Commander Gen. James K. Woolnough expressed dismay over the inability of Vietnam-bound Regular Army officers to undergo stressful patrol training in an unusually frank letter to General Haines in the Pentagon that October:

> This high attrition rate among new Regular Army officers deeply concerns me as, on one hand, I don't want to see the standards lowered and, on the other hand, I don't want to see the stamp of failure in a required course put on this number of brand-new Regular Army officers. I think we have to take a new hard look at the impact of our current requirements, and this I intend to do. In the meantime, we will continue close surveillance of attrition rates in subsequent classes and recommend corrective action if indicated.[11]

The ranger school attrition dilemma caused great concern. Senior Army officials understood career "ticket punching" and realized that any military school failure, even in the harsh ranger course, would inhibit officers at the very outset of their Army service. In addition, Army recruitment of officer-quality scholars from civilian universities was already being complicated by the Vietnam war's unpopularity, and the prospect of required ranger training further discouraged many prospects. These misgivings might have been counterbalanced by the desperate need for well-trained lieutenants in Vietnam, especially those imbued with ranger spirit, but the adverse effects were profound.

The Army's training base in the United States was rapidly eroded by the seemingly interminable demands of the Vietnam conflict, and the ranger course was no exception. The institution of the "Regular Army drafted ranger" concept only aggravated ranger department difficulties. The school received high-level pressure to ease course standards and improve graduation statistics. This slippage of prewar standards was exacerbated by instructional staff shortages, as the need for expert ranger personnel on the front in Vietnam and Thailand denuded the school of many superior lane instructors. Casualties and continual levies for new ranger units prevented significant cadre refurbishment.

The ranger program was not reexamined seriously until the beginning of 1970, when reduced Army presence in Vietnam gave General Westmoreland, now Army chief of staff, an opportunity to review training policies. On 28 January he ordered the Infantry School to thoroughly appraise the ranger course, including the validity of requiring attendance by all newly commissioned Regular Army combat-arms officers. The survey resulted in several corrective measures, including dropping of "armed swimming" prerequisites (an applicant swam fifteen meters while carrying basic combat gear and a rifle) and the award of the ranger tab (an insignia previously denied bottom-level graduates) to all personnel who successfully completed the course.

Most important, on 23 April 1970, General Woolnough of the Continental Army Command declared that the requirement for compulsory ranger course attendance should be rescinded. In September 1970, General Westmoreland approved reverting the ranger course to voluntary attendance, but only if the basic officer schools could incorporate ranger-type subjects in their own course work. On 21 October the ranger department began preparing instructional packets, and these materials were distributed to the various school commandants in December.[12]

General Haines succeeded General Woolnough as the new CONARC commander and halted all revisions aimed at returning the school to its prewar voluntary status. Haines had originated the mandatory ranger program for new officers, and he wanted the school retained in its present form. In February 1971 he warned that substituting ranger instruction in the basic officer schools would be cost-ineffective, and on 21 June, Westmoreland disapproved modifying the ranger course on that basis. This decision effectively retained involuntary wartime ranger course criteria for the duration of the Army's service in Vietnam.[13]

MACV RECONDO SCHOOL: AN INTERIM SOLUTION

The ranger school at Fort Benning, Georgia, taught master patrolling techniques for Army-wide application. For much of the period of American military involvement in Vietnam, the ranger school was supplemented by the Vietnam-based MACV Recondo

School. The latter was based at Nha Trang and functioned as a combat theater academy specializing in Vietnam-specific reconnaissance practices. The recondo course was essentially a three-week, 310-instructional-hour crash course in wartime patrolling. The school was not a ranger substitute, but it served an essential role improving reconnaissance and ranger operations in Vietnam.

U.S. Army Special Forces Project Delta began conducting internal long-range reconnaissance training in May 1964. During the following year, arriving conventional army forces learned of the program and began sending selected soldiers to attend Special Forces instruction at Nha Trang. The 1st Brigade of the 101st Airborne Division sent ten troops through the training in September 1965, and awareness of the Project Delta recon course spread. More formations sent soldiers, and by August 1966 the Nha Trang Special Forces course totaled fifty-two students per class.

MACV commander General Westmoreland decided to formalize the Vietnam-oriented Special Forces recon course. He favored the term "recondo"—derived from "reconnaissance," "doughboy," and "commando"—that his own 101st Airborne Division recondo school used while under his command in 1958–1960. His division recondo school had prepared patrol leaders by physical hardening, cliff rappelling, land navigation, stream crossings, and woods survival. General Westmoreland now directed Special Forces to create a three-week Vietnam recondo school, based on its successful model program. Project Delta officer-in-charge Maj. A. J. Baker formulated the basis for the academy and hand-selected the cadre.

On 15 September 1966, General Westmoreland officially opened the MACV Recondo School at Nha Trang, Vietnam. Maj. Edward S. Rybat became the first assistant commandant (the school commandant position was honorarily reserved for the 5th Special Forces Group commander). The recondo school staff was limited to five officers and forty-one sergeants at its inception, and only eight positions were added to this number during the war. The hand-selected instructors combined qualities of expert teachers, recon team advisers, and aggressive field leaders. Master Sgt. Lonnie L. Ledford was credited as Recondo Instructor #1, and Recondo Instructor #311 Sgt. William G. Mihaly Jr. became the final school cadre member. Some foreign liaison personnel were also assigned, including staff instructors from Australia, Korea, the Philippines, Thailand, and Vietnam.[14]

The standards for student selection were contained in USARV Regulation 350-2: All students had to be volunteers; possess a combat military occupational specialty; be in excellent physical condition; have a minimum of one month in Vietnam; have six months retainability in Vietnam; have an actual or anticipated assignment to a long-range reconnaissance patrol unit; and be proficient in general military subjects.

The MACV Recondo School pocket patch was worn by instructors and course graduates and represented an outgrowth of the 101st Airborne Division recondo school patch originally approved by General Westmoreland. The latter was an elongated arrowhead patch pointing downward to symbolize air-to-ground operations, and colored white and black for night and day capability. It could only be worn under limited circumstances, but the school's prominence and its badge came to symbolize recondo capability throughout the Army.[15]

The MACV Recondo School patch was a subdued version based on the arrowhead design, but was olive green instead of white and featured an inner black "V" (for Vietnam) instead of "101." The black letters "RECONDO" were printed across the upper arrowhead base. This design was intended as the basis for Army-wide recon standardization. For example, a modified patch having the inner V but deleting RECONDO was used to denote members of Vietnam patrol units who never completed the MACV Recondo School. Graduates of stateside recondo schools wore patches without the V signifier but with the word RECONDO. Finally, a plain green arrowhead patch devoid of inside inscriptions was intended for non-school-trained long-range reconnaissance patrol members outside Vietnam. This logical scheme was accepted for several years, despite Army Department disapproval of all "unofficial recondo-type pocket insignia."[16]

The MACV Recondo School was considered by Vietnam-based soldiers as both intensive and immediately applicable to jungle warfare. Honor recondo graduate Sp4 Russell Woodrum, who started with seventy-one soldiers in the twenty-day cycle and graduated first among the forty-one who completed, typically understated the demanding course in soldier fashion: "Recondo School was not easy."[17]

The first phase of training consisted of academic classroom subjects and conditioning exercises. Students were administered a standard airborne physical training test on the second day. They also climbed and descended knotted ropes on the forty-foot rappelling tower to prepare them mentally for helicopter extraction practice. A swimming test was also administered during the opening session. Each school morning started at 4:30 A.M. and covered the Army "daily dozen" exercises plus a lot of extra sit-ups, pull-ups, and push-ups. The students then donned full rucksacks, combat equipment, and weapons and completed forced marches that started at five kilometers and added a kilometer daily, until their hikes reached nine kilometers with full gear. Basic instruction included sixteen hours of map reading, six hours of medical training, ten hours of radio handling and field-expedient antenna erection, and over seven hours of combat intelligence.

During the second week the physical training continued early each morning, but now the combat-loaded students had to jog five kilometers instead of walk, until they were running eight kilometers at a time. The field coursework expanded to include weapons familiarization, enemy mines and booby traps, landing zone selection, and adjusting artillery and mortar fire. The patrol training covered patrol preparation, tracking, security, using special equipment, techniques of helicopter infiltration and extractions, and "break-contact" immediate action drills.

The third week of the course climaxed in a long-range reconnaissance four- or five-day patrol in VC-contested mountains west of Nha Trang or on deserted islands like Hon Tre. Because the final patrol was spent in hostile territory—where students were subjected to life-and-death situations—only individuals who achieved overall proficiency in reconnaissance techniques were permitted to participate.

The dangers of this final patrolling were proved on several occasions. In early April 1967, eight student teams of MACV Recondo Class R-10-67 were infiltrated into a mountainous region covered by scattered boulders and patches of thick foliage. On the early afternoon of 4 April a Viet Cong portage party suddenly exchanged fire with team 6 as it stepped off a well-used trail, killing one student and wounding three others. Gunships responded and covered the team as helicopter-dropped McGuire rigs were used to extract the troops. Sfc. Thomas R. Lane led the school's reaction platoon to recover the American body and discovered a dead Viet Cong nearby. The fallen VC, dressed in black peasant attire with rubber sandals, had dropped his SKS rifle and forty-pound bag of rice along with a letter that he had started to write home—evidence that the encounter was a mutual surprise.[18]

The April 1967 incident also reemphasized the severe disadvantages of McGuire rig extraction. The recon team 4 patrollers had to await lowering of the rigs before being able to prepare themselves for extraction, stood up in exposed positions while getting into the harnesses, and were unable to operate their radios and weapons or use their hands for protection while being dragged through the trees.

Additionally, it proved difficult to retrieve wounded members of the patrol.

The school staff began working on a new extraction rig that could be worn as a field harness-belt combination around the body, thus enabling a person to hook up to extraction ropes from any position while keeping both hands free. This recondo-school-developed device became known as the "STABO Rig" in honor of its instructor inventors: Maj. Robert L. Stevens, Capt. John D. H. Knabb, and Sfc. Clifford L. Roberts. The Stabo extraction harness was first demonstrated on 1 October 1968 and proved to be one of the most useful innovations in reconnaissance hardware produced during the Vietnam war.[19]

Another important, but lesser-known, recondo school contribution was the August 1968 adoption of the "Gorwoody" antenna system for patrol communications. This device was the brainchild of Sfc. Jason T. Woodworth and Sp4 William E. Gorris. It was constructed of a PRC short-whip antenna cut at the first joint and flexibly connected silver-coated copper wires, cut to frequency, looped at the end to facilitate hanging in jungle shrubbery.[20]

The high standards of the MACV Recondo School caused sixty percent attrition rates in normal classes. In one case, from September 1966 to July 1967, only thirty-five troops of the separate 1st Brigade, 101st Airborne Division, were graduated from the course. Brigade commander General Matheson became alarmed over the high number of course failures, especially among privates and young specialists needed most urgently for patrol duty. He sent a liaison team to Nha Trang, and they reported that instruction was intended as refresher training for experienced reconnaissance personnel. Based on this report, General Matheson restricted student selection to sergeants and those about to be promoted. He also sent a message to higher headquarters suggesting that MACV Recondo School requirements be altered to produce more scouts among the lower ranks.[21]

In August 1967, Maj. David W. Ranger took over the recondo school from Major Rybat. That October he was succeeded by Maj. Robert G. Lunday, who immediately had to suspend regular classes through December in order to train two newly formed field force reconnaissance companies at General Westmoreland's direction. The recondo instructors first trained Company F (Long Range Patrol), 51st Infantry (Airborne), for II Field Force Vietnam. The next complete company sent through the special recon unit training cycles was Company E (Long Range Patrol), 20th Infantry (Airborne), of I Field Force Vietnam.[22]

Regular recondo school classes resumed in January 1968, only to be seriously disrupted by the unexpected communist Tet-68 offensive that started at the end of the month. The school provided emergency patrols and secured the outer Nha Trang complex during heavy fighting. General Westmoreland did not want to use valuable school resources in regular infantry assignments, but the emergency demanded that all available combat resources be utilized on the front.

The MACV Recondo School returned to normalcy in the spring, except that its patrols continued to brush more frequently with enemy forces. On the evening of 28 May 1968 a Combat Orientation Course patrol was lying in ambush along a section of irregular rice paddies. Student officer Lt. Merrill D. Reich was posted in the adjacent thickets to cover the patrol's right flank. He spotted a North Vietnamese point squad silently stalking the patrol's main position and saw that his comrades were unaware of the enemy approach.

Lieutenant Reich realized that the proximity of the rapidly approaching enemy force prevented enough time for a warning. He jumped up with his rifle blazing and killed the lead North Vietnamese riflemen at point-blank range. Reich was hit in return and fell severely wounded, but continued to fire into the startled enemy force. He tenaciously held his position in spite of rocket and machine gun fire until mortally wounded, thus giving the thirteen other Americans enough time to shift their positions and counter the platoon-sized surprise attack. On 26 October 1968 the recondo school training area on Hon Tre Island was memorialized in honor of Reich's inspirational courage.[23]

The presence of North Vietnamese infiltration parties constantly menaced the recondo school's forward training locations. Maj. Robert L. Stevens took over the school in June 1968. At the end of the month, eight student teams of MACV Recondo Class R-21-68 infiltrated various recon zones southwest of My Loc outpost and found an elaborate system of enemy way stations and supply points. The recondo insertions included one rubber boat landing by recon team 4. The recondo patrols determined that contingents of the 18B NVA Regiment were dispersed in the area but that an extensive security net, consisting of numerous two-to-three-man listening posts and small three-to-eight-man local patrols, shielded the enemy against unwanted contacts.[24]

In November 1968, Maj. James H. Morris became MACV Recondo School assistant commandant, and he hosted the long-range reconnaissance patrol leaders' conference in April of the following year. The seminar participants came from all Marine and Army divisions and brigades in Vietnam and exchanged recon ideas and lessons learned. The combat recon disparity between tactical operating areas naturally created many different operating methods, and the conference allowed the sharing of many professional techniques.[25]

Maj. Joe A. Rodriques took over the MACV Recondo School in September 1969, and by the time Maj. Gary W. Bowles assumed the assistant commandant's position in July 1970, the academy was already being scheduled for inactivation. The last ceremony for the MACV Recondo School was held on 31 December 1970, when the guidons were cased. During the Vietnam war, the academy graduated a total of 5,625 reconnaissance personnel—including 296 Koreans, 193 Thais, 130 Vietnamese, 18 Australians, and 22 Filipinos.[26]

The 4th Infantry Division typified American formation experiences with MACV Recondo School availability. The formation sent its first volunteers to MACV Recondo School on 6 November 1966. When the division pressed into battle, however, it became imperative to insert authorized recon teams immediately and forgo the time-consuming requirement of sending soldiers to the recondo course. In December the division created its own mini-school, the 4th Division Recondo Preparation Course, which taught basic patrol methodology and hardened selected soldiers for the increased stress of highland scouting. These troops were then either sent directly to the field or, if operational intervals permitted, given advanced instruction at the MACV Recondo School. Both courses demanded mental alertness, superior soldiering qualities, and physical excellence. In actuality, battlefield demands and dropout rates combined to make formally qualified graduates of either course a field rarity.[27]

The MACV Recondo School possessed all the benefits and flaws implicit in an expedient training organization serving a wartime theater. Among its advantages were Special Forces combat veterans of elite Project Delta as instructors, soldier-students who were eager to learn and sharpen their combat skills, and operational instruction that culminated in a week of actual reconnaissance against Viet Cong "not in the lesson plan." Unfortunately, these advantages were offset by the school's understaffing and resulting inability to train enough personnel to sustain divisional and brigade reconnaissance units. The school was an interim solution and failed to bridge the "ranger gap" that General Westmoreland intended to fill on an emergency basis.

FROM RANGER COMPANIES TO BATTALIONS

By 1967, escalating demands of Vietnam combat overshadowed all other American military considerations. The "limited war" had already depleted the Army force structure, and the drain on personnel and equipment being sent overseas into Southeast Asia appeared interminable. Within the United States, most installations were used as training centers to prepare Vietnam-bound replacements. Many formations were no longer able to perform fully as fighting units, because they were filled with transient soldiers either going to Vietnam or returning. This situation dominated the organization and employment of stateside reconnaissance and ranger assets.

Only one infantry long-range patrol company existed in the entire United States. This unit, Company E (LRP) of the 30th Infantry, had been active since 25 August 1966 and was stationed at Fort Rucker, Alabama. The company was reserved for global response as part of the Strategic Army Forces and maintained at Priority I level with 208 members, in the event that combat reconnaissance was needed during a general war.

Unfortunately, Company E strike capabilities were undercut by competing training demands imposed by the Vietnam war. Fort Rucker was the home of the Army Aviation Center and School, and the patrol company became immersed in the Army school for fixed-wing and helicopter pilots. Company E remained committed to the Army Strategic Forces, but it was used in an entirely different manner: "supplying personnel to portray aggressors in the student pilot escape-and-evasion problem presented by the aviation school survival committee every two weeks."[28]

Heightened stateside training requirements also existed for long-range patrol instruction. There was an urgent need to produce more infantrymen, capable of serving as scouts for Vietnam-based combat recon units. Unfortunately, adequate facilities were lacking. The normally available but minuscule ranger course was hopelessly swamped by the wartime emergency. The depleted cadre of the parachute and infantry schools could not fulfill this additional requirement either.

This dilemma caused General Woolnough of the Continental Army Command to borrow a quick-fix idea from Vietnam—where divisions and brigades had created their own field schools to supplement the understaffed MACV Recondo School. General Woolnough decided to augment the formal ranger school with various patrol schools set up at posts throughout the country.

On 22 July 1967 he ordered every stateside division, separate brigade, and armored cavalry regiment to establish a long-range patrol course. Exceptions were made only for units engaged in other school training support. Enough recon-experienced Vietnam veterans existed to make General Woolnough's substitute patrol schools a workable program. Soldiers with the proper background were identified and taken out of their normal assignments. Even "short-timer" troops about to leave the service were pressed into the new courses.

Two recon academies started functioning in 1967. In the east, the 82d Airborne Division started the Third Army "Raider School" at Fort Bragg, North Carolina. At Fort Carson, Colorado, the 5th Infantry Division (Mechanized) commenced a Fifth Army "Long Range Patrol" School that graduated ninety new recon personnel by the end of the year. However, the Fourth Army experienced so much fluctuation among individual reassignments that it declined to establish a planned school at Fort Hood. The Sixth Army in the west expressed no enthusiasm for the project and reported having no units assigned to perform the mission.

In 1968, more infantry recon units within the United States were planned, but they never materialized. The main culprits were a combination of Vietnam-generated troop requisitions and the continuing need for training assets. Original projections to activate two long-range patrol companies for the Strategic Army Forces in February, one at Fort Hood and the other at Fort Bragg, were shelved. Company E (LRP) of the 30th Infantry continued to languish in its training role for the aviation school at Fort Rucker. During the year, Company E (LRP) of the 21st Infantry was activated at Fort Benning, Georgia, but it remained only a paper organization. The unit was carried at zero strength while its personnel spaces were used for installation school support slots.[29]

The year 1968, however, proved decisive in preparing the groundwork for revitalizing ranger units and the role of combat reconnaissance in Army doctrine. During the early part of the year, even as the battles of Tet-68 were raging in Vietnam, the Continental Army Command published unit-structure charts governing the organization and equipment for infantry long-range patrol units. These "tables of organization and equipment," known as the TOE 7-157 series, formed the basis for all infantry patrol companies and later ranger companies throughout the Army (see Appendix C). During August the Continental Army Command also developed and distributed a revised field manual on long-range patrol tactics.

These documents established the final working basis of Vietnam-era ranger structure and tactics.[30]

On 3 July 1968, General Westmoreland became the chief of staff of the United States Army. He reemphasized the vitality of combat reconnaissance instruction in the United States. General Westmoreland was a staunch advocate of recon training, a preference dating from his creation of the first divisional recondo school while commanding the 101st Airborne Division, as well as the MACV Recondo School in Vietnam. He believed strongly in the value of using small independent patrols as a training tool for better infantry leadership, especially at squad level.

General Westmoreland wanted to institute a solid program of patrol training at the installations where divisions, brigades, and armored cavalry regiments were located. He also wanted the combat recon schools harmonized into one uniform program. In September, General Westmoreland issued a letter of instructions establishing a model program for all long-range patrol/recondo schools. In May 1969 the courses were formally designated as the 82d Airborne Division Raider-Recondo School, the 5th Infantry Division Raider School, and the III Corps Recondo School. Each was producing ten yearly classes, with a student capacity of forty-five, 150, and thirty respectively, by the end of the year.[31]

In the meantime, during 1968, the Army began a massive pullout from Europe code-named Operation REFORGER (Redeployment of Forces, Germany). The withdrawal proceeded despite the communist invasion of Czechoslovakia in August, and that month both European-stationed infantry long-range patrol companies were returned to the United States as part of REFORGER reductions. The "Victory Lerps" of Company D (LRP), 17th Infantry, relocated at Fort Benning, Georgia, at less than half strength. The loss of skilled personnel and mission-essential equipment forced Capt. Harry W. Nieuwboer to rebuild his unit practically from scratch. The difficulty of this task was compounded by the conditions in the United States, in which the military fixation on Vietnam and lack of any immediate Soviet threat fostered command indifference to Captain Nieuwboer's NATO-oriented company and hindered his ability to secure qualified replacements. Captain Nieuwboer reconstructed the unit slowly, in stages, starting with cadre retraining on 15 September and followed by recommencement of basic long-range patrol training on 18 November. In similar fashion the understrength "Jayhawk Lerps" of Company C (LRP), 58th Infantry, deplaned at Fort Riley, Kansas, and were subsequently transferred to Fort

Carson, Colorado, for rebuilding. Both units, along with other RE-FORGER forces, were reserved for NATO response.[32]

On 2 December 1968, General Westmoreland gave final approval to reorganizing the 75th Infantry—the modern descendant of "Merrill's Marauders"—in the combat arms regimental system as the parent regiment for Army long-range patrol companies and detachments. With few exceptions, such units were redesignated as ranger companies of the 75th Infantry. The orders became effective in February 1969 and affected fifteen long-range patrol units on a worldwide basis.[33]

On 21 February 1969, Company A (Airborne Ranger), 75th Infantry, was activated at Fort Benning under Capt. Thomas P. Meyer with an authorized strength of 216 personnel. The company absorbed the assets of Company D, 17th Infantry, as well as its RE-FORGER mission. The new ranger company thus maintained a "short-fuze capability" to deploy back to V Corps in Germany and execute deep penetration missions within a 110-mile communications range. If Europe was threatened by war, ranger Company A was slated to infiltrate into East Germany to ascertain Soviet dispositions in the Bad Hersfeld, Fulda, Bad Kissingen, and Coburg corridors.[34]

Capt. Dennis R. Foley was shifted from his job commanding the Fort Benning Honor Guard (Company C, 1st Battalion, 29th Infantry) to command the new company soon after its activation. The rangers were hand-selected, and almost every member was a parachute-qualified Vietnam veteran patroller. Because the 75th was a regiment of separately operating companies (Companies A–P), there was no real headquarters. Company A became the de facto regimental headquarters for administrative tasks, such as heraldic insignia and ranger standardization procedures. The director of the ranger school, Col. John Geraci, was the honorary regimental commander.

Ranger Company A performed a variety of important duties at Fort Benning. The company supported the ranger patrolling committee and other ranger department tasks. Col. Willard Latham, commanding the 197th Infantry Brigade, also placed the rangers in charge of his brigade "Drug Rehabilitation Program" for soldiers with drug problems. The rangers removed drug users from Martin Army Hospital and placed them through two-week rehabilitation cycles that resembled unofficial company punishment. The rangers placed the soldiers in guarded platoon bays within the two brick Company A barracks and reconditioned them with physical training, rifle drill, and hard labor chores.

On 10 February 1969, Company B (Ranger), 75th Infantry, was activated at Fort Carson, Colorado. It used the personnel and equipment of the inactivated Company C (LRP) of the 58th Infantry. Company B operated at less than half the strength of Company A and suffered more organizational problems. The company was still maintained in a REFORGER reaction mode. Under the Army Strategic Capabilities Plan the rangers were programed to reenter Germany under VII Corps and perform extended patrolling in the Fürth and Hof corridors.

On 27 February 1969, shortly after both stateside ranger companies were activated, U.S. Army Vietnam requested that a ranger company be readied for Vietnam deployment that November, in order to replace the National Guard ranger company (Company D, 151st Infantry) scheduled to leave combat at year's end. This sudden overseas demand for a nonprogrammed combat unit of elite quality generated major Defense Department concern, because the Army was obligated to keep ranger Companies A and B on REFORGER status.

Prospects for raising a fresh ranger company were bleak. The ranger and paratrooper school cadre were already operating at diminished levels. Continental Army Commander General Woolnough estimated that it would require nearly half a year (twenty-two weeks) to activate, train, and fully equip an entirely new ranger company for overseas combat. He indicated that Company A (Airborne Ranger) could be ready in thirteen weeks, but release from its REFORGER commitment would have to be granted under emergency authority. The preparation of any ranger company for Vietnam duty would also force a temporary curtailment of the entire ranger school program.

Based on General Woolnough's input, General Westmoreland communicated to USARV commander General Abrams that the earliest availability date for a stateside-trained ranger replacement unit was 10 January 1970. Westmoreland suggested that a ranger company could be raised more easily in Vietnam, using troops already in the pipeline or from other experienced recon assets. The latter course of action was finally adopted, and Company D of the 75th Infantry (see chapter 11) was subsequently formed in the Republic of Vietnam during November 1969.[35]

During mid-June 1969 the United States Army withdrawal from Vietnam began. Budgetary and stationing restrictions kept emphasis on retention of regular line formations, and the wartime ranger companies were abolished inside Vietnam. Within the United States, there were only two companies capable of extended reconnaissance patrolling: the 75th Infantry's Companies A and B. The Fort Rucker-based Company E (Airborne Pathfinder), 30th Infantry, was no longer functioning as a patrol company but as a post Honor Company with the school pathfinder element, 5th Infantry Detachment, attached. In October, Company E was again reorganized and became a standard rifle company with responsibilities for school support and burial details.[36]

During February 1970, Company A (Airborne Ranger) of the 75th Infantry was shifted from Fort Benning to Fort Hood, Texas, to begin Project MASSTER (Mobile Army Sensor Systems Test, Evaluation, and Review). The ranger company was attached to the 1st Armored Division and upgraded to a new authorization of 268 personnel. The ranger work was difficult and inglorious and involved the constant testing of surveillance, target acquisition, seismic intrusion detectors, and night observation equipment across the windswept central Texas plains. This dedicated ranger pioneering work paved the way for improved systems that superbly benefited the Army performance in the Gulf War twenty years later.[37]

Army personnel levels continued to decline over the next few years as personnel turbulence, heavy levies for European-deployed forces, and poor readiness conditions plagued the entire Army establishment. General Westmoreland officially launched the Modern Volunteer Army program on 13 October 1970 in anticipation of the end of the draft. In late 1971 the 156-man Company B (Ranger), 75th Infantry, was deployed from Fort Carson to Europe in Exercise REFORGER III. The company demonstrated its patrolling capabilities inside Germany during this crucial test of ranger response.

Just before the end of the Vietnam war, ranger service in the United States Army was bolstered by the expansion of the two active ranger companies, A and B, to battalions during October 1974. The 1st Battalion (Ranger) of the 75th Infantry was activated at Fort Stewart by using the assets of inactivated ranger Company A, but it was assigned the heritage of the Vietnam-honored field force rangers of Company C. On 1 November the 2d Battalion (Ranger) of the 75th Infantry was activated at Fort Lewis, Washington, from ranger Company B and acquired the lineage of the Company H airmobile cavalry rangers. During the spring of 1975, while the new battalions were still organizing, an all-out North Vietnamese invasion overwhelmed and destroyed the Republic of Vietnam.

LESSONS OF VIETNAM COMBAT RECONNAISSANCE

The Army waged a prolonged combat reconnaissance campaign in Southeast Asia as a result of battlefield circumstances. The unforeseen nature of territorial control and area warfare operations within Vietnam, for which the Army was doctrinally ill-prepared, demanded sustained ground patrols that ventured forward of conventional battlefront reconnaissance sectors, but stayed on operations-level and tactical assignments. The Army long-range patrol and ranger endeavor during the Vietnam conflict was thus largely unexpected and characterized foremost by the field-expedient and decentralized nature of most regular formation recon units.

The Special Forces, charged with strategic reconnaissance, had contained recon elements since 1964. The Regular Army, however, sent its main contingents into Vietnam without sufficient capability to conduct extended foot reconnaissance. To provide a scouting adjunct for their maneuvering units, the Army's field forces, divisions, and brigades created special combat reconnaissance units out of battlefield necessity.

Patrol missions demonstrated the supreme value of the human being as an intelligence-collection agent. During the Vietnam era, patrol personnel were more reliable at gathering information than the primitive electronic warfare and aerial photographic apparatus being placed on the battlefield. As the war progressed, however, teams relied increasingly on remote detection and firing mechanisms. Mechanical items remained only supplemental and never replaced the infiltration of people to determine targets and perform reconnaissance missions.

The ad hoc nature of combat recon units, initially assembled outside the authorized structure of regular formations, placed them well within the traditional legacy of Rogers' Rangers. The units were also akin to the tactical ranger companies of the Korean war, but far removed in methodology from the ranger battalion strike forces of World War II and the current Army.

The sudden necessity for combat recon in Vietnam created a tremendous and unexpected increase in personnel on such missions, often at the expense of quality and desired training. For example, from November 1966 until November 1967, MACV recorded the increase in patrollers needed by region (excluding Special Forces). Within I Corps Tactical Zone the 1,256 Marine recon, stinger patrol, and SEAL personnel present during late 1966 increased to 1,328 such personnel by the following year. Within the

Vietnamese Central Highlands a total of thirty-four authorized patrollers during 1966 rose dramatically to 556 recon members committed by 1967. In the III Corps Tactical Zone the total allocation of seventy-two recon members increased to 650 members during 1967. These strength comparisons between 1,362 and 2,534 authorized patrollers represented an 88 percent increase in personnel posted to specialized extended combat recon duty, in just one year.[38]

Long-range patrols were given the normal mission of entering a specific area within hostile territory and observing and reporting on enemy dispositions, installations, and activities. In addition to military intelligence collection, the patrols were also used on many combat tasks, such as ambushing enemy courier and liaison personnel, capturing prisoners, and a myriad of other command-directed special assignments.

The I Field Force Vietnam commander, Lt. Gen. Charles A. Corcoran, concluded his opening remarks at the April 1969 MACV Recondo School conference with a valuable observation:

> Our long-range patrols should not be frittered away by sending them chasing after ghosts. We should strike to develop our own ideas of how the enemy's [maneuver and logistical] system works. Then, having some clear idea of his routes and critical points, we should use our long-range patrol capability in a systematic way, with one patrol's mission related to what the other patrol is doing. Once we develop in detail how the enemy's system works, then we have the forces and the mobility to move in and destroy it rather quickly.[39]

Unfortunately, politically imposed limitations on military action left the enemy's "Ho Chi Minh trail" lifeline unchallenged by American maneuver formations and their tactical recon elements, except at its various terminals and forward depots. Many recon missions were doomed to repetitive sorties against the same replenishable enemy base areas and infiltration corridors throughout the war.

A common tactical failing of Vietnam-based patrolling was excessive dependence on airmobility. The use of helicopters, with all their attendant strengths and weaknesses, was the mainstay of Army operations during the Vietnam conflict, and long-range patrolling was no exception. Recon teams employed helicopters routinely for insertion, extraction, and firepower support. As a result, jungle clearings and landing fields often served as the Vietnam-era scouting equivalents of road junctions and bridges in previous wars. Helicopters could overfly inhospitable terrain and deliver teams on pinpoint locations, but they were extremely noisy and highly visible. No matter how many ruses were developed to shield helicopter-inserted patrols, the enemy was often alerted to recon team presence.

The limited duration of most "extended" reconnaissance patrolling in Vietnam caused a decline in intelligence-collecting capability. The United States Army Vietnam compiled statistics, through mid-1968, for all long-range patrols that revealed one-third of all patrols were actually less than twenty-four hours in length, one-third of patrols were between twenty-four and seventy-two hours, and the remaining one-third of the patrols lasted seventy-two hours or longer. Some formations, typified by the 4th Infantry Division, had planned their patrols to last five days in dry weather conditions and three days during the rainy season.[40]

The large expanse of patrolling territory increasingly assigned with the extension of allied security efforts introduced many complexities in fielding area and point reconnaissance. Problems for extended patrols included the shortage of helicopters for immediate reaction or extraction during emergency situations, the heavy weight of individual loads carried by patrol members, and the necessity for a stand-down of several days following a long-duration mission. There were also disadvantages inherent in reconnoitering the same area over an extended period of time. When the enemy became aware of continuous recon efforts in a particular zone, counter-raider and patrolling impairments were established that diminished recon team effectiveness.

Misuse by higher commands constituted a significant handicap for many long-range patrol and ranger units in Vietnam. In many cases, the operational control of long-range patrol and ranger elements was assigned to brigades and even battalions. Patrol leaders of teams responsible to the unit intelligence sections generally believed that their teams were properly employed. In contrast, patrol leaders of teams misused as security forces, point elements, and on infantry reaction or economy-of-force operations invariably worked under commanders and operations officers who were unfamiliar with the capabilities and limitations of combat reconnaissance.[41]

The failure of reconnaissance schooling also worked against patrolling proficiency in Vietnam. Throughout the conflict, the preparation of reconnaissance troops depended more on chance than plan. Wartime patrol and ranger units needed soldiers who, at the very minimum, could read military maps, could understand compasses, and had some ability to administer first aid. Some soldiers with previous combat infantry or reconnaissance experience in jungle warfare were actually unwanted, because they had learned bad habits or were more interested in fighting than gathering intelligence. This reduced the available pool of volunteers.

Improper training opportunities aggravated the inherent soldiering handicaps of one-year service tours. The effects of the annual rotation policy, another politically mandated necessity, almost crippled sustained combat reconnaissance proficiency. Most new patrol members were recent arrivals in Vietnam with only a general indoctrination to field conditions. In many cases, the new recon members were teamed up with an "old hand" who was often only a nineteen-year-old youth with twenty missions under his belt. Recon training consisted of keeping newer members close to the base on short-range missions and then gradually unleashing them on longer and more complicated patrols. Neither the ranger school nor the MACV Recondo School did much to alleviate such hazardous "learning on-the-job" scenarios.

Incredibly, despite these handicaps, most Army long-range patrollers performed their missions in Vietnam with good results. Combat reconnaissance units in support of the field forces, divisions, and brigades gathered intelligence, located and tracked enemy units, and produced a field record of many successes. Considering the circumstances, their failures were few.

The overall ability of Army patrol forces in Vietnam was a result of sound soldiering professionalism, close team bonding, the common pride in ranger legacy, an understanding of patrol principles, individual courage, physical stamina, and mental alertness. These characteristics enabled Army recon teams of the Vietnam war to perform important intelligence and raiding tasks against a battle-hardened adversary in a difficult jungle warfare climate, and added another milestone in United States Army ranger development.

APPENDIX A

LONG RANGE PATROLLERS AND RANGERS MISSING IN ACTION

Champion, James Albert, Private First Class, Ranger scout of team Cubs, Company L (Airborne Ranger), 75th Infantry, 101st Airborne Division (Airmobile). Born 16 November 1949 at Houston, Texas; entered service at Houston, Texas; established residence at Houston, Texas.

Missing in action since 25 April 1971, when his ranger radio relay team was battling enemy forces near Hill 809 in the A Shau Valley of Thua Thien Province near the Laotian border. Throughout the night of 24–25 April, Private First Class Champion guarded the wounded crew of a helicopter shot down by enemy fire on the previous day. He was last seen at 5:00 A.M. by crew chief Pfc. Clarence D. Allen, who watched him depart the crash site to find water for the dehydrated and painfully injured airmen.

Cochrane, Deverton Carpenter, Staff Sergeant, team leader of team 52, Company H (Airmobile Ranger), 75th Infantry, 1st Cavalry Division. Born 15 December 1948 at Boston, Massachusetts; entered service at Boston, Massachusetts; established residence at Brookline, Massachusetts.

Missing in action since 17 June 1970, when his ranger team was surprised by enemy machine gun fire from a bunker at the edge of a forest clearing southeast of O'Rang, Cambodia. Staff Sergeant Cochrane was hit in the opening burst of fire and said, "Oh my God, I'm hit." He fell to the ground on his stomach, with his hand to his neck and blood flowing profusely, and was seen suffering respiratory distress. The patrol survivors fought to break contact with the enemy force for fifteen minutes. Staff Sergeant Cochrane was last seen lying on the forest floor near Sp4 Carl J. Laker (who was later declared dead although his body was also never recovered) as the other rangers retreated.

Finley, Dickie Waine, Private First Class, team leader of team 28, Company E (Long Range Patrol), 58th Infantry, 4th Infantry Division. Born 29 June 1947 at East Prairie, Missouri; entered service at Sweet Springs, Missouri; established residence at Sweet Springs, Missouri.

Missing in action since 21 October 1968 near Ban Me Thuot, Darlac Province. He fell from the skid of the extraction helicopter at an altitude of fifty feet over an area of broken jungle, and search efforts failed to locate him.

Fitzgerald, Joseph Edward, Private First Class, patrol member of 3d Brigade, 25th Infantry Division Long Range Reconnaissance Patrol Contingent, Task Force Oregon. Born 25 November 1948 at St. Johnsbury, Vermont; entered service at Springfield, Massachusetts; established residence at Northbridge, Massachusetts.

Missing in action since 30 May 1967, when his patrol was annihilated along a ridge of Nui Gio (mountain), northeast of Special Forces Camp Ha Thanh in Quang Ngai Province. Last radio contact with the patrol was made at 8:30 P.M. that evening, and a search unit later found the bodies of two other patrol members. Evidence at the scene indicated that patrol destruction occurred about 3:00 A.M. on 31 May 1967.

Jakovac, John Andrew, Sergeant, patrol member of 3d Brigade, 25th Infantry Division Long Range Reconnaissance Patrol Contingent, Task Force Oregon. Born 10 April 1947 at Ontonangon, Michigan; entered service at Lansing, Michigan; established residence at Detroit, Michigan.

Missing in action since 30 May 1967, when his patrol was annihilated along a ridge of Nui Gio (mountain), northeast of Special Forces Camp Ha Thanh in Quang Ngai Province. Last radio contact with the patrol was made at 8:30 P.M. that evening, and a search unit later found the bodies of two other patrol members. Evidence at the scene indicated that patrol destruction occurred about 3:00 A.M. on 31 May 1967.

* * *

Lancaster, Kenneth Ray, Specialist Fourth Class, student patrol member of MACV Recondo Patrol #3 while on temporary assignment from Company E (Long Range Patrol), 50th Infantry, 9th Infantry Division. Born 24 June 1946 at Washington, District of Columbia; entered service at Silver Spring, Maryland; established residence at Silver Spring, Maryland.

Missing in action since 3 September 1966 twenty miles northwest of Nha Trang, near Hon Ong mountain west of Ninh Hoa in Khanh Hoa Province. He fell from the skid of the extraction helicopter at an altitude of 1,000 feet over an area of dense jungle, and search efforts failed to locate him.

Malo, Issako Faatoese, Private First Class, ranger scout of team Cubs, Company L (Airborne Ranger), 75th Infantry, 101st Airborne Division (Airmobile). Born 18 October 1950 in American Samoa; entered service at Oakland, California; established residence at San Francisco, California. [Malo returned from captivity 27 March 1973.]

Missing in action since 24 April 1971, when his ranger radio relay team was battling enemy forces near Hill 809 in the A Shau Valley of Thua Thien Province, near the Laotian border. Private First Class Malo was wounded but stayed on the landing zone with WO1 Frederic Behrens, an aviator who was crippled by enemy fire after his helicopter was shot down. Malo was last seen moving from the field late in the afternoon to secure assistance for Behrens.

McGar, Brian Kent, Private First Class, patrol member of 3d Brigade, 25th Infantry Long Range Reconnaissance Patrol Contingent, Task Force Oregon. Born 17 August 1947 at Turlock, California; reenlisted at Fort Wainwright, Alaska; established residence at Ceres, California.

Missing in action since 30 May 1967, when his patrol was annihilated along a ridge of Nui Gio, northeast of Special Forces Camp Ha Thanh in Quang Ngai Province. Last radio contact with the patrol was made at 8:30 P.M. that evening, and a search unit later found the bodies of two other patrol members. Evidence at the scene indicated that patrol destruction occurred about 3:00 A.M. on 31 May 1967.

Newton, Donald Stephen, Sergeant, forward observer of Long Range Reconnaissance Patrol Platoon, 1st Brigade, 101st Airborne Division. Born 8 July 1942 at San Pedro, California; entered service at Los Angeles, California; established residence at San Pedro, California.

Missing in action since 26 February 1966, when directed to scout the next ridge 250 yards ahead of the reconnaissance patrol west of Tuy Hoa, Phu Yen Province. Sergeant Newton was later observed on 1 and 2 March 1966 as a Viet Cong captive by several reliable Vietnamese witnesses who saw him being paraded through Phu Sen, Phung Hau, and Thanh Hoi villages, with his name tag still on his tunic. The Vietnamese reported their sightings to South Vietnamese intelligence officer Lt. Tran Huu Tien of the Tuy Hoa District headquarters and stated that Newton was later taken by his captors across the river into Heiu Xuong district of the same province.

AUTHOR'S NOTE: Appendix A was adjusted to conform with the official Missing-In-Action (MIA) list maintained by the Department of Defense and does not include *bodies not recovered* (BNR) and other losses that may remain in dispute because of unexplained circumstances.

APPENDIX B

LONG RANGE PATROL AND RANGER MEDALS OF HONOR

Rabel, Laszlo, Staff Sergeant, team leader of team Delta, 74th Infantry Detachment (Airborne Long Range Reconnaissance Patrol), 173d Airborne Brigade. Born 21 September 1939 in Budapest Hungary; entered service at Minneapolis, Minnesota; established residence at Bloomfield, New Jersey.

At 10:00 A.M. on 13 November 1968, Staff Sergeant Rabel's patrol was located on a steep mountainside of Hill 819, covered with forty-foot jungle canopy, along the Nuoi Luong river northwest of Landing Zone English in Binh Dinh Province. The weather was 103 degrees Fahrenheit and raining. The team was watching a suspected enemy infiltration zone when movement was heard downhill in front of the defensive position. Staff Sergeant Rabel and another team member were preparing to search the vicinity when an enemy grenade suddenly landed inside the small patrol perimeter. Staff Sergeant Rabel jumped without hesitation on the grenade and absorbed the full explosive blast, saving his comrades from death. He never regained consciousness and died eight hours later.

Law, Robert D., Specialist Fourth Class, pace man of team 3, Company I (Ranger), 75th Infantry, 1st Infantry Division. Born 15 September 1944 at Fort Worth, Texas; entered service at Dallas, Texas; residence established at Forth Worth, Texas.

At 8:54 A.M. on 22 February 1969, Specialist Law's team was located on both sides of a small footbridge over the Suoi Ong Bang, a marshy tributary stream of the Song Be, east of Fire Support Base

304

Thunder outside Ap Bau Long in Phuoc Thanh Province. The weather was moderately warm and partially overcast. An enemy patrol exited the dense jungle and detected the rangers, resulting in a brief firefight. During the action, Specialist Law moved to a more advantageous firing position and saw an enemy grenade land in the midst of the ranger flank position. He jumped on the grenade without hesitation and absorbed the full blast of the explosion, saving two nearby comrades from death or injury, at the cost of his own life.

Littrell, Gary L., Sergeant First Class, light weapons infantry adviser of advisory team 21 (Airborne Ranger), U.S. Military Assistance Command, Vietnam. Born 26 October 1944 at Henderson, Kentucky; entered service at Los Angeles, California; established residence at Dahlonega, Georgia.

On 4 April 1970, Sergeant First Class Littrell was an adviser with the Army of the Republic of Vietnam 23d Ranger Battalion when it occupied a defensive perimeter in the double-canopy tropical rain forest on Hill 763 near Dak Seang, Kontum Province. An enemy mortar barrage killed the Vietnamese commander and seriously wounded all the advisers except Sergeant First Class Littrell, who took charge of the beleaguered defense during the next four days. Despite intense enemy fire, he repeatedly abandoned positions of relative safety to direct artillery fire and mark the defensive perimeter for aerial support. Sergeant First Class Littrell moved continuously to defensive sectors most threatened by enemy attack, redistributed ammunition, and shouted encouragement to the South Vietnamese in their own language. The rangers responded to his leadership and personal example by repulsing a series of concentrated enemy assaults until superior enemy forces finally rendered the mountain position untenable. Sergeant First Class Littrell prevented widespread disorder and successfully led the retreating column through numerous enemy ambushes, enabling the ARVN 23d Ranger Battalion to reach allied lines intact on 8 April.

Pruden, Robert J., Staff Sergeant, team leader of team Oregon, Company G (Ranger), 75th Infantry, 23d Infantry Division (Americal). Born 9 September 1949 at St. Paul, Minnesota; entered military service at Minneapolis, Minnesota; established residence at St. Paul, Minnesota.

At 10:30 A.M. on 20 November 1969, Staff Sergeant Pruden's team was establishing a combination ambush-prisoner snatch position along a trail in the rice paddies west of Duc Pho, Quang Ngai

Province, when one of the team members was spotted and pinned down by fire from an enemy squad. Staff Sergeant Pruden performed a heroic solitary charge that diverted enemy fire from the pinned-down soldier while the rest of the patrol fought off a second enemy element. Staff Sergeant Pruden kept running and firing despite being twice wounded, until finally stopped by a third bullet. The enemy squad, unnerved by his lone attack, withdrew from the area. Staff Sergeant Pruden then issued patrol instructions until succumbing to his mortal wounds.

APPENDIX C

RANGER ORGANIZATIONAL ALLOWANCES

1. DIVISION-LEVEL INFANTRY LONG RANGE PATROL OR RANGER COMPANY

a. Personnel

	HEADQUARTERS	PLATOON HQ × 2	PATROLS × 16	TOTAL
Officers	1	1	—	3
Enlisted	17	1	6	115
Total Personnel	18	2	6	118

b. Equipment

M16 Rifles	116	PRC-25 radios	16
M79 Grenade Launchers	32	PRC-64 radios	8
.45-cal. Pistols	2	URC-10 radios	16
		TA-312 telephone sets	5
¼ ton trucks	9		
¼ ton trailers	6		

SOURCE: U.S. Army MTOE 7-157E.

307

2. RANGER COMBAT ADVISORY TEAMS

TEAM PERSONNEL	ARVN RGR GP	ARVN RGR BN
Team Commander / G1542	1 Lt. Col.	1 Major
Deputy Team Commander / G1542	1 Major	1 Captain
Operations Adviser / G2162	1 Captain	—
Intelligence Adviser / G9301	1 Captain	—
Artillery Liaison Officer / 01193	1 Captain	—
Asst. Operations Adviser / 11F4H	1 SFC	—
Asst. Intell Adviser / 96B4H	1 SFC	—
Medical Adviser / 91B4H	1 SFC	—
Light Weapons Adviser / 11B4H	—	1 SFC
Operations-Intell Adviser / 11B4H	—	1 SSG
Communications Chief / 31Z40	1 SSG	—
Radio Telephone Operator / 05B30	4 Sp4	
Total Personnel	13	4

3. REPUBLIC OF VIETNAM RANGER BATTALION (1965–1967)

a. Personnel

	HEADQUARTERS	COMPANIES × 4	TOTAL
Officers	8	5	28
Enlisted	79	138	631
Total Personnel	87	143	659

b. Equipment

M1 Carbines	98	2.5 ton trucks	1
M2 Carbines	309	1 ton truck	6
M1 Garand Rifles	139	¼ ton trucks	11
Recoilless Rifles	2		
Browning Auto Rifles	36	SB-22 switchboards	1
M79 Grenade Launchers	38	GRC-87 radio sets	7
.45 cal Pistols	77	PRC-6 radios	64
Light Machine Guns	10	PRC-10 radios	34

SOURCE: BDQ Battalion Headquarters TOE BB-150 dtd 31 Aug 63; BDQ Company TOE BB-149 dtd 27 Apr 65.

4. ARMY OF THE REPUBLIC OF VIETNAM RANGER GROUP (1968–1972)

a. Personnel

	HQ Co	RECON Co	TRANS Co	ENGINEER Co	RGR BN	RGR BN	RGR BN	TOTAL
Officers	24	9	6	6	31	31	31	138
Sergeants	65	25	13	16	101	101	101	422
Privates	124	77	95	100	613	613	613	2,235
Total	213	111	114	122	745	745	745	2,795

b. Equipment

Rifles	2,415	2.5 ton trucks	24
Grenade Launchers	242	¼ ton trucks	67
Machine Guns	46	¼ ton ambulances	8
Mortars	25		
Bayonets	2,766	SB-22 switchboards	5
Entrenching Tools	2,440	GRC-87 radio sets	24
Demolition Kits	1	PRC-25 radios	149
		WD1 field wire rolls	70

SOURCE: BDQ Group Headquarters TOE 5-202A dtd 11 Oct 67; BDQ Battalion Headquarters TOE 5-641 dtd 11 Oct 67; BDQ Company TOE 5-742 dtd 11 Oct 67; BDQ Transportation Company TOE 5-772 dtd 8 Jan 68; BDQ Engineer Company TOE 12-775 dtd 22 May 68; BDQ Reconnaissance Company TOE 4-770 B dtd 3 Oct 69.

5. REPUBLIC OF VIETNAM RANGER TRAINING CENTER (1968–1972)

a. Cadre Personnel

	HQ	POLITICAL WARFARE BRANCH	SUPPORT BRANCH	TRAINING BRANCH	TOTAL
Officers	4	5	18	105	132
Sergeants	3	10	106	136	255
Privates	—	15	140	35	190
Total	7	30	264	276	577

b. Demonstration and Control Units

	301ST RGR CO	302ND RGR CO	305TH MP DET	TOTAL
Officers	3	3	1	7
Sergeants	19	19	7	45
Privates	110	110	13	233
Total	132	132	21	285

c. Training Items

BB-Guns	234
M1 Rifles	519
M1 Carbines	661
M2 Carbines	872
2.5 ton trucks	30
1 ton trucks	12
¼ ton trucks	variable
¼ ton ambulances	variable
Water Trailers	9
Rubber Boats	20

SOURCE: ARVN TOE 5-020 dtd 7 Apr 66, as amended by Memorandum #584-TTM/P3/TC/4/K-TTM/TCTV/KHCT dtd 18 Mar 68.

APPENDIX D

BUDGETED EXPENSES FOR A RANGER COMPANY

ITEM VALUE	VIETNAM SERVICE	STATESIDE SERVICE
Supply Value	$1,109,065	$1,109,065
Electronic Value	415,336	415,336
Vehicular Value	175,001	175,001
Weapons Value	40,876	40,876
Equipment Value	631,213	631,213
Permanent Unit Value	$2,371,491	$2,371,491

ANNUAL COSTS	VIETNAM SERVICE	STATESIDE SERVICE
Annual Personnel Costs	1,049,300	500,400
Annual Ration Costs	135,700	92,400
Annual Supply Costs	242,100	75,600
Annual Petroleum Costs	108,900	18,300
Annual Ammunition Costs	12,200	10,300
Annual Equipment Maintenance	67,600	32,800
Total Annual Costs	$1,615,800	$729,800

NOTE: Annual personnel and petroleum costs for ranger companies in Vietnam service were much higher because of combat pay and aviation fuel allocation for airmobile operations. The annual ammunition costs for stateside-based ranger companies was still equivalent to Vietnam expenditures because of the need to include stockage for wartime deployment.

SOURCE: U.S. Army AMSAA Technical Memorandum No. 88 dtd Nov 70.

311

APPENDIX E

U.S. ARMY RANGER
SERVICE IN VIETNAM

Combat Command	1965	1966	1967
173d Airborne Brigade			Ⓐ
II Field Force, Vietnam			
1st Brigade, 101st Airborne Division			Ⓓ
I Field Force, Vietnam			
1st Cavalry Division (Airmobile)			
1st Infantry Division			
25th Infantry Division			
4th Infantry Division			
9th Infantry Division			
199th Infantry Brigade			
196th Infantry Brigade			Ⓔ
23d Infantry Division (Americal)			
101st Airborne Division (Airmobile)			
3d Brigade, 82d Airborne Division			
1st Brigade, 5th Infantry Division			

Notes

A   173d Abn Bde LRRP Platoon personnel transf to II FFV in Sep 67; skeletal LRRP
     Platoon in service until 20 Dec 67.

B   Part of Co F, 51st Inf, transf to 71st Inf Det in Dec 67.

C   In Dec 68 personnel fm Co F, 51st Inf, formed Provisional Field Force LRRP Co, which
     service overlapped as troop transfers formed the basis of 78th and 79th Inf Dets., and was
     finally discontinued with creation of ranger companies O and P.

D   1st Bde, 101st Abn Div, LRRP Platoon assets transf to I FFV in Sep 67; skeletal LRRP
     Platoon in service until 10 Jan 68.

E   196th Inf Bde LRPD absorbed by Americal LRPD in Nov 67.

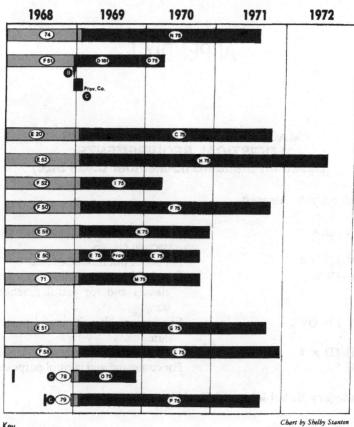

Chart by Shelby Stanton

Key

Formation Headquarters Arrival in Vietnam
Long Range Reconnaissance Patrol unit {4th Inf Div: Recondo}
Long Range Patrol Detachment
Infantry Company or Detachment (Long Range Reconnaissance)
Infantry Company (Ranger)

APPENDIX F

MACV RECONDO SCHOOL CLASS
LOGISTICAL REQUIREMENTS
(Based on Standard 65-Member Class Size)

Category A. Aircraft

UH-1D × 2	For rappelling and emergency extraction classes
UH-1D × 4	For patrol insertion purposes
UH-1B × 2	For aerial gunship adjustment fire classes and for patrol reaction standby
OV-1 or OV-2	For forward aircraft control procedures class
UH-1D × 4	For insertion purposes
OH-5A	For command and control purposes

Category B. Vehicles and Boats

¼-ton Truck × 4
¼-ton Truck Ambulance × 1
¾-ton Truck × 2
2½-ton Truck × 2
15-man Aluminum Assault Boat × 1 with Evinrude 40 hp. engine

Category C. Munitions

5.56 mm Ball × 8 cases
40mm HE × 2 cases
M18A1 Claymore × 65
C4 or TNT Explosive × 60 lbs.
Time Fuze × 50 feet
Grenades, Fragmentation × 170
Grenades, Smoke/CS × 65
81mm Mortar HE × 180 rounds
81 mm Mortar WP × 40 rounds
81mm Mortar Illum × 20 rounds
Detonating Cord × 200 feet
Non-electric Blasting Caps × 60
Grenades, Smoke × 65

Category D. Team Equipment (with 8 student patrol teams fielded)

AN/PRC-25 radio set × 8
HT-1 radio set × 8
Antenna, field-expedient × 8
Camera, 35mm Polaroid × 8
AN/GSS-9 anti-intrusion device × 8
Solution, Ringers, in 300cc transfer pack w/ accessories × 8
AT/892 antenna × 8
RT-278A or URC-10 radio × 8
Light, strobe × 16
Binoculars (7 × 35) × 8
Marker, panel × 8

Category E. Individual Equipment (per student and instructor)

STABO Harness × 1
CAR-15 or M16 × 1
Signal instructions × 1 set
Pack, First Aid, w/Bandage × 1
Canteen, 1-Quart × 2
M16 ammunition pouches × 2
M16 magazines × 18
Rope, Swiss, 6-foot length × 1
Boots, jungle, pair
Hat, Jungle camouflage × 1

Ground sheet × 1
Map, with protective plastic
Darvon tablets × 12
Knife, K-Bar, Navy × 1
Mirror, signal × 1
Compass, lensatic × 1
Injection Kit, Morphine × 2
Purification tablets, Bottle
D-Ring, Snap link × 2
Rucksack, indigenous × 1
Uniform, jungle fatigues, set
Towel, Olive-drab × 3
Poncho, indigenous × 1
Gloves, heavy duty leather
Notebook, with plastic cover
Codeine tablets × 24
Dextroamphetamine tablets × 6
Chloroquine-Primaquine tablets × 8
Polymagma tablets × 12
Cold tablets × 12
Dapsone tablets × 24
Tetracycline tablets × 24

APPENDIX G

REPUBLIC OF VIETNAM RANGER
COMPANY LOCATIONS
(Posted as of 1 July 1963)

I Corps

Thua Thien Province

1 Co-11 Bn, 2 Co-11 Bn,
3 Co-11 Bn, 4 Co-11 Bn,
105 Co

II Corps

Binh Dinh Province

205 Co, 211 Co

Pleiku Province

1 Co-21 Bn, 2 Co-21 Bn,
3 Co-21 Bn, 4 Co-21 Bn,
206 Co

Transferred to Duc My for new
22 Ranger Bn

201 Co, 202 Co, 204 Co,
207 Co, 208 Co, 209 Co

III Corps

Binh Duong Province

1 Co-32 Bn, 2 Co-32 Bn,
3 Co-32 Bn, 4 Co-32 Bn,
318 Co-33 Bn, 319 Co-33 Bn
322 Co-33 Bn,
339 Co-33 Bn, 367 Co

III Corps *(cont.)*

Binh Tuy Province	311 Co, 317 Co, 333 Co, 341 Co
Khanh Hoa Province	2 Co-11 Bn, 301 Co, 302 Cc
Saigon Capital Area	306 Co, 307 Co, 308 Co, 309 Co, 310 Co
Long Khanh Province	323 Co
Phuoc Long Province	312 Co, 313 Co, 320 Co, 329 Co, 342 Co
Phuoc Thanh Province	1 Co-31 Bn, 2 Co-31 Bn, 3 Co-31 Bn, 4 Co-31 Bn, 314 Co, 321 Co, 324 Co, 330 Co, 335 Co, 336 Co, 338 Co, 343 Co, 350 Co
Tuyen Duc Province	210 Co

IV Corps

An Giang Province	360 Co, 366 Co
An Xuyen Province	315 Co, 365 Co, 370 Co
Ba Xuyen Province	362 Co, 363 Co, 364 Co, 369 Co
Chuong Thien Province	361 Co
Dinh Tuong Province	334 Co
Kien Hoa Province	1 Co-41 Bn, 3 Co-41 Bn, 353 Co, 354 Co
Kien Phuong Province	347 Co, 348 Co
Kien Tuong Province	351 Co, 355 Co
Long An Province	2 Co-41 Bn, 356 Co, 357 Cc
Phong Dinh Province	368 Co
Vinh Long Province	4 Co-41 Bn

APPENDIX H

PARATROOPER ASSIGNMENT TO LONG RANGE PATROL UNITS
(USARV Adjutant General 28 March 1968 Position Paper)

I. PERSONNEL STATUS OF MAJOR USARV-ASSIGNED AIRBORNE COMBAT UNITS

UNIT	AUTHORIZED TOTAL	ACTUAL TOTAL	PARATROOPERS
101st Abn Div	14,594	14,654	5,791
173d Abn Bde	5,400	5,619	5,403

II. PERSONNEL STATUS OF I AND II FFV LONG-RANGE PATROL UNITS

UNIT	AUTHORIZED TOTAL	ACTUAL TOTAL	PARATROOPERS
Co E, 20th Inf	221	221	204
Co F, 51st Inf	221	221	211

III. RECOMMENDATION

Airborne qualified MOS 11B (infantry) personnel should be assigned to LRP units on a priority basis to maximize combat effectiveness. Corps-level LRP companies have almost 100% airborne qualified personnel but none have been assigned to division- and brigade-level LRP companies by USARV. There are 140 airborne troops pending assignment at the replacement battalions and 900 airborne troops on the May 68 requisition for LRP units. The proposed distribution of the 140 airborne troops presently on hold at the replacement activities is:

MOS 11B (AIRBORNE) PACKET	LRP RECIPIENT UNITS
22-Man Packet × 3:	Co E, 52nd Inf; Co F, 52nd Inf; Co E, 58th Inf
21-Man Packet × 3:	Co E, 50th Inf; Co F, 50th Inf; Co E, 51st Inf
11-Man Packet × 1:	Co F, 51st Inf

AUTHOR'S NOTE: Appendix G presented to depict the high command interest in sustaining long-range patrol units with at least partial parachute capability in Vietnam, in order to meet various contingencies demanding airborne insertion over enemy-held territory.

APPENDIX I

SURVEY OF DECORATIONS IN TYPICAL LRP/RANGER UNIT
(USARV Adjutant General 1 July 1969 Position Paper)

I. ANNUAL INDIVIDUAL DECORATIONS IN TYPICAL LRP/RANGER UNIT

Decoration	FEB 68 TO APR 68	MAY 68 TO JUL 68	AUG 68 TO OCT 68	NOV 68 TO JAN 69	FEB 69 TO APR 69	MAY 69 TO JUN 69
Medal of Honor	–	–	–	–	–	–
Distinguished Service Cross	–	–	1	–	–	–
Silver Star	–	1	2	–	12	9
Legion of Merit	–	–	–	–	–	–
Distinguished Flying Cross	–	–	–	–	–	–
Soldier's Medal	–	–	1	–	–	–
Bronze Star (V)	3	27	18	7	34	10
Bronze Star	19	2	6	13	44	18

321

Decoration	FEB 68 TO APR 68	MAY 68 TO JUL 68	AUG 68 TO OCT 68	NOV 68 TO JAN 69	FEB 69 TO APR 69	MAY 69 TO JUN 69
Air Medal (V)	–	–	–	–	–	5
Air Medal	–	2	1	–	2	103
Army Commendation Medal (V)	3	15	30	3	–	–
Army Commendation Medal	6	2	23	14	55	27
Purple Heart*	–	5	5	20	22	11

II. RECOMMENDATION

A USARV survey of a typical Long Range Patrol/Ranger company (Co E, 50th Infantry, later redesignated as Co E, 75th Infantry) was conducted in response to allegations that certain U.S. Army units received more favorable consideration. The survey results are summarized in (I) above and offer conclusive evidence that the number of individual awards are well within the normal expectations of infantry combat units. In fact, considering the elevated danger of many patrol and ranger missions, it appears that decorations are more judiciously dispensed than those in some other units. Accordingly, allegations of "award inflation" for long-range patrol/ranger personnel are without merit.

*Incomplete records: not correlated with hospital reports.

AUTHOR'S NOTE: Appendix H presented to depict the high command interest in fair distribution of awards among all units and the equitable treatment accorded long-range patrol and ranger organizations compared to other Army forces serving in Vietnam.

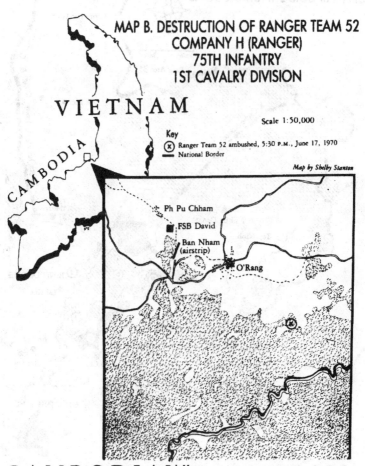

MAP B. DESTRUCTION OF RANGER TEAM 52
COMPANY H (RANGER)
75TH INFANTRY
1ST CAVALRY DIVISION

VIETNAM

Scale 1:50,000

Key

Ⓧ Ranger Team 52 ambushed, 5:30 P.M., June 17, 1970
━━ National Border

Map by Shelby Stanton

CAMBODIA

Ph Pu Chham

FSB David

Ban Nham
(airstrip)

O'Rang

CAMBODIA Dak Huyt
(river) VIETNAM

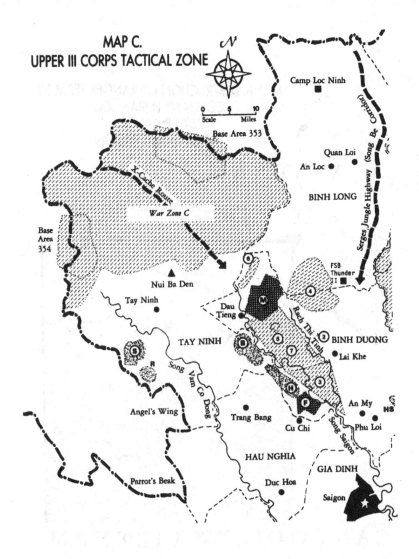

MAP C.
UPPER III CORPS TACTICAL ZONE

N

0   5   10
Scale   Miles

Camp Loc Ninh

Base Area 353

Quan Loi
An Loc

BINH LONG

X-Cache Route

Serges Jungle Highway (Song Be Corridor)

War Zone C

Base
Area
354

FSB
Thunder
II

Nui Ba Den

M

Tay Ninh

Dau
Tieng

Rach Thi Tinh

2   BINH DUONG

TAY NINH

B

6

7

Lai Khe

S

Song Vam Co Dong

R

H

3

An My

HS

F

Angel's Wing

Trang Bang

Cu Chi

Phu Loi

Song Saigon

HAU NGHIA

GIA DINH

Parrot's Beak

Duc Hoa

Saigon

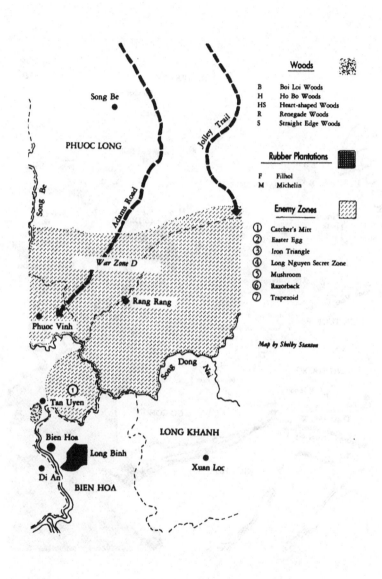

Map by Shelby Stanton

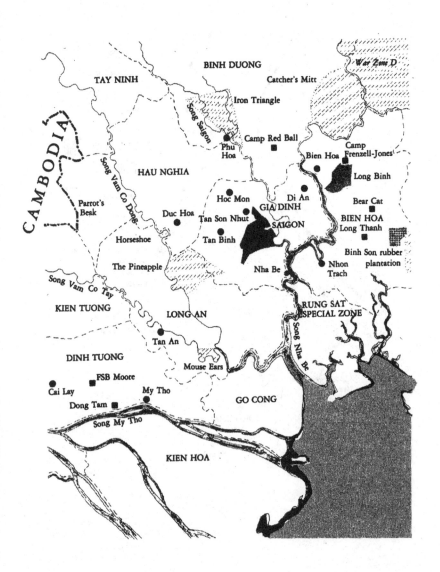

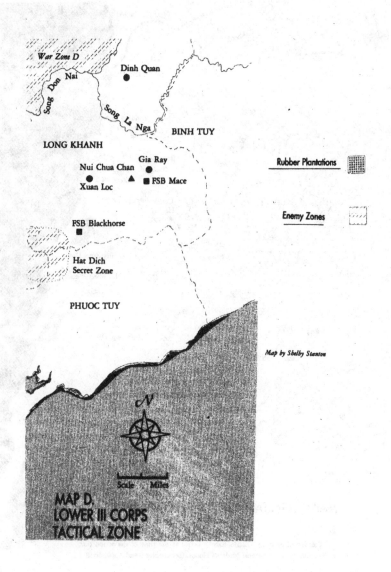

War Zone D

Dinh Quan

Song Don Nai

Song La Nga

BINH TUY

LONG KHANH

Nui Chua Chan   Gia Ray

Xuan Loc   ▲   ■ FSB Mace

FSB Blackhorse ■

Hat Dich
Secret Zone

PHUOC TUY

Rubber Plantations

Enemy Zones

Map by Shelby Stanton

N

Scale   Miles

MAP D.
LOWER III CORPS
TACTICAL ZONE

MAP E. COASTAL BINH DINH PROVINCE

Map by Shelby Stanton

Key
(X) Position of Staff Sgt. Laszlo Rabel's patrol at the time of the action that
earned him the Congressional Medal of Honor. (See chapter 9 and Appendix B.)

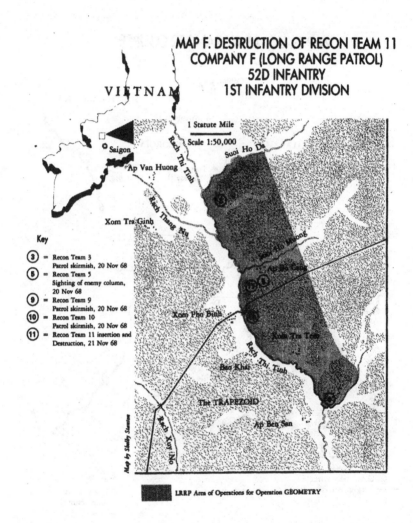

MAP F. DESTRUCTION OF RECON TEAM 11
COMPANY F (LONG RANGE PATROL)
52D INFANTRY
1ST INFANTRY DIVISION

VIETNAM

1 Statute Mile
Scale 1:50,000

Saigon
Ap Van Huong
Xom Tra Ginh

Key

(3) = Recon Team 3
Patrol skirmish, 20 Nov 68
(5) = Recon Team 5
Sighting of enemy column,
20 Nov 68
(9) = Recon Team 9
Patrol skirmish, 20 Nov 68
(10) = Recon Team 10
Patrol skirmish, 20 Nov 68
(11) = Recon Team 11 insertion and
Destruction, 21 Nov 68

Rach Thi Tinh
Suoi Ho Da
Rach Thang Nu
Xom Pho Binh
Ben Khat
The TRAPEZOID
Rach Thi Tinh
Ap Ben San
Rach Xuy No

Map by Shelby Stanton

LRRP Area of Operations for Operation GEOMETRY

MAP G. U.S. ARMY RANGER COURSE

Dahlonega
(Phase II)

SOUTH CAROLINA

• Atlanta

ALABAMA

GEORGIA

Fort Benning
(Phase I)

Fort
Stewart

Eglin
Air Force Base
(Phase III)

FLORIDA

Map by Shelby Stanton

Ranger Training Area,
Florida
(Area "O")

Crestview

De Funiak Springs

① ⑥

③

⑤

②

Valparaiso

⑩

⑦

④

Eglin AFB

Niceville

⑥

East
Bay

Choctawhatchee Bay

⑨

Santa Rosa Island

Fort Walton Beach

GULF OF MEXICO

①—⑩Auxiliary Airfield
------- Eglin Air Force Base perimeter and interior ranges

Primary ranger
swamp training
area as of 1965

NOTES

CHAPTER 1

1. Robert K. Wright Jr., *The Continental Army*, U.S. Army Center of Military History: 1983, pp. 8, 72, 73.
2. Shelby L. Stanton, *Order of Battle: U.S. Army, World War II*, Novato, Calif.: Presidio Press, 1984, pp. 262, 268, 621. In addition to the 1st–6th Ranger Infantry Battalions, the 29th Provisional Ranger Battalion was formed 20 December 1942 in England with cadre from both the 1st Ranger Battalion and the 29th Infantry Division.
3. *The Army Lineage Book, Vol. 2, Infantry*, Office of the Chief of Military History, Washington D.C.: 1953, p. 796.
4. War Department General Order 54 dtd 5 Jul 44 and War Department Military Intelligence Division, *Merrill's Marauders*, Washington D.C.: June 1945, p. 114.
5. Army Forces Far East (AFFE) Military History Section, *A Brief History of the 75th Infantry Regiment*, dtd 4 Oct 54.
6. John K. Mahon and Romana Danysh, *Army Lineage Series: Infantry, Part I: Regular Army*, Office of the Chief of Military History (OCMH), Washington, D.C.: 1972, p. 762, and *Nippon Times* dtd 30 Oct 54.
7. When the Eighth Army Ranger Company arrived in Korea, it was dispatched to IX Corps effective 10 Oct 50 and four days later it was attached to the 25th Infantry Division. See Eighth Army General Order 237 of 1950, and Eighth Army G-3 War Diary for October 1950.
8. On 28 Mar 51 the Eighth Army Ranger Company, then attached to the 25th Infantry Division, was discontinued as the 5th Ranger Company arrived in Korea on 24 Mar 51 and then assigned to replace it as the divisional ranger contingent effective 31 Mar 51. Reference Eighth Army General Order 172 of 1951 and information furnished by Charles Crockett, then a major in the Eighth Army G-3 Troop Control Section.
9. Shelby Stanton, *America's Tenth Legion: X Corps in Korea, 1950*, No-

331

vato, Calif.: Presidio Press, 1989, contains further details on the actions of the provisional raider company.

10. Eighth Army Historical Monograph Vol. III, Part 14, p. 81–82, and Ranger Company (Tentative) Manual, Ranger Training Center, Fort Benning, Ga., dtd 13 Nov 50 with Revision No. 1, dtd 28 Mar 51.

11. EUSAK G-3 Rpt, Subj: Future Employment of Ranger Companies in Korea, dtd 1 May 51, Para 2a and 2b (Capabilities).

12. CG 2d Inf Div Ltr fm BG G. C. Stewart dtd 5 Apr 51.

13. CG 3d Inf Div Ltr Subj: Comments on Proposed Employment of 3d Ranger Company, dtd 3 Apr 51.

14. CG 7th Inf Div Msg ST 239 dtd 8 Apr 51 and 187th Abn RCT Ltr, Subj: Ranger Companies, dtd 1 Apr 51.

15. CG 24th Inf Div Msg 121910 I dtd 12 Apr 51 and EUSAK 4th Hist Det Rpt, *Action on Hill 628,* dtd 15 Apr 52.

16. CG 25th Inf Div Ltr Subj: Employment of Ranger Company, dtd 1 Apr 51, and CG I Corps Ltr dtd 1 Apr 51.

17. Eighth Army Command Report Narrative, Jan 51; 4th Hist Det After Action interview with 4th Ranger Inf Co Capt. Dorsey B. Anderson; 3d Hist Det Hwachon Dam After Action Interviews, and Eighth Army Historical Monograph, Vol. III, Part 14, p. 82.

18. EUSAK G-3 DF Subj: Future Status and Employment of Ranger Units, dtd 14 May 51.

19. EUSAK CG Ltr Subj: Organization of Ranger Battalion, dtd 17 May 51.

20. CG CINCFE Msg CX 63926 dtd 2 Jun 51. In the message General Ridgway stressed, among other contributory factors to ranger ineffectiveness, their "inability to overcome language and racial recognition barriers *which are greater here than in European areas.*"

21. DA Msg 95587 dtd 5 Jul 51.

22. EUSAK G-3 Rpt, Subj: Future Employment of Ranger Companies in Korea, dtd 1 May 51, Para 2c (Limitations) and Para 3a (Discussion).

23. Sec of the Army FY 1961 Annual Rpt with special annexes, and DA Annual Rpt FY 65, p. 120.

24. US Army Europe Cable SX-6812 to Seventh Army dtd 5 Dec 60.

25. The two LRRP companies were organized under separately numbered Tables of Distribution (3779) and (3780). The Army specified, "The TD number used in parenthesis after the unit designation will not be considered an integral part of the unit designation but is there for [Table of Distribution] identification purposes only." *AGAO Directory and Station List of the United States Army,* Section I-b. The 15 Feb 62 edition of this directory contains the proper named titles of both U.S. Army LRRP companies on p. 173 and p. 508. Improper designations (such as 3779th and 3780th U.S. Army LRRP Companies) are incorrect.

26. US Army Europe DCS for Opns DF dtd 17 May 61, Subj: Long Range Reconnaissance Patrol Companies; US Army General Order 149 dtd 19 Jun 61; and 9th MHD Rpt dtd 15 Nov 61.

27. Company D previously served as the Eighth Army's separate honor guard

rifle company at Yongsan, Korea, from 24 June 1960 until 26 December 1964.

CHAPTER 2

1. 196th Inf Bde Opn Rpt dtd 7 Mar 67, p. 20.
2. USARV After Action Rpt dtd 27 Feb 67.
3. USARV After Action Rpt dtd 20 Mar 67.
4. USARV After Action Rpt dtd 1 Apr 67, p. 7.
5. 196th Inf Bde Opn Rpt dtd 22 Sep 67, p. 36 and 196th Inf Bde Opn Rpt dtd 10 Nov 67.
6. USARV After Action Rpt dtd 17 Jul 67, p. 8.
7. 196th Inf Bde Combat Interview dtd 7 Aug 67.
8. 196th Inf Bde Opn Rpt dtd 10 Nov 67.
9. Source of detachment activation and actual title is Americal Division General Order 1341 dtd 22 Nov 67. A divisional yearbook-style publication, published for veteran consumption several years later, referenced the unit erroneously as "Detachment A (Long Range Patrol)" instead of using the full title, Americal Long Range Patrol Detachment. This abbreviation mistake has been perpetuated by some postwar accounts.
10. 11th Inf Bde Unit Hist, 1 Jan–31 Jan 67, Appendix 7 to Annex B. This account clarifies the fact that the 70th Inf Det did not contribute to the forming of any Americal Division patrol unit.
11. 23d Inf Div Senior Officer Debrief dtd 13 Jun 69, p. 9.
12. USARV After Action Rpt dtd Feb 68, p. 7.
13. Americal Div Organization and Equipment Reference Data Book, p. 91.
14. USARV After Action Rpt dtd 29 Sep 69, p. 5.
15. MACV Command History: 1970, p. G-12.
16. Army Materiel Test Directorate Rpt dtd 28 Apr 69 with supplements.
17. Americal Div Recommendation for Award dtd 27 Dec 69 with statements.
18. Co G, 75th Inf, Opn Rpt dtd 31 Mar 70, p. 4.
19. Ibid., p. 5.
20. Co G 75th Inf, dtd 10 May 70, p. 5.
21. 23d Inf Div Opn Rpt dtd 15 Nov 70, p. 31.

CHAPTER 3

1. The organization and tactics of the 1st Cavalry Division in Vietnam are treated extensively in Shelby L. Stanton, *Anatomy of a Division: The 1st Cav in Vietnam,* Novato, Calif.: Presidio Press, 1987.
2. 1st Cav Div Opn Rpt dtd 15 Nov 67, p. 18.
3. 1st Cav Div Memo for Record: Opn Pershing, dtd Feb 68, p. 9.
4. 1st Cav Div Opn Rpt dtd 17 Mar 68, p. 6.
5. 1st Cav Div Opn Rpt dtd 20 Aug 68, Tab E.
6. 1st Cav Div Opn Rpt dtd 6 Dec 68, Tab E.
7. 1st Cav Div Opn Rpt dtd 17 Mar 68, p. 16.
8. Co H, 75th Inf, Ltr dtd 1 Sep 69.
9. 14th MHD, Opn Liberty Canyon Rpt, dtd 30 Jan 69, p. 31.

10. USARV After Action Rpt dtd 24 Feb 69, p. 5.
11. Co E, 52d Inf Ltr dtd 2 Jan 69, Subj: Grenade Incident.
12. Co H, 75th Inf, Ltr dtd 7 Mar 69, Subj: Exceptional Valorous Conduct.
13. Co H, 75th Inf, Ranger Newsletter 9-69, Item 5.
14. Paccerelli Ltr to author dtd 26 Apr 85.
15. EOD Rpt of Incident 99-1031-69, dtd 25 Jul 69, and 1st Cav Div CID Rpt dtd 24 Jul 69.
16. Co H, 75th Inf, Ltr dtd 16 Jul 69.
17. Co H, 75th Inf, Opn Rpt dtd 15 Feb 70.
18. 14th MHD Cbt Rpt dtd 20 Feb 70.
19. Co H, 75th Inf, Opn Rpt dtd 15 May 70.
20. 1st Cav Div Cambodian Opn Rpt, dtd 15 Feb 71, Annex K-3.
21. 1st Cav Div MIA Board Proceedings dtd 28 June 70.
22. 3d Bde, 1st Cav Div, Opn Rpt dtd 13 Nov 71, p. 22.
23. USARV Recomm for Decoration, dtd 12 Jun 72.
24. USARV Gen Order 1518 dtd 4 Jul 72.

CHAPTER 4

1. 1st Inf Div After Action Rpt dtd 26 Aug 67, p. 5.
2. 1st Inf Div Opn Birmingham Rpt and Society of the First Division Ltr dtd 2 Sep 67, Subj: Scholarship for Nuñoz family.
3. 1st Inf Div After Action Rpt dtd 4 Feb 67, p. 7. Lt. Col. Lazzell commanded the British parachute company in Aldershot, England, as part of an officer exchange program with the U.S. Army.
4. 1st Inf Div After Action Rpt dtd 25 Feb 67, p. 3.
5. 1st Inf Div After Action Rpt dtd 13 May 67.
6. 1st Inf Div After Action Rpt dtd 7 Jan 67, p. 1.
7. 1st Inf Div Opn Rpt dtd 25 Mar 68, pp. 2, 22.
8. 1st Inf Div After Action Rpt dtd 4 Nov 67, pp. 1, 7.
9. 1st Inf Div After Action Rpt dtd 11 May 68, p. 2.
10. 1st Inf Div After Action Rpt dtd 6 Apr 68, p. 6.
11. 1st Inf Div Opn Rpt dtd 27 May 68, p. 5.
12. 1st Inf Div After Action Rpt dtd 15 Mar 68, p. 3.
13. 1st Inf Div After Action Rpt dtd 4 May 68, p. 8.
14. 1st Inf Div After Action Rpt dtd 6 Jul 68, p. 1.
15. 1st Inf Div Rpt of Investigation of Facts and Circumstances Surrounding the Death of MG Ware and Others on 13 Sep 68.
16. 1st Bde, 1st Inf Div, Rpt of Investigation dtd 25 Nov 68, Witness statement of Capt. Lindman at Tab C.
17. 1st Bde, 1st Inf Div, Rpt of Investigation dtd 25 Nov 68, Witness statement of LTC Bunn at Tab C. Lieutenant Colonel Bunn was the brigade executive officer who also recommended against inserting team 11. His statement merely cited division staff rationale for the board's convenience.
18. 1st Bde, 1st Inf Div, Rpt of Investigation dtd 25 Nov 68, Witness statement of Maj Haley at Tab C.
19. 1st Bde, 1st Inf Div, Rpt of Investigation dtd 25 Nov 68, Para 6: Conclusions.

20. 1st Inf Div Opn Rpt dtd 15 May 69, p. 8.
21. 1st Inf Div Opn Rpt dtd 29 Aug 69, p. 7; 1st Inf Div General Order 2533, dtd 9 Apr 69.
22. 1st Inf Div Opn Rpt dtd 1 Dec 69, p. 20.
23. 1st Inf Div Opn Rpt dtd 10 Mar 70.
24. 1st Inf Div Opn Keystone Bluejay Rpt dtd 7 Apr 70.

CHAPTER 5

1. 4th Infantry Division territorial responsibilities fluctuated during the war, but were never under 5,000 square miles. The division operations report of the quarterly period ending 30 April 1968 (the peak of combat activities) states that its "extremely large division area of operations" was 8,000 to 10,000 square miles. 4th Inf Div Opn Rpt dtd 21 May 68, p. 63.
2. 4th Inf Div Opn Sam Houston Rpt dtd 16 May 67, pp. 36–37.
3. 4th Inf Div After Action Rpt dtd 12 May 67, p. 5.
4. 4th Inf Div Opn Rpt dtd 15 Jun 67, p. 12.
5. 4th Inf Div Opn Francis Marion Rpt dtd 25 Nov 67, p. 9.
6. 4th Inf Div After Action Rpt dtd 11 Jun 67, Annex: 2d Bde LRRP.
7. USARV Cbt Intell Review dtd 23 Jan 68, p. 21.
8. 4th Inf Div After Action Rpt dtd 11 Jun 67, Annex: 2d Bde LRRP.
9. 4th Inf Div After Action Rpt dtd 5 Nov 67.
10. USARV After Action Rpt dtd 17 Jun 67, p. 1.
11. 4th Inf Div Opn Francis Marion Rpt dtd 25 Nov 67, p. 10, and USARV Cbt Intell Review dtd 23 Jan 68, p. 25.
12. 4th Inf Div Opn Rpt dtd 7 Mar 68, pp. 1, 8.
13. 4th Inf Div Opn Rpt dtd 21 May 68, p. 12, 18 Aug 68, p. 12, and 15 Nov 68, p. 11.
14. 4th Inf Div Opn Task Force Mathews Rpt dtd 13 Jun 68.
15. 4th Inf Div After Action Rpt dtd 6 Oct 68.
16. 4th Inf Div Ltr dtd 17 Sep 68, p. 4.
17. 4th Inf Div Ltr dtd 17 Sep 68, Subj: Tactical Notes: Employment of Short Range Patrol Screen.
18. 4th Inf Div Report of Inquiry dtd 27 Nov 68, Hamby testimony.
19. Ibid., Pisarcik testimony.
20. Ibid., Hancock testimony.
21. DA MIA Board dtd 8 Oct 69 and Rpt of Casualty dtd 11 Mar 71.
22. 4th Inf Div After Action Rpt dtd 15 Dec 68, p. 3.
23. 4th Inf Div Senior Off Debrief: MG Donn R. Pepke, dtd 10 Nov 69, p. 17.
24. 4th Inf Div MIA Board dtd 17 Feb 69.
25. Co K, 75th Inf, Opn Rpt dtd 5 Apr 70.
26. 4th Inf Div Senior Off Debrief: MG Donn R. Pepke, dtd 10 Nov 69, Incl. 9.
27. 4th Inf Div Cbt Rpt dtd 24 Nov 69.
28. Co K, 75th Inf, Opn Rpt dtd 5 Apr 70, p. 3.
29. USARV After Action Rpt dtd 22 Dec 69, p. 7.
30. 4th Inf Div Opn Rpt dtd 31 May 70, pp. 13–15.

31. Ibid., p. 16.
32. 4th Inf Div Opn Rpt dtd 20 Aug 70, p. 20.
33. Co K, 75th Inf, Opn Rpts dtd 5 Apr 70, 4 May 70, and 31 Jul 70.
34. 4th Inf Div Opn Rpts dtd 20 Aug 70, p. 36, and 20 Nov 70, p. 40.
35. 4th Inf Div Keystone Robin-B Rpt dtd 13 Dec 70, D-1-1.

CHAPTER 6

1. U.S. Army Medical Dept, *Internal Medicine in Vietnam*, Vol. 1, Office of the Surgeon General: 1977, pp. 13, 64.
2. Footwear and clothing adjustments for the Mekong Delta are covered in Shelby L. Stanton, *U.S. Army Uniforms of the Vietnam War*, Harrisburg, Pa.: Stackpole Books, 1989.
3. The Vietnamese, and those in Viet Cong units, did not suffer the same degree of susceptibility to medical hardships because they wore lighter clothing and sandals, could dry their skin at night, and were better acclimatized to tropical conditions.
4. USARV After Action Rpt dtd 29 Apr 67, p. 11.
5. Fulton, Maj. Gen. William B., *Vietnam Studies: Riverine Operations*, Dept. of the Army, Washington, D.C.: 1973.
6. USARV After Action Rpt dtd 5 Aug 67, p. 11.
7. 9th Inf Div Opn Rpt dtd 31 Jul 67, p. 20.
8. 9th Inf Div Opn Rpt dtd 23 Dec 67, pp. 13, 31.
9. USARV After Action Rpt dtd 2 Sep 67, p. 2.
10. USARV After Action Rpt dtd 28 Oct 67, p. 10.
11. USARV After Action Rpt dtd 26 Aug 67, p. 3. Army Special Forces was involved in sampan warfare much earlier, but not in this particular sector of the Mekong Delta.
12. 9th Inf Div Opn Rpt dtd 15 Feb 68, p. 119.
13. 9th Inf Div Opn Rpt dtd 15 Feb 68, pp. 3, 11.
14. USARV After Action Rpt dtd 6 Jan 68, p. 13.
15. USARV Investigation Rpt dtd 12 Jan 68, DA MIA Board dtd 24 Mar 71.
16. 9th Inf Div Opn Rpt dtd 15 Feb 68, p. 202.
17. 9th Inf Div Opn Rpt dtd 12 May 68, p. 16.
18. 9th Inf Div After Action Rpt dtd 1 May 68, p. 8.
19. 9th Inf Div Opn Rpt dtd 20 Aug 68, pp. 13, 14.
20. 9th Inf Div After Action Rpt dtd 18 Sep 68, p. 3.
21. DA Army Concept Team in Vietnam Final Rpt dtd 23 Feb 68.
22. 1st Bde, 9th Inf Div, Opn Rpt dtd 31 Oct 68, p. 8, and 9th Inf Div After Action Rpt dtd 7 Aug 68, p. 6.
23. 9th Inf Div Opn Rpt dtd 15 Nov 68, p. 13.
24. 1st Bde, 9th Inf Div, Opn Rpt dtd 29 Jan 69, p. 5.
25. 9th Inf Div After Action Rpt dtd 11 Dec 68.
26. 9th Inf Div Opn Rpt dtd 15 Feb 69, pp. 11, 12.
27. 9th Inf Div Opn Rpt dtd 15 May 69, pp. 16, 17.
28. 1st Bde, 9th Div Opn Rpt dtd 30 Apr 69, p. 3.
29. 1st Bde, 9th Inf Div, Opn Rpt dtd 30 Jun 69, p. 3.
30. 9th Inf Div After Action Rpt dtd 18 Jun 69, p. 3.

31. 9th Inf Div Redeployment After Action Rpt dtd 27 Aug 69.
32. 3d Bde, 9th Inf Div, Opn Rpt dtd 1 Dec 69.
33. Co E, 75th Inf, Opn Rpt dtd 31 Jan 70.
34. 3d Bde, 9th Inf Div, Opn Rpts dtd 14 May 70 and 15 Aug 70.
35. 3d Bde, 9th Inf Div, Keystone Robin Rpt dtd 8 Oct 70.

CHAPTER 7

1. 25th Inf Div Opn Rpt dtd 30 Aug 66, pp. 13, 22.
2. 25th Inf Div Opn Rpt dtd 18 Nov 66, p. 12. Actual patrol number from August to October 1966 was twenty-six patrols.
3. 25th Inf Div Gadsen Opn Rpt and After Action Rpt dtd 27 Feb 67, p. 8.
4. 25th Inf Div Opn Rpt dtd 19 May 67, p. 17.
5. 25th Inf Div "Join LRRP!" notice dtd 22 May 67.
6. 25th Inf Div After Action Rpt dtd 22 May 67, p. 8.
7. 135 MI Group Rpt, Subj: Purported American Personnel Held by Hostile Foreign Elements, dtd 1 Aug 67.
8. 4th Inf Div Board Proceedings dtd 28 Jun 67; 135th MI Group DA Form 339 dtd 19 Jul 67, and DA MIA Rpts dtd 11 Mar 71.
9. 25th Inf Div Opn Rpt dtd 14 Nov 67, p. 49.
10. 25th Inf Div Opn Rpt.
11. 25th Inf Div After Action Rpt dtd 19 Feb 68.
12. 25th Inf Div Opn Rpt dtd 14 Feb 68, p. 7.
13. Co F, 50th Inf, After Action Rpt dtd 6 Apr 68.
14. Co F, 50th Inf, After Action Rpt dtd 9 Apr 68.
15. 25th Inf Div After Action Rpt dtd 3 Jun 68, p. 3.
16. 18th MHD After Action Rpt dtd 30 May 68.
17. 25th Inf Div After Action Rpt dtd 5 Aug 68.
18. 25th Inf Div After Action Rpt dtd 23 Dec 68; Co F, 50th Inf, Rpt dtd 30 Nov 68.
19. 3d Sqdn, 4th Cav, Opn Rpt dtd 31 Jan 69, p. L-2.
20. 25th Inf Div Opn Rpt dtd 1 Feb 69, Sec I-B; Co F, 50th Inf, After Action Rpt dtd 19 Dec 68.
21. 25th Inf Div Senior Officer Debriefing Rpt dtd 1 Apr 70, p. 39.
22. 18th MHD After Action Rpt dtd 19 Oct 69.
23. 25th Inf Div Opn Rpt dtd 31 Jul 70; Co F, 75th Inf, Opn Rpt dtd 1 May 70.
24. 18th MHD After Action Rpt for Opn dtd 2–6 Apr 70, pp. 1–7, Inclosures 4, 5, and 8.
25. Co F, 75th Inf, Opn Rpt dtd 1 May 70: Lessons Learned Annex.
26. 25th Inf Div Opn Rpt dtd 31 Jul 70.
27. 25th Inf Div Ltr of Instruction: Combat Operations Ranger Company, dtd 28 Jun 70.
28. 25th Inf Div Opn Rpt dtd 31 Oct 70, p. 33.
29. 25th Inf Div Opn Rpt dtd 31 Jul 70, p. 52; Keystone Robin Bravo After Action Rpt dtd 15 Dec 70, Tab A.
30. 2d Bde, 25th Inf Div, Redeployment Rpt dtd 28 Apr 71, pp. 14, 54.

CHAPTER 8

1. On 9 June 1965 the 1st Brigade, 101st Airborne Division, was reorganized before departure from the United States to the TOE (Table of Organization and Equipment) 57-F series with an authorized strength of 223 officers, twenty-two warrant officers, and 3,868 enlisted troops. Third Army General Order 9 dtd 9 Jun 65 and Troop List No. 23 dtd 31 Jul 65.
2. 322d MID Hist Rpt, p. 46.
3. Dennis Foley Ltr to author dtd 20 Sep 90.
4. Lt. Jim Gardner received the posthumous Medal of Honor for his actions in this battle. Details of Tiger Force participation in these battles can be referenced in David H. Hackworth, *About Face*, New York: Simon & Schuster, 1989, pp. 501, 519.
5. 322d MID Rpt "First Brigade in the RVN: Jul 65–Jan 68" and 1st Bde, 101st Abn Div, After Action Rpt, 3 Mar 68, p. 3.
6. Dept Army MIA Board Ltr dtd 29 Oct 71. Donald Stephen Newton of San Pedro, California, was not heard of again and remains missing.
7. 1st Bde, 101st Abn Div, Opn Rpt dtd 13 Aug 66, Incl 1.
8. 1st Bde, 101st Abn Div, After Action Rpt dtd 6 Mar 67.
9. 1st Bde, 101st Abn Div, After Action Rpt dtd 17 Apr 67.
10. 1st Bde, 101st Abn Div, After Action Rpt dtd 19 Jun 67, p. 3.
11. 101st Abn Div Opn Rpt dtd 31 Jan 68, pp. 19–20.
12. Co L, 75th Inf, Transmittal of Unit Hist Supplement, dtd 19 Mar 69, p. 1.
13. 101st Abn Div After Action Rpt dtd 19 Aug 68, p. 6.
14. 101st Abn Div After Action Rpt dtd 3 Mar 69, p. 6.
15. 101st Abn Div "Rendezvous with Destiny," Fall 70, p. 9.
16. Co L, 75th Inf, Opn Rpt dtd 19 Mar 70, Para 1.
17. Co L, 75th Inf, Opn Rpt dtd 1 Apr 70.
18. Co L, 75th Inf, Opn Rpt dtd 20 Aug 70.
19. 101st Abn Div Senior Off Debrief dtd 15 Jan 71 with annexes.
20. Co L, 75th Inf, Opn Rpt dtd 5 Nov 70.
21. Co L, 75th Inf, Opn Rpts dtd 31 Aug 70, 30 Nov 70, and 31 Dec 70.
22. Co L, 75th Inf, Opn Rpts dtd 1 Mar 71 and 1 Apr 71.
23. Co L, 75th Inf, Opn Rpt dtd 1 May 70 and USARV MIA Rpt dtd 29 Jun 71.
24. Co L, 75th Inf, Opn Rpt dtd 4 Nov 71.
25. Co L, 75th Inf, Ranger Team Debrief dtd 7 Sep 71.
26. Co L, 75th, Inf Opn Rpt dtd 4 Nov 71, p. 5.
27. Co L, 75th Inf, Opn Rpt dtd 26 Nov 71.

CHAPTER 9

1. 173d Abn Bde Opn Rpt dtd 15 Oct 66, p. 1.
2. 173d Abn Bde Opn Rpt dtd 15 Feb 67, Tab C, pp. 12, 13.
3. 173d Abn Bde Opn Toledo Rpt, dtd 15 Dec 66, pp. 16–33.
4. 173d Abn Bde Opn Waco Rpt dtd 2 Jan 67, p. 5.
5. Troop E, 17th Cav, After Action Rpt dtd 25 Feb 67, pp. 14–15.

6. Ibid., pp. 15–16.

7. 173d Abn Bde Incident Rpt dtd 15 Nov 67, p. 10.

8. 173d Abn Bde Opn Rpt dtd 15 Nov 67, p. 17.

9. 173d Abn Bde, Battle of Dak To Rpt, dtd 10 Dec 67, pp. 6, 10.

10. Presidential Unit Citation for the period 6–23 Nov 67 by authority of DA General Order 42 of 1969 and 5 of 1970, as amended. The orders refer to the LRRP Platoon by its later title of the 74th Infantry Detachment, which was in fact not activated until after the above-cited time interval.

11. 173d Abn Bde Opn Rpt dtd 15 May 68, p. 39.

12. 173d Abn Bde Opn Rpt dtd 15 Aug 68.

13. 173d Abn Bde Opn Rpt dtd 15 May 68, p. 46.

14. 173d Abn Bde After Action Rpt dtd 11 Nov 68, p. 1.

15. 173d Abn Bde Opn Rpt dtd 15 Nov 68, p. 33.

16. 173d Abn Bde Incident Rpt dtd 25 Nov 68.

17. The Vietnam records in the custody of the National Archives reflect much wartime disorientation, created by 173d Airborne Brigade requirements from I Field Force Vietnam to support both ranger companies, so that documents pertaining to Company C and N at both field force and brigade level must be carefully analyzed.

18. 173d Abn Bde Recommend for Award dtd 9 Jun 69.

19. Ibid., Narrative Summary.

20. Co N, 75th Inf, Opn Rpt dtd 29 Mar 70, and 173d Abn Bde Opn Washington Green Rpt, p. 20.

21. The Remote Firing Device was a box implanted in the ground. One of its two wires was tied into the detonating cord that connected the claymore mines, while the other wire was strung up in shrubbery or trees like an antenna. The camouflaged claymores and the buried boxes were aligned along a trail or ambush zone, and then the rangers would take up distant positions, up to 1,000 feet away, with hand-held actuators. As long as the rangers had a clear visual line of sight to the boxes, they could "fire" the boxes by adjusting the firing device switches on their actuators to match desired box codes. For example, if a ranger wanted to fire Box "A-10" he put one switch to "A" and the other to "10" and pushed the activator switch. In this manner, a ranger team could set up an ambush kill zone along a trail at the base of a hill and facing into the slope, then take up positions on top of the hill and ambush enemy troops using the trail below them.

22. Co N, 75th Inf, Opn Rpt dtd 3 Aug 70, Para 2. The rangers connected a trip wire, placed across a likely approach route, to a clothespin-type electrical activator. The electrical device was hooked up to a small power source and then to a daisy chain of claymore mines or grenades. The mine could be easily disarmed by removing the system's power unit.

23. Rope ladders could not be used where forest canopies exceeded forty feet, or where injured or overloaded team members had difficulty climbing. The Special Forces–invented McGuire rigs also had problems (see chapter 14). Company N rangers reported their preference for ropes and ladders fitted with working red-filtered flashlights attached to the ends of the lines,

even in daylight. The lights made it easier for the rangers to see separate ropes being lowered, and pilots were able to judge hover altitude as the lights neared or touched the ground.

24. John Lawton Ltr to author dtd 18 Mar 91.
25. I FFV Gen Order 228 dtd 6 Mar 70 and Lawton Ltr to author dtd 18 Mar 91.
26. 173d Abn Bde After Action Rpt dtd 14 Sep 70, p. 1.
27. 173d Abn Bde After Action Rpt dtd 9 Nov 70, pp. 1, 8.
28. 173d Abn Bde After Action Rpt dtd 14 Feb 71, p. 3.
29. 173d Abn Bde Brightlight After Action Rpt dtd 20 Feb 71.
30. 173d Abn Bde After Action Rpt dtd 29 Mar 71, p. 3 (b).
31. 173d Abn Bde After Action Rpt dtd 12 Apr 71, p. 2.
32. 173d Abn Bde After Action Rpt dtd 26 Apr 71, p. 6.
33. 173d Abn Bde After Action Rpt dtd 12 Apr 71, p. 3.
34. 173d Abn Bde After Action Rpt dtd 21 Jun 71, p. 7.
35. Technically, this distinction was earned by Company N alone because both the ranger company and its parent 173d Airborne Brigade remained on parachute status throughout their Vietnam service. Company L of the 75th Infantry was also parachute-qualified, but its parent 101st Airborne Division had been removed from jump-status capability during July 1968.

CHAPTER 10

1. Shelby L. Stanton, *Vietnam Order of Battle*, Millwood, N.Y.: Kraus Reprints, 1986, contains a detailed overview of Army organization and responsibilities in Vietnam.
2. Shelby L. Stanton, *Green Berets at War: U.S. Army Special Forces in Southeast Asia, 1956–1975*, Novato, Calif.: Presidio Press, 1985, provides a narrative history of wartime Special Forces that explains their somewhat complex operational demands and relationships with the rest of the Army in Vietnam.
3. JCS Document 2472/99 dtd 22 Jun 67 and MACV Command History: 1967, Vol I, p. 158.
4. USARPAC General Order 170 dtd 19 Sep 67 specified "maximum number of personnel required by this action [230 men] will be assigned from locally available resources without MPA-PCS costs; the remainder will be procured through application of normal personnel requisitioning procedures."
5. USARV General Order 4916 dtd 26 Sep 67; I FFV Letter of Instruction 2-67 dtd 23 Sep 67; and I FFV Opn Rpt dtd 15 Nov 67. Company E of the 20th Infantry had served over five years previously, from 24 June 1960 until 1 January 1966, as a separate rifle company at Sihung-Ni, Korea.
6. Co E, 20th Inf, Hist Rpt dtd 6 Apr 68.
7. Ibid., and 4th Inf Div Opn Rpt dtd 26 Dec 67. USARV General Order 5271 dtd 14 Oct 67 attached Co E (LRP), 20th Inf, to the 4th Inf Div "for administration and logistics" effective 15 Oct 67.
8. Co E, 20th Inf, Hist Rpt dtd 6 Apr 68, p. 4.
9. II CTZ MSFC Opn Summary dtd 31 Dec 67.

10. Co E, 20th Inf, Hist Rpt dtd 6 Apr 68, p. 5.
11. I FFV Opn Rpt dtd 15 Feb 68, p. 5.
12. 4th Inf Div After Action Rpt dtd 10 Mar 68.
13. I FFV Opn Rpt dtd 15 May 68, p. 3. In mid-July recon training for the 22d ARVN Division was taken over by the 173d Airborne Brigade, leaving Company E with responsibility for one division plus the Duc My ranger course.
14. 5th SFG II CTZ Mike Force After Action Rpt dtd 18 Apr 68.
15. I FFV Opn Rpt dtd 15 May 68, p. 4; I FFV Opn Rpt dtd 15 Aug 68, pp. 3, 8.
16. USARV After Action Rpt dtd 24 Feb 69, p. 7.
17. I FFV Opn Rpt dtd 15 Nov 68 and I FFV dtd 15 Feb 69, pp. 8, 9.
18. USARV Gen Order 542 dtd 16 Feb 69.
19. I FFV Opn Rpt dtd 15 May 70, p. 11.
20. 173d Abn Bde Opn Washington Green Rpt, pp. 8, 11.
21. I FFV Opn Rpt dtd 15 Aug 69, p. 9.
22. Co C, 75th Inf, Opn Rpt dtd 23 Feb 70.
23. I FFV Opn Rpt dtd 15 Nov 69, p. 11.
24. Task Force South After Action Rpt dtd 30 Sep 69.
25. I FFV General Order 1133 dtd 31 Dec 69.
26. Co C, 75th Inf, After Action Rpt dtd 24 Nov 69.
27. *Typhoon*, I Field Force Vietnam magazine published by 5th PID, Vol. IV, No. 5 (May 1970 issue), p. 2.
28. Co C, 75th Inf, After Action Rpt dtd 23 Dec 69.
29. I FFV Opn Rpt dtd 15 May 70, p. 8.
30. Co C, 75th Inf, Opn Rpt dtd 3 Jun 70., Para 2-b and 2-c.
31. Co C, 75th Inf, Opn Rpt dtd 3 Jun 70.
32. 4th Inf Div Opn Binh Tay dtd 21 Jul 70, p. 10.
33. 4th Inf Div Opn Binh Tay I Rpt dtd 21 Jul 70.
34. I FFV Opn Rpt dtd 15 Aug 70, pp. 6, 10; 4th Inf Div Opn Rpt dtd 20 Aug 70, pp. 21, 29.
35. Co C, 75th Inf, Patrol Rpt dtd 31 May 70.
36. Co C, 75th Inf, Opn Rpt dtd 5 Aug 70.
37. USARV Tech Rpt of Army Aircraft Accident dtd 1 Jun 70.
38. 4th Inf Div Opn Rpt dtd 20 Nov 70, pp. 21–23; 173d Abn Bde Opn Washington Green Rpt, p. 20.
39. USARV Gen Order 5079 dtd 17 Nov 70.

CHAPTER 11

1. Organizational details and functions of U.S. Army units can be referenced in Shelby L. Stanton, *Vietnam Order of Battle*, Millwood, N.Y.: Kraus Reprints, 1986.
2. General Westmoreland was faced with an urgent requirement to increase reconnoitering efforts across the border into Cambodia and decided to withdraw Project Sigma from Major General Weyand's control and transfer it to MACV-SOG for strategic theater-level application. Westmoreland

informed Weyand that this transfer was to become effective 1 November 1967.

3. Details on the Special Forces reconnaissance transactions are further addressed in Shelby L. Stanton, *Green Berets at War: U.S. Army Special Forces in Southeast Asia, 1956–1975*, Novato, Calif.: Presidio Press, 1985.

4. USARPAC General Order 170 dtd 19 Sep 67 and USARV General Order 4916 dtd 26 Sep 67.

5. II FFV Opn Rpt dtd 31 Oct 67, p. 36.

6. II FFV Opn Rpt dtd 21 Feb 68, p. 22.

7. II FFV Opn Rpt dtd 15 Aug 68, p. 41.

8. II FFV Opn Rpt dtd 26 Feb 69, p. 36.

9. Dennis Foley Ltr to author dtd 20 Sep 90.

10. II FFV Opn Rpt dtd 31 Jan 69, p. 39.

11. Company F was a field force asset and was available for deployment in III Corps Tactical Zone and IV Corps Tactical Zone. There were some small patrols conducted in the northern part of IV Corps Tactical Zone, but the lack of concealment in that region discouraged the company from patrolling there.

12. II FFV Opn Rpt dtd 31 Jan 69, p. 5.

13. USARPAC Annual Hist Summary: 1 Jan–31 Dec 68, p. 219.

14. Ibid., p. 220.

15. USARV Rpt dtd 27 Jan 68, p. 13, and II FFV Opn Rpt dtd 31 Jan 69, p. 58.

16. CG USARV Message to CG II FFV Subj: Personnel Guidance for D/151st Inf (LRP) dtd 0934Z 10 Jan 69. The Army corps-level ranger company table of organization called for a major in command instead of a captain, and captains leading the platoons instead of lieutenants.

17. AVHGA-PO DCS DF, Subj: Commander of D Co, 151st Inf (LRP), dtd 15 Feb 69.

18. USAF Seventh Air Force DOI Release 4345.

19. II FFV Opn Rpt dtd 30 Apr 69, p. 33.

20. USARV After Action Rpt V-19, p. 12.

21. II FFV Opn Rpt dtd 30 Apr 69, p. 5; II FFV Opn Rpt dtd 31 Jul 69, p. 6.

22. USARV After Action Rpt dtd 15 Sep 69, p. 8.

23. *Hurricane*, II Field Force Vietnam magazine published by 16th PID No. 25 (Nov 69 issue), p. 36.

24. II FFV Opn Rpt dtd 17 Nov 69, p. 37.

25. Co D, 75th Inf, Opn Rpt dtd 15 Feb 70.

26. Co D, 75th Inf, Opn Rpt dtd 2 Apr 70.

27. II FFV Opn Rpt dtd 14 Feb 70, p. 6; II FFV Opn Rpt dtd 30 Apr 70, p. 6.

CHAPTER 12

1. USARV After Action Rpt dtd 11 May 68, p. 3.

2. 199th Inf Bde Opn Rpt dtd 30 Apr 69.

3. 199th Inf Bde Opn Rpt dtd 31 Jul 69.

4. USARV After Action Rpt dtd 29 Sep 69, p. 16.

5. Co M, 75th Inf, Opn Rpt dtd 13 Mar 70, p. 4.
6. Co M, 75th Inf, Opn Rpt dtd 15 May 70.
7. 199th Inf Bde After Action Rpt: Opn Keystone Robin, dtd 12 Oct 70, p. 125.
8. 3d Bde, 82d Abn Div, Opn Rpt dtd 12 May 68.
9. USARV IO Rpt V-5 dtd 3 Feb 69, p. 13.
10. 3d Bde, 82d Abn Div, Opn Rpt dtd 15 May 69, p. 6.
11. 3d Bde, 82d Abn Div, Opn Rpt dtd 31 Jul 69, p. 8.
12. 3d Bde, 82d Abn Div, Opn Rpt dtd 20 Nov 69.
13. DA Gen Order 204 dtd 4 Aug 70.
14. Company O, 75th Inf, Unit Hist Rpt dtd 12 Feb 71, Classified Overview segment.
15. Company O, 75th Inf, Unit Hist Rpt dtd 12 Feb 71, p. 11.
16. Headquarters U.S. Army Alaska Information Office Press Release No. 2-8-38, dtd 12 Feb 71.
17. Co O, 75th Inf, 1972 Unit History, Section II-6.
18. Co O, 75th Inf, 1972 Unit History, Section III-7.
19. 1st Bde, 5th Inf Div, Opn Rpt dtd 30 May 69, with statistical compilations carried through Opn Rpt of 30 Apr 70.
20. USARV IO Rpt V-13 dtd 31 Mar 69, p. 13.
21. USARV After Action Rpt dtd 16 Jun 69, p. 16.
22. USARV After Action Rpt dtd 2 Jun 69, p. 5.
23. 1st Bde, 5th Inf Div, Keystone Oriole (Bravo) Rpt dtd 19 Aug 71.

CHAPTER 13

1. SF MTT Rpt fm Col Ewald to Col Blackburn dtd 22 Jun 60.
2. USARV Rpt I-26 dtd 7 Aug 65, p. 1.
3. MACV After Action Rpt dtd 26 Jun 65, p. 5.
4. PUC Recomm dtd 26 Apr 65.
5. Jeffrey J. Clarke, *Advice and Support: The Final Years (U.S. Army in Vietnam)*, U.S. Army Center of Military History: 1988, pp. 102, 177.
6. MACV After Action Rpt dtd 7 Aug 68, p. 1.
7. MACV After Action Rpt dtd 17 May 67, p. 3.
8. MACV After Action Rpt dtd 24 May 67, p. 5.
9. MACV After Action Rpt dtd 12 Jul 67, p. 1.
10. USA Adv Gp II CTZ After Action Rpt dtd 2 Jun 68.
11. MACV Duc My Ranger Training Center Ltr dtd 21 Feb 69, p. 2.
12. Ibid., p. 1.
13. Statistical data and quotes throughout the discussion of the 3d Ranger Group situation during 1969 are derived from RVN JGS Inspector General Rpt #5624/TTM/TTQL/STT/K dtd 8 Dec 69.
14. Co. Le Quang Hien Inspec Gen Rpt dtd 8 Dec 69, Para 5d, Logistics.
15. Ibid., Para 5d (d), Barracks and Housing.
16. Ibid., Para 5 (e), Mess Service and Commissary Management.
17. Ibid., Para 5 (g), Problems and Recommendation of IG Team: Classes.
18. Ibid., Para 5 (c), Psychological Operations.
19. Ibid., Para 8 (Conclusion).

20. Recomm for MOH dtd 11 Sep 70 with supporting statements.
21. HQ Delta Mil Assistance Cmd Rpt dtd 8 Dec 70, with attachments.
22. Jeffrey J. Clarke, *Advice and Support: The Final Years (U.S. Army in Vietnam)*, U.S. Army Center of Military History: 1988, p. 458.
23. Quote from PACOM Summary #64-60 dtd 1 Apr 60, p. 9.
24. Origins of Thai ranger program based on 1973 correspondence between General Tienchai Sirisumpan and author, to include Thai MOD Order 46/12682 establishing the RTA Field Ranger Battalion and directives governing the changes in the Royal Thai Army Special Warfare Center. The author was a ranger officer of Detachment A-41 (Ranger) and was wounded in action while on a patrolling mission near Nam Yu, Laos.

CHAPTER 14

1. DA Field Manual 21-50, Ranger Training and Ranger Operations, Jan 62, and Ranger Dept Standard Operating Procedures dtd 1 Jun 60 and 1 Feb 64, with Change 1 dtd 8 Feb 65.
2. HQ Third Army TD 61-315 dtd 26 Apr 60 and 1960 Ranger Dept SOP. From 1960 to 1965 the ranger department was authorized ninety-eight officers, 169 enlisted men, and eight civilians. During the Vietnam years, the ranger department was organized under TDA (Table of Distribution and Allowances) 3A-3151 with seventy-five officers, one warrant officer, 224 enlisted men, and eleven civilians. Of these 311 personnel, 117 were posted to Fort Benning, ninety-nine to the Army mountain ranger camp, and ninety-five to the Florida ranger camp.
3. USAIS Hist Supplement dtd 28 Mar 66, p. 8, and 21 Mar 67, p. 10. During April 1965 ranger instructors were trained in helicopter rappelling by the 11th Air Assault Division (Test), but helicopter shortages at Fort Benning prevented teaching the tactics to ranger students until the following year.
4. Frostbite and trench foot cold-weather injuries accompanied every winter ranger class. A tightening of ranger safety standards was imposed, however, after several ranger deaths occurred in back-to-back classes during the winter of 1970-71.
5. Critique of Fort Benning ranger problems 8630 and 8635 in USAIS files for 1965-66. During the 1966 "ranger searches," a total of thirteen scout dog platoons were involved (25th, 26th, 34th, 35th, 38th–42d, 44th, 48th, 49th, and 50th).
6. Ranger Dept Ltr dtd 26 Aug 65, Subj: Relocation of Florida Ranger Camp and USAIS Hist Supplement, dtd 28 Mar 66, p. 38. Following the creation of the ranger department in October 1951, a Third Army team completely surveyed available military terrain in the eastern United States from the Atlantic coast to the Mississippi River. This team had originally selected the Fort Benning, Dahlonega, and Eglin Auxiliary Field #7 ranger camp sites. Ranger Dept DF File No. GNKEAD-J, Subj: Report of TDY Trip to Ranger Camp, Eglin Field, and Camp Stewart, Ga., dtd 4 Dec 53.
7. CONARC 1966 Hist Supplement, p. 33, and BG J. T. Corley Ltr to MG R. H. York dtd 11 Mar 66.

8. DA DCSPER-SED Ltr dtd 16 Aug 66, Subj: Report of DA Board to Review Army Officer Schools.

9. USAIS Hist Supplements, dtd 28 Mar 66 and 21 Mar 67, Appendix I.

10. CONARC Annual Hist Summary, 1 July 1966–30 June 1967, p. 175.

11. CONARC Ltr to Army Vice of Staff Gen. Ralph E. Haines Jr. dtd 14 Oct 67, p. 3.

12. DA ODCS Indiv Tng Semiannual History, Jan–Jun 70, Section III.

13. CONARC Annual Hist Summary, FY 1971, p. 246.

14. 5th SFG MACV Recondo School Field Grade Officer Debriefing Rpt dtd 1 Nov 68, p. 2; MACV Recondo School Instructor Lists dtd 19 Jan 67 and 10 Dec 70.

15. William C. Westmoreland, *A Soldier Reports,* Garden City, N.Y.: Doubleday, 1976, p. 31.

16. DA Institute of Heraldry correspondence files with MACV Recondo School Ltr AVGB-RS Ltr Subj: Recondo Badge, dtd 1 Nov 68, with DA disapproval.

17. 25th Inf Div After Action Rpt dtd 29 Jan 68, p. 1.

18. 5th SFG MACV Recondo School After Action Rpt to OPORD R-10-67 dtd 7 Apr 67, with annexes.

19. Shelby L. Stanton, *U.S. Army Uniforms of the Vietnam War,* Harrisburg, Pa.: Stackpole Books, 1989, pp. 149, 150. This reference has illustrations and more details about the Stabo extraction harness and its employment.

20. MACV Recondo School Radio Communications Techniques, dtd 27 Aug 68.

21. 1st Bde, 101st Abn Bde, Opn Rpts dtd 31 Jul 67, p. 29, and 2 Oct 67, pp. 27–28.

22. More details on training the field force patrol companies is contained in chapters 11 and 12.

23. 5th SFG Recondo School Ltr dtd 26 Oct 68, Subj: Naming of Combat Orientation Course Site on Hon Tre Island.

24. 5th SFG MACV Recondo School After Action Rpt to OPORD R-21-68 dtd 5 Jul 68, with Annex A (Intelligence).

25. MACV Recondo School Ltr dtd 28 May 69, Subj: LRRP Commanders' Conference.

26. The nationality breakdown for MACV Recondo School students was 4,966 Americans; 296 Koreans; 193 Thais; 130 Vietnamese; 22 Filipino; and 18 Australians. Source: MACV Recondo School Unit History S/C 4.

27. 1st Bde, 4th Inf Div, Opn Rpt dtd 31 Jan 67, p. 17. The Recondo Preparatory Course was initially a two-day program, but was expanded during fall 1967 into a five-day course. Reference 4th Inf Div Opn Rpt dtd 26 Dec 67, p. 10.

28. USA Avn Center 1967, 1968, and 1969 Annual Hist Supplements, pp. 96–97.

29. U.S. Continental Army Command (CONARC) Ltr dated 14 Oct 67 in Fort Monroe historical files and Fort Benning Annual Hist FY 1968.

30. DA Office of the Chief of Staff for Operations Training Division, Semiannual Historical Reports for Jul–Dec 67, Tab E, and Jan–Jun 68, Tab E.

31. CONARC Ltr ATOPS-TNG-CA to CONUSA dtd 9 Sep 68, Subj: Ltr of Instructions, and Office of the Deputy Chief of Staff for Operations, Training Div Semiannual Hist Rpts for Jul–Dec 68 and Jan–Jun 69, Tab D. Note that the Third, Fourth, and Fifth Armies thus offered Long Range Patrol/ Recondo training at Forts Bragg, Hood, and Carson, but the First and Sixth Armies had no LRP/Recondo schools.

32. DA Deputy Chief of Staff for Operations, REFORGER Weekly Report No. 27 dtd 4 Oct 68.

33. Excluded from the 75th Infantry were the National Guard's Company D (Ranger), 151st Infantry, because it was not a Regular Army component. Company E, 30th Infantry, at Fort Rucker, was no longer considered an LRP unit and also excluded.

34. DA Message 893755 to USARPAC, 161447Z Jan 69, Subj: Redesignation of Long Range Patrol (LRP) units; TOETMTB-69 Annex VI, MPPGD, p. 138.

35. CONARC Msg 54564 to Third Army dtd 041828Z Apr 69, Subj: Replacement Unit for Co D (Ranger) 151st Inf in RVN, and Third Army Msg 04978 to CONARC dtd 081534Z Apr 69, same subject.

36. USA Aviation Center 1969 Annual Hist Supplement, pp. 96, 97. On 5 October 1969 the 53d Aviation Battalion was organized at Fort Rucker and Company E, 30th Infantry, was placed under the new unit with an operating strength of 122 soldiers as a standard rifle company. At the end of 1970, commanding Captain Wiley wrote, "Company E has taken part in over 150 burial details from 1 January to 1 December 1970, and received several letters of appreciation for their appearance and devotion to duty from the next of kin." Reference USA Aviation Center 1970 Hist Supplement, p. 96.

37. CONARC Msg 181832Z Mar 70, Subj: Stabilization of Project MASSTER personnel.

38. MACV Strength Comparisons of Reconnaissance Assets: Briefing Rpt for LRP Company Activations, dtd 20 Dec 67.

39. MACV Recondo School LRRP Commanders Conference transcription of 9 Apr 69 Opening Remarks by LTG Corcoran, CG I FFV.

40. USARV Patrol Summary Statistics dtd 1 Jul 68.

41. MACV LRP Command Conference Rpt dtd 28 Mar 68.

INDEX

Page numbers in **boldface** refer to maps.

347

SHELBY L. STANTON is a noted military historian. During the conflict in Vietnam, he was commissioned as an infantry officer of the U.S. Army and completed the Airborne, Ranger, and Special Forces Officer courses. His six years on active military duty included service throughout Southeast Asia, where he earned the Vietnam service and campaign medals. He was also decorated for advisory duty in direct support of Cambodian operations. After being wounded in Laos, he was medically retired with the rank of captain.

Stanton received a B.A., M.Ed., and J.D. from Louisiana State University. He is also the author of *Green Berets at War*; *The Rise and Fall of an American Army: U.S. Ground Forces in Vietnam, 1965–1973*; *Vietnam Order of Battle*; and *Order of Battle: U.S. Army, World War II*.

Printed in the United States
by Baker & Taylor Publisher Services

Printed in the United States
by Baker & Taylor Publisher Services